Created and Directed by Hans Höfer

INSIGHT GUIDES
GREAT BRITAIN

Edited by Roger Williams
Editorial Director: Brian Bell

HOUGHTON MIFFLIN COMPANY

APA PUBLICATIONS

GReaT BRiTaiN

Sixth Edition (2nd Reprint)
© 1994 APA PUBLICATIONS (HK) LTD
All Rights Reserved
Printed in Singapore by Höfer Press Pte Ltd

Distributed in the United States by:	Distributed in Canada by:	Distributed in the UK & Ireland by:	Worldwide distribution enquiries:
Houghton Mifflin Company	**Thomas Allen & Son**	**GeoCenter International UK Ltd**	**Höfer Communications Pte Ltd**
222 Berkeley Street	390 Steelcase Road East	The Viables Center, Harrow Way	38 Joo Koon Road
Boston, Massachusetts 02116-3764	Markham, Ontario L3R 1G2	Basingstoke, Hampshire RG22 4BJ	Singapore 2262
ISBN: 0-395-66172-2	ISBN: 0-395-66172-2	ISBN: 9-62421-025-X	ISBN: 9-62421-025-X

ABOUT THIS BOOK

This is a completely revised and restructured edition of Apa Publications' first European guide, initially published in 1985. At that time, the Singapore-based company was renowned for its mould-breaking guides to Asia and the United States, and it was logical that it should next apply its unique combination of stunning photography and journalistic analysis to Europe. Since then, Apa has published 60 Insight and City Guides to various parts of Europe, both West and East, including nine to various parts of the British Isles (Scotland, Wales, London, Oxford, Edinburgh, Glasgow, Ireland, Dublin and the Channel Islands), and the experience gained in that remarkable explosion of travel publishing is reflected in this book.

Centre of Europe

The original *Insight Guide: Great Britain* also introduced to Apa two writers who subsequently established a London editorial office to spearhead production of the new European guides. **Brian Bell**, now Apa's associate publisher for Europe, wrote the chapter on the Northeast for that first edition, and **Andrew Eames**, now managing editor of the London office, wrote the chapter on East Anglia and Cambridge.

Bell joined Apa from *The Observer*, Britain's oldest Sunday newspaper, where he had been deputy editor of its colour magazine. Eames, author of books on Asia and Scotland, brought with him wide writing and editing experience on national newspapers such as *The Times* and *The Independent*. Given this background, it wasn't surprising that they emphasised the guides' already strong photojournalistic approach. Too many guidebooks, they believed, contented themselves with anodyne prose and picture-postcard images. Yet a country's warts, they argued, can be just as interesting as its beauty spots and usually make it more enticing to the adventurous traveller.

The project editor to the original edition was **Merin Wexler**, a classics graduate from Harvard on a Frank Knox fellowship to Oxford where she read English Literature. Wexler was recruited by **Hans Höfer**, Apa's founder and publisher. A designer and photographer, Höfer spent several weeks touring Britain with his camera and many of the colourful pictures in this book are his.

Wexler is now back in the US, so Bell and Eames called on **Roger Williams** to bring the guide bang up to date for the 1990s. Williams, a widely experienced journalist who had just edited *Insight Guide: Catalonia*, was quick to point out his suitability for a project about Britain: although he was born and bred in London and is now resident in the rural south, his grandparents on his father's side came from Ludlow, on the Welsh borders, and his mother's father was born in the shadow of Edinburgh Castle.

Pam Barrett, who squeezed several thousand years of British history into a manageable size, has a history degree from London University. She otherwise works as a freelance editor for book publishers and reviews books for London's *Sunday Times*.

Joseph Yogerst, who wrote the chapters on London and the Thames and on the West Country, was born in California, but his travel writing has taken him all over the world and he has written guides to destinations as diverse as Paris and Bangladesh. He

Bell

Eames

Wexler

Williams

Barrett

has a degree in both geography and journalism, and he likes to take photographs as he goes.

Roland Collins wrote on the Southeast, the Southwest and the chapter on Oxford to Stratford. Collins approaches his travel writing with a painterly eye: he has exhibited at the Royal Academy in London and at the Royal Watercolour Society, and his deep knowledge of English history and architecture has enhanced several Insight Guides.

The Lake District was given the expert attention of **William Ruddick**, a former professor of English Literature at the University of Manchester. A Wordsworth specialist, he does work for the Wordsworth Society and has made a study of guidebooks and tours of the Lakes in the 18th and 19th centuries.

Scotland was covered by **Iain Crawford**, a Scotsman born in Inverness whose long career in journalism has embraced every aspect of the media. He has been publicity director of the Edinburgh Festival and Scottish Opera and his by-line has appeared in just about every quality daily paper in Britain. When he is not working or travelling, he makes the best of Scotland's great golfing opportunities.

The chapters on Wales were covered by **Gwyneth Lewis**, who was doing the reverse of Wexler: she was on a two-year fellowship at Harvard and Columbia when they met. A native of Cardiff, Lewis is a writer and broadcaster and her poems have been published in Welsh. She is also a keen gardener and her essay on the subject is included in the *Culture from A to Z* section.

Alphabetic approach

The A–Z section, designed to allow readers to dip into many aspects of British culture, is new to this edition. It enabled the editors to give full rein to their hobby-horses, and contributions also came from several experienced London-based freelance journalists. **Angela Wilkes** writes on Foxhunting, Sex, Tea and the Weather; she was brought up in Chelsea and her father never set out to catch a bus for work in the morning, she says, without first listening to the weather forecast. **Richard Johnson** is a young writer with his finger on the pulse of Britain's youth, and he writes about the Youth culture, as well as the BBC. **Daniela Soave** is a Scot, though she now lives in London. Her contributions are on Elections, Lords and Vicars. The items on the Monarchy and on Pubs, updated from the first edition, were written by **Alan Hamilton**, chief royal watcher of *The Times*.

The onerous task of updating the Travel Tips at the back of the book was cheerfully undertaken by **Beverley Harper**, who cut her teeth on *City Guide: London*. She lives in London with the photographer Kim Faroukh, but still sometimes looks to the advice of her mother who works in a tourist office in the Cotswolds where Beverley grew up.

Collins

Lewis

Hamilton

Harper

History and People

Culture from A-Z

—by Brian Bell, Richard Johnson, Daniela Soave, Angela Wilkes and Roger Williams

Places

Maps

TRAVEL TIPS

Compiled by Beverley Harper

*For detailed information
see page 345*

Millions of people in Britain, wrote George Orwell in 1947, "willingly accept as their national emblem the bulldog, an animal noted for its obstinacy, ugliness, and impenetrable stupidity." A foreigner, he went on, would find the salient characteristics of the common people to be "artistic insensibility, gentleness, respect for legality, suspicion of foreigners, sentimentality about animals, hypocrisy, exaggerated class distinctions, and an obsession with sport."

The Welsh and the Scots would point out that Orwell was thinking primarily of the English – a distinction that would never occur to the English themselves, who, to the fury of the Welsh and Scots, persistently equate the terms "British" and "English". Stung by England's self-centred attitude, nationalists from both Celtic fringes call for a greater degree of self-government – perhaps even independence – for Wales and Scotland, but the demands become more muted during periods of economic difficulty and rhetoric has so far not resulted in action.

Confusion reigns: But then the English have a gift for ambiguity. As a character in Alan Bennett's play *The Old Country* put it: "In England we never entirely mean what we say, do we? Do I mean that? Not entirely. And logically it follows that when we say we don't mean what we say, only then are we entirely serious."

If that seems contradictory, there's worse to come. The British embrace marriage more frequently than any other European nation, yet their divorce rate is second only to Denmark's. On average, they work more hours per week than any other European Community country (43.9 hours for men), yet their productivity is lowest. They have 54,600 churches, but by far the lowest active church membership in Europe (14 percent of the total population). They laud family life, yet many prefer to send their children off to boarding school as soon as possible and park their aged parents in old people's homes.

Preceding pages: detail, Holborn Viaduct, London; Cornish fishing village; Leeds Castle, Kent; winter, north of England; oast houses, Kent. **Left,** friendly publican. **Right,** dressed to shop.

They love animals, yet enthusiastically pursue blood sports. They pride themselves on their solidarity in war, yet cling to a divisive class system in peacetime. They are famed for their tolerance and sense of humour, yet, as the writer Paul Gallico observed: "No one can be as calculatedly rude as the British, which amazes Americans, who do not understand studied insult and can only offer abuse as a substitute."

Britain's nearest neighbours can be just as amazed as Americans. André Maurois ad-

vised his fellow countrymen: "In France it is rude to let a conversation drop; in England it is rash to keep it up. No one there will blame you for silence. When you have not opened your mouth for three years, they will think, 'This Frenchman is a nice quiet fellow'."

The truth, as always, is more complicated. If Maurois had been in Liverpool or in Leeds, in Glasgow or in Cardiff, he might not have got a word in. The Englishman who has "all the qualities of a poker except its occasional warmth" probably lives in the overcrowded south-east, where standoffishness is a way of protecting precious privacy.

But certain generalisations can be made.

Because Britain is an island, its people retain their bachelor outlook despite having married into the European Community. Because it has not been successfully invaded for nearly 1,000 years, Britain remains deeply individualistic. On the one hand, its people perhaps overvalue tradition – a substitute for thought, critics say; on the other hand, they tend not to kill one another in civil conflict and they have absorbed, with relatively little civic pain, large numbers of their former imperial subjects.

Wales fights back: To the English, the Welsh appear a much more homogeneous group than themselves: ebullient, warmhearted and emotional but also rather sly and different from the English – "Mediterraneans in the rain" broadcaster René Cutforth called them.

Within Wales itself, the people seem anything but homogeneous. Many in North Wales, where Welsh is still widely spoken, look down on people from South Wales whose blood is much more mixed and whose habits are thought too anglicised. Naturally, South Walians return the compliment by regarding North Walians as less progressive and less sociable.

Whether their preferred tongue is English or Welsh, however, there is no denying that the Welsh are voluble. "It is not so long ago," remembers the poet Dannie Abse, "that the

extremely garrulous. A certain amount of antipathy exists. Evelyn Waugh, for instance, claimed in his novel *Decline and Fall*: "We can trace almost all the disasters of English history to the influence of Wales." And Shakespeare poked fun at Welsh hyperbole by having the Welsh hero Owain Glyndwr boast, in *Henry V*, "I can call spirits from the vasty deep" – only to be put down by Hotspur, who replies, "So can any man; but will they come?" The Welsh, for their part, have had to work hard, like many minority nations, to protect their self-esteem and culture from a strong, self-confident neighbour. Certainly, they are distinctively

trains leaving from London for South Wales consisted of separate carriages – that is, they were not open-planned. Then, half a dozen strangers would look out of the window, or suck their mints, or read their newspapers, but they would not speak to each other. It was not the 'done' English thing. The English are happy with few words and like to keep strangers at a comfortable distance from themselves. And in a train leaving England for Wales, who knows who is not English? Only when the train had passed through the Severn Tunnel, only when the passengers felt themselves to be safely in Wales, only then would the carriage suddenly hum with conversation." Because Wales, particularly in the 19th century, was fertile ground for preachers and trade union leaders, this gift of the gab was nourished.

Scotland the Brave: In contrast, the Scots are seen by the English as "dour", though they'd be hard put to justify the claim in a noisy Glasgow pub. English literature is peppered with anti-Scots aphorisms, ranging from Dr Samuel Johnson's claim that "the noblest prospect that a Scotchman ever sees is the high road that leads him to England" to P.G. Wodehouse's observation that "it is never difficult to distinguish between a Scotsman with a grievance and a ray of sunshine."

The Scots' principal grievance is that the ingenuity of Scots played a major role in creating the British Empire.

Unlike the English and Scots, the Scots were never conquered by the Romans, and they also avoided Norman centralisation after the Conquest in 1066. Their religious experience also differentiated them: while England absorbed the Reformation with a series of cunning compromises, Scotland underwent a revolution, replacing the panoply of Roman Catholicism with an austere Presbyterianism designed to put the ordinary people directly in touch with their God. No man was deemed inherently better than the next – and that included the clergy, who were directly answerable to their congregations.

London-based parliament treats them as second-class citizens, especially when implementing its economic policies. This is far from being a new complaint, having been echoed long before the two nations united in 1707 in what most Scots still regard as a shotgun marriage. Indeed, when the future Pope Pius II visited the country in the 15th century, he concluded: "Nothing pleases the Scots more than abuse of the English." Not that the Scots can't cooperate with the English when it suits them: the work ethic and

In many ways, the Scots character confuses the English. It combines sourness and humour, meanness and generosity, arrogance and tolerance, cantankerousness and chivalry, sentimentality and hard-headedness. One aspect of these contradictions was caught by a *Punch* cartoon showing a hitchhiker trying to entice passing motorists with a sign reading "Glasgow – or else!"

Come again: To understand Great Britain, its people will tell you, will take many visits. This, bearing in mind their inability to say exactly what they mean, translates as: "Although we regard tourism as terribly vulgar, we do rather need the repeat business."

<u>Left</u>, Welsh couple at the Eisteddfod, Llangollen. <u>Above</u>, spectators at a Highland games.

DECISIVE DATES

Prehistory
250,000 BC First evidence of human life.
5000 BC Britain becomes an island.
3000 BC Stone-age people arrive, probably from the Iberian peninsula.
2000 BC Stonehenge built.
700 BC Celts arrive from central Europe.
Roman occupation (55 BC–AD 410)
55 BC Julius Caesar heads first Roman invasion.
AD 43 Conquest begins under the emperor Claudius.
AD 61 Rebellion of Boudicca, Queen of Iceini in East Anglia, crushed.
AD 119 Hadrian's Wall built to keep back Picts and Scots.
Anglo-Saxon & Danish Kings (AD 449–1066)
449–550 Arrival of Jutes from Jutland, Angles from south of Denmark and Saxons from Germany, around Hanover.
563 St Columba establishes monastery on island of Iona, Scotland.
597 St Augustine arrives to convert English and becomes first Archbishop of Canterbury.
700 Lindisfarne Gospels illuminated.
779 King Offa builds dyke to keep out Welsh.
843 Kenneth MacAlpine unites Picts and Scots.
897 Danish Vikings are defeated at sea by Alfred the Great, generally regarded as being the founder of the British navy.
980–1016 Viking invasions renewed.
1017 Canute, first Danish king, chosen by the Witan (council).
The Normans (1066–1154)
1066 Conquest of England by William, Duke of Normandy. Authority and parcels of land are given to French-speaking Norman barons.
1080–1100 Great monastery and cathedral building begins.
1086 Domesday Book, a complete inventory of Britain, is completed.
1124 David I succeeds to Scottish throne and establishes capital at Edinburgh.
1167 Oxford University founded.
The Plantagenets (1154–1399)
1154 Henry II, descendent of Geoffrey of Anjou, inherits the throne, thus starting the line of Angevin kings. He owned more land in France than he did in Britain.
1170 Archbishop Thomas Becket murdered.
1215 The Barons force King John to sign the Magna Carta.
1265 The first House of Commons.
1277–88 English conquest of Wales. Llewellyn ab Gruffydd, the country's last prince, is killed.
1306 Robert Bruce crowned King of the Scots.
1348–49 The Black Death plague kills nearly half the population.
1337–1453 Hundred Years' War with France.
1350–1550 Gothic perpendicular flourished.
1381 Peasants' Revolt.
1387 Chaucer's *Canterbury Tales* published.
The Houses of Lancaster and York (1399–1485)
1415 Owain Glyndwr, Welsh hero, dies.
1455–85 Wars of the Roses between the competing Houses of York and Lancaster.
1412 St Andrew's University founded.
1469 Orkney and Shetland islands recovered from Norway.
1476 William Caxton sets up Britain's first printing press.
The Tudors (1485–1558)
1485 Henry VII, grandson of the Welsh Owain Tudor, crowned king.
1509 Henry VIII succeeds to the throne.
1514 Hampton Court Palace begun.
1534 Papal authority in England abolished.
1535 Henry VIII becomes Supreme Head of the Church of England.
1536–39 Destruction or closure of 560 monasteries and religious houses.
1536 Act of Union joins England and Wales.
1558 Under Queen Mary, England's last possession on the Continent, Calais, falls to France.
1558 Elizabeth I, daughter of Henry VIII, begins 45-year reign.
1558 John Knox, Scottish disciple of Calvin, launches *First Blast of the Trumpet against the Monstrous Regiment of Women*.
1580 Sir Francis Drake (*pictured above*) completes circumnavigation of the world.
1585 William Shakespeare begins his dramatic career in London.
1587 Mary Queen of Scots is executed.
1588 The Spanish Armada is defeated.

The Stuarts (1603–1714)

1603 James VI of Scotland, son of Mary Queen of Scots, is crowned James I of England, uniting the two kingdoms.

1605 Guy Fawkes tries to blow up parliament.

1620 Pilgrim Fathers set sail for America.

1642–49 Civil War between Royalists and republican Roundheads. Many castles and fortified houses razed. Defeated, Charles I is beheaded.

1660 Monarchy reinstated with Charles II.

1665 The Great Plague of London.

1666 The Great Fire of London.

1672–1700 St Paul's Cathedral, in London, built by Sir Christopher Wren.

1694 Bank of England established.

The House of Hanover (1714–1936)

1714 George I of Hanover, Germany, is invited to take the throne. He speaks no English and shows very little interest in his new subjects.

1721 Sir Robert Walpole becomes Britain's first prime minister, a new parliamentary concept.

1739 Wesley begins to preach Methodism.

1759 Quebec captured from the French.

1775 James Watt makes the first steam engine.

1786 Robert Burns dazzles Edinburgh society.

1802 J.M.W. Turner elected to Royal Academy aged 27, the same year John Constable first exhibits at the Academy.

1802 Sir Walter Scott's *Border Minstrelsey* is published.

1805 Death of Admiral Lord Nelson at the crucial Battle of Trafalgar.

1807 Abolition of the slave trade.

1815 Duke of Wellington defeats Napoleon Bonaparte at Battle of Waterloo in modern Belgium.

1830 Liverpool to Manchester railway opened.

The Victorian Age (1837–1901)

1837 Victoria becomes Queen, aged 18. She marries Albert of Saxe-Coburg three years later and wears only black after he dies in 1861.

1851 The Great Exhibition held in London.

1853–56 Crimean War against Russia, the first major war to be photographed.

1857 Indian Mutiny results in Britain taking over administration of the East India Company.

1872 Composer Ralph Vaughan Williams born.

1876 The Queen becomes Empress of India.

1890–96 Cecil Rhodes, founder of Rhodesia, becomes prime minister of Cape Colony, south Africa. His ambition is to see British territory extend across the whole continent.

1898–1902 Boer War to settle South Africa between British and Dutch.

The Edwardian Era (1901–10)

1909 Charles Rennie Mackintosh completes Glasgow School of Art.

1909 Old age pensions introduced.

1909 Bleriot flies the English Channel.

1914–18 World War I. More than 1 million Britons and Allies killed, mainly in the trenches of northern France; 400,000 killed gaining 9 miles (15 km) in the First Battle of the Somme.

1918 Universal suffrage (except for women under 30) achieved.

1926 General Strike paralyses the nation.

1927 The BBC is founded.

The House of Windsor (from 1936)

1936 Edward VIII abdicates so that he can marry a divorcee, Mrs Wallis Simpson.

1939–45 World War II. Fewer military casualties than World War I, but many civilian casualties from heavy bombing of ports and cities.

1946 National Health Service established.

1947 Edinburgh Festival begun, Welsh Eisteddfod re-established.

1947 India and Pakistan gain independence.

1951 Festival of Britain.

1953 Coronation of Queen Elizabeth II.

1954 Dylan Thomas's *Under Milk Wood* read on radio by Richard Burton.

1961 South Africa leaves Commonwealth because of apartheid policy.

1962 The Beatles enter the pop charts with their first hit, *Love Me Do*.

1965 Capital punishment abolished.

1969 Sectarian strife breaks out in Northern Ireland; troops sent in.

1972 Northern Ireland government removed and replaced with direct rule from Westminster.

1973 Britain finally becomes a member of the European Community.

1976 Bill for devolution of Scotland and Wales defeated in parliament.

1979 Margaret Thatcher becomes Britain's first woman prime minister.

1981 Prince of Wales weds Lady Diana Spencer.

1982 Argentinian troops beaten off the Crown Colony of the Falkland Islands.

1984 IRA bomb aimed at the government in conference at Brighton kills five people.

1990 Tory party sacks its leader, Margaret Thatcher. Britain rejoins the Continent as Channel Tunnel is broken through.

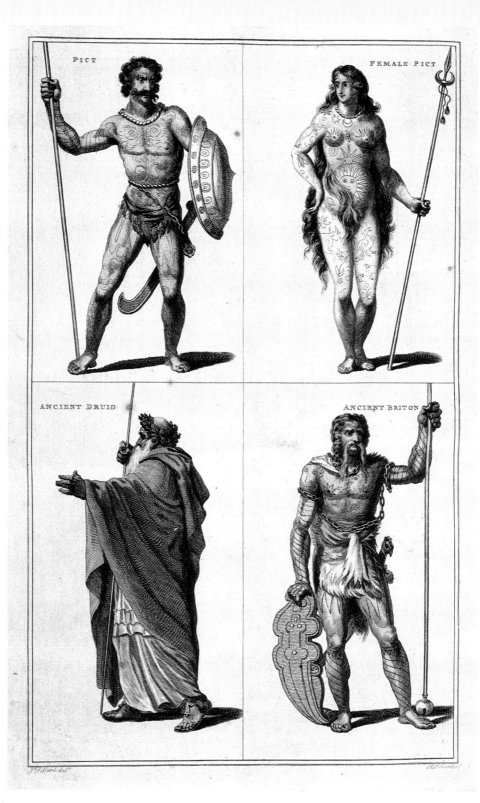

PICT

FEMALE PICT

ANCIENT DRUID

ANCIENT BRITON

When French and British construction workers met beneath the English Channel in 1990, Britain became linked to Continental Europe for the first time in 7,000 years. For it was then, when the last Ice Age ended, that melting ice flooded the low-lying lands, creating the English Channel and the North Sea, and turning Britain into an island. This fact of being "set apart" from Europe was one of two seemingly contradictory factors which would affect every aspect of the country's subsequent history. The other was a genius for absorbing every invader and immigrant, creating a mongrel breed whose energies would establish an empire incorporating a quarter of the population of the planet.

Early settlers: A race of nomadic hunter-gatherers were the earliest inhabitants. By about 3000 BC tribes of Neolithic people had crossed the water from Europe, probably from the Iberian peninsula, now Spain. They were farming folk who kept animals and grew crops. The barrows which can still be found, mostly in the chalky lands of Wiltshire and Dorset, were their huge communal burial mounds.

More dramatic monuments were the henges, the most important of which was Stonehenge in Wiltshire, constructed before 2000 BC. Exactly why it was built is unknown but it must have had religious and political significance; the massive undertaking involved in bringing bluestones all the way from Wales for part of its construction suggests that its builders had a substantial power base. Although in popular mythology Druids are associated with Stonehenge, they were Celtic priests who arrived much later. They met in sacred groves, usually near water, the symbol of fertility, and there is evidence that they made human sacrifices.

At about the time Stonehenge was built another race arrived from Europe. With them they brought the art of pottery making, the ability to fashion bronze tools and the custom of individual burial. Because decorated pottery beakers have been found in

their graves, they are known as Beaker people. They appear to have accepted the existing culture and many were buried at Stonehenge. But they developed their own farming society and built hill forts which took over the role of henges. These forts, of which Maiden Castle in Dorset is one of the finest examples, became small fortified towns.

As far as can be known – and, by definition, very little can be known about prehistory except through archaeological finds and modern dating methods – the next wave

of immigrants were the Celts. They began to arrive about 700 BC and kept coming until the arrival of the Romans. They may originally have come from eastern and central Europe and they probably became dominant because, being ironworkers, their weapons were superior. They seem to have been a more sophisticated people altogether. They drained much of the marshlands and built houses of wood and wickerwork with a weatherproof coating of mud. The Celtic tribes are ancestors of the Highland Scots, the Irish and the Welsh, and their languages are the basis of both Welsh and Gaelic.

We have been left with a rich legacy of

Preceding pages: Stonehenge, finest monument of early Britain; Sir Francis Drake; 18th-century cartoon map. Left, early Britons. Right, early map.

intricate and beautiful Celtic metalwork, some purely decorative, some with religious significance and many fine examples can be seen in London's British Museum.

The Celts have given history an undeniably famous figure: Boadicea (or Boudicca) queen of the Iceni in what is now East Anglia. She is said to have been tall, red-haired and fearsome, and she attempted to drive the Romans from Britain in AD 61. She succeeded in destroying their capital, Londinium, before being defeated. Her bravery and that of other female warriors was reported by her Roman enemies.

The Romans: British recorded history begins with the Roman invasion. Julius Caesar

first crossed the English Channel and arrived in Britain in 55 BC but, meeting resistance and bad weather, he returned to Gaul. The successful invasion did not take place until nearly a century later, in AD 43, headed by the Emperor Claudius. This time, the land they knew by its Greco-Roman name, Pretani, was subdued with relative ease, apart from the country in the far north they called Caledonia (now Scotland). To repel persistent raids by the warlike Picts, or "painted ones", the Emperor Hadrian had a wall built right across the north of England. Much of the wall still remains, running from Carlisle to Newcastle, but the border with

Scotland is now further north. When raids continued, a second wall was built by the Emperor Antoninus Pius, linking the firths (estuaries) of the Forth and the Clyde, but this also failed to contain the Picts.

The Romans remained in control of Pretani, renamed Britannia, for nearly 400 years. Then, with barbarians at the gates of Rome, under repeated attacks from Picts and also from the Scots (the "tattooed ones" who invaded from the north of Ireland) and needing to set up a new military front on the east coast to repel the Germanic Saxon tribes invading from Europe, they pulled out.

Behind them they left a network of towns, mostly walled, many on the sites of Celtic settlements or their own military camps. The suffix -caster or -chester in English place names – Lancaster, Winchester and Chester itself – derives from castra, the Latin word for camp. The Roman capital was London (Londinium), York had been created as a northern stronghold and Bath (Aquae Sulis) rapidly developed because of its waters. Many of these centres were linked by a network of roads, so well constructed that they survived for centuries and became the routes of other, much later, highways. Their main purpose was military, but they also encouraged trade by enabling goods to be moved rapidly about the country. The most famous, Watling Street, stretched from Dover to Chester, and passed through London.

The Romans also utilised Britain's natural resources, mining lead, iron and tin and manufacturing pottery. They constructed baths, temples, amphitheatres and ornate and beautiful villas, some with rudimentary under-floor central heating, the remains of which can still be seen today. They also brought literacy to the country, the use of the Latin language and the new religion, Christianity. This came at first by indirect means, probably brought by traders and soldiers, and was quite well-established before the first Christian Emperor, Constantine, was proclaimed in AD 306. But the majority of the indigenous people continued to live much as they had before Roman rule and, when the conquerors left, their influence faded surprisingly fast. Buildings crumbled through lack of repair and language, literacy and religion soon disappeared.

Anglo-Saxon assault: The new wave of invaders from central Europe, Saxons, Angles and Jutes, gradually pushed the native Celts westward into Wales and north into Scotland. The Saxons established their kingdoms in Essex, Sussex and Wessex (which covered most of the West Country), the Jutes were confined to Kent, and the Angles settled in East Anglia, Mercia (which covered the Midlands and the Welsh borders) and Northumbria, which reached to the Scottish border. This border was still well-defended and a Northumbrian attack on Scotland in the 7th century was swiftly repulsed.

For the next four centuries the Anglo-Saxons battled it out among themselves. Offa, the King of Mercia (AD 757–797), emerged as a strong leader and built Offa's

strong enough to defeat them and come to a relatively amicable agreement. The Danes, who established a large settlement in York, were to control the north and east of the country, ("the Danelaw"), while Alfred would rule the rest. Alfred is known as "the father of the British navy" as he founded a strong fleet which first beat the Danes at sea, then protected the coasts and encouraged trade. He also reorganised the *fyrd* (the Saxon army), making it more efficient.

Although the Anglo-Saxons were a ferocious bunch, constantly squabbling, they laid the foundations of the English state. They divided the country into shires (which the Normans later called counties) and de-

Dyke along the border with Wales to contain the Celts in this mountainous region. But, after his death, Wessex became the dominant kingdom. In Scotland, the Picts and Scots were finally united into a kingdom under King Kenneth MacAlpin.

In the mid-9th century the Danes or Norsemen, popularly known as Vikings, who had been raiding the country for almost a century and taking their booty home, decided it was time to settle. Of the local leaders, Alfred of Wessex (AD 871–901) was the only one

Left, Victorian depiction of Caesar's arrival in Britain. **Above**, Roman mosaic from Dorset.

vised the narrow-strip, three-field farming system which continued until the agricultural revolution in the 18th century. They also established the manorial system, whereby the lord of the manor collected taxes, and organised the local army. And they created the Witan, or council, to advise the king, the basis of the Privy Council which still exists today.

Religious change: The Anglo-Saxons brought their own Teutonic religion. Among their gods were Woden, king of heaven, Thor, the god of storms, and Freya, goddess of peace. The names Wednesday, Thursday and Friday derive from these gods.

Christianity soon disappeared, except among the Celts of Cornwall, Wales, Scotland and Ireland. In AD 563 on the island of Iona, off the west coast of Scotland, a monk called Columba established a monastery which was to be responsible for much of the Christian conversion of the people of the north. Under its influence a monastery was founded at Lindisfarne in Northumberland and another at Kells in Ireland, and many smaller ones sprang up throughout the Celtic areas. The earlier decorative traditions of the Celts were continued, under Christian auspices. Lindisfarne produced its beautifully illustrated *Gospels*, now in the British Museum; the Irish abbey created the exquisite

try and became places of learning. In Jarrow-on-Tyne a monk called Bede (AD 673–735) wrote the *Ecclesiastical History of the English People*. Bede's work, and the *Anglo-Saxon Chronicle*, compiled under the direction of King Alfred the following century, are the principal sources of knowledge for this period. An 8th-century epic poem, *Beowulf*, captures the essence of courtly life of the time and is the first poem written in a European vernacular language.

Alfred, who is said to have taught himself Latin at the age of 40, translated Bede's work into English. A learned man himself, he encouraged learning in others, established schools and formulated a legal system. This,

Book of Kells, much of it executed at Lindisfarne; it is now on display in Dublin, in the Irish Republic. Even so, Christianity remained a fringe belief.

At the end of the 6th century the monk Augustine (who was once heard to remark "O Lord make me chaste, but not yet") was sent from Rome to convert the Anglo-Saxons. He went to Canterbury, in Kent, and became its first archbishop. He was remarkably successful in converting the king and the nobility, but the conversion of the common people was largely due to the missionary activities of the monks in the north. Monasteries sprang up throughout the coun-

as well as his sterling work with the army and the navy, makes him worthy of his title "Alfred the Great".

After the great king's death, trouble broke out again. His successors reconquered the Danelaw, but in 980 Viking invasions recommenced. King Ethelred tried paying them to stay away by imposing a tax, called the *danegeld*, on his people. But Ethelred, whose title "The Unready" was as well earned as Alfred's, was a poor psychologist. The Danes merely grew more predatory while he grew more confused.

When his death left no strong Saxon successor, the Witan chose Canute, the Danish leader, as king. Canute proved to be a wise ruler. He divided power between Danes and Saxons and, to protect his northern border, compelled Malcolm II, king of the Scots, to recognise him as overlord. Some 20 years later, Malcolm's grandson, Duncan, would be murdered by Macbeth, Lord of Moray, who was greedy for power. Macbeth, in his turn, was killed and the throne restored to Duncan's son, who became King Malcolm III. Thus the bones of Shakespeare's plot for *Macbeth* are true, although his scheming Lady and Banquo's ghost are less well authenticated. Had Canute's sons, Harold and Hardicanute, not died within a few years of him, the whole history of Britain might have

favourites and appointing a Norman priest Archbishop of Canterbury. He is also said to have promised the English throne to William, Duke of Normandy. But, when Edward died, the Witan chose Harold, son of Godwin, as king.

Harold's reign lasted less than a year. In October 1066 William of Normandy came to claim the throne. He landed at Pevensey on the Sussex coast, near the great Roman fort of Anderida, and defeated Harold in battle on Senlac Field, near Hastings. The Norman Conquest of 1066 is perhaps the best-known event in English history and probably remains so important because England has never been invaded since.

been very different. As it was, the succession passed to Edward, son of Ethelred, who had spent most of his life in Normandy, the part of France settled by the Vikings.

The Norman Conquest: Edward (1042–66), known as the Confessor, was a pious man who built Westminster Abbey to the glory of God. He was also far more Norman than Saxon and soon upset his father-in-law, Earl Godwin, by filling his court with "foreign"

William was crowned king in Westminster Abbey on Christmas Day and set out to consolidate his kingdom. Many Saxon nobles had died in battle while others fled to Scotland. Their coming intensified the anglicisation of Scotland which had begun with the marriage of King Malcolm III to Margaret, an English princess. William filled the vacuum with Norman barons and strengthened and formalised the feudal system which had begun before his arrival.

His barons received their land in return for a promise of military service and a proportion of the land's produce. The barons then parcelled out land to the lesser nobles,

<u>Left</u>, Canute counters his courtiers' flattery by showing he cannot keep back the sea. <u>Above</u>, William the Conqueror sets sail for England, as depicted in the Bayeux Tapestry.

knights and freemen, also in return for goods and services. At the bottom of the heap were the villeins or serfs, unfree peasants who were little better than slaves.

William's influence was strongest in the south. Faced with combined Saxon-Danish rebellion in the north, he took swift and brutal action in what has been called the "harrying of the north", devastating the countryside and destroying much of the Roman city of York. He then buttressed his power with a string of defensive castles, and replaced the Witan with the Great Council of his new tenants-in-chief, which met three times a year in the southern cities of Winchester, Westminster and Gloucester.

William needed to know exactly who owned what in his new kingdom, the amount of produce he could expect and the taxes he could demand. So he sent his clerks to compile a property record. This collection, called the *Domesday Book* because it seemed to the English not unlike the Book of Doom to be used by the greatest feudal lord of all on Judgment Day, was completed in 1086. Today, *Domesday Book* is kept in the Public Records Office in London, and is a fascinating document of early social history.

The early Norman kings had trouble keeping peace on their borders. William's son, Henry I, tried a pacific approach to Scotland:

he married King Malcolm III's daughter, Matilda. He died in 1135, leaving no male heir. His daughter, who was also called Matilda, had married Henry Plantagenet, Count of Anjou, and became embroiled in a civil war against the followers of her cousin, Stephen. This war ended in 1153 with Stephen in control of the Crown but forced to accept Matilda's son, Henry, as joint ruler. On Stephen's death the following year, Henry, founder of the Angevin dynasty (the dynasty of Anjou), usually known as the Plantagenet dynasty, became king and went on to rule for 35 years.

The great monasteries: While battles raged and kings connived, there was another side to life in this period, which has been described as "the flowering of Norman culture on English soil". The monasteries, both Benedictine and Cistercian, formed the new cultural centres; Canterbury, Westminster and Winchester were among the most active in the south, as were Fountains Abbey and Rievaulx in the north and Strata Florida in mid-Wales. In Scotland the great monasteries at Melrose, Dryburgh, Jedburgh and Kelso were all built in the reign of Malcolm III's son, David I (1124–53), who also established the nation's capital at Edinburgh.

These great houses produced erudite historians and scholars, some of whom went in search of other branches of learning in European monasteries, but they made no attempt to educate those outside the Orders.

Benedictine monasteries were a vital part of the feudal system, some gradually becoming almost indistinguishable from the great landed estates. Their abbots lived very well indeed, eating and drinking with great abandon. The Cistercian orders were not feudalised and their members were far less self-indulgent. Located in remote spots, many in the Yorkshire dales and Welsh valleys, they lived a far more spiritual life and supported their communities through sheep farming. The Cistercians were the founders of the wool trade, which was to become the country's main source of wealth. The Benedictines would also become involved in this profitable business a century later.

Both Black and White monks, as the Benedictines and Cistercians were called, after the colours of their habits, offered hospitality to travellers and charity to the poor, although the Abbot of Evesham may have been unusual in "washing their feet, giving clothes to some and money to others". A constant stream of pilgrims also had to be provided for, because pilgrimages were a feature of the age. Two pilgrimages to St David's in Wales were deemed the equivalent of one to Rome.

Chaucer's *Canterbury Tales* was not written until the 14th century; but his characters, a group of pilgrims travelling towards Canterbury, would have been a common enough sight at any time in the Middle Ages. They might not all have had such bawdy tales to tell but the popularity of Chaucer's book shows that a ribald sense of humour was appreciated at the time and that women, if his

Arthur probably existed and may well have been a Celtic leader of the 6th or 7th century. But it was Geoffrey of Monmouth, a 12th-century historian, who invented many of the legends which surround him, his magical sword, Excalibur, and the wizard Merlin. Tintagel Castle in Cornwall, supposedly Arthur's birthplace, was not built until the 12th century – but there is no need to let historical facts spoil a good story.

As more people learned to read, curiosity about the history of Britain grew and, as there were few historical details to go on, it is understandable that writers should embellish, romanticise and quite simply invent. Geoffrey attributed one of Britain's early

Wife of Bath is anything to go by, were expected to be as lascivious as men.

King Arthur and Albion: But Chaucer's knight, his "verray parfit gentil knight", shows another side of medieval life: the courtly tradition and the code of chivalry. The highly exaggerated, romantic ideals of knights who would fight and die to win a smile from their pure and unblemished ladies first gained popularity in the 12th century at the time of the Crusades. From this tradition sprang the Arthurian myth.

<u>Left</u>, illuminated 12th-century psalter from York. <u>Above</u>, pilgrims on their way to Canterbury.

names, Albion, to the fact that the country had first been ruled by Albina, daughter of a Roman Emperor, Diocletian. More sober writers believe the name comes from the Latin for white, *alba*, and refers to the cliffs at Dover, the Romans' first sight of Britain.

In the 15th century William Caxton, the printing pioneer, published a book which blended historical fact and fantasy, myth and legend, in a fascinating account called *The Description of Britain*. A century later, Raphael Holinshed compiled a history of Britain, called simply *Chronicles*, which features the story of King Lear, later adapted and dramatised by Shakespeare.

1   2   3   4   5   6   7

8   9   10   11   12   13   14   15

16   17   18   19   20   21   22   23

For his Histories, William Shakespeare drew on the lives of the Plantagenet and Tudor kings who ruled from 1154 to 1547. These were the King Henrys, the Richards and King John, around whom he wove fanciful plots, bloody deeds and heroic tales. He did not tackle the first of the Plantagenet kings, Henry II: that was left for T.S. Eliot, in the 20th century, who made a classic drama out of the king and his archbishop in *Murder in the Cathedral*.

Henry cemented the Anglo-Norman state. Through his mother's line he was the rightful king of England and through his father he inherited the title Count of Anjou. With his marriage to Eleanor of Aquitaine he also gained control of her lands, which stretched down to the Pyrenees. Scotland, Ireland and Wales, however, formed no part of his kingdom. In order to consolidate his power, he introduced administrative reforms and instigated the system of common law which still operates today, distinguishing English from Continental and Scottish legal systems.

But relations between the Church and the State became increasingly strained during Henry's reign. As part of his legal reforms, he tried to end the Church's monopoly of jurisdiction over members of the clergy who committed secular crimes, and to bring clerics under the law of the land. Thomas Becket, his strong-willed Archbishop and erstwhile friend, balked at this and tension between the two leaders mounted. In 1170 four knights of the royal household took literally the king's wish that someone would "rid me of this meddlesome priest" and murdered Becket on the altar steps of Canterbury Cathedral. Sheer outrage resulted; the Pope placed England under an Interdict and removed it only when Henry agreed to do penance at Becket's tomb and be publicly whipped for his sins.

When Henry II died in 1189, his son Richard came to the throne. Richard has always been one of England's most popular kings even though – or maybe because – he

Preceding pages: costumes from medieval Britain and the 14th century. **Left**, brave King Henry V. **Right**, bad King John.

spent most of his time in the Holy Land fighting Crusades against the Infidel. Known as Coeur de Lion (Lionheart) for his bravery, he was deeply mourned when killed in France, despite the domestic mess into which his prolonged absence and expensive exploits had plunged the country. It was the injustice at home, presided over in part by Richard's brother and successor John, that produced the legendary Nottingham outlaw, Robin Hood, who, with his Merry Men, preyed on the rich to give to the poor.

Magna Carta: Every English schoolchild knows that King John was a Bad King. He quarrelled with the Pope over his practice of siphoning off the revenues of ecclesiastical estates and over the Papal appointment of Stephen Langton as Archbishop of Canterbury. This resulted in another Interdict and John's excommunication.

He also caused a rising tide of resentment among the barons, chiefly because he failed to protect their Norman lands from the advances of the French king, Philip Augustus. Another important grievance was that John had imposed high taxes, undermined the power of the feudal courts and taken for himself the fines of offenders which had previously been part of the barons' income.

Angered by the king's contempt of them, the barons threatened to take up arms against John unless he agreed to a series of demands on behalf of the people. These became the basis of the Magna Carta (Great Charter) signed at Runnymede near Windsor in 1215. Under its terms, the Church was given back its former rights. The Charter also limited royal power over arrests and imprisonments and prevented the king from expropriating fines. For the barons the main interest was to stop him encroaching on their feudal rights and privileges.

Although history sees the Charter as a

milestone, the document on which British freedoms are based, it brought no immediate solution. The Pope condemned it and John defied it and his barons; as soon as he could, he raised troops and ravaged the north. The barons retaliated by turning to Louis of France for help, but John died in 1216 before he could cause any more trouble.

His son, who became Henry III, proved little better. He filled all the highest posts in Church and State with foreign favourites who flocked to England after his marriage to Eleanor of Provence. In 1242 he embarked on a disastrous war with France which ended with the loss of the valuable lands of Poitou.

The barons, under Simon de Montfort, rebelled and the king was defeated at the Battle of Lewes (now the county town of East Sussex). In 1265 de Montfort summoned a parliament, which represented all the chief towns and boroughs and has been called the first House of Commons, although anything approaching a fair system of representation was still centuries away. But de Montfort's lust for power soon lost him the support of the barons and in 1266 Henry was restored to the throne where he reigned peacefully, if not very well, until his death six years later.

Under Edward I, Henry's son, Wales was conquered and came under the English Crown. Llewellyn, Prince of Wales, was killed in the Battle of Builth on the River Wye and his brother David was captured and executed. The Statute of Wales in 1284 placed the country under English law and Edward presented his newborn son to the Welsh people as Prince of Wales, a title held by the heir to the throne ever since.

Scotland's independence: Scarcely had Wales been subdued than the struggle with Scotland began. More than a century earlier King David had united the country – apart from the islands, which were still controlled by the Danes. Gaelic was still the language of the Highlands, but elsewhere most people spoke English and trade links between the two countries had been established. But this did not mean that the Scots had to like the English.

When Alexander II died in 1286, rival claimants to the throne arose. The first, John Balliol, son of the founder of Balliol College, Oxford, was persuaded to accept the throne as England's vassal and was crowned at Scone Abbey in Perthshire. But he resented owing allegiance to England and soon made a treaty with Edward's enemy, the king of France, then crossed the border and ravaged Cumberland. Edward diverted his attentions from France to Scotland, Balliol was captured and imprisoned and the sacred kingmaking Stone of Scone was taken to Westminster Abbey.

The struggle against English domination was later renewed by Robert Bruce (1274–1329), one of Scotland's greatest heroes. Defeated by the Earl of Pembroke, he became a fugitive but re-emerged to be crowned at Scone, and in 1314 defeated the English at Bannockburn in Stirlingshire.

Scottish independence was recognised. Robert's daughter Margery married Walter Stewart and their son Robert II came to the throne in 1371, the first Stuart King.

In England, the reign of Edward II had little to commend it. His defeat by Bruce paved the way for a Scottish invasion of Ireland. He lost Gascony and thoroughly upset his own barons by appointing his unsuitable friends to high office. Even his wife eventually deserted him and joined his enemy, Roger Mortimer. The pair assumed power and in 1327 Edward was deposed by Parliament, who named his young son king. Edward was later murdered, unmourned, in Berkeley Castle in Gloucestershire.

side to the other. At the Battle of Crécy more than 30,000 French troops were killed and the Massacre of Limoges, led by England's Black Prince, left 3,000 dead. But by 1371 the English had lost most of their French possessions. After a long peaceful lull, Edward's claim was revived by his great-grandson, Henry V, immortalised by Shakespeare (and, later, by the actor Laurence Olivier) as Prince Hal. With miraculously few English casualties – although rather more than Shakespeare claimed – Henry defeated the French at Agincourt and starved Rouen into submission four years later. By the time of his death in 1422 he was in control of all northern France.

As soon as he was old enough, young Edward III, showing little filial loyalty, had his mother incarcerated for life in Castle Rising, Norfolk, and Mortimer executed. Much of his long reign was spent fighting the Hundred Years' War with France, which actually lasted from 1337 to 1453 with several periods of peace.

These protracted hostilities began when Edward, whose maternal grandfather was Philip IV of France, claimed the French throne. The fortunes of war shifted from one

Left, knight's coat of arms. **Above**, the Battle of Agincourt, where Henry V defeated the French.

Plague and Poll Tax: On the domestic front, times were also hard. The Black Death, which reached England in 1348, killed nearly half the population. Followed by lesser epidemics during the next 50 years, it had reduced Britain's population from four million to two million by the end of the century. This had far-reaching effects. By leaving so much land untended and making labour scarce, it gave surviving peasants, and those who came after them, a better bargaining position. But it also meant that some landlords, unable or unwilling to pay higher wages, tried to force peasants back into serfdom. The more affluent peasants of

Kent and East Anglia began to flex their economic muscles and when a Poll Tax was introduced in 1381 they rose in rebellion, both against the tax and against the land-lords' oppressive treatment. "When Adam delved and Eve span/Who was then the gentleman?" the people sang, publicly suggesting for the first time that the social order had not been created by God.

Wat Tyler and Jack Straw were the most prominent leaders of the Peasants' Revolt, which gained the support of the urban poor and briefly took control of London. (A pub called Jack Straw's Castle does a thriving trade on London's Hampstead Heath.) Soon the rebellion was brutally suppressed and

living from the often poor pieces of land and convert them, as they gradually did, into valuable smallholdings.

In 1399 the Lancastrian Revolution over-threw Richard II and put Henry IV, Duke of Lancaster, on the throne. It was during his reign that the first English heretic was burned at the stake. He was William Sawtrey, Rector of Lynn, in Dorset, and his heresy was preaching the Lollard Doctrines. Lollards were the followers of John Wycliffe, who rejected the authority of the Pope and had the Bible translated into English so that any literate person could understand it. The persecution of the Lollards continued into the next reign when the move-

Richard II reneged on his promise to abolish serfdom. But this manifestation of the power of the people had made their lords and masters nervous and landlords became more wary about enforcing villeinage. Gradually the feudal system withered until it died.

The "Yeomen of Old England" who feature in some patriotic songs also emerged as a result of the 14th-century plagues. Landlords found it more profitable to rent out much of their land rather than pay labourers to tend it and in so doing they created a whole new class of yeomen farmers. The name originally meant simply "young men", presumably those with the energy to scratch a

ment, not strong or organised enough to withstand the pressure, went underground. The demands for change and reform in the Church would resurface successfully 100 years later, when they suited the purposes of the king.

Wars of the Roses: Times were rarely peaceful during these centuries. Foreign wars were fought to gain or retain land and glory, while at home periodic attacks on the throne by rival contenders were equally bloody. Henry IV had to contend with the Rebellions of the Perceys, a powerful North-umberland family, and the guerrilla warfare conducted by Owain Glyndwr (Owen

Glendower, 1354–1416), a self-declared prince who was pressing for independence for Wales.

Henry IV's son, Henry V (1413–22), faced a conspiracy led by the Earl of Mortimer and, in 1455, after Henry VI had gone completely insane and government put into the hands of a Protector, rivalries between the powerful Dukes of York and Somerset led to the romantically named Wars of the Roses. This name was, in fact, coined by the great 19th-century novelist Sir Walter Scott, but it has become the accepted way of referring to these battles between the great House of York, symbolised by the white rose, and that of Lancaster, symbolised by

was the number of people who were executed, with or without a trial, off the field of battle. Perhaps the best known of these murders was that of the young princes, Edward and Richard, said to have been smothered while imprisoned in the Tower of London in 1483. The guilt of their uncle, Shakespeare's hunchbacked Richard III, has never been proved and there is today a society dedicated to proving his innocence.

The circumstances of Richard's own death are also well known. He was killed during the Battle of Bosworth, in Leicestershire, where Shakespeare had him offering his kingdom for a horse, while his crown came to rest ignominiously in a nearby haw-

the red.

Edward IV (1461–83) reigned for most of the duration of these wars. He has been called "a man of gentle nature and cheerful aspect", although he did not extend his gentleness towards his brother, the Duke of Clarence, who incurred the king's displeasure, was found guilty of treason in 1478 and drowned in a butt of Malmsey wine.

One of the nastiest things about these wars

Left, Wat Tyler beheaded by the Lord Mayor of London after the Peasants' Revolt, watched by King Richard (also seen on the right inspecting his troops). Above, medieval jousting.

thorn bush.

The wars ended with the marriage of Henry VII (1485–1509), part-Welsh grandson of Owen Tudor and descendant of John of Gaunt, Duke of Lancaster, to Elizabeth of York. This united the opposing factions and put the country under the rule of the Tudors. Henry was something of a financial wizard and, determined to enrich a throne impoverished by years of war, proceeded to extort money wherever possible.

Through loans, subsidies, property levies and fines he refilled the royal coffers but, regrettably, most of the money was squandered by his son, Henry VIII on a series of

French wars. These renewed hostilities gave the Scots an opportunity to ally themselves with the French and invade England. But they were terribly defeated at the Battle of Flodden Field, a name still familiar to every Scot, when James IV and 10,000 of his men were slaughtered.

The break from Rome: Henry VIII is the most famous of British kings. He was the hugely fat, gluttonous and licentious ruler who married six times, divorced twice and beheaded two of his wives. He is also famous as the man who brought about the Reformation, which made England a Protestant rather than a Catholic country, because the Pope refused to annul his marriage to Catherine of

Aragon, who could not oblige him by producing a male heir.

There are other well-known characters in this drama: one is Thomas Wolsey, Archbishop and Lord Chancellor, who had Hampton Court Palace built as an exhibition of his wealth and who was later charged with high treason for not giving sufficient support to his King. Another is Sir Thomas More, beheaded for refusing to recognise Henry as Supreme Head of the Church of England; and a third is Thomas Cromwell who, between 1536 and 1539, carried out the King's drastic wish to destroy the country's monasteries. But he made the mistake of taking

Protestantism too far for Henry's liking and was rewarded with decapitation on Tower Hill, while all the monastery lands and riches went to his ungrateful monarch.

The causes of the English Reformation were not, of course, quite so simple. Papal dispensation for the divorce was only withheld because Pope Clement VII was living in fear of Charles of Spain, the Holy Roman Emperor and Europe's most powerful monarch, who happened to be Catherine's nephew. A desire for change and reform in the Church had been growing for many years and now, encouraged by the success of Martin Luther (1483–1546), the great German reformer, many believed its time had come. The privilege and wealth of the clergy were also resented, even by those who had no doctrinal quarrels with the Church. And, of course, Henry needed the money which the vast amounts of seized monastic lands and property would bring him.

Under Henry, Wales was joined with England in the 1536 Act of Union, which gave it representation in parliament. When he died in 1547, Henry was succeeded by his only male heir, Edward, a sickly 10-year-old who died six years later. His half-sister Mary then came to the throne and won herself the nickname "Bloody Mary", proving that a woman could be just as ruthless as a man when the occasion demanded. A devout Catholic, she restored the Old Religion and raised fears that her marriage to Philip II of Spain would lead to undue Spanish interference and the introduction of the dreaded Inquisition. During her rule the Marian Persecution, as it was called, saw at least 300 Protestants burned as heretics, including Archbishop Cranmer, who died at Oxford after first thrusting into the flames "the unworthy hand" which had earlier signed a recantation.

Mary is also remembered as the monarch who lost the French port of Calais, the "brightest jewel in the English crown" and the last British possession on the Continent, during a renewed war with France. More remorseful, it seems, about the loss of territory than the loss of so many lives, she declared that when she died the word "Calais" would be found engraved on her heart.

Left, Cardinal Wolsey, Archbishop and Chancellor to Henry VIII (right). Wolsey was one of those beheaded by the much-married king.

The Elizabethan Age has a swashbuckling ring to it: the Virgin Queen and her dashing courtiers at the palace in Whitehall; the defeat of the Spanish Armada and the exploits of the "sea dogs", Frobisher and Hawkins. Sir Walter Raleigh brought tobacco back from Virginia; Sir Francis Drake circumnavigated the world. In this age of the renaissance man, even the great poets Sir Philip Sidney and John Donne spent time before the mast – although William Shakespeare, born six years after Elizabeth had been crowned queen, stayed at home, entertaining the crowds at the Globe Theatre in Southwark. Poetry, plays and pageants were the thing, and they accompanied the Queen on her tours of the country.

Elizabeth I, Henry VIII's daughter by Anne Boleyn whom he beheaded, may have had an interesting life at court but in fact she spent nearly 20 years of her long reign (1558–1603) resisting Catholic attempts to either dethrone or assassinate her. She had re-established Protestantism but was constantly challenged by those who wished to put Mary Stuart, Queen of Scots, on the throne and return to the Old Religion.

Mary had a colourful background. Sent to France as a child, she returned a young widow and in 1565 married her cousin, Lord Darnley. But she became far too friendly with her secretary, Rizzio, who was stabbed to death by her jealous husband at Holyrood Castle in Edinburgh (tour guides will point out the exact spot where it happened – some can even discern traces of faded bloodstains). Shortly afterwards Darnley himself was killed and, as Mary rather too swiftly married Lord Bothwell, suspicions were aroused, a rebellion mounted and Mary had to abdicate in favour of her son, James.

On fleeing to England, however, she was promptly incarcerated by Elizabeth and languished in prison while plots were fomented, mostly involving the assistance of Spain. The trial and execution of Mary in 1587 removed the conspirators' focal point and

the defeat of the Armada the following year put an end to Catholic conspiracies against Elizabeth. It also gave England naval supremacy, which laid the foundations for the years of flourishing trade, expansionism and colonisation which were to come.

When Elizabeth died without an heir she was succeeded by Mary's son, James. He was James VI of Scotland, but James I in England, where he was the first of the Stuarts to take the throne. His succession brought a temporary union of the two countries but his

reign, too, was bedevilled by religious controversy. The Puritans became prominent, believing that the Reformation had not gone far enough and calling for a purer form of worship. And the Catholics engineered a number of plots, one of which resulted in Sir Walter Raleigh's 13-year imprisonment in the Tower of London (his well-appointed rooms can be visited). Ironically, Raleigh was released by James who was short of money and sent in search of gold in Guiana. The expedition failed and Raleigh was accused of treason and executed at Winchester.

Plots and protests: The most famous of the Catholic conspiracies was the Gunpowder

Plot of 1605, when Guy Fawkes attempted to blow up the Houses of Parliament. The immediate result was the execution of Fawkes and his fellow-conspirators and the imposition of severe anti-Catholic laws. The long-term result has been an annual celebration on 5 November, when Fawkes is burned in effigy throughout the land and thousands of pounds-worth of fireworks go up in smoke.

The Puritan protests were more peaceful, but James had little sympathy with their demands. A new translation of the Bible into English (known thereafter as the "Authorised" or "King James" Version) was one of the few concessions. James declared that he would "make them conform or harry them

became England's first important colony.

The Stuart period was one of conflict between Crown and Parliament. James I, a staunch believer in the Divine Right of Kings, a belief held by most European rulers of the time, would have preferred no Parliament at all and actually did without one for seven years. But, once recalled in 1621, the House of Commons renewed its insistence on political power in return for the taxes it was constantly asked to raise.

The Civil War: Under Charles I, relations with Parliament went from bad to dreadful. In 1628 he reluctantly accepted the Petition of Right, regarded as one of the most important documents in British history, which for-

from the land". Some left of their own volition. Going first to Holland, a small group who became known as the Pilgrim Fathers set sail in the *Mayflower* in 1620 and founded New Plymouth in North America, Britain's first settlement in the New World.

Meanwhile, in Ireland, events were taking place which would leave a long and bloody legacy. The lands of northern Irish lords had been seized in Elizabeth's reign after a series of rebellions had been brutally suppressed. Now they were redistributed among English and Scottish settlers. The county of Derry was divided up among 12 London merchant guilds and renamed Londonderry. Ulster

bade arbitrary arrest and imprisonment and deemed that taxes should be raised only by an act of Parliament. But a year later he dissolved Parliament and initiated an 11-year period of absolute rule. Surprisingly, he managed very well and might have continued indefinitely had it not been for the over-zealous attempts of William Laud, the anti-Puritan Archbishop of Canterbury, to impose the English Book of Common Prayer on the Scottish Church, or Kirk.

Influenced by the great French theologian, John Calvin (1509–64), the Scottish Church had become strictly Puritan, and was called Presbyterian because its elders were Presbyters, not Bishops. Laud's intransigence provoked a massive popular rebellion. The Covenanters, so-called because they had signed a National Covenant "to resist Popery", formed an army and invaded England.

Short of money and trained men, Charles was unable to cope. He was forced to summon a Parliament, but King and Commons were constantly at each other's throats and in 1641 discontented Irish Catholics took advantage of their disarray to attack the settlers who had taken their land. Thousands were massacred and the outcry in England was heightened by a belief that Charles had backed the Irish Catholic side. This belief, together with Charles's attempt to arrest the

– either destroyed completely or made indefensible. The Civil War has been heavily romanticised, with the King and his Cavaliers being shown more sympathy than Cromwell and his Roundheads – so called because of their short haircuts. A society flourishes today which regularly re-enacts the principal battles of the war.

King Charles's execution in 1649, on a scaffold erected outside Inigo Jones's new Banqueting House in Whitehall, has also become the stuff of which legends are made. He reputedly wore two shirts, so that he would not shiver in the January cold and cause people to think he was afraid. The poet Andrew Marvell, deeply moved by the

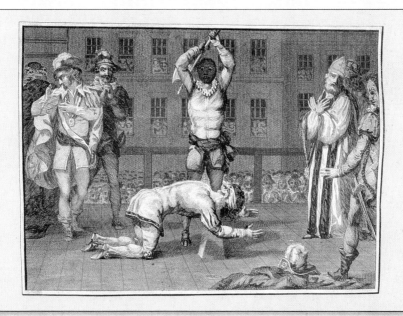

five members of Parliament most openly opposed to him, precipitated the Civil War.

Charles gained the support of the north and west of the country and Wales. Oliver Cromwell, member of Parliament for Cambridge and a stout defender of the Puritan cause, became leader of the Ironsides, backed by London and the southern counties and later joined by Scottish troops. An enormous amount of damage was done to castles, churches and fortified houses during the war and when it was over many were "slighted"

Left, the execution of Mary Queen of Scots.
Above, the execution of Charles I.

event, wrote: "He nothing common did or mean/Upon that memorable scene."

As so often in politics, making a martyr of the enemy proved a big mistake. There was public outrage at home while in Scotland Charles's son and namesake was crowned king. Young Charles, however, was not happy with the Presbyterian religion he was pledged to uphold. He marched into England where he was defeated at Worcester, was pursued south and, after many adventures, finally escaped to France.

Meanwhile, Cromwell and "the Rump" – the Parliamentary members who had voted for Charles's execution – declared England a

Commonwealth. One of Cromwell's first acts was to exact reprisals for the massacres in Ireland by killing all the inhabitants of the towns of Drogheda and Wexford. Another was the suppression of the Levellers, a group within his own army who did not believe that his democratisation had gone far enough. In 1653 Cromwell dissolved Parliament, formed a Protectorate with himself as Lord Protector and ruled alone until his death in 1658. Without him republicanism faltered and, in 1660, Charles II was declared king.

Britain prospered under Charles (1660–85), of whom it was said that he "never said a foolish thing nor ever did a wise one". True or not, one unwise thing Parliament was

Code after their instigator. Two of the most famous literary works of the late 17th century were written by Puritans: John Bunyan's *Pilgrim's Progress*, which he wrote while in prison for "unlicensed preaching", and the blind poet John Milton's *Paradise Lost*, which was a thinly-veiled lament for the Puritan cause.

Whigs and Tories: Fear of the monarchy ever again becoming too powerful led to the emergence of the first political parties. Both were known by nicknames: Whigs was a derogatory name for cattle drivers, Tories an Irish word meaning thugs. Loosely speaking, the Whigs opposed absolute monarchy and supported the right to religious freedom

afraid he would do was become a Catholic. They therefore passed the Test Act, which excluded all Catholics from public office of any kind. In 1678 Titus Oates (whose house can still be seen in the narrow high street in Hastings in Sussex) disclosed a bogus "Popish Plot" to assassinate the king. In the resultant hysteria, thousands of Catholics were imprisoned and the Disabling Act forbade anyone of their religion to sit in the House of Commons – an act that was not repealed for nearly 300 years.

Puritans, now known as Nonconformists, also aroused paranoia and were subject to a series of severe laws called the Clarendon

for Nonconformists, while Tories were the upholders of Church and Crown, the natural successors of Charles I's Royalists. The Whigs were to form a coalition with dissident Tories in the mid-19th century and become the Liberal Party. The Tories were the forerunners of the Conservative Party, which still bears the nickname today.

In 1685 Charles was succeeded by his brother. James II (1685–89) was not a success. Within a year he had imposed illegal taxation and tried to bring back absolute monarchy and the Catholic religion. Rebellions led by the Dukes of Monmouth and Argyle were savagely put down and, in their aftermath, Judge Jeffreys, known as the Hanging Judge, was sent to the West Country on the Bloody Assize to deal with Monmouth's followers who had landed in Dorset. Some 300 people were hanged and many more were sold into slavery to the West Indies.

In desperation, Whigs and Tories swallowed their differences and invited James's daughter, Mary, and her husband, the Dutch prince William of Orange, to defend the country. James fled and the crown was offered to William and Mary in 1688. This became known as the Glorious Revolution and, although bloodless, a revolution it certainly was. By choosing the new monarch,

Parliament had proved itself more powerful than the Crown. This power was spelled out in a Bill of Rights, which limited the monarch's freedom of action and ushered in a new era in which Divine Right and Absolute Monarchy would never again be possible.

But James II had not yet given up hope. Backed by the French, he landed in Ireland in 1689, believing that the disaffected Irish Catholics would support his cause. This they did, but with disastrous results for both sides.

Left, William of Orange defeats the Irish in the Battle of the Boyne. **Above**, portrait of John Churchill, Duke of Marlborough.

At Londonderry 30,000 pro-William Protestants survived a siege lasting 15 weeks, but were finally defeated. Their Loyalist descendants still call themselves "Orangemen", and "No Surrender" is the Protestant rallying cry heard in Ulster's streets today. The next year, William's troops defeated James at the Battle of the Boyne. James fled to France, the south of Ireland was subdued and Protestant victory complete.

War with France dragged on throughout this period, to be transformed in Queen Anne's reign into the War of the Spanish Succession, the aim of which was to put Charles, Archduke of Austria, on the Spanish throne. John Churchill, Duke of Marlborough, won a famous victory at Blenheim in 1704, for which he was rewarded with Blenheim Palace in Oxfordshire. In the same year Gibraltar was taken. Still in British hands, this remains a source of dispute with the Spanish government of today. The Treaty of Utrecht ended the war in 1713 and the Queen died without an heir the next year.

It was during Anne's reign that the name Great Britain came into being when, in 1707, the Act of Union united England and Scotland. The motives for this union were largely economic: the Darien Scheme, which was to have facilitated Scottish trade with the Indies, had failed, largely through opposition from the immensely powerful English-owned East India Company, and the duties on goods traded between Scotland and England had become exorbitant. Under the Act the two countries were to share the same monarch and parliament while trade and customs laws were to be standardised, though Scotland was to retain its own Church and legislature. The Act did not, however, bring about instant friendliness and accord between the two nations, and it was largely the cause of the Jacobite Rebellions a few years later.

Handel's Britain: On Anne's death, a reliable Protestant monarch was needed in a hurry and George of Hanover, great-grandson of James I on his mother's side, but a Hanoverian through his father's line and German in language, upbringing and outlook, was invited to Britain. Throughout his 13-year reign he never learned to speak English fluently, nor did he have any great liking for his subjects. Some good, however, came of the king. The composer George Frederic

Handel had been a musician at George's court in Hanover but had come to London before his master to try his luck. This had annoyed George and, when he was appointed king, Handel wrote the *Water Music* for a river procession to placate him. Handel became a quintessentially English composer and is buried at Westminster Abbey.

The Hanoverian dynasty, under the four Georges, spanned a period of nearly 115 years. It was a time of wars with France and Spain, of expanding empire, industrialisation and growing demands for political reform. It also saw the last violent attempts to overthrow a British monarch, in the shape of the two Jacobite Rebellions in support of the

Laws were subsequently imposed which removed the jurisdiction of the clan chiefs, forbade the wearing of national dress and ended the traditional Highland way of life forever. Charles roamed the highlands for several months as a fugitive before escaping to France with a huge price on his head. Seldom has any figure captured the popular imagination quite so thoroughly as the Bonnie Prince, who became a legend both to his own countrymen and to the country which defeated him and his cause.

No more "Pretenders" arose. From then on power struggles would be political ones, for it was with politicians and Parliament that real power lay. Monarchs were gradually

"Pretenders", descendants of James II.

The first rebellion, in 1715, raised by the Earl of Mar in favour of James, the "Old Pretender", was defeated near Stirling and its leaders forced to flee to France. Thirty years later English war with France encouraged the Jacobites to try again. Charles, the "Young Pretender", popularly known as Bonnie Prince Charlie, returned from France, raised a huge army and marched into England. Finding little support from English Jacobites, he returned north of the border where his Highland troops were savagely defeated in battle at Culloden by the Duke of Cumberland, nicknamed "the Butcher".

becoming titular figures. Historians may talk about the importance of the reign of George III, but it was the policies of William Pitt or Lord Liverpool which mattered. Similarly, the Victorian Age was really the age of Peel and Palmerston, Gladstone and Disraeli.

Early 18th-century London: What was London like when George and his queen, Sophia, arrived from Hanover in 1714? It was a city of great contrasts. Despite the ravages of the Great Plague of 1665 which killed 100,000 people in the metropolis, and a high infant mortality rate, the population had more than doubled since 1600 and now stood at 550,000. This was largely due to migrants from poor rural areas who came in search of work, and their numbers would increase substantially as new farming techniques and machinery made them redundant.

The city had been partially rebuilt after the Great Fire of 1666, which started in a baker's shop in Pudding Lane and destroyed two-thirds of the cramped, timber-built city. But the subsequent elegant buildings of Sir Christopher Wren (1632–1723), of which St Paul's Cathedral is the jewel, were a far cry from the overcrowded and insanitary slums in which the majority of the population lived in poverty and discontent. In the more affluent parts of London some streets were widened to allow carriages to pass and rudimen-

happened when the South Sea Bubble burst in 1720. In return for exclusive trading rights in the area, the South Sea Company had agreed to pay off part of the vast National Debt. But the shares crashed spectacularly and the City's first financial scandal left thousands ruined. Whig politician Robert Walpole (1676–1745) stepped in to sort it out and restore public confidence, which he did so well that he subsequently became Chancellor of the Exchequer and, the following year, Britain's first Prime Minister.

A flourishing trade and financial sector also created work for craftsmen and artisans, to furnish homes, build carriages and make clothes. At the same time it brought in serv-

tary street lighting was introduced in the mid-18th century. Westminster Bridge was illuminated by gaslight for the first time in 1813. But in the slums there were few improvements and the squalor and degradation captured in William Hogarth's famous picture *Gin Lane* was probably typical.

London was then, as now, the country's leading commercial centre and fortunes were made in colonial trade which stimulated banking, insurance and share dealing. Quickly made fortunes could also be lost, as

Left, the defeat of the Jacobites at Culloden. Above, *Gin Lane* **by William Hogarth.**

ice industries to cater for the *habitués* of the theatres, concert halls and the coffee houses which were springing up in the more fashionable parts of town.

London was also the centre of court life and the seat of political power. The royal families spent their time at Buckingham House, Kensington Palace and at Hampton Court. George III was the first monarch to live in Buckingham House and George IV had it redesigned by John Nash into a Palace. A system of patronage flourished around Parliament, which met at Westminster, although not in the present building, which was rebuilt after a serious fire in 1834.

The treaty signed at the end of the Seven Years' War with France in 1763 allowed Britain to keep all its overseas colonies. This made it the leading world power. The empire had been growing since the beginning of the 17th century. In 1607, Virginia, the first British colony in America, had been established. In 1620 English Puritans had settled in Massachusetts and other settlements were made later in the century. By 1700 most were governed by a Crown official and incorporated into Britain's Atlantic Empire.

Throughout the 17th century the demand for goods – furs, rice, silk, tobacco, sugar – led to a series of wars with the Dutch and the French from which Britain emerged in control of much of West Africa, Newfoundland and Nova Scotia and some of the Caribbean islands. French and English battled for supremacy in Canada and India during the 18th century. By 1760 England had proved the clear winner: General James Wolfe's capture of Quebec ended French power in Canada and Robert Clive had beaten both Indians and French for control of the Indian subcontinent, a victory which made the East India Company a private colonial power.

Britain's loss of its American colonies in 1783 was made easier to bear by the opening up of the Pacific. Captain Cook reached Tahiti in 1768 and then went on to New Zealand and Australia, where he landed at Botany Bay. When American Independence deprived Britain of a place to send its convicts, the harsh, undeveloped lands of Australia were the obvious alternative.

Colonial trade, unfortunately, went hand in hand with slavery. European traders bought slaves in West Africa, shipped them to the Americas under appalling conditions and sold them to plantation owners, often in exchange for produce which they took back home. The raw materials would then be converted into finished products and exported to other parts of the Empire. It was a neat trade triangle which resulted in high profits for some, misery and degradation for

Left, the Battle of Trafalgar, as painted by Turner. **Right**, bustling trade with the New World from the quays of the Port of Bristol.

others. It was not until 1807 that the tireless efforts of William Wilberforce made the trade illegal and another 27 years before slavery itself was finally abolished in all British colonies.

The road to riches: Radical changes took place in the English countryside in the late 18th century. Since Saxon times large areas of land had been cultivated in narrow strips by tenant farmers, and common land had been used for grazing. Little was known about crop rotation or fertilisation and land

would be worked until it was exhausted.

During the late 18th and early 19th centuries this system ended when the Enclosure Acts empowered wealthier landowners to seize any land to which tenants could prove no legal title and to divide it into enclosed fields. This accounts for the patchwork quality of much of Britain's countryside today, and the paintings of Suffolk by John Constable (1776–1837) show that in some parts of the country little has changed.

A system of crop rotation meant land could be exploited to the full while the cultivation of fodder crops enabled livestock to be kept through the winter months. Artificial fertilizer and new agricultural machinery, such as the seed drill invented by Jethro Tull, also made arable farming more efficient and more profitable. But for the tenants evicted from their lands by the enclosures and the labourers thrown out of work by mechanisation, it was a disaster. Riots erupted in many areas but they could not prevent the march of progress. Many dispossessed peasant farmers were forced to leave their homes and look for work in the towns, which rapidly became hopelessly overcrowded. In Ireland and the Scottish Highlands the agricultural revolution led to mass emigration, particularly to the New World, and to lasting resentment.

Those who had done well out of new

Industrialisation: The first steam engine was devised at the end of the 17th century but it was only when the Scottish inventor James Watt (1736–1819) modified and improved the design in the 1770s that steam became an efficient source of energy, which would power trains and ships as well as factory machinery and make many later developments possible. The new steam pumps, for example, allowed speculators to drain deep coal mines, which vastly increased coal production, an important factor when the country's opencast and shallow mines were nearly exhausted.

Textiles had long been a vital part of Britain's economy and the invention of the

farming methods began to look for ways to invest their capital. They soon joined flourishing city bankers and merchants who had been made prosperous by international trade, to finance what we now call the Industrial Revolution.

This surfeit of capital was one reason why Britain was the first country to industrialise, but it was also helped by relative political stability, the security which came from being an island, from natural resources and from good trade arrangements. These fortunate circumstances combined to produce a genuine revolution, so rapid and complete were the changes it made.

Spinning Jenny and the power loom in the 1770s and 1780s opened the way to mass production. As in agriculture, mechanisation destroyed the livelihood of those who could not invest in it. Handloom weavers, many of them women and children, were obliged to leave their homes and work in these "dark satanic mills". Attempts to destroy the hated machines were made by "Luddites", named after Ned Ludd of Leicestershire, the first to try it, but were severely repressed and cottage industry virtually died out.

Perhaps the most important element in speeding industrialisation was the breakthrough which came when Abraham Darby of Coalbrookdale, Shropshire, succeeded in smelting iron with coke, instead of charcoal. This hugely increased the production of iron which was used for machinery, railways and shipping. Here, in 1776, the world's first cast-iron bridge was constructed and can still be seen. Cast steel was first produced in the mid-18th century but it was another 100 years before the Bessemer process made the cheap mass production of steel a possibility.

It was, of course, pointless to produce goods or materials unless they could reach a market, so improved transportation ran parallel with production. The 18th century saw massive outlay on canal building. By 1830

after its inventor, the blind Scot John Macadam, and gave us the road surface called "tarmac". By the early 19th century, men such as Macadam and Thomas Telford, whose masterpiece is the magnificent Menai Strait Bridge in North Wales, had created a road network of some 125,000 miles (200,000 km).

The Railway Age: But above all this was the age of the railways, when iron and steam combined to change the face of the country, and were romanticised in such vivid paintings as *Rain, Steam and Speed* by J.M.W. Turner (1775–1851). Isambard Kingdom Brunel (1806–59), who also designed the elegant Clifton Suspension Bridge across

all the main industrial areas were linked by waterways and Scotland was sliced in two by the Caledonian Canal. Unfortunately, most of these would fall into disuse when the new railways proved faster and more efficient, but today, cleared out and cleaned up, they provide thousands of miles of leisure boating. There are more miles of canal in Birmingham than there are in Venice.

New roads were built. A process involving crushed stones and a layer of tar was named

Left, coal mine in the Midlands at the start of the Industrial Revolution. **Above**, Turner's *Rain, Steam and Speed*, 1844.

the Avon Gorge, laid down the Great Western Railway. The Stockton and Darlington line, designed by George Stephenson, inventor of the *Rocket*, was the first steam line to open, in 1825, followed five years later by the first inter-city line, from Liverpool to Manchester. This historic occasion was marred when William Huskisson, the President of the Board of Trade, was accidentally killed while officiating at the opening.

In the 18th and 19th centuries a whole new class of industrialists and entrepreneurs made fortunes to rival those of the aristocracy, who in turn looked down on them as *nouveaux riches*, with no breeding. But what about the workers? The new factories and mines certainly provided employment, but working conditions were dreadful. Fatalities in the new deepcast mines were high and those who survived sudden death often had their lives shortened by pneumoconiosis. Children as young as four were employed underground and women worked alongside the men. In factories, too, employees of all ages were treated abominably, working 15-hour days in poor light and deafening noise.

It was not until 1833 that the first Factory Act made it illegal to employ children under nine and for women and under-18s to work more than 12 hours a day. Sixty years were to pass before another act dealt with health and

safety at work, and then in a very minor way. These early industrial reforms were the initiatives of enlightened, liberal-minded men, acting on behalf of the under-privileged, often arousing great opposition from members of their own class for their "interference". It would be some time before working people would be able to achieve benefits on their own behalf.

The Combination Acts of 1824 allowed workers to "combine" together to improve wages, but nothing else. The case of the Tolpuddle Martyrs, six Dorset men sentenced to deportation for their attempts to organise a more comprehensive union, dem-

onstrated the need for workers to protect themselves against exploitation, but it was not until 1868 that the first Trades Union Congress met. Unions then went from strength to strength, although for a long time they largely benefited the so-called "Triple Alliance" of miners, railwaymen and transport workers, and they did little for workers in other areas.

Time for change: The two events which most alarmed the British ruling classes in the closing decades of the 18th century were the American War of Independence and the French Revolution. In the former, people proved themselves willing to fight and die for equality, national identity and political representation. In the latter, they were prepared to remove the heads of the aristocracy and anyone else who denied them liberty, equality and fraternity.

Radical thinkers such as Edmund Burke (1729–97) and Tom Paine (1737–1809) enthused over the American people's struggle and Paine also supported the ideals of the French Revolution, although he later became sickened by its excesses. *The Rights of Man*, which he published in 1792, defended the right of the people to reform what was corrupt. It attracted a lot of like-minded followers and seriously worried the government. Freedom of the press was suppressed, many radical leaders imprisoned, and Paine escaped to France to avoid retribution.

The fear of revolution was exacerbated by wars with France and Spain and the dissatisfaction provoked by the heavy taxes and loss of trade they caused. Known as the Napoleonic Wars, these hostilities began with the threatened French invasion of Belgium and Holland in 1793 and rumbled on, with only three years' break, until 1815.

These were wars which gave Britain two of its greatest heroes, Admiral Lord Nelson (1758–1805) and the Duke of Wellington (1759–1852) and some of its most famous victories. There was the Battle of the Nile in 1798, when Nelson annihilated the French fleet; the Battle of Trafalgar, where he himself was killed after reminding his men that "England expects that every man will do his duty"; Sir John Moore's inspired strike at Corunna, and Wellington's victory at Waterloo, which ended the war and Napoleon's career, in 1815.

However, political change in England was

to come not through revolution but gradual reform. Between 1832 and 1884 three Reform Bills were passed. The first abolished "rotten boroughs", places which returned members to Parliament but had few or no inhabitants, and redistributed parliamentary seats more fairly among the growing towns. It also gave the vote to many householders and tenants, which was based on the value of their property.

The later reform acts extended the franchise more widely, but it was still property-based. Only in 1918 was universal suffrage granted and, even then, it was not quite universal: women under 30 were excluded and had to wait another 10 years. It is un-

votes for the working class, were regarded as dangerous revolutionaries, but their movement collapsed in disarray in 1848.

The Emancipation Act, passed in 1829, which allowed Catholics to sit in Parliament, was another measure which frightened many of the old school, who feared it might pave the way for Popish plots and undermine both Church and State. And the Repeal of the Corn Laws – the heavy taxes on imported corn which were crippling trade and starving the poor – caused such controversy that it split the ruling Conservative Party. The "Peelite" faction, followers of Prime Minister Sir Robert Peel, who favoured repeal, soon joined with Whigs to form the embry-

likely that women would have been enfranchised until much later had it not been for the determined and sometimes violent efforts of the suffragettes, led by Emmeline Pankhurst, and the role women had played in the workforce during World War I.

However limited the 19th-century reforms now appear, they provoked enormous opposition from people who believed that the whole structure of society was being changed – and not for the better. The Chartists, who lobbied for a secret ballot and

Left, naval hero Admiral Lord Nelson. **Above**, industry produced a new urban working class.

onic Liberal Party. This new grouping was committed to free trade, religious tolerance and a growing conviction that Ireland should be granted Home Rule.

The trouble with Ireland: The "Irish Question" was one to which no satisfactory answer could be found. The resentment of centuries bubbled to the surface after the potato famine of 1848, when about 20 percent of Ireland's population died of hunger and more than a million people emigrated to escape a similar fate. Hostility to Britain and all things British manifested itself in sporadic outbreaks of violence over the next decades. In 1885, after the extension of the franchise, 86 members of the Irish Party were elected to Parliament.

Under the leadership of Charles Parnell, the "Uncrowned King of Ireland", and with the backing of Prime Minister Gladstone and many of his Liberal Party, it seemed that their demands for Home Rule would be met. But Gladstone's bills were defeated and Parnell brought down by a personal scandal. It was not until 1914 that Britain agreed to establish an Irish parliament. But World War I intervened, delaying action, and Irish nationalists, tired of waiting, decided to fight.

At Easter 1916 a group of nationalists staged a rebellion. It was savagely repressed and the ringleaders executed. The severity of

Britain, and an influential and vocal minority continued to believe that their aim, a united Ireland, could be achieved by violence. After years of relative peace, this violence exploded on the streets of Belfast in 1969, sparked by civil rights protests. Since then, British troops have been stationed in Ulster and the IRA (Irish Republican Army) has regarded itself as at war with Britain.

The age of Dickens: In 1848, famine raged in Ireland and revolution broke out all over Europe. In Britain, once fear of the Chartists was quashed, the country entered a period of self-confidence and relative domestic harmony, despite the polarisation of rich and poor which Benjamin Disraeli, a later Con-

the reprisals swung Irish public opinion firmly behind the rebels, who established their own parliament, the Dail, and fought a guerrilla campaign against the British. This prompted a compromise: in 1921 Ireland was partitioned. The Irish Free State in the south was given Dominion status, not full independence, and obliged to accept the loss of Ulster in the north. This led to civil war in Ireland. In 1932, a new party, Fianna Fail, won the election and five years later the Prime Minister, Eamon de Valera, declared southern Ireland a Republic.

But bitterness grew, polarised between Protestants and Catholics as well as against

servative prime minister, called "the two nations" in his mid-century novel, *Sybil*.

The Crystal Palace was designed by Joseph Paxton to house the Great Exhibition of 1851. This showcase for Britain's industrial and technical achievements was conceived by Queen Victoria's beloved Consort, Prince Albert, and it was a roaring success. But many of London's inhabitants at this time might well have wondered when they would benefit from these achievements. For them, the squalor and crime which Charles Dickens (1812–70) portrayed so evocatively in his novels – which were first written for serialisation in popular newspapers – were all too real. Fortunately, Dickens was not the only one who saw a need for improvement. Change, although slow, was on the way. The idea that public health was a public responsibility was gradually taking hold. After a cholera epidemic in 1832 claimed thousands of lives, health officials were appointed and measures taken to provide drainage and clean water.

The police force which Sir Robert Peel had established in 1829, and which took the nickname "bobbies" from him, was helping combat crime in London and other large towns. At the same time, Peel had abolished the death penalty for many petty crimes, such as pocket-picking, influenced perhaps

ment, which began in 1844 in Rochdale, Lancashire, was run on self-help lines, providing cheap goods and sharing profits with its members. Methodism, founded by John Wesley (1703–91), who established the first Methodist chapel in Bristol, had become the religion of the working class. It is often said that the British Labour Party owes more to Methodism than to Marxism.

The working class: It is certainly true that working-class people, on the whole, were not attracted by revolutionary struggle and preferred to pursue their aims through trade union organisation and representation in Parliament. The first working-class member of Parliament in 1892 was John Keir Hardie,

by the ideas of Jeremy Bentham, the utilitarian thinker who believed there should be a balance between reward and punishment. Bentham was the founder of University College, London and his corpse, fully clothed, still sits in a glass case in the entrance hall.

A newly created class of clerks, tradespeople and artisans were adopting the values of thrift, sobriety and self-improvement which Samuel Smiles exhorted in his famous work, *Self-Help*. The Co-Operative Move-

Left, election meeting in Blackburn, in the new industrial Midlands. Above, print by William Morris, who revived medieval arts and crafts.

the Scottish miners' leader, and 14 years later the British Labour Party won its first parliamentary seats. Although Karl Marx (1818–83) lived and worked in London for much of his life – his tomb can be seen in London's Highgate Cemetery – his ideas were known and shared only by a relatively small group of middle-class intellectuals.

Also largely ignored by the working man for whom he hoped to speak was John Ruskin (1819–1900), one of the founders of the Pre-Raphaelite Brotherhood of painters and writers which flourished in the late 19th century. William Morris, who devoted himself to the revival of medieval arts and crafts, shared Ruskin's anger at the social deprivation caused by capitalism. Examples of his decoration and furnishings can be seen at Kelmscott Place, near Oxford, which was for a time the centre of the Brotherhood's activities. Fellow Pre-Raphaelites were Edward Burne-Jones, John Millais and Dante Gabriel Rossetti, artists who were perhaps less concerned with the social ills of the 19th century but equally convinced of the need to return to pre-Renaissance art forms. They eventually became establishment figures and their work is spread through the galleries of London, Birmingham, Manchester and Liverpool.

Ruskin and Morris were among a growing

number of those who believed that the lot of working people would only be improved through education. Despite fears in some quarters that education for the masses was a dangerous thing, two Education Acts were passed towards the end of the century which made schooling free and compulsory up to the age of 13. The educational provision may have been rudimentary, but at least it was there – which put England on a more equal footing with Scotland, which had had state education since 1696.

Working-class life improved considerably during the last quarter of the 19th century. Many homes had gas lighting and streets were cleaned by the new municipal councils. The music hall provided inexpensive entertainment in towns. Bicycles became a common method of transport and day trips by train to seaside resorts were the highlight of summer, even if most could not afford the bathing machines which allowed more affluent visitors to get into the water without any great loss of modesty.

Middle-class life was comfortable and pleasant. Improved transport, including the underground railway in London, which opened in 1900, enabled people to work in towns but live in leafy suburbs. Most of their new homes were built with bathrooms and the majority had a maid.

Art and drama were flourishing. Aubrey Beardsley's fluid, sensual drawings were creating a stir. The Art Nouveau movement had reached Britain and influenced the work of Charles Rennie Mackintosh (1868–1928), who founded the Glasgow School at the end of the century, where he created his own strikingly simple style. At the theatre, audiences were being entertained by the plays of two Anglo-Irish writers: George Bernard Shaw believed in combining education with entertainment and introduced some of his radical politics into his work; Oscar Wilde, who would soon end his glittering career in a prison cell on charges of homosexuality, poked sophisticated fun at London's high society.

So Britain was feeling quite pleased with itself by the time of Queen Victoria's Diamond Jubilee in 1897, and continued to do so for another decade or so.

The Jubilee celebrated 60 years on the throne for the woman who had spent much of her reign as a black-clad widow and who had given her name to the age. She ruled over the biggest empire in the world. Atlases of the time showed vast areas coloured red, signifying that they were British colonies. The Punjab and much of Southern Africa had been added to earlier possessions. Egypt and the Sudan had become colonies – in practice if not in name – after Britain invaded in 1882 to protect its shipping routes to India through the newly built Suez Canal. Britannia did indeed rule the waves.

Left, four generations of royalty: Victoria with George V, Edward VII and Edward VIII. **Right**, the Crystal Palace, built for the Great Exhibition.

AUGUSTUS BUTLER, DEL.T ET LITH.   THE GUIDES AT THE CRYSTAL PALACE, OCT.R 28.TH 1854.   STANNARD & DIXON, IMP

All good things must come to an end. The Boer War of 1899–1902 ended in victory for Britain in South Africa but damaged its international reputation. France, Germany and America were becoming powerful competitors for world markets. The newly united German state was emerging as the biggest threat. Its education system put it far ahead of Britain in scientific and technological developments. It had good reserves of coal and iron and was becoming the world's biggest producer of steel, which it was using to build battleships to rival those of the British navy.

Fear of Germany's growing strength forced Britain and France into an alliance. This, together with an earlier treaty which promised to guarantee Belgium's neutrality, plus the fear that Germany would overrun Europe and gain control of parts of the Empire, brought Britain into World War I in 1914. The Edwardian era, sandwiched between the turn of the century and the outbreak of war, is looked back on as the zenith of prosperous stability, but its foundations had been shifting for some time.

World War I claimed over a million British casualties, most of them under the age of 25. The scale of the carnage shocked even such patriots as the writer Rudyard Kipling (1865–1936) who had been firmly committed to the aims of the war. But there were other effects, too. Men who had fought in France and been promised a "land fit for heroes" were disillusioned when they found unemployment and poor housing awaited them at the war's end. Women who had worked in factories while the men were away were not prepared to give up any of their independence.

There were strikes on the railways and in the mines and political unrest led to four general elections in just over five years, including one which brought the Labour Party to power for the first time. In 1926 a general strike paralysed the country but the unions' demands were not met and the men

returned to work, much disgruntled and worse off than before.

Jazz age: There was another side to life, of course. For some, unaffected by gloomy financial reality, these were the Roaring Twenties. Women with cropped hair and short dresses drank cocktails and danced to the new music, jazz, which had crossed the ocean from America. Silent films, another American import, were the wonder of the age. Writers such as Virginia Woolf and D.H.Lawrence were opening new horizons

for the curious and daring – although it would be another 30 years before Lawrence's *Lady Chatterley's Lover* won the legal right to be published in Britain.

The New York Stock Market crash of 1929 looked as if it would bring the party to an end. The effects soon spread throughout Europe and by 1931 Britain was entering the Great Depression. It ruined a few fortunes, but the principal victims of the recession were in the industrial areas of northern England, south Wales, and Clydeside in Scotland. Some three million people lost their jobs and suffered real misery with only the "dole", a limited state benefit, to keep them

Preceding pages: Sir Winston Churchill, Britain's great war-time leader. **Left,** bathing belles. **Right,** Emmeline Pankhurst, arrested campaigning for votes for women outside Buckingham Palace.

from starvation and homelessness. Walter Greenwood's classic 1933 novel, *Love on the Dole*, is perhaps the best book written about this period.

In the south of England and the Midlands, the depression hit less hard and recovery was faster, mainly due to the rapid growth of the motor, electrical and light engineering industries. The bold, geometric designs of Art Deco, which began in Paris in 1925, could soon be seen adorning the spanking new factories which lined main roads, roads which were beginning to fill with small, family cars.

In 1936, following the death of George V, the country had been rocked by an unprece-

end all wars" still fresh in people's minds, there was great reluctance to enter another conflict. But by 1939 the policy of appeasement of German aggression was no longer tenable and war became inevitable. Although Britain's island status protected it from invasion, it was a war which involved civilians in a way that had never happened before. German bombing raids destroyed many cities. Coventry was particularly badly hit; its present cathedral, with its renowned John Piper windows, was built to replace the one that was lost.

The Blitz radically changed the face of London for the first time since the Great Fire nearly three centuries earlier. Ports and ship-

dented crisis. Edward VIII succeeded his father but was obliged to abdicate when family, Church and Government united in their refusal to let him marry the twice-divorced Mrs Wallis Simpson. The couple married in France and remained in permanent exile as the Duke and Duchess of Windsor. Edward's brother came to the throne and, as George VI, became one of Britain's most popular monarchs, not least for the support which he and his Queen, Elizabeth, later the Queen Mother, gave to their subjects during the Blitz, as the German air raids were called.

World War II: With memories of the "war to

yards around the country were battered by repeated raids. Much of the modern building in British towns, not always blending too harmoniously, has been erected on bomb sites.

Many London families spent their nights in the underground stations, the safest places during an attack, and a lot of people from cities and industrial areas were evacuated to the countryside during the worst of the Blitz. For children, sent to live with strangers while their parents remained behind, it was both a time of great loneliness and the first glimpse many of them had ever had of green fields and woodlands. For some of the country families on whom they were billeted, it may have been their first glimpse of the effects of urban deprivation.

Sir Winston Churchill had received massive popular support as a war leader, and he is still regarded by many people as Britain's greatest prime minister. But when hostilities ended in 1945 the electorate returned a Labour government, hoping that it would be able to sort out the problems of the war-torn country. The basis of the welfare state was laid during these years, providing free medical care for everyone and financial help for the old, the sick and the unemployed. The Bank of England, coal mines, railways and steelworks were nationalised. But these

Trinidad did not gain independence until 1962, but they were two islands whose people were among the first black immigrants to Britain in the early 1950s, when work was plentiful and immigrants were welcomed to fill the labour gap. Newcomers from the Caribbean settled mainly in London at first, while later immigrants from the Indian subcontinent made their homes in the Midlands, where textiles and the motor industry offered employment.

The post-war years were ones of uneasy peace. Britain joined the war against North Korea in 1950 and its troops, still a conscripted army, fought there for four years. In 1956, following Egyptian nationalisation of

were hard years and wartime rationing of food, clothing and fuel continued as the country struggled back to its feet.

End of empire: One of the most far-reaching consequences of the war was that it hastened the end of Britain's empire. Starting with India's independence in 1947, the colonies one after another achieved autonomy during the next two decades, although many remained in the Commonwealth, with the Queen as their titular head. Jamaica and

Left, Underground stations were used as bomb shelters during London's Blitz (<u>above</u>) through which St Paul's Cathedral miraculously survived.

the Suez Canal, British and French forces attacked Egypt. The action was widely condemned both at home and abroad and led to the resignation of the Prime Minister, Sir Anthony Eden.

These were also the years of the Cold War between the Soviet Union and the West, which prompted Britain to become a nuclear power. The first British hydrogen bomb was tested in 1957, two years after the world's first nuclear power station had opened in Cumberland (now Cumbria). The Campaign for Nuclear Disarmament was born in response and organised annual marches from the Atomic Weapons Research Establishment at Aldermaston, Berkshire, to London.

But all was not gloom and doom. In 1947 Edinburgh had a highly successful festival of music and drama, which has gone from strength to strength. At the same time the first annual International Music Eisteddfod was held in Llangollen in Wales. Four years later the Festival of Britain was held in the newly built Royal Festival Hall on London's South Bank – the National Theatre was added to this massive and controversial concrete complex in 1964.

The Festival was designed to commemorate the Great Exhibition 100 years earlier and to celebrate the beginning of the end of austerity. More than eight million people

labour-saving devices. Car ownership was rising too, congesting roads and leading to the construction of Britain's first motorway, the M1, between London and Birmingham, which opened in 1959.

Several new universities were built, with the aim of making higher education a possibility for more than just the privileged elite. Most people had two weeks' paid holiday a year and, alongside the traditional seaside resorts, holiday camps blossomed, offering inexpensive family holidays with basic accommodation, swimming pools, sports facilities and dance halls under one brightly-coloured roof.

Social attitudes were changing too, re-

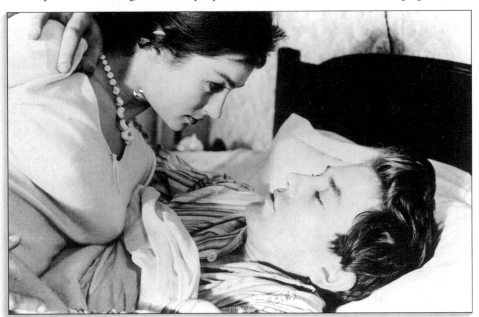

visited the Exhibition, which had a heartening effect on the morale of the country. In 1953 there was another event to celebrate: following the death of her father the previous year, Princess Elizabeth was crowned Queen Elizabeth II in Westminster Abbey, the coronation being watched by millions on the wonderful new invention, television.

By the latter half of the decade things were definitely looking up. Harold Macmillan, the Conservative prime minister, declared in a famous speech that people had "never had it so good": unemployment was low, average living standards were rising. Increasing numbers of people owned television sets and

flected in the rise of a group of writers known as "angry young men", including John Osborne and Arnold Wesker, whose plays challenged conventional attitudes and values. The popularity of these writers also marked the beginning of a move away from the dominance of the middle class in literature and of America in popular culture.

The 1960s saw an explosion of new talent, much of it from the north of England. Alan Sillitoe and Stan Barstow wrote about working-class life in a way no one had done before. Northern actors, such as Albert Finney, achieved huge success and, in the cinema, directors Lindsay Anderson and

Karel Reisz (best known for *If* and *Saturday Night and Sunday Morning*) made British films big box-office attractions. Pop music, as it was now called, underwent a revolution when the Beatles became world famous ("we're probably more famous than Jesus" said John Lennon) and turned their home town of Liverpool into a place of pilgrimage.

This was the Swinging Sixties, the permissive age. Not yet permissive enough, in 1963, to save Cabinet Minister John Profumo from disgrace over his widely publicised affair with Christine Keeler, popularly referred to as a "call girl". But long before the end of the decade a relaxation of attitudes and the introduction of the contra-

in 1966 England's footballers had even won the World Cup. It was during the winter of 1973, when an oil embargo and a miners' strike provoked a State of Emergency and brought down Edward Heath's Conservative Government, that the honeymoon appeared to be over. That was the same year that Britain, with somewhat mixed feelings, finally became a full member of the European Community, which was then called the Common Market.

The country entered a more subdued phase. The optimism of the 1960s evaporated, rising oil prices pushed up the cost of living, high inflation was taking its toll, unemployment was rising and an IRA bomb-

ceptive pill had prompted a sexual revolution. As Philip Larkin, one of Britain's most respected modern poets, put it:

Sexual intercourse began
In nineteen sixty-three
(Which was rather late for me)
Between the end of the Chatterley ban
And the Beatles' first LP.

Not everyone was swept along with the fashions, but this was a decade of optimism and national self-confidence was infectious:

Left, Shirley Ann Field and Albert Finney starring in *Saturday Night and Sunday Morning*. **Above**, oil rig in the raging North Sea.

ing campaign brought home the seriousness of the situation in Northern Ireland. Oil was discovered in the North Sea but, although the construction of oil rigs provided employment and towns like Aberdeen grew prosperous, the revenues from oil did not create an economic miracle.

The 1970s also saw the growth of nationalism in Wales and Scotland. Plaid Cymru (pronounced *Plied Cumree*) became a political force to be reckoned with. Through its pressure on central government Wales earned itself television and radio channels in Welsh and the language was reintroduced into schools, although it is still spoken by less than 20 percent of the population.

In Scotland support grew for the Scottish Nationalist Party (SNP). In national elections it overtook the Conservatives and began to threaten the Labour Party, which had always done rather better north of the Border. In 1976 a Devolution Bill was introduced, proposing a far greater degree of regional control for Scotland and Wales. But referenda held in both regions failed to produce the required number of votes in favour, and the Bill never became law.

The Thatcher years: By 1979, unemployment had reached 3½ million and a wave of strikes plunged the country into what was called "the winter of discontent" – the media

has a tendency to quote Shakespeare in times of crisis. The country lost confidence in its Labour government and an election returned the Conservatives to office under their new leader, Margaret Thatcher.

The impact of the western world's first woman prime minister was enormous, but her personal popularity soon began to fade. It was dramatically revived in 1982 by the Falklands War when an invading Argentinian force was beaten off these South Atlantic islands, remnants of the empire.

The 1980s became known as the Thatcher decade. For many it was a decade of increased prosperity. Docklands in Cardiff,

Liverpool and Hull tried to emulate the chic shopping centre that Eliza Doolittle's flower and vegetable market in Covent Garden had become, and even some of the north's satanic mills were given facelifts. Most ambitious of all was the development of London's once-bustling docklands area which established a small airport and turned disused warehouse sites into prestigious housing for young City professionals. Docklands became a symbol of the decade.

But as the 1990s began, the City was no longer riding so high. Recession returned and many newly constructed luxury apartments remained empty. For others, particularly in the north, where steelworks, shipyards and mines had closed and much of the infrastructure of Britain's industry had collapsed, the 1980s was a grim decade, and Disraeli's description of Britain as "two nations" was recalled. A long and acrimonious miners' strike in 1984 weakened the unions, and coal mines, including most of those in South Wales, were subsequently closed.

Scotland, also badly hit, showed its dissatisfaction clearly in the 1987 election when only 10 Tory MPs were returned to Parliament. Most of Britain's nationalised industries were sold off, a move which ex-Prime Minister Harold Macmillan – himself a Conservative – likened to "selling the family silver", but which was greeted with enthusiasm by the thousands who flocked to buy shares in the companies.

Although twice re-elected, Mrs Thatcher was finally removed in November 1990, not by the electorate, but by her own party who thought she had lost touch with the country, particularly over its role within the European Community, and might therefore lose them the next election. She was replaced by a less combative leader, John Major.

The problems did not change, though. The economy remained weak, distrust of the European Community did not abate, nationalism in Wales and Scotland increased, the conflict in Northern Ireland continued, and the Royal Family's private life continued to obsess the tabloid press. It was business as usual, in fact – which, in a country obsessed by continuity, was immensely reassuring.

Above, Margaret Thatcher, who dominated a decade. **Right**, construction of the Channel Tunnel, linking Britain with continental Europe.

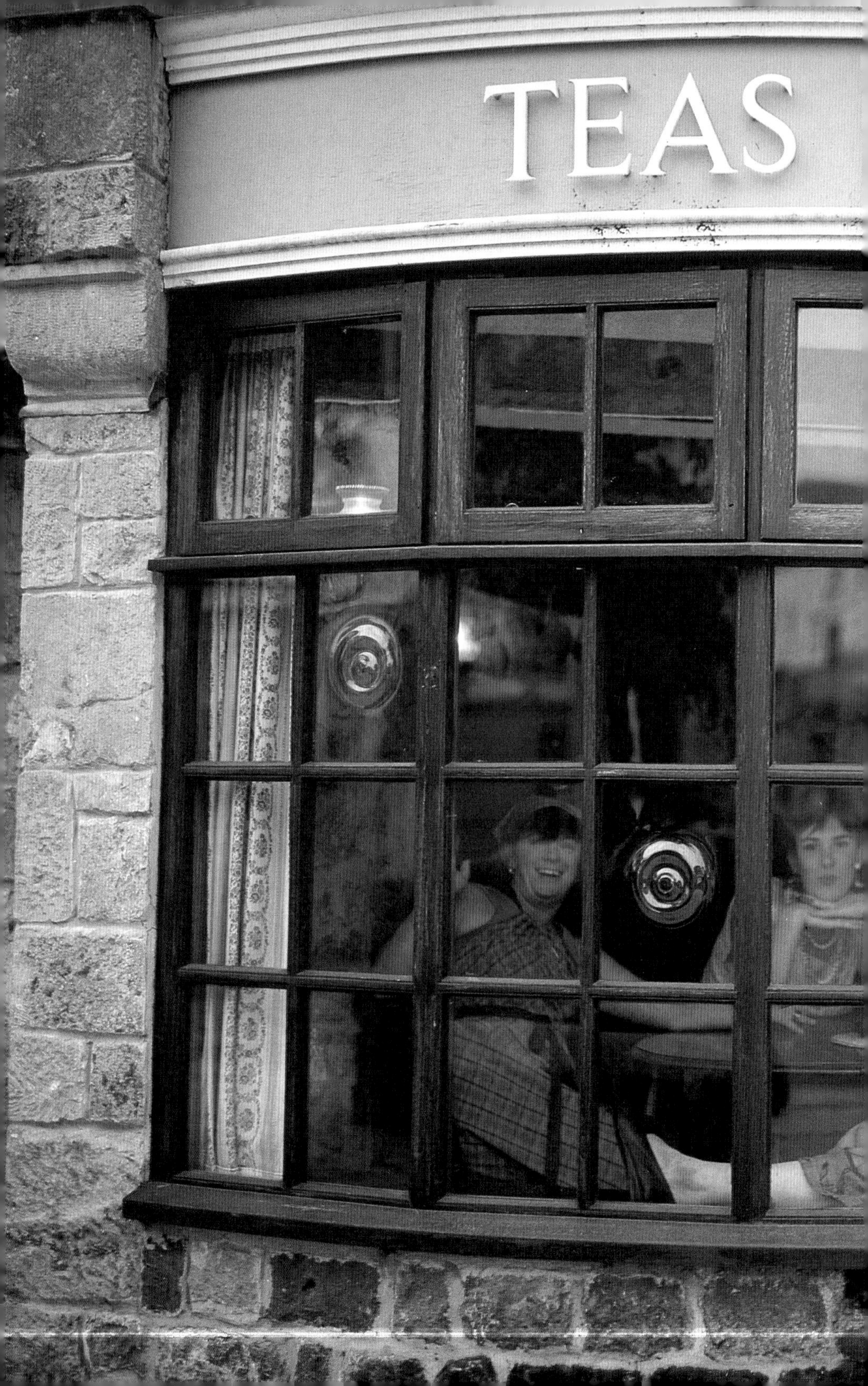
TEAS

CULTURE FROM A TO Z

The British take a masochistic delight in hearing how bleak their outlook is. As Sir Winston Churchill put it, they "are the only people who like to be told how bad things are – they like to be told the worst." And it's certainly a conspicuous characteristic. Noel Coward lampooned it in the song "There are bad times just around the corner" – which, of course, became immensely popular.

Visitors find it hard to sympathise this self-deprecation, suspecting that it is really a cloak for rampant arrogance and realising that few countries are as rewarding to dip into. Take a pin and put it down on a map of Britain and you will find a different experience each time: different people, different houses, different scenery, different accents, different values, different views. Together they make up an astonishing island race, in whom the culture and customs are inextricably mixed; a character that is the sum of so many parts.

The A to Z of the nation and its foibles on the following pages can also be dipped into. These 26 short essays look at the ruling establishment of government, knights, lords and monarchy, and the role of the BBC. They examine the country's preoccupations with vicars, the weather and official secrets. They look at its hang-ups about accents, class and sex. They extol its gardens, its theatre and its pubs. They explain the particular peculiarities of tea-drinking, fox-hunting and forming queues. The nation's notorious xenophobia is confronted head on. And the section finishes by trying to analyse the peculiar zeitgeist that has gripped post-imperial Britain – this "soggy little island huffing and puffing to keep up with Western Europe", as the American novelist John Updike once characterised it.

This alphabetical analysis does not explain everything that goes on either in public or behind closed doors between John O'Groats and Land's End. But it may shed light on some of the shadier areas of a society renowned for curious customs, mild eccentricities and an erstwhile ambition to rule half the world.

Preceding pages: tea-shop photo-call; the Queen on ceremonial parade with Prince Philip and Prince Charles. **Left**, modern choir girl.

Accents

When, in *Pygmalion* (later to be reborn as *My Fair Lady*), George Bernard Shaw set Professor Henry Higgins the task of passing off Eliza Doolittle, a common Cockney flowerseller, as a duchess at an ambassador's dinner party, there was no question about Higgins's first priority: he had to change her accent. Then, as now, a person's origins, class as well as locality, could be identified by the way he or she speaks and, as Shaw observed, "it is impossible for an Englishman to open his mouth without making an-

other Englishman despise or hate him."

Although such snobbery is most associated with the English, the Welsh and Scots are not immune. The linguistically alert can detect a range of class differences between the North Welsh and the South Welsh, for instance, and the ambassador would much prefer to welcome to his dinner party a guest who greeted him in the soft-spoken tones of middle-class Edinburgh than in the rough vernacular of working-class Glasgow.

The paradox is that, although there is no "national" accent, many Britons are remarkably hostile to regional accents which differ from their own. Only 3 percent of the popu-lation consistently uses the generally accepted "Received Pronunciation" associated with BBC announcers, yet the BBC is inundated with complaints when it employs on its national news bulletins an announcer with a noticeable regional accent.

In a way it is remarkable – given these social pressures, the small size of Britain and the smoothing influence of television – that a vast variety of regional accents can continue to flourish. Yet they do: two Britons, one with a strong West Country accent and the other from Newcastle upon Tyne, would scarcely understand each other.

The royal family has sought to maintain a degree of impartiality by coming up with an accent all of its own. A variant on the aristocrat's accent, it turns "stone" into *stain* and finds Prince Charles *abite the hice* when most people are "about the house". If nothing else, it is a gift to impersonators.

With Asian and West Indian immigrants having added to the variety of speech patterns in Britain, consensus about what constitutes "proper English speech" remains as elusive as ever. Pity the manufacturers of digitised voice generators: who in Glasgow wants their cooker to inform them in a Surrey accent that their roast is ready, or what Oxfordshire driver wants his car to tell him in a Norfolk accent to fasten his seat-belt? The same unsatisfactory solution again presents itself and machines, like BBC announcers, embrace Received Pronunciation.

BBC

The voice of Britain is often thought to be the voice of the BBC. Its tone is exemplified in its ponderous, impeccably pronounced radio World Service which broadcasts in 38 languages from Bush House in London's Aldwych. Its cultural aspirations are conveyed in the costume-drama exports of classic television sagas.

The British Broadcasting Corporation, set up in 1927, does not have a monopoly of the air waves, but it does have a good slice. It has the only national radio channels plus a countrywide network of local radio stations, and two of the four terrestrial TV channels.

As an advertisement-free public service

organisation, its powers and obligations are vested in the Board of Governors appointed by the government. These are exercised through a permanent staff headed by the Director General and the Board of Management. It must be impartial and free from political interference.

That is the theory. In practice, interested parties constantly tot up the number of minutes' reporting of each side of an issue, looking for bias. The Left calls the BBC elitist and Conservative. The Right refers to the Bolshevik Broadcasting Corporation. But, having packed the Board of Governors with like-minded souls, the government of the day usually has less cause for complaint.

BBC's first director-general, who shared the pioneering producers' passion to educate. A concession to audience taste was made in 1936 in one of the first variety programmes. It included a Chilean tap-dancing duo, the Lai Founs Chinese jugglers and Miss Lutie and her pantomime horse. No wonder the "Aunty" image stuck.

There have been eccentricities, too – evidence that the Corporation is merely the nation talking to itself. One of television's early stars was Joseph Cooper and his silent piano; a long-running hit was a radio ventriloquist and his dummy, Archie Andrews.

But the BBC began to shrug off its Aunty image under Sir Hugh Greene, the director

The Home Secretary has the power to intervene directly in broadcasting, as he did with the banning of interviews with members of terrorist organisations (aimed primarily at the IRA and its political wing, Sinn Fein). But government control is usually restricted to a quick chat, a nod and a wink, which can leave the BBC looking ridiculous.

Unconcerned with pleasing advertisers, the BBC can give its audience what it should have rather than what it necessarily wants. Certainly that was the aim of John Reith, the

Traditional bastions of "proper" English, at Oxford (left) and at the BBC (above).

general during the 1960s, when satire bit deeply in *That Was the Week That Was*, hosted by David Frost and featuring such new young talents as John Cleese. Since then funny BBC programmes have won large audiences and awards, but they have, in the main, been undemanding. The most biting show of recent years, *Spitting Image*, is transmitted by a commercial channel.

Audience ratings still matter to the BBC, which is called to account when justifying the viewer's annual licence fee. Satellite television has been slow to take off but it will eventually threaten audience figures. Still resolutely refusing to take advertising, the

Corporation is constantly looking at ways of funding its output, from index-linked licences to pay-as-you-view TV. Always reliant on government for its funding, it must tread carefully; its future is never certain.

Class

A newspaper cartoon cunningly caught the British confusion over its social attitudes. "I don't believe in class differences," its well-heeled gentleman was explaining, "but luckily my butler disagrees with me."

threats to civilised society as Mick Jagger consort with the royal family. In the 1980s, the consensus among classes seemed again to be threatened, this time by Thatcherism, whose economic policies created stark inequalities between the regions and swelled the ranks of the disgruntled unemployed; but, before any permanent damage could be done, the Conservative Party replaced Mrs Thatcher with the mollifying John Major.

Mr Major's humble origins suggested that any working-class boy who applied himself diligently could become prime minister – surely a threat to the power of the upper classes? In reality, however, the true aristocrat is unperturbed by such irrelevancies,

The implication is that the lower classes, far from being revolutionaries, are as keen as anyone to maintain the status quo, and that they still embody the attitude to the upper classes parodied more than a century ago by W.S. Gilbert in *Iolanthe*:

Bow, bow, ye lower middle classes!
Bow, bow, ye tradesmen, bow, ye masses!

From time to time, the class rigidities seem set to crumble, but the promise is never quite fulfilled. mainly because the British have a genius for absorbing dissenters into "the system" as surely as a spider lures a fly into a web. The Swinging Sixties promoted a new egalitarianism; but 30 years later such former

regarding a prime minister as the nation's equivalent to his butler.

The monarchy cements the social hierarchy; fringe aristocrats define their social standing in relation to their closeness to royalty, and the elaborate system of honours – from peerages and knighthoods to Companionships of the British Empire – transform achievement into much sought-after feudal rank because the titles (even though generally decided by the politicians of the day) are bestowed in person by the monarch.

Strangely enough, Britain's aristocracy is not especially ancient; it is said that only two families (the Ardens and the Berkeleys) can trace back their ancestry with any certainty to before the Norman Conquest of 1066. Many later knights, barons, earls, dukes, marquises and viscounts purchased their honours from kings or governments.

Within the aristocracy, intellectual ability is not highly valued – few intellectuals receive honours – and a fondness for noisy, drunken and disorderly parties is common. As the essayist Hilaire Belloc put it:

Like many of the upper class
He liked the sound of broken glass.

Snobbery, "the pox Britannica", values attitude and position in society over money and the ability to make it. "Old" money, handed down over generations, is held to be superior to "new" money acquired through vulgar commerce. Thus a poor duke will rank higher in the social pecking order than a successful businessman. Within the middle classes, rank is assigned partly by a person's ability to act and speak like an aristocrat.

The ruling class is a pragmatic coalition of middle and upper-class members. Generally, "they" (the people who seem to make all the decisions) remain strangely amorphous; common speech refers constantly to the fact that "they" have built an inadequate new motorway or that "they" have allowed some hideous glass skyscraper to be placed next to a Gothic cathedral – a peculiar dissociation from power in an avowedly democratic society. But "they" have certain characteristics in common: they tend to have been educated at any one of a dozen public schools and then to have progressed to either Oxford or Cambridge universities. From then on, the network is firmly in place and, with the help of dinner parties, country-house weekends and college reunions, the bush telegraph of power keeps lines of communications open. The "old school tie" has a durable knot.

Drama

In spite of its reputation, the West End of London is not always the place to find the country's dramatic cultural pearls. Here the tradition is as much of the theatre as of

Left, Eton-Harrow cricket match. **Right**, William Shakespeare, still pulling the crowds.

performances. This is where velvet and gilt Victorian playhouses were designed so that most of the audiences would peer down over the cast, where "the gods" (the seats high at the back) bring on vertigo and a concern that, had the buildings been thought of today, fire regulations would have ensured they never left the architects' drawing boards.

Nevertheless, the West End is still the place where companies aspire to put on their productions, because that is where the money is. Catering for audiences by the coachload, impresarios look to musical spectacles, revivals, and to plays that will please the widest range of tastes. As a result, such middle-of-the-road creative persons as

Andrew Lloyd Webber and the playwright Alan Ayckbourn have become both famous and very rich.

In general, the 1990s are showing no signs of danger. Peter Hall, the young genius who brought Beckett's *Waiting for Godot* to the stage and who had an inspired reign at the National Theatre in London's South Bank, now directs more cautiously, casting his Shakespearean characters among sets that might be taken from paintings by Watteau or Fragonard.

The new caution is in part due to the limited government subsidy, but it has more to do with trends. Funding, an annual complaint, need not affect quality and there is undoubtedly a continuing tradition of high-quality, committed drama throughout the country.

Shakespeare is certainly alive and well. The Royal Shakespeare Company, based in Stratford-upon-Avon and in the Barbican in the City of London, is basking beneath bright new directors such as Deborah Warner and Katie Mitchell and, as always, there is another wave of talented actors coming through. The theatre's continuing strength is highlighted as the curtain rises on a third generation of the great acting families, the Cusacks, Redgraves and Richardsons, while the tradition of acting companies which

manage and direct themselves, as they did in Shakespeare's day, has been reintroduced by Ian McKellen and Kenneth Branagh.

The National Theare in London can still offer surprises (and comfortable seats), and notable productions can regularly be found at the Young Vic, the Gate, the Almeida and the Royal Court in Sloane Square, where Max Stafford-Clark has kept the avant-garde reputation with a stable of writers including David Hare and Caryl Churchill.

The backbone of British theatre lies beyond London, in the repertory companies of the provinces. The Manchester Exchange, Leicester Phoenix, Glasgow Citizens' and the Edinburgh Traverse all have good reputations and in Liverpool a hive of talent has included the playwright Willy Russell and the actress Julie Walters. And, of course, the summer Fringe Festival in Edinburgh is where myriad actors and comedians clamour to show their earliest promise.

Britain's film industry, like the theatre, is continually short of cash, and only 40 or so films are produced each year. Increasingly television has not only bridged the gap between the two, but has also pushed drama into more exciting areas.

Both independent televison and the BBC have commissioned films which would otherwise never have been made. Sometimes they are shown both on television and on the circuit, such as Peter Greenaway's *The Draughtsman's Contract*, now a cult on the Continent. Others are only shown on television after they have been distributed in the normal way, such as Granada Television's *My Left Foot*, which brought its star, Daniel Day-Lewis, international acclaim.

At the end of the day, theatre remains the great pull, and however far actors, directors and writers drift from it and feed the other media, there always seems to be a desire to return. Why, even old Joan Collins, famous beyond the dreams of avarice, has gone back to Britain's boards to find real success.

Elections

There are two main parliamentary political parties in Britain, Labour and Conservative, with the Liberal Democrats, Plaid Cymru (Welsh nationalists), the Scottish Nationalists and Ulster Unionists trailing a long way behind. But at election time there can be numerous hopeful (and eccentric) parties, including the Greens, the Rainbow Alliance, The Monster Raving Loony Party and Sausages Against HP Sauce.

Any British citizen can form a political party. All that is required is a name for the party and a person to second the registration – and £500, placed as a deposit, which is forfeited if the party receives less than 5 percent of the constituency vote. This is designed to deter frivolous candidates.

The House of Commons, parliament's

Lower House, is furnished with green seats, which distinguishes it from the red seats of the Lords in the Upper House. It can just about hold all 650 MPs, though the amount of committee work means there are often no more than a handful of members in the chamber at any one time. Like most British institutions, parliament is a male-dominated preserve with the air of a public school. Raucous behaviour is encouraged, although the Speaker, with his weary cries of "Order! Order!", endeavours to stamp out the worst excesses.

Unpardonable sins include accusing fellow MPs of lying (though they can be mendacious or "economical with the truth"). As recompense, they are free to libel members of the public without fear of prosecution – so long as they don't repeat the libel outside the House, in which case the courts are liable to take them for every penny they have. The ministers are answerable to the House and the prime minister answers questions on Tuesdays and Fridays. The business of actually getting a question asked is lengthy and an MP may spend years without once speaking.

Parliament has no written constitution. It relies on statutes and acts which have been passed over the centuries. The monarch has a right of veto but, wisely, none has used it since the 18th century. The Queen is not allowed to set foot in the chamber unless she is invited – which she is at the start of each session at the beginning of November, when she reads a speech prepared by ministers and civil servants outlining her government's plans for the nation's future.

A government may be in office for five years and the prime minister can call an election at any time within that period, giving six weeks' notice of the date.

Fox-hunting

Along with politics, sex and religion, fox-hunting is a conversational topic best avoided at polite dinner parties. Mere mention of it will invoke foaming hatred from

Left, Laurence Olivier, star of his own *Henry V.*
Right, fox-hunter in southern England.

those who believe, along with Oscar Wilde, that chasing a small russet dog-like creature to exhaustion constitutes the unspeakable in full pursuit of the uneatable. Others will snort that they don't know what all the fuss is about: nature is harsh and, apart from giving the fox a good run for his money (he often gets away, don't you know), it's fun for the hounds and bally fine exercise for the horses. Hunt balls are jolly affairs, they say.

Fox-hunting may or may not be a sport – the hushed-up practice of catching and "bagging" foxes the night before a hunt never qualified by anyone's standards – but its nostalgic image appeals to those who wish to believe in a mythical Merrie England. The

subject of much table-mat art and mainstay of Christmas cards, it conjures a pleasing persona: true Britisher as bluff squire. The John Peel or Jorrocks of literary tradition has an unvarnished heart-of-oak and enjoys a simple, healthy, outdoor pleasure – pitting his wits and horsemanship against the wiles of crafty Reynard.

Peel lived from 1776 to 1854 and, for 40 years, ran a famous Cumberland pack of hounds. Mr Jorrocks was the florid, funny fantasy of 19th-century author Robert Surtees and was not a high-born huntin', fishin' and shootin' man but an adventurous Cockney grocer.

These days *Vulpes vulpes* is increasingly becoming the quarry of the vulgar Volvo-owning classes, *nouveaux-riches* townies whose names are swelling waiting lists throughout the country. Belonging to a hunt has always carried a certain social cachet – though it has to be a famous-name one, like Quorn in Leicestershire or Belvoir (pronounced *Beever*) in Lincolnshire, to really count. Humbler folk – working farmers, village blacksmiths and the like – always hunted alongside the leisured aristocracy, but they traditionally shared a common knowledge of country lore. Critics of the new hunting breed say this is lamentably lacking, but where does pragmatism end and snobbery begin?

New or old, money is vital for anyone wanting to ride to hounds regularly. Horse and tack apart, a hunt subscription fee can cost up to £1,000 a season, depending on how many times a week and on which days you wish to hunt. If you only turn out on a limited number of occasions, you'll pay a lesser fee, the "cap".

Cub-hunting begins in September, fox-hunting proper runs from the first Saturday in November to mid-March. Fox-hunts also attract foot followers, prepared to tramp a hearty 8 or 10 miles – and hunt saboteurs. The saboteurs use horns to confuse and lure hounds from their quarry, and aniseed sprays to mask the fox's scent. Clashes can be violent and frequently result in injury and arrest. Some landowners resent the damage a hunt can inflict on their property.

As an effective means of fox population control, hunting comes a poor second to the motor car. A survey by Bristol University calculated that, despite an average 12,000 to 13,000 foxes and cubs killed every season, these losses only accounted for 2½ percent of the population each year. It is a tough sport for the fox-hounds, too. Some 7,000 are put down each year, halfway through their natural lives.

Otter hunting has been banned in Britain for several years – otters have enough problems with a poisoned environment. But hares (hunted on foot with beagles), deer (the West Country has three packs of staghounds) and mink are still fair game. The National Trust is considering a ban on deer hunting on over half of its 625,000 acres.

In the 1930s, writer A.G. Street described fox-hunting as the only remaining bit of truly rural pageantry. "Folk-dancing, maypoles and the like are merely revivals by townsfolk; fox-hunting is a survival." Perhaps it, too, will soon seem another quaint anachronism. In today's increasingly urbanised Britain, the fox is becoming as familiar a night-time dustbin scavenger as the alley cat.

Gardens

"A garden is a lovesome thing, God wot!" wrote the 19th-century poet Thomas Edward Brown. Most Britons would agree. The climate is temperate, rain falls all year and the sun often shines in summer. The grass is sumptuously green, plants grow easily and gardening is the nation's favourite hobby. The Royal Horticultural Society's annual flower show in Chelsea, southwest London, is always packed, while every village in the country holds competitions for blooms, flower arranging and vegetable growing. Nearly 3,000 humble homes open their front gates to the inquisitive public under the National Gardens Scheme.

Formal gardens of great houses have followed fashion and set the style. In medieval times, fruit trees, roses and herbs were grown in walled enclosures; Elvaston Country Park, Derbyshire, is a good example. In Elizabeth I's reign, aromatic plants were incorporated in "knots" (carpet-like patterns). Tudor gardens (like those at Hatfield House in Hertfordshire, Packwood House in Warwickshire and the Tudor House Museum in Southampton) were enclosed squares of flowers in geometric patterns bordered by low hedges and gravel paths.

The Renaissance gardener also liked snipping hedges into shapes. The maze at Hampton Court, west of London, is famous, and the most inventive are at Hever Castle in Kent. A taste for small flower beds persisted through the 17th and 18th centuries when fountains and canals began to be introduced.

But is was the landscape garden that made British gardens pre-eminent. Called *le jardin anglais*, the style came about as a direct reaction to the formal gardens made in France for Louis XIV at Versailles. The idylls of landscape painters soon became the idylls of gardeners, too. In the 1740s a rich banker called Henry Hoare was inspired by Continental painting during his Grand Tour and he turned his garden at Stourhead in Wiltshire into a series of lakes dotted with grottoes and buildings in the classical style. Castle Howard, in Yorkshire, soon followed suit, employing architects to add temples.

A master of this developing style, "the monarch of the landscape", was Lancelot Brown (1715–83) who rode from one aristocratic client to the next pointing out "capabilities to improvement" which earned both his fee and his nickname, "Capability Brown". Brown's forte was presenting gardens in the natural state. He had been in-

Oxford are among the best of his 200 works.

Brown was also involved with the gardens at Kew, Britain's principal botanical establishment just outside London, which is recovering from the ferocious storm of 1987 which blew down many of its fine trees. There are botanical gardens, arboretums and pinetums all round the country, reflecting the public's interest. Many large houses, like Powis Castle in Wales, have gardens of horticultural importance. Scotland's botanical gardens are in Edinburgh. Even though pines, spruce and fir take over the farther north one goes, there are balmy enclaves, such as Inverewe Gardens in the Grampians, where some tropical plants can grow.

volved with the gardens at Stowe in Buckinghamshire, which the National Trust today describes as "Britain's largest work of art". Stowe was one of the first places to use a "ha-ha". This peculiarly-named device was simply a narrow ditch dug near a house to keep out livestock, so the parklands could come right up to the house and the view would be uninterrupted by fences or hedges. Brown was particularly ingenious with water and he liked to create elegant lakes for his parks. The lake and gardens at Blenheim Palace in

Above, the topiary garden at 16th-century Levens Hall in Cumbria.

Heritage Industry

One reason why the British appear to live so much in the past is that they've got so much of it. Yet not until the 1980s, when corporatism and Mrs Margaret Thatcher took Great Britain Ltd by the throat, did anyone realise that The Past needed to be ruthlessly revalued on the national balance sheet. What's more, it needed a bright new image. So it changed its name. It became Heritage.

The tourist map of Britain took on a new

aspect. Instead of the familiar counties and areas, there appeared Robin Hood Country, James Herriott Country, Rob Roy Country, Brideshead Country, Poldark Country… Soon any area without such slick identification sought it. The depressed northeast, for instance, baptised itself Catherine Cookson Country – much to the confusion of tourists who turned up in South Tyneside in search of the mean streets that Ms Cookson had captured so well in her novels, only to find that they had long since been bulldozed.

Almost every week, somewhere in this economically declining country, a new museum opens. No aspect of life, it seems, can escape being removed, rearranged, sanitised and preserved for profit. As the iron and steel industries wither away, the Ironbridge Gorge Museum flourishes. As coal mines close throughout Wales, the Big Pit mining museum at Blaenavon kits out tourists in hard hats and miners' lamps.

Critics complain that recreated "heritage" is often bogus history. Many new-wave industrial entertainments, said a former director of the Ironbridge Gorge Museum, tend to create a "curious, nostalgic, rose-coloured picture of a sort of Pickwickian industrial past which bears no relation to reality, but which we like to imagine. A lot of what is presented isn't based on scholarship at all but on attitude and emotion."

And not all the redeployed industrial workers take to being guides. "I'm glad I've got a job, but it isn't real work," said a former Big Pit miner. "Coal mining was hard but there was a sense of doing something; and there were good times with your pals."

In the end, there are distinctions to be drawn. "Places like Jorvik in York, Beamish industrial museum in Durham and Ironbridge in Shropshire offer you 'real' artefacts as well as reconstructions," says Gordon Marsden, editor of *History Today* magazine. "But a themed museum like, say, the Oxford Story in Oxford is more like an Easter egg – hollow inside. You get a quick whisk through the past but then come out with nothing real to relate to."

It's all becoming rather Orwellian, people sometimes say. But even George Orwell might be taken aback to find that the subject of his 1930s study of recession in *The Road to Wigan Pier* has now become –what else? – the £3.5 million Wigan Heritage Centre.

Islands

Great Britain is the largest of the British Isles, an archipelago made up of around 2,000 islands. It is distinguished from the United Kingdom (of Great Britain and Northern Ireland) by the specific exclusion of any part of Ireland, and from the British Isles by the exclusion of the self-governing Isle of Man and Channel Islands.

The Isle of Man, in the Irish Sea midway between England and Ireland and 16 miles (25 km) from the Scottish coast, has a population of some 50,000. Its parliament, the

House of Keys, is said to be the world's oldest. The Manx language, from the same root as Gaelic, was spoken by half the inhabitants at the end of the 19th century, but it has now died out. The island is famous for the tail-less Manx cat, and for the use of the birch, an instrument of corporal punishment employed by the courts.

On the Channel Islands, in the Gulf of St Malo off the French coast and much closer to France than to Britain, French and English are both official languages. Popularised by the *Bergerac* television detective series, the islands are a tax haven and a residency is hard to obtain, even for Britons. The two main islands are Jersey (45 sq. miles/117 sq. km) and Guernsey (24 sq. miles/62 sq. miles). The 2 sq.-mile (5 sq.-km) island of Sark is a feudal remnant, ruled over by an hereditary seigneur.

The idea of being a king of an island is clearly an attractive one and whole islands do occasionally come up for sale. They are almost exclusively on the western side of the country, running from the Scilly Isles off Land's End in Cornwall, past Anglesea in Wales to the more prolific Western Isles of Scotland beyond its dramatic fjords. In the far northwest are the Hebrides; flying off the northeast are the Orkney and Shetland islands, where Britain's most northerly inhab-

their own private airstrips for the use of new owners. From having been traditionally the property of the landed aristocracy, many are now being bought by film stars, rock musicians, property speculators and tycoons. Owning an island still has a poetic appeal, no matter what the cost. Accordingly, prices have spiralled. The islanders have grown nervous; when an island is sold, the futures of its residents hang in the balance.

Even so, after all the money in the world has been spent and the new owner has taken possession, he is only the lord of all he can see when the tide is high. When the tide is low, he is surrounded by the Crown, because the monarch owns the foreshore.

ited island, Muckle Flugga, is manned by brave lighthouse keepers.

Inter-island transport in these remote places is sometimes difficult and often exhilarating. With Caledonian MacBrayne, the Scottish ferry company, it is possible to island-hop through 22 of the Western Isles. Loganair has the shortest scheduled flight in the world – a two-minute flight between two Orkney islands – and uses fields and even beaches as landing strips.

Some of the Scottish islands are getting

Left, St Michael's Mount, off the coast of Cornwall.
Above, Benny Hill in his television heyday.

Jokes

For a slightly objective view of something so intensely subjective as humour, one could do worse than seek the opinion of George Mikes, a Hungarian who moved to England where he became a humorous writer. "Britain is the only country in the world which is inordinately proud of its sense of humour," he said. "In other countries, if they find you inadequate or they hate you, they will call you stupid, ill-mannered, a horse-thief or hyena. In England, they will say that you have no sense of humour. That is the final condemnation, the total dismissal."

Yet no monolithic British sense of humour exists. There are many varieties, of which five are most common:

Irony. To justify their view of themselves as good losers, to whom playing the game is more important than winning it – fortunately, given their usual performance – the British have developed a sophisticated self-mockery. It is a virtue, for instance, to be able to laugh at oneself.

Satire. The satirist, who laughs at others, is nourished by the prevalence of hypocrisy in national life. Also, given the rigidity and conservatism of most national habits and institutions, it's easier to joke about them than to change them. Political pamphleteering nourished that habit, which continued in such TV programmes as *Yes, Prime Minister*. The great visual tradition of vicious caricature, which reached its peak in the 18th and 19th centuries with James Gillray, George Cruikshank and William Hogarth, is alive and kicking today in the TV puppet show *Spitting Image*.

Smut. Farces in which hilarity often relies on males losing their trousers remain popular theatre. Because the British are repressed about sex, dirty jokes abound and comedians such as the late Benny Hill built careers on a limited range of innuendo. "Mark my words," warned playwright Alan Bennett, "when a society has to resort to the lavatory for its humour, the writing is on the wall."

Absurdity. Perhaps as a palliative against the national failings of formality and pomposity, surreal humour is highly developed. Lewis Carroll is the greatest literary exemplar, and there is a long tradition of nonsense verse. Modern examples are the radio *Goon Shows* of the 1950s (in which Peter Sellars made his name) and the *Monty Python's Flying Circus* TV comedies of the 1970s. Cruelty and sadism figure heavily in this form of British humour, allowing people to channel nastiness and frustration into a socially acceptable outlet, smiling politely.

Wit. Shakespeare is full of it and Dr Johnson is still endlessly quoted ("A second marriage is the triumph of hope over experience"). The richness of the English language, with its wealth of homonyms and synonyms, encouraged verbal acrobats such as Oscar Wilde ("He hasn't a single redeeming vice.") and George Bernard Shaw ("An Englishman thinks he is moral when he is only uncomfortable."). But there's also ready wit to be found in most areas of national life, even in Parliament. In one famous exchange, Lady Astor spat at Sir Winston Churchill: "If the Rt. Hon. Gentleman were my husband, I'd put poison in his tea." To which Churchill replied: "If the Hon. Lady were my wife, I would drink it."

Knights

Twice a year, at New Year and on the Queen's official birthday in June, British newspapers carry two pages of tiny type – the Honours List of medals given out to the good, the worthy, the dedicated, the long-serving. Some simply receive medals, a few are made lords, others will be made knights, to be called, for ever after, Sir or Dame.

This is what is left of the system of patronage and chivalry upon which wars were fought, taxes levied and monarchs, however mad or bad, could guarantee a faithful following. In the Middle Ages there were two kinds of knight: religious and secular. Religious orders, such as the Knights Templar, took monastic vows and devoted themselves to crusades against the infidel, while the secular knights enrolled in the services of noblemen. By the 14th century, however, knights had become merely wealthy landowners and anyone holding property worth more than £20 a year could buy a title.

There is no evidence of titles being bought in modern times, but a certain amount of sucking up to the political parties, including generous donations to party funds, should not go amiss. The Honours List is compiled by the civil service for the government of the day. Those to be knighted are invited to Buckingham Palace, where the Queen dubs them on each shoulder with a cermonial sword in the time-honoured way.

There is something rather predictable about the recipients, for the most part unknown beavers, busybodies and bureaucrats. Headlines are reserved for the sprinkling of knighthoods for people in the arts, since the public might at least have heard of them. There is always a frisson of controversy: the actor Ian McKellen was attacked for accepting a knighthood in Margaret Thatcher's final Honours List, as she had done so little to support gays. The award to Band Aid's organiser, Bob Geldof, surprised some, given his attacks on Thatcher's government (being Irish, he is not entitled to be called "Sir Bob"). When the Beatles were given their Orders of the British Empire (knighthoods not included), disgusted colonels sent their medals back to the Queen.

There are 10 different orders of knighthood. There is a better chance of becoming a lowly Knight Batchelor than joining one of the more obscure orders, such as The Most Eminent Order of the Indian Empire, a title

ostrich and heron's feathers, gold collars, silver stars and enamelled broaches of St George. And on the blue-and-gold garter, gripping His left calf and Her left arm the motto is emblazoned: *Honi Soit qui Mal y Pense* (Shame on him who thinks evil of it).

Most would be content with a less chivalrous Baronetage or Knightage with a title of Sir and, for Sir's wife, Lady, and the knowledge that they have joined an exclusive club of around 4,500. Membership is for life unless, as in the case of the odd financier and businessman, they are jailed ("detained at Her Majesty's pleasure" is the euphemism), in which case Her Majesty can show her displeasure by demanding the title back.

not conferred on anyone since 1947. And there is no chance at all of joining Europe's oldest chivalrous order, The Most Noble Order of the Garter, which belongs to the Chapel of St George at Windsor Castle and dates from 1358. It is limited to 24 members, of which the Queen is Sovereign, and half a dozen reigning monarchs are Extra Knights Companion.

Purchase of the required regalia alone would preclude all but monarchy and millionaires from joining. The taffeta-lined blue velvet mantle is set off by diamond bands,

Above, Roxburgh, a Scottish duke at home.

Lords

Some Britons are born lords, some achieve their lordships, and some have lordships thrust upon them, but no longer is the monarch predisposed to carve up parcels of the kingdom for some lordly pals, for the kingdom has long since been accounted for.

All Briton's aristocrats are lords, but not all lords are aristocracy. The pecking order of the nation's nobility, at last count, goes like this: royal dukes 5 (Edinburgh, Cornwall, York, Gloucester, Kent), ordinary dukes 24, marquesses 35, earls 204, viscounts 127 and barons 500. Kindly address a duke as "Your Grace" and a marquess as "Most Honourable". For the rest, "Right Honourable Lord" will do. What separates a duke from a baron is one yard of velvet and 3 inches of ermine trim, the difference between the length of train on the ceremonial robe each is entitled to wear.

In general, English lords take precedent over Scottish lords, of whom there are a disproportionate number; they include the Duke of Atholl, the only man in the realm allowed to keep a standing army, which he does in his 100-strong Atholl Highlanders. Lords are not all rich and powerful. Every now and again a newspaper discovers one living in a bedsit or working for British Rail. But death and taxes apart, they don't have too much to complain about. One of Britain's wealthiest men is the Duke of Westminster who inherited his many millions-worth of Westminster and Belgravia property before he was 30, making him an exceptionally eligible bachelor.

Many lords still live in their stately homes and among them are sumptuous museums of art and architecture, harbouring collections that would put many a big-city gallery to shame. Most can now be visited. The burden of death duties, and of maintaining these crumbling piles, turned them into theme parks from the 1960s onwards. Otherwise, floating the odd old master or piece of furniture on to the art markets keeps them going for a year or two.

There are some 800 peers of the realm in all. With few exceptions their titles pass through the male side of the family. The heirs to a large chunk of Britain will undoubtedly attend a top public school, but not go to university, preferring instead officer training at the Royal Military Academy, Sandhurst, after which they would hope to be commissioned into one of the army's prestigious Guards regiments.

At the age of 21, they can take their places in Parliament's Upper House, the House of Lords. There they can make speeches and pass or amend legislation sent up to them for approval by the House of Commons. Theoretically they may speak their minds, but a degree of conformity is expected. When John, Viscount Amberley, Lord Russell, spoke in the House in 1978 demanding the abolition of prisons, free goods in shops, free houses for girls aged 12 and the abolition of marriage, he was not allowed even to finish his speech.

In order to try to get some sense out of this place, and to try to bolster party support, Life Peers are created in the annual Honours List (*see Knights*). These peerages are often handed out to former politicians from the House of Commons who have been "kicked upstairs" for reasons either of age or of political expediency. More properly called Life Barons, this is a junior award, made only for the holder's own lifetime and no title is passed on to the children.

There are around 400 Life Peers, added to which are the Archbishops of Canterbury and York plus 24 bishops, making up the Lords Spiritual, and 19 Law Lords, judges who are Lords of Appeal. That makes a total of more than 1,200 entitled to sit in the House of Lords, though at its most crowded (such as the day television cameras were first switched on) there will be barely 300 there. Lords own so much of the country they can't be expected to run the damn thing, too.

Monarchy

"Her majesty's speech delivered upon the reassembling of parliament was, as usual, insipid and uninstructive. Its preferred topic was her majesty's approaching marriage, a matter of little importance or interest to the country, except as it may thereby be burdened with additional and unnecessary expense." That curt dismissal of Queen Victoria was written by a correspondent of *The Times* a century and a half ago. Since then the tribes of Britain have become noticeably more democratic, more pluralistic, more educated, more informed and far more reverential to the family whom they continue to crown with the world's most valuable single piece of jewellery.

Her Majesty Queen Elizabeth II, descendent of both Kings Egbert of Wessex (AD 827–39) and McAlpine of Scotland (1057–93), and relative of the half-dozen remaining monarchs of Europe, earns around £1.8 million a day. It takes only the briefest whistle-stop tour of Britain's major palaces to realise that she is the world's richest woman and is the custodian of the world's largest private collection of art. Yet she and her close family also benefit from the Civil List, which provides millions of pounds of taxpayers' money a year towards their expenses.

Sometimes there is an outcry if lesser royals are seen to be living off the fat without putting in time on what can be an arduous stream of official engagements. But the British still regard the monarchy as a useful and desirable institution. By its very age it is a potent symbol of national identity; by being above party politics and not subject to election, it provides the State with a sense of last-bastion hope against the incompetence of

people want. Never mind that, as builders, art patrons or setters of style, they have often seemed uninspired dullards.

The Queen passed retiring age in 1986 and she has made it known that, should the public want it, she would go. But opinion polls show that she is the one member of the royal family who wins almost universal approval. The same cannot be said of her son and heir, Charles III (as he would be). Much mud was flung during the break-up of his marriage to Princess Diana, and people suggested that he should stand aside from the succession in favour of his eldest son, Prince William.

The ideal "image" of the royals in the 1990s is still a matter of debate. Nobody

often uninspiring politicians; and not least it is a darned good show.

Unlike Queen Victoria, who tried to interfere with her democratically elected prime ministers and became so disenchanted with the whole business of politics that she seriously considered packing her bags and ruling the Empire from Australia, her descendents who have reigned this century as the House of Windsor have been adept at two things: keeping clear of the political arena and judging what style of monarchy the

wants them to return to being the remote figureheads they were until the 1960s, but many question whether the insistence of Britain's tabloid press in treating the family as the cast of an action-packed soap opera, reporting sexual indiscretions in a way undreamt of a decade ago, will destroy the mystique necessary to enable an hereditary monarchy to prosper in a democratic age. A savage TV puppet show, *Spitting Image*, has lampooned them mercilessly, depicting Princess Margaret as a gin swiller, Prince Charles as an ecology freak and Princess Diana as a brainless blonde inseparable from her Sony Walkman. But the scandals sur-

Above, Her Majesty Queen Elizabeth II, the richest woman in the world.

rounding the separations of Andrew and Fergie and Charles and Diana made the TV show seem almost restrained. So will the royals survive into the 21st century? Will Charles ever make it to the throne? Stay tuned for tomorrow's exciting episode…

Newspapers

After listening to a journalist passionately defending the importance of a politically free and unfettered press in a modern democracy such as Britain, a character in Tom

Independent, the *Financial Times*), it also has some of the worst *(The Sun, The Star)*.

By "worst", one means that objective news is consistently subordinated to highly imaginative stories about the sex lives of TV personalities, pop stars, footballers and the royal family, and that the few columns of genuine news are grotesquely sensationalised. Rupert Murdoch is generally credited with having started the downward slide with *The Sun*, best known for its photographs of topless models and its robust patriotism (its page-one headline after the sinking of the *Belgrano* during the Falklands War, with the drowning of many Argentine sailors, read simply "Gotcha!"). Significantly, *The Sun*

Stoppard's play *Night and Day* replies: "I'm with you on the free press. It's the newspapers I can't stand."

Many share that ambivalence, and opinion polls show that journalists are rated in public esteem somewhere below tax inspectors and secondhand car salesmen. The old Humbert Wolfe rhyme is often quoted:

You cannot hope to bribe or twist,
thank God, the British journalist.
But, seeing what the man will do
unbribed, there's no occasion to.

One reason for such cynicism is that, while Britain has some of the best newspapers in the world (*The Times, The Guardian, The*

remains the country's best-selling daily, with a circulation of nearly 4 million. That success makes it hard to ignore, but its critics can console themselves with the words of another Tom Stoppard character: "Junk journalism is the evidence of a society that has got at least one thing right, that there should be nobody with the power to dictate where responsible journalism begins." Even so, governments (whether Conservative or Labour) periodically threaten legal curbs when they feel the press is against them.

Above, avid readers of the world's best and the world's worst newspapers.

The saving grace is the diversity of Britain's papers. Eleven national dailies (total daily sale: 15 million) and 10 Sundays (total sale: 17 million) are distributed throughout the length of the country, augmented by a host of regional dailies and local weeklies.

One worry is concentration of ownership: Rupert Murdoch alone owns five national papers – including the top-selling Sunday scandal-sheet, the *News of the World* (circulation: nearly 5 million) and the top-selling Sunday quality, the *Sunday Times* (1.2 million).

Another often voiced complaint is that the majority of national newspapers remain politically right of centre. Such worries are probably overemphasised: all the evidence is that the British are every bit as cynical about politicians as they are about journalists and will vote according to their best interests, regardless of what their favourite newspaper advises them to do.

Official Secrets

Officially, there are lots of secrets in Britain, but no-one knows quite what they all are. The Official Secrets Act has the notorious catch-all phrase "against the national interest", which can even be used about information compiled from officially published government sources.

Parliament is free to discuss everything except the secret services, MI5 and MI6. Even the name of the head of British intelligence, which can be worked out from published sources by anyone with half a brain, could for many years only be mentioned in a whisper on the top of Ben Nevis for fear of prosecution. This is somewhat ironic, since during the Cold War the whole shooting match leeked like a sieve, notoriously leading to the defection of Kim Philby in 1963. He had been in British Intelligence since World War II, and had risen so high in the ranks he had been tipped to become chief of the Secret Intelligence Service.

Nor, until 1982, did GCHQ exist. This is the government's code-cracking, eavesdropping station in Cheltenham, which used to be signposted as an Experimental Radio Station. But when one of its senior officers confessed to assaulting three schoolgirls he didn't stop there. Geoffrey Prime, it turned out, had been telling the Soviets everything that went on at GCHQ for more than a decade. He was sentenced to 35 years for that, plus three years for the schoolgirls.

This idea of a "mole", an insider who is working for the other side, has provided the most intriguing material for the enormously popular spy books of Len Deighton and John Le Carré, whose thriller *The Spy Who Came in From the Cold* was published the year Philby defected. The Czech-born playwright Tom Stoppard even wrote a play in which a British spy, in retirement, could no longer remember which side he worked for. It sounded entirely plausible.

In the US, information is freely available about some aspects of Britain which is not available here. The government spent millions pursuing an official secrets case against the former intelligence officer Peter Wright after his book *Spycatcher* had been published in half the countries of the world.

In the post-Cold War years, secrecy is unlikely to go away. It seems ingrained in the way government and business work. Parliament conducts a lobby system in which selected political journalists are summoned and briefed by ministers at regular meetings. The journalists are then not allowed to say who they got their information from.

There is what is called a "Nanny knows best" attitude towards the public. It is an attitude which was most shockingly used in World War I when the people of Britain had no idea that a whole generation was being wasted in the mud of France.

Pubs

The best pub in England is called The Moon Under Water, and it hides down an unprepossessing side street in an old northern industrial town not far from Manchester. It has that indefinable richness of atmosphere that comes in part from its customers, who are mostly regulars and who attend not only for the beer but equally for the conversation, and in part from its uncompromisingly Victorian architecture and fittings, its dark-grained mahogany, ornamental mirrors and sparkling etched glass, its cast-iron fire-places and ceiling stained yellow-brown by decades of nicotine, all combining to create the solid comfortable ugliness of the 19th century.

It has games, particularly darts, in its public bar, and good solid plain food at prices that would bankrupt a restaurant. It has barmaids who know everyone by name, and a delightful garden where, in summer, the customers drink under the shade of plane trees, while their children play at a decent distance on swings and slides.

The Moon Under Water is entirely free from modern miseries: from piped music or piano, from plastic panels masquerading as

What makes a perfect pub is a personal, subjective judgement and remains, for the most part, an elusive goal. But there are certain well-defined ground rules for what makes a *good* pub, and of those there is no shortage. The rules are clearly defined for all to see by author Michael Jackson in the English beer-drinker's Bible, the annual *Good Beer Guide:* "In a good pub, the greatest attention is given to the drink, and in particular to the beer. Sociability, on both sides of the bar, comes a close second. A good pub encourages social intercourse, and is not dominated by cliques. A good pub has a caring, responsive landlord, not an uninterested time-server or an arrogant buffon. In a

oak, from sham roof beams and glass-topped tables. It is always quiet enough to talk, if only to praise the excellence of the fine traditional English ale, and to marvel at the reasonableness of its price.

The Moon Under Water does not exist, and never did. It was a figment of the imagination of George Orwell, who 50 years ago played a round of that perennially popular English game – dreaming of the perfect pub. There are 70,000 pubs in England and Wales and several thousand more in Scotland. The immense richness of their variety means that some are a great deal closer to perfection than others.

good pub, whatever further services are offered, there is always one bar (and preferably two) to accommodate those people who simply want to drink and chat without the distraction or inhibition induced by overbearing decor, noisy entertainment, or intrusive dining."

Every country has its drinking shop, but none has an institution quite like the British pub. The essence of a good pub (which modern buildings hardly ever achieve) is a feeling of intimacy. It must have nooks and crannies, corners and snugs, where conversations and assignations can take place without the whole world listening in.

The beer must be pumped into the glass. Still alive and fermenting, it is drunk at the temperature of the cool dark cellar without benefit of refrigeration. It has no carbon dioxide gas added to make it fizz, and it is brewed only from barley, hops and pure clear water. It should be golden or straw-coloured, and crystal clear when held up to the light.

Most pubs have at least two separate bars: the "public bar" which is the basic drinking shop; and the "lounge bar" which will probably have a carpet on the floor and rather more plush decoration. There may be a difference of a few pence in the drink prices, although all pubs are required by law to put their price lists prominently on display.

Some would say that the public bar is for serious, usually male, drinkers, or for workers in dirty overalls. It will probably have a bare floor and a dartboard, for darts remains the most popular of pub games, although it is being seriously challenged by pool. Conventionally, the lounge bar is for sitting down, for entertaining women, for an evening out. It may have a piano or piped music, both of which are an abomination because they interfere with the primary purpose of a pub (apart, of course, from drinking) which is conversation.

The word "pub" is merely a shortened form of "public house", an indication that the earliest ale houses were simply private homes where the occupant brewed beer and sold it at the front door or across a table in the living room. To indicate that the house sold ale, the owner would hang out a sign, not saying "Ale", as the average Saxon peasant never graduated to literacy, but a pole topped with a bough of evergreen.

There is no shortage of claimants to be the Oldest Pub in Britain, but one with a stronger case than most is the Trip to Jerusalem, hacked into the rock beneath the walls of Nottingham Castle, and certainly in business at the time of the 13th-century Crusades to drive the Saracen from the Holy Land, hence its name. Like so much else in British life, the pub reached its zenith in Victorian times and the country is still immensely rich in opulent pub interiors from that period, despite all the efforts of philistine brewery corporations to

rip them out in the name of "modernisation". Landlords, keen to rise above the squalid image of the gin shops and penny beer parlours, built magnificently: in mahogany and brass, marble and ceramic tile, exquisitely etched glass and decorative mirrors. It made the new electric light dance and sparkle like a fairy grotto.

Pubs have been changing over the past few decades. More and more of them sell good, inexpensive food and are competing strongly with restaurants. Tea and coffee are often on offer and children are being made more welcome. The law says that no one under 14 may enter a pub, and between 14 and 18 they must be accompanied by an adult and may

not buy or consume liquor. In reality some pubs, especially in country districts, welcome whole families. Some set aside special rooms for children and where there are gardens they are almost always welcome. It is, in the end, up to the absolute discretion of the landlord, and how strictly the local police chief applies the law.

The most radical change, however, came about in the 1988 licensing laws which allowed pubs in England and Wales to open not just at lunch time and in the evening, but all day, from 11am to 11pm. (Scottish laws already permitted all-day opening). About a third of the pubs take advantage of this,

Left and **above**, the perfect pub has friendly faces and is also a place for quiet reflection.

though Sunday hours remain 12–3pm and 7–10.30pm (12.30–2.30pm and 6.30–11 pm in Scotland). Twenty minutes' "drinking up" time is officially allowed after the closing time, half an hour for those who have had a meal.

Whatever the government legislates, the most important thing to understand about British pubs is that, although certain common factors prevail, every one is different in architecture, atmosphere and clientele.

Queues

"A man in a queue is as much the image of a true Briton as a man in a bull-ring is the image of a Spaniard or a man with a two-foot cigar of an American," wrote humorist George Mikes. "An Englishman, even if he is alone, forms an orderly queue of one."

This willingness to wait patiently in line even extends to driving. Approaching a roundabout (a much used traffic management device that caters for the urge to queue), drivers will seldom jostle for position or cut across other traffic as would, say, an Italian.

Queue-jumping incurs severe social disapproval, though this takes no more serious form than tut-tutting and loud remarks such as: "I say, don't they know there's a queue?" The easiest response is to pretend one is a foreigner; the affronted queuers will then sigh resignedly, knowing that you know no better, poor soul, having been deprived of their cultural conditioning.

Some think that the orderly behaviour of most crowds is the only rational behaviour when one lives in a small, overpopulated island. Others see such conspicuous respect for order as the Germanic traits never far below the surface in the British character (the presence of which helps explain why, even when the British and Germans were at loggerheads in two world wars, they continued to regard each other with respect).

Ralf Dahrendorf, a German who became head of the London School of Economics, may have got to the heart of the matter when he said: "I have a feeling that this island is uninhabitable, and therefore people have tried to make it habitable by being reasonable with one another."

Race

Britons have the blood of many people coursing through their veins. Even before history was written, tribes were coming in from Iberia, central Europe and the Indian subcontinent. Romans were followed by waves of Jutes, Angles, Saxons, Scandinavians and Normans (originally Scandinavian Norsemen). What Prince Llewellyn was fighting for in Wales was not the original Celtic heritage, but the last bastion of a tribe driven up from Iberia and finally stopped by the Irish Sea. Robert the Bruce,

champion of the Scots, was descended from Robert de Bruis, a French Norman knight who arrived with William the Conqueror.

Trade, persecution and war brought Flemish weavers, French Huguenots, Chinese sailors, White Russians, patriotic Poles and German Jews. Hunger brought, among others, the Irish. In the 1950s Commonwealth citizens were enticed to Britain with job offers, but when they arrived, mostly from the West Indies, they found a welcome not quite as warm as they had been led to expect. There are around half a million West Indians now; many have become assimilated into British culture, although some of the latest generation have begun to reassert their Afro-Caribbean heritage. Four black politicians were elected to parliament in 1987.

Asians came, too, from Africa and the Indian subcontinent, heading for the manufacturing cities of Birmingham, Bradford and Leicester. In 1972 Asians thrown out of Uganda were reluctantly allowed into Britain: increasingly, Her Majesty's Principal Secretary of State for Foreign and Commonwealth Affairs did not want to allow its Commonwealth citizens the right of abode and the word "immigrant" began to be used as a euphemism for coloureds or blacks.

Many Ugandan Asians were professional businessmen and, though they had to start

100,000 from Bangladesh. The 125,000 Chinese may well increase in 1997 when the lease of the Crown Colony of Hong Kong expires. Other ethnic minorities include 12,000 Africans and 73,000 Arabs.

Coloured ethnic groups make up just over 3 percent of Britain's 54.5 million population. Racial intolerance is not endemic but some nasty incidents are reported now and then, particularly against Asians. Sometimes poor black communities are provoked; sometimes they erupt. In surveys over the past 15 years, race has been seen as a diminishing social problem, but the country still has a long way to go before it feels comfortable as a multi-racial society.

their lives again with nothing, some were able to build up highly successful companies which their sons are now inheriting. On a smaller scale, newsagents and local grocers' shops with long opening hours are often Asian-run; in towns and villages everywhere there are Indian restaurants, usually owned or managed by people from Pakistan or Bangladesh. Also noticeable are the traditional fish-and-chip shops run as Chinese takeaways. There are around 800,000 Indians in Britain, 400,000 Pakistanis and

Left, 3 percent of Britain's population is coloured. **Above**, safe sex in the park.

Sex

Time to consult George Mikes again. "Continental people," he said, "have a sex life; the English have hot-water bottles." The description is probably just as true of the Scots and Welsh, though of course there are exceptions, and the nation did have a brief affair with sex in the Swinging Sixties. But in the AIDS era, the pendulum has swung back: *No Sex, Please, We're British* enjoyed an exceptionally long run in the West End.

Britons prefer their sex to be safe, a bit of

a naughty joke rather than a dangerous affair. There is a parallel with British eating habits: performed when needs dictate, with minimum flair. Just as Continental caterers have found scant competition in setting up the smaller, best-run restaurants and cafés, so generations of Continental men, faced with the British female on holiday, must wonder when their luck is going to run out.

Why should the most insincere, banal compliment, even when garnished with a foreign accent, produce such instant success year after year? It must be because, whatever other qualities it may possess, British sexuality is sorely lacking in flattery and flirtation. More often an initial encounter will

involve insulting banter. Two young men, for instance, may approach two young women in the following manner. One youth will target the woman of his choice and give his companion a grotesque nudge. "Here!" he will shout merrily. "Don't think much of your one!" From this exchange, the young lady in question will understand that her swain fancies her very much indeed.

Other "come-on" phrases may include "Watcha, Thunderthighs! What jumble sale did you get that in?" (a reference to any item of a young woman's clothing). And, designed to melt the heart, "Don't look so glum! Cat got your tongue, then?" No won-

der British women tend to fall on their backs when they hear their first sunny "Hello, preety lady" from a Continental. They have probably fainted with shock.

Traditionally, the attitude of the British to sex is prudish and repressive. They are supposed to be secretly addicted to spanking and other forms of corporal punishment for which public school has instilled a taste. They send each other postcards of a somewhat childish nature, showing, perhaps, a puny, henpecked husband, his obsessively fat and unattractive wife and a beautiful big-busted bikini-clad passer-by. The printed jest is double entendre of the "Ooh, what a lovely pear" variety.

This is by no means old-fashioned humour, as any click of the radio or television switch will reveal. There is no better crash course of British sexuality than the *Carry On* films (28 in all, full of cosy sexual stereotypes, from tarty, pneumatic blondes to outrageously effeminate homosexuals) or a *Benny Hill Show*. Our Benny always played the archetypal buffoonish innocent abroad, leering hopelessly at lovely women.

The British do not like overt sex displays. Not for them the garish shop windows of Dutch and German red-light districts. Every taste is catered for, particularly in the capital, but it is all reasonably discreet. No longer do street-walkers of both sexes ply their trade around Piccadilly Circus. The women left that scene decades ago and the boys' meat-rack was swept away by big police clean-ups more recently. But no telephone kiosk in town is without its "calling cards" tucked into every crevice, advertising a Roman-orgy range of vices for those who care to call.

Sex has never been a legitimate excuse for a crime of passion in Britain, but it haunts politicians. In 1963 the Profumo Scandal hastened the end of Harold Macmillan's Conservative government. The country was enthralled by the saga ("War Minister shares delights of call girl with Soviet naval attaché") and it still excited enough interest to be a successful film, *Scandal*, a quarter of a century later. In 1973 two lords, Lambton and Jellicoe, resigned from the government after admitting to having associated with prostitutes. The Conservative cabinet minister Cecil Parkinson, whom many believed Margaret Thatcher saw as her heir, blew his chances when he got his secretary pregnant.

Tea

On average, Britons drink five cups of tea a day, consuming about one third of the total tea export market every year. The "real" cup of tea is, however, not always easy to find. Places to go looking are posh hotels that cater for the better-off tourist, low-budget cafés of the fish-and-chip variety that thrive in seaside towns, and native British homes that have not gone over to teabags.

The finest tea is made from the bud and first two leaves of the tea bush. They should be steeped in boiled water for between three all methods involve mysterious and magical warmings and stirrings of the pot, exact timings and individual blends. Up North, they tend to put the tea in first, then add milk; down South they do the reverse and both halves of the country swear blind that theirs is the only way to make tea. Anyone with Far or Near East connections may well add a sneaky pinch of cardamom.

Notoriously cold British bedrooms inspired the Teasmade, a weird, rather outdated contraption – part alarm-clock, part Thermos, part eyesore – that promised a preprogrammed steaming cup of tea upon wakening. The taste does not live up to its technology, alas, but the idea of a solitary or

and five minutes. Traditionally, very strong Indian tea, rigid with tannin and probably jaw-clenchingly sweet, is favoured by burly men who work with their hands, while women, children and effete males like their cuppa watery-weak and China. But an occasional macho workman called out to fix something in a British home has reportedly voiced approval of delicately scented, pale Earl Grey.

There are as many ways of making a cup of tea properly as there are British residents and

Left, Christine Keeler caused a scandal that rattled many an afternoon cup of tea (above).

marital cup taken in bed suits the national isolationism – in contrast, for example, with the early morning Italian espresso downed sociably, standing elbow to elbow with strangers.

Dipping a biscuit, cake or burger in your teacup (dunking), or drinking from the saucer and blowing on your tea to cool it are socially out of order. It is also bad form to borrow someone else's spoon. Locals may call tea "tiffin", "char", "Rosie" (tea rhymes with Rosie Lee) or a "cuppa". They make it as a form of displacement activity, rather as a confused cat resorts to an unnecessary wash, at moments of high and emotional drama in their lives. Births and deaths require several gallons.

The Chinese were the first tea drinkers, thousands of years ago. Legend has it that a philosopher discovered its delights when leaves fell into his campfire pot of boiling water. Diarist Samuel Pepys found his first cup of China tea such a novelty in 1660 that he gave it a special entry. In its early days, it was so expensive that it had to be locked away in metal caddies to stop the servants helping themselves. Adding to the price was the cost of transportation from the Far East on such speedy clippers as the *Cutty Sark*, now in dry dock at Greenwich, in London.

The habit of afternoon tea with cakes was started around 1840 by the Duchess of Bedford. For a traditional afternoon tea, try a big hotel like the London Ritz, though it is necessary to book. The West Country's rich cream teas, with scones, jam, whipped double cream and cakes to accompany the pot of tea, is inexpensive, delicious in a sickly way and packed with cholesterol.

A cup of tea, without sugar or milk, contains only about four calories. Its stimulating effect is due to caffeine (weight for weight, tea leaves contain more than twice the caffeine of coffee beans), its astringency and colour come from the tannin content, and its flavour is produced by volatile oils.

High Tea is a full meal, eaten in the north of England – an early supper which may contain ham and eggs, bread-and-butter with various spreads and a good helping of cakes. To work one off, find a Tea Dance where you can do the foxtrot to such nostalgic inter-war orchestral numbers as *Blue Moon* and *Smoke Gets In Your Eyes*. Such dances were once highly fashionable and are still popular with older people, the occasional member of parliament and anyone else with a little free time in the afternoon.

Union Jack

The flag of Great Britain is the same as the flag of the United Kingdom, which includes Northern Ireland. Most Britons do not know its proper name and they call it the Union Jack. Better informed people, such as writers on *The Times*, call it the Union Flag, though

a further name for it is the Great Union (not to be confused with the Grand Union, a pleasant north London canal).

The Union Flag was first designed after the union between England and Scotland in 1606, combining the red cross of St George (heraldically speaking, cross gules in a field argent) with Scotland's cross of St Andrew, a white diagonal cross on a blue background (saltire argent in a field azure). In 1801 Ireland introduced St Patrick, adding his red diagonal cross (saltire gules in a field argent). No room is left for Wales's St Dewi, or David, whose emblem is a dove.

The constituent parts of the kingdom also have animals and plants for their own flags

and heraldic devices: lions for both England and Scotland and a dragon for Wales; a rose for England, a thistle for Scotland and a leek for Wales.

Although it is not immediately apparent, the Union Flag is a bit lopsided and may only be flown one way up. If hoisted incorrectly, particularly at sea, where mariners are well informed in these matters, it may be taken for a distress signal. The flag of any country hoisted on the jackstaff of a ship's bows is called the Jack. When the Union Flag is hoisted on a jackstaff it can be called the Union Jack. Tearing up or burning the Union Flag is impolite, but not an offence.

Vicars

"What a pity it is that we have no amusements but vice and religion," said Sydney Smith. As a journalist as well as a clergyman, Smith, who was born in Essex in 1771, knew both the failings and the predelictions of the British. And, nearly two centuries after his death, the vicar is still portrayed as an object of affectionate ridicule. He is the stuff that farces are made of: a blathering, upper-class nincompoop who regularly looses his trousers or is otherwise compromised through misunderstandings. Or he is the sorry figure

it is the Church of England, with the Queen as its head, that is the backbone of Britain's moral society. The sovereign's role, established by Henry VIII, gives her power to appoint (these days to approve) the two archbishops, of Canterbury and York, who are in turn responsible for their bishoprics and for the church's ruling body, the General Synod, which regulates church matters subject to parliament and royal assent.

On the whole, the Church of England, though rather stuck with a typically British misogynous establishment unkeen on the ordination of women, is pretty easy-going. It has a liberal, ecumenical approach and prefers compassion to fire and brimstone.

the tabloid press triumphantly produces, accused of sins of the flesh.

In reality, the vicar who pops in for afternoon tea and lives in an enormous grace-and-favour vicarage is a disappearing breed. Although a slight upturn was detected in congregations at the beginning of the 1990s, they have dwindled, and Britain cannot be called a nation of churchgoers. The Church is, however, a microcosm of society. Mosques, synagogues and temples co-exist beside cathedrals, churches and chapels. But

Left, patriotic painted face. **Above**, the Scots Presbyterian minister, made of sterner stuff.

Not so its Welsh and Scots counterparts. The Scots Presbyterian Church is a stern church, Calvinist in its beliefs. Worshippers in the remoter parts of the country still regard cooking, washing up or reading a newspaper on Sundays as a cardinal sin. Scots Catholics, too, are far stricter than English ones.

Nor is there such a liberal tradition among the ministry of Wales, where the loveless and utilitarian "chapel" is well attended. The chapels are Methodist, a movement founded by the 18th-century evangelist John Wesley, which urged thrift and hard work and appealed to the working class. It took hold in the working populations of north-east England, parts of Cornwall and, particularly, Wales where, linked with the Welsh language, Calvinistic Methodism evolved.

Unlike their English counterparts, none of these serious-minded clerics who watch from the side chapels of the realm are liable to be caught with their trousers down. If they were, it would be no laughing matter.

Weather

"When two Englishmen meet, their first talk is of the weather," wrote Dr Samuel Johnson.

Two centuries later, this relatively harmless national obsession is still going strong and no weather-related phrase is considered too banal or boring to merit use as a conversational opening gambit between strangers. Try "Hot/cold enough for you, then, is it?" "Looks like rain", "All right if you're a duck" and "Don't suppose this will hold much longer" – all useful, widely used phrases.

Why should the British be so interested in the vagaries of their climate? The key lies in its unpredictability. Its swings of mood don't bear out its dull reputation at all. Far from always having the drizzly, mediocre sum-

mers and mild, wet winters of popular misconception, British weather can switch rapidly from drought to flood, damp cold to oppressive heat. Each dramatic change catches Britons on the hop.

The summer of 1976 contained the longest spell of continuous heat, while in August 1990 temperatures reached the highest ever recorded: 98.8° F (37.1° C). Hurricanes in 1987 and 1990 caused several deaths and uprooted thousands of trees, Western film-style dust "devils" have blown through the lanes of Surrey, and waves higher than a double-decker bus submerged a seaside town in Wales.

Such violent extremes are made all the harder to bear because national habits, buildings and clothing are simply not designed to cope with them. Few homes or offices have fans or air conditioning to alleviate the summer's heat. In winter, heating and insulation systems work at half-cock, while road and rail networks inevitably come to a standstill in anything more than an inch of snow (British Rail, brought to a halt by one light snowfall, said it was the "wrong kind" of snow). Unwary motorists, villagers and livestock disappear under mounds of drifting snow in a manner that puzzles Continentals used to handling such seasonal hazards.

The British have a strange pride in describing their childhood bedrooms in winter. These were often of such incredible coldness that parental false teeth and pet goldfish supposedly froze solid in their water overnight. They like to pretend to ignore the weather. They would prefer to pit themselves against the worst the elements can throw at them, rather than make themselves comfortable, which would be wimpish.

So, in summer's oven heat, they do not hide in tree-shaded piazzas or close their shutters to keep the tiled floor cool. Their cities are designed to ensure that streets become sweltering canyons, while over-furnished homes become more stuffy. In winter, people frequently dress inadequately, as if out of bravado. Women slush through icy pavements to the shops wearing carpet slippers. Men sweat in summer traffic jams in heavyweight synthetic suits, tie only slightly loosened.

Hats (other than those expensive designer creations shown off at Ascot) are generally not taken seriously. Anyone spotted wearing something large and shady to fend off sunstroke or stop precious body heat seeping away is probably foreign.

Global warming may change British weather forever, creating very hot, long, dry summers. The writer Virginia Woolf thought that such weather might turn us all into outgoing Mediterraneans. But relentless, reliable sunshine is far more likely to provoke deep Scandinavian gloom, making us all sadder than SAD – Seasonal Affective Disorder, a condition diagnosed by doctors and normally produced by too little, rather than too much light.

For although the British have always dreamed of an empire upon which the sun plastic rainhat, furled down to the size of a condom and secreted in the handbag, is still favoured today by older ladies with tightly permed, snowy hair.

One famous British weather feature is, happily, dead and gone: the noxious, sulphuric fog that used to blanket cities in chest-clogging yellow fumes and cause hundreds of deaths each year. It got everywhere, including the auditorium of the Royal Opera House, Covent Garden, where it was once so bad the audience could not see the stage. It became a film stock favourite, usually wafting across lamplit, cobbled streets to denote 19th-century London. A sinister, cloaked stranger would collide with cheery police-

never sets, dependable good weather spoils their "just-in-case" philosophy. Umbrellas, extra woollens and fold-up plastic raincoats are much-loved accessories. British women might have been considered as chic as Parisiennes were it not for their just-in-case cardigans flung inelegantly over summer dresses. In the days before golfing umbrellas were big and country people waxed their coats, ugly folding plastic macs used to make rainswept holidaymakers look like film-wrapped, self-basting chickens. The small

Left and above, come snow or sunshine the weather is a constant topic of conversation.

man: "Terrible night, Guv, a real pea-souper." Another horrible murder was only moments away. In real life, the 1956 Clean Air Act put an end to these killer smogs.

Britons today keep a keen weather eye on their climate by frequently tuning in to radio and television forecasts. Television weathermen and women, civil servants from the Meteorological Office in Bracknell, Berkshire, are given cult status and are loved for their blend of ordinariness and eccentricity. Odd voices, peculiar glasses, bad-taste jumpers and silly names (like Michael Fish, famous for not predicting the 1987 hurricane) ensure superstardom.

Xenophobia

Like many island peoples, the British – and especially the working classes – have a profound distrust of outsiders, perhaps equating them unconsciously with invaders. It is not by chance that it took them so long to agree, reluctantly, to help finance a tunnel beneath the English Channel.

The writer Nancy Mitford expressed an extreme version of this narrow-mindedness: "Abroad is unutterably boring and foreigners are fiends." The actor Robert Morley was more circumspect: "The British tourist is always happy abroad so long as the natives are waiters."

Even when dealing with their fellow Europeans, the British fall back on stereotypes. David Frost and Anthony Jay, in their book *To England With Love*, definitively summed up hell for the British as "a place where the Germans are the police, the Swedish are the comedians, the Italians are the defence force, Frenchmen dig the roads, the Belgians are the pop singers, the Spanish run the railways, the Turks cook the food, the Irish are the waiters, the Greeks run the government, and the common language is Dutch."

Youth

The teenager was invented in 1945 as a category of market research by 19-year-old Eugene Gilbert. Gilbert set up his copywriting company while still a student and made a fortune in America out of strategic use of phrases such as "dig this", "far out" and "groovy daddyo" to an impressed advertising industry. But when his London office opened and closed in the same year, his explanation was that "teenagers in Britain haven't found enough freedom or money to be commercially interesting."

The postwar world economy was built around the United States – the symbol of the future. Britain's wannabe rock-and-rollers even sounded as if they came from half-way across the Atlantic. But the authorities didn't make it easy for them to practise their accents: they banned Marlon Brando's 1954 film *The Wild One* for 13 years, and felt their caution justified when cinema riots greeted Bill Haley's *Rock Around the Clock*.

Teenagers began to be more commercially interesting as the 1950s melted into the 1960s, a result of full employment. They surprised their elders and betters by not only dancing to Tutti Frutti but by being able to spell it, too. They were better built, fed, clothed, housed and educated than ever before. Between 1938 and 1956 the number of children in secondary and higher education had doubled.

With education came a conscience, a rejection of materialism, nuclear arms and parental values. In life as well as literature, the anti-hero was "in". For a youth subculture on the campus, students in duffle coats (toggle-fastening, coarse wool coats with hoods) distinguished themselves by refusing to get into fights – even if somebody made fun of their garb.

Fighting was left to two gangs, the Mods and the Rockers, usually at seaside resorts on Bank Holiday weekends. The rockers were oily bikers on Harley-Davidsons or British machines, the Mods had short hair, wore suits and rode Italian motorscooters. Their encounters were seen as two mutually exclusive visions of the future: Europe's and America's. It was cappuccino versus Coca-Cola. Blood was spilt but no clear winner emerged.

The Merseybeat, amounting to little more than The Beatles and their lookalikes from Liverpool, pulled the spotlight away from the capital for a while. But Mary Quant's fashions and the Rolling Stones soon had London swinging again. Hippies and glam rockers in platform boots and glittery jackets came and went in the 1970s.

Then, just as things were beginning to look boring, in the long hot summer of 1976 punk arrived. The music was loud and live and, like the clothes, designed to shock. Serious rebels adorned their bodies with safety pins and tattoos and opted for day wear associated with dirty sex – rubber, leather or bondage. Swastikas, swearing and spitting were the order of the day and everyone spoke with a fake working-class accent.

By the early 1980s punk had become a spiky-haircut postcard image to sell the tourists. Thatcher's children were growing up to become the Me generation of 18-year-old merchant bankers and stockbrokers who drove Porsches and lived in developments that rose from London's filled-in docks. These teenagers led the revolution of new money which supposedly would sweep the class system away.

But by the end of Thatcher's 1980s, the cycle of unemployment and inflation ushered in a more caring Britain. Even Thatcher, by her third term of office, suddenly became concerned about the environment. Other "young" issues, such as disarmament and the Third World, were the concern of all the political parties. In post-Thatcher Britain a new school, which surfaced in Liverpool and Manchester, began to talk once more about

Zeitgeist

Taking a nation's spiritual temperature is as precise an art as palmistry, but a clue to Britain's confusing symptoms since World War II was provided by Dean Acheson, a US Secretary of State, who declared: "Great Britain has lost an Empire and has not yet found a role." Instead, it has embraced a wide repertoire of roles: in the 1950s, that of a respectable, middle-class spinster, strapped for cash but determined to maintain her dignity; in the 1960s, that of a buoyantly optimistic, fashion-conscious good-time

global love and to exhort each other to "dig this, man". Flared trousers were seen. British youth had turned another circle.

Today teenagers have freedom. They can join the army and get married at 16, the age of consent; at 18 they can vote and get drunk. They are commercially interesting to car manufacturers, record companies and food chains. Even parents listen to what they say. But Britain's politicians will never take the young 'uns seriously – not until they get a job, a vote and a haircut.

Above, seaside Bank Holiday Mods who fought it out with big-bike Rockers.

girl; in the 1970s, that of a lonely woman beset by financial worries, spurned by America and regarded by Europe as dowdy and old-fashioned; in the 1980s, a career woman, inspired by Margaret Thatcher to embrace a red-blooded success ethic.

But where are the good roles in the 1990s for an ageing player on the world stage? There was a high-profile supporting role in America's 1991 action blockbuster *War in the Gulf*. But the future may lie in European co-productions, sharing the smaller-print billing with her Continental counterparts. It hasn't the glamour of Hollywood, but times change – and well, a girl's got to eat.

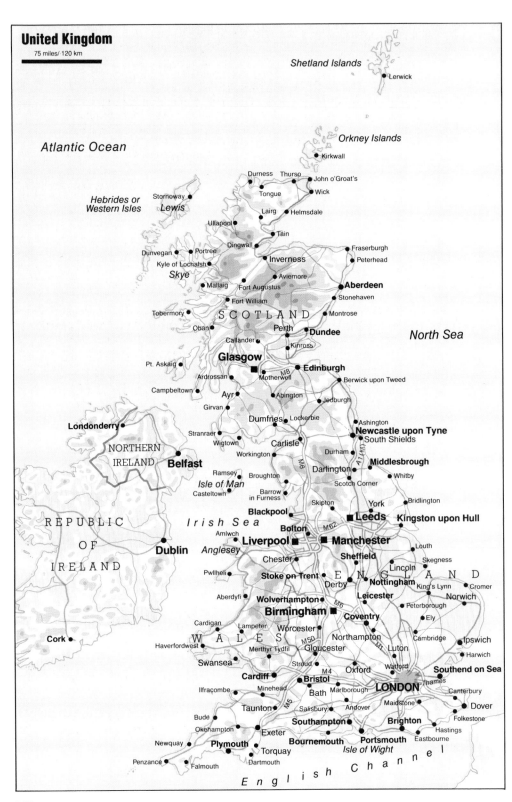

United Kingdom

75 miles/ 120 km

Shetland Islands
● Lerwick

Atlantic Ocean

Orkney Islands
● Kirkwall

Hebrides or
Western Isles   Lewis
● Stornoway

Durness Thurso
● ● John o'Groat's
Tongue ● Wick
Lairg ● Helmsdale
Ullapool ●
● Tain
Dingwall ●
● Fraserburgh
Dunvegan ● Portree ● Peterhead
Kyle of Lochalsh ● Inverness
Skye ● Aviemore
● Mallaig Fort Augustus
Fort William ● Aberdeen
● Stonehaven
Tobermory ● S C O T L A N D ● Montrose
Oban ● Perth ● Dundee
Callander ● North Sea
● Kinross
Pt. Askaig ● Glasgow ● Edinburgh
Ardrossan ● Motherwell M8
Campbeltown ● ● Berwick upon Tweed
Ayr ● Abington
Girvan ● ● Jedburgh
Dumfries ● Lockerbie
Londonderry ● ● Ashington
● Newcastle upon Tyne
Stranraer ● ● South Shields
Wigtown ● Carlisle
NORTHERN Workington ● Durham ● ● Middlesbrough
IRELAND Darlington ● Whitby
Belfast Broughton ● Scotch Corner
Ramsey ● M6
Isle of Man ● Skipton ● Bridlington
Barrow ● York
Castletown ● in Furness
Blackpool ● ● Kingston upon Hull
REPUBLIC Irish Sea ● Leeds
Bolton ● M62
OF Amlwch ● Liverpool ● Manchester
Dublin Anglesey ● Louth
IRELAND Chester ● Sheffield ● Skegness
Pwllheli ● Lincoln
Stoke on Trent ● E N G L A N D ● Cromer
Aberdyfi ● Derby ● Nottingham King's Lynn
Wolverhampton ● Leicester Norwich
Cardigan Birmingham ● Peterborough
Lampeter Worcester ● Coventry ● Ely
Cork ● W A L E S ● Northampton Cambridge ● Ipswich
Haverfordwest Merthyr Tydfil M50 Luton ● Harwich
Gloucester ● Watford
Swansea ● Stroud M1
Cardiff ● Bristol Oxford ● Southend on Sea
Ilfracombe ● Minehead Bath Marlborough LONDON Thames
M4 ● Canterbury
Taunton ● M5 Salisbury ● Andover Maidstone ● Dover
Bude ● Folkestone
Okehampton ● Southampton ● Brighton ● Hastings
Newquay ● Exeter ● Bournemouth Portsmouth Eastbourne
Plymouth ● Torquay Isle of Wight
Penzance ● Falmouth Dartmouth
E n g l i s h   C h a n n e l

In the early 1960s, before jogging and trainers were invented, Dr Barbara Moore began a brief craze of walking the length of the country, 874 miles (1,408 km) from John O'Groats in the northeast of Scotland to Land's End in Cornwall. (Even in this land of eccentrics she was thought rather crazy.) Though it took several weeks, it made the island seem small. Today a motorist could make the trip in not much more than a day, and it seems to have shrunk still further. But within that short distance there is an extraordinary variety of landscape, of peoples and places to see.

Apart from winter in the blizzard-blown Highlands of Scotland, getting around the country is very easy, particularly by car, and minor roads have always been good. Britain is, however, a crowded island: traffic can be bumper to bumper on motorways, especially such arteries as the M1, M4 and M6 and on London's orbital M25, while in the capital itself the average speed of traffic is the same as it was in the days of horse-drawn carriages.

Britain has its own favourite holiday haunts: the Lake Dictrict in the northwest, the Peak District in the Midlands, Devon and the Cornish Riviera in the West Country and the Pembroke Coast in South Wales. The Scots tend to head for the West Coast which is big enough to diffuse most crowds, while Blackpool, Britain's favourite seaside resort, creaks a bit under its 6 million annual visitors.

The tourist, rightfully, wants to see the classic sites, to visit the historic buildings, the university towns, to go on literary and artistic pilgrimages, to enjoy the splendour of castles, gardens and country houses. There is, however, pressure on these places and there is a continuing debate about limiting numbers. (Oxford, for instance, the third most visited city in Britain after London and Edinburgh, is concerned at the effect of around 3½ million visitors a year; it may follow the example of a Cambridge college which is is trying to reduce the numbers by charging an entrance fee.)

While this guide gives all the necesssary information about these important and popular historic centres, it also suggests a host of other places to visit, places that are often missed but which give just as much insight into the life and culture of Britain. The chapters have been divided geographically in a way that makes each area easy to explore, and the Travel Tips section at the back of the book contains further recommendations that will help you gain an insight into Britain both on and off the beaten track.

Preceding pages: Knights of The Most Noble Order Of The Garter at Windsor Castle; Victorian elegance at a Welsh fair; wedding in Exeter. Following pages: Big Ben and the Houses of Parliament.

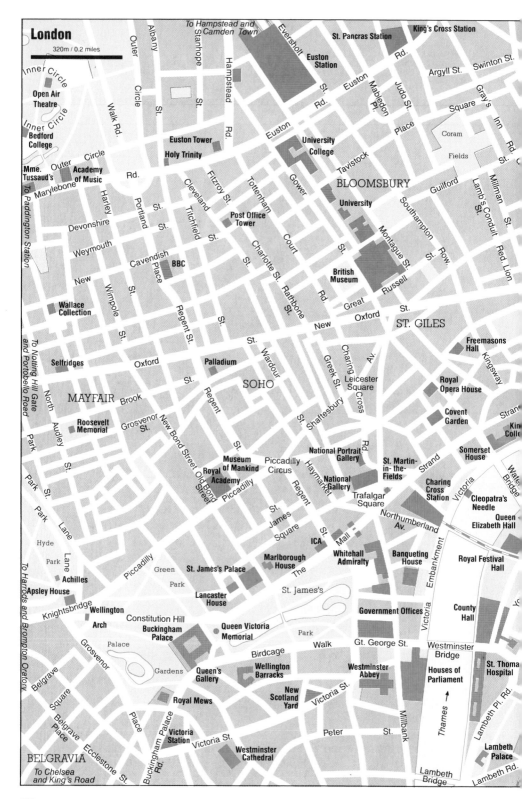

London

320m / 0.2 miles

To Hampstead and Camden Town

Inner Circle
Outer Circle
Open Air Theatre
Inner Circle
Bedford College
Mme. Tussaud's
Academy of Music
To Paddington Station
Marylebone Rd.

Albany St.
Stanhope St.
Hampstead Rd.
Walk Rd.
Circle

Eversholt St.
Euston Station
Euston Rd.
Euston

St. Pancras Station
King's Cross Station
Rd.
Euston Rd.
Argyll St.
Swinton St.
Mabledon Pl.
Judd St.
Gray's Inn Rd.
Square
Coram Fields

Euston Tower
Holy Trinity

University College

BLOOMSBURY

Tavistock

University

Guilford
Lamb's Conduit St.
Milman St.
Red Lion

Devonshire
Weymouth
Harley St.
Portland St.
Cleveland
Titchfield St.
Fitzroy St.
Cavendish Place
BBC

Tottenham Court Rd.
Charlotte St.
Rathbone St.

Gower St.
Montague St.
Southampton Row.
Russell
St.

Wallace Collection
New
Wimpole St.
Regent St.

Post Office Tower

British Museum

Great Oxford St.
New
St. GILES

To Notting Hill Gate and Portobello Road
Selfridges
Oxford St.
MAYFAIR
Brook
Grosvenor St.
Roosevelt Memorial
North Audley St.
Park Lane
Hyde Park
Park Lane
Achilles

Palladium
Regent St.
SOHO
Wardour St.
Greek St.
Shaftesbury
Charing Cross Rd.
Leicester Square
Av.
Freemasons Hall
Kingsway
Royal Opera House
Covent Garden
Strand
King's College
Somerset House

New Bond Street
Old Bond Street
Museum of Mankind
Royal Academy
Piccadilly
Piccadilly Circus
Regent St.
Haymarket
National Portrait Gallery
National Gallery
St. Martin-in-the-Fields
Charing Cross Station
Victoria
Strand
Cleopatra's Needle
Queen Elizabeth Hall
Trafalgar Square
Northumberland Av.
Water Bridge

To Harrods and Brompton Oratory
Apsley House
Knightsbridge
Wellington Arch
Constitution Hill
Grosvenor
Palace
Belgrave Square
Belgrave Place
Eccleston St.

St. James's
ICA
Marlborough House
The
St. James's
Mall
Whitehall
Admiralty
Banqueting House
Embankment
Victoria
Royal Festival Hall
County Hall

Piccadilly
Green Park
St. James's Palace
Lancaster House
Park

Buckingham Palace
Queen Victoria Memorial
Birdcage Walk
Gardens
Queen's Gallery
Wellington Barracks
Royal Mews
New Scotland Yard
Victoria St.

Government Offices
Gt. George St.
Westminster Abbey
Westminster Bridge
Houses of Parliament
Thames
St. Thomas Hospital
Lambeth Pl. Rd.

BELGRAVIA
To Chelsea and King's Road
Buckingham Palace Rd.
Victoria Station
Victoria St.
Westminster Cathedral
Peter St.
Millbank
Lambeth Bridge
Lambeth Palace
Lambeth Rd.

122

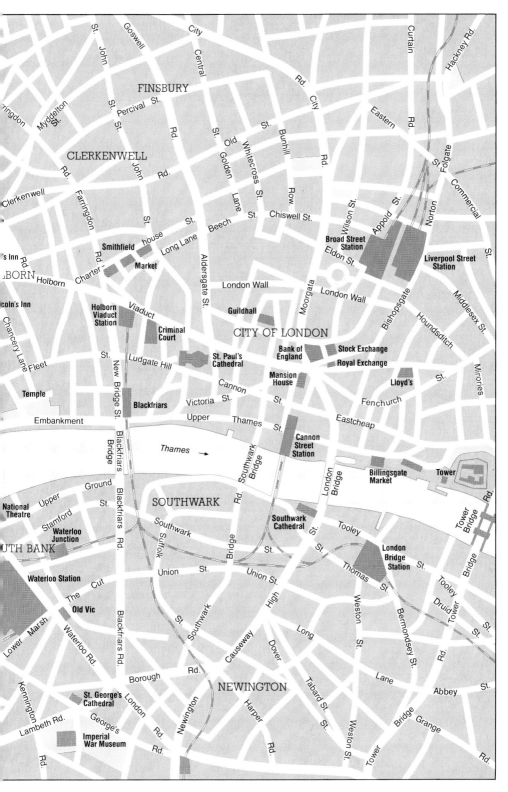

LONDON

London, thou great emporium of our isle,
O though too bounteous, thou too fruitful Nile!

— John Dryden

Not every visitor to London has come away enthusiastic. Henry James, witnessing the squalor of London's slums in the 19th century, called the city "a horrible numerosity". Dostoyevsky, sharing James's opinion, described London as "vast as an ocean… a Biblical symbol, some prophesy of the apocalypse." Thomas De Quincey's disaffection was more mundane: "A duller spectacle the earth of ours has not to show than a rainy Sunday in London."

There is, however, the flip side of the coin, the London that has delighted and enchanted visitors and residents for at least five centuries. And no one has captured in words the excitement of London as well as Samuel Johnson, the doctor who had a literary cure for just about everything: "When a man is tired of London he is tired of life, for there is in London all that life can afford."

Today, 200 years later, Johnson's words still ring true. There are few cities that offer such a variety of sights and sounds, few places that present a mood to suit just about any whim. London is there for the taking, so take and enjoy.

Trafalgar beginnings: The pigeon-filled precinct called **Trafalgar Square** is a good starting point. Sitting at the core of London as one of the most impressive public squares in the world. Trafalgar was laid out in 1829 by Sir Charles Barry and dedicated to the memory of Admiral Lord Nelson and his brilliant victory over Napoleon's fleet off Cape Trafalgar in 1805. The square is a paragon of the Classical style, enclosed by graceful white facades and dominated by the 164-ft (50-metre) **Nelson's Column** and four bronze lions. This is the strategic heart of London. The financial wizards of the City work to the east; the entertainment empire of the West End lies directly to the north; and the government palaces of Whitehall and Westminster stretch to the south.

Trafalgar Square is a transportation hub, traversed by a dozen bus lines and five different Tube lines. The square is also the scene of London's annual New Year's Eve bash and it has been the site of political demonstrations for more than 100 years. And in case there's trouble, the smallest police station in England sits in a lamppost at the southeast corner, with a direct telephone link to Scotland Yard.

The French Crown Jewels are said to be buried beneath Trafalgar Square: Madame du Barry, the mistress of Louis XV, brought them to London in 1793 and, the legend goes, buried the stones in the grounds of the old Royal Mews, later demolished to make way for Trafalgar Square. Madame du Barry returned to France and lost her head upon the guillotine – but she never disclosed the whereabouts of the missing jewels.

The **National Gallery** runs along the north flank of Trafalgar Square. Inau-

Left, Georgian town house. **Right**, St Martin-in-the-Fields, the oldest building in Trafalgar Square.

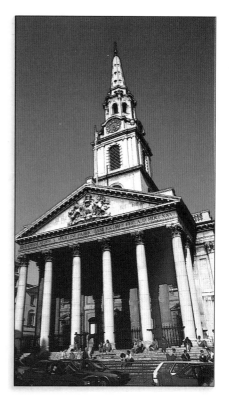

gurated in 1838 as a storehouse for British art, the gallery has since grown into one of the most outstanding and comprehensive collections in the world, with a list of masters ranging from da Vinci and Rembrandt to El Greco and Van Gogh. In 1991 the architecturally controversial "Sainsbury Wing", designed by Robert Venturi, was opened. It is the latest of a number of extensions to this grand neoclassical building which have been necessary due to the increasing growth of its collection.

Around the corner is the superb **National Portrait Gallery**, established in 1856. Presenting an illustrated British history, it now contains the faces of over 9,000 famous Britons.

St Martin-in-the-Fields church is the oldest surviving structure on Trafalgar Square, built along simple but elegant lines by James Gibbs in the early 18th century. The church became well-known during World War II as a refuge from the Blitz. St Martin is still the parish church for Buckingham Palace, with royal boxes at the east end. It might remind Americans of a New England country church because its distinctive style was copied widely in the 13 colonies before their independence.

Serendipitous Covent Garden: Northeast of Trafalgar Square begins the maze of narrow streets and tiny alleys called **Covent Garden**, now the hub of entertainment London but once a notorious red-light district and criminal haunt. There has been some type of market on this spot for more than 300 years, but the name actually derives from the convent garden that occupied the area until Henry VIII's Dissolution. At the centre of Covent Garden lies a cobblestone square and superb steel-and-glass market pavilions constructed in the 1830s to house flower, fruit and vegetable stalls. The market was moved to new quarters south of the river at Nine Elms in 1974, and the old district passed into several years of poverty and neglect. But in the early 1980s, Covent Garden was refurbished into an area of restaurants, shops and cafés. It's now a showplace for buskers, or street entertainers, and a summer mecca both for office workers at lunchtime and for tourists.

London's Busking Festival takes place at Covent Garden the last two weeks of July each year to celebrate the first Punch and Judy show, staged here in the 18th century. The popular Jubilee Market on weekends offers a colourful hodgepodge of arts and crafts, food stalls and puppet shows. But the action at Covent Garden really heats up at night. Those with a taste for English tradition might imbibe at the many ancient pubs in the area such as the **Lamb and Flag**, a 16th-century pub known in its more sinister days as the "Bucket of Blood". Tutton's Café is good for a quiet chat, while the **Rock Garden** offers an ear-shattering array of live music.

Covent Garden is also synonymous with British theatre, for the district plays host to the best of London's drama, music and dance. Some of the names associated with Covent Garden's past are Sarah Bernhardt, Charlie Chaplin, Richard Sheridan, George Bernard Shaw and Margot Fonteyn. The **Theatre Royal** was established on Drury Lane in

Saxophonist playing for his supper, Covent Garden.

1663 and is still a showcase for musicals. Nearby stands the majestic **Royal Opera House**, home of both the Royal Opera and Ballet Companies. Covent Garden is also popular for afternoon shopping, especially cobblestoned **Neal Street** with its unique collection of speciality shops. One shop sells only kites; another deals in shells.

Bibliophiles usually make haste for **Charing Cross Road**, which marks the western boundary of Covent Garden district with a solid wall of bookshops. They range from **Foyle's** (the largest bookstore in London) to tiny specialist enclaves like **A. Zwemmer** (graphic design and photography), **Silver Moon** (feminist books and literature at No. 68), plus the usual mainstream bookshop chains (such as **Waterstone's**).

For a change of scene, take a stroll through the **Photographer's Gallery** in Great Newport Street with its changing exhibitions of historic and contemporary photographs. The gallery doubles as a café, so it's also a perfect place to quench a thirst or rest tired feet.

Just beyond Charing Cross Road is **Leicester Square**. This is the domain of an odd assortment of tourists, pigeons and drunks, a gaudy place filled with flashing neon and throbbing music that's home to another form of London entertainment – the cinema. More than a dozen movie houses are scattered around its leafy confines, and there's a statue of London-born Charlie Chaplin as The Little Tramp in the southwest corner.

High-class club land: A much different atmosphere is found in **Pall Mall**, a sedate and elegant avenue that runs through the heart of the St James's district to the west of Trafalgar Square. This is London's "Club Land" – the exclusive gathering place of English gentlemen behind the closed doors of the Athenaeum, White's, the Carlton and a dozen other private enclaves. The street takes its name from *paille maille*, a French lawn game imported to England in the 17th century and played by Charles I on a long green which once occupied this site.

Wedged between the wood-panelled

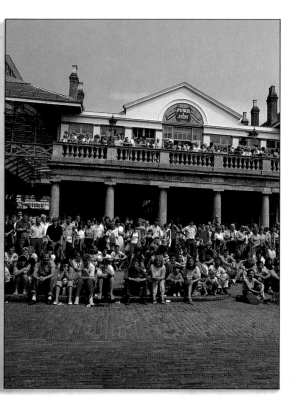

Left, Waiting for the street show to begin, Covent Garden. **Right**, a Royal Horse Guard in Whitehall.

halls of Pall Mall and the leafy landscape of Green Park are a number of stately homes. The most impressive of these is **St James's Palace**, built by Henry VIII in the 1530s. This was the official royal residence until Queen Victoria moved court to nearby Buckingham Palace in 1837. St James's is now occupied by royal servants, although foreign ambassadors are still appointed to the Court of St James's. This cluster of royal mansions also includes **Marlborough House**, **Clarence House** and **Lancaster House**, where Chopin played a royal command performance for Queen Victoria.

The Mall is London's impressive ceremonial way, a broad tree-lined avenue that runs from Buckingham Palace to the Admiralty Arch. The spectacular Trooping the Colour takes place on the Mall each June, as Queen Elizabeth rides sedately down the avenue in a horse-drawn carriage with an escort of Household Cavalry as part of a 200-year-old ceremony to mark the official birthday of the monarch. The legions mass on **Horse Guard Parade**, a huge open space behind Whitehall, where the various royal units troop their regimental flags to the tune of marching music and thundering drums. The Household Cavalry can also be seen at 11.30 a.m. daily (alternative days in winter), as they ride down the Mall on their way to and from the changing of the guard at Buckingham Palace. They also mount a guard outside the old palace entrance on Whitehall.

Overlooking the Mall is the **Institute of Contemporary Arts**, a continually changing showcase for the cutting edge of modern painting, sculpture and the performing arts, housed within the incongruous setting of Georgian-style Nash House.

Londoners have a love-hate relationship with **Buckingham Palace**. To some, it's one of the ugliest buildings in the capital, but it's also held in esteem as the symbol of Britain's royalty. The palace arose within a mulberry grove in the early 18th century as a mansion for the powerful Duke of Buckingham. It

The Guards at Buckingham Palace.

was later purchased by George III (who preferred to live in St James's Palace). George had some improvements made to it in the 18th century. However, it wasn't grand enough for George IV (the Prince Regent) and when the building came into his control he commissioned his favourite architect, John Nash, to rebuild it on a more magnificent scale. The marble triumphant arch was no longer large enough and had to be removed to where it now stands on the corner of Hyde Park. Neverthless, despite all these alterations the palace wasn't occupied until Victoria became queen and made it the official royal residence in London.

Visitors gather at 11.30am in front of Buckingham Palace for the Changing of the Guard and perhaps to snatch a glimpse of the Queen, who is in residence when the standard is flying. Otherwise, only two sections of the palace are open to the public: the **Royal Mews** (stables), and the **Queen's Gallery**, which displays a rotating sample of paintings from the Royal Collection.

Bounding Buckingham Palace on the north and east are two of London's renowned green spaces – the arboreal tracts of St James's Park and Green Park. **St James's** in particular has lush vegetation and a tranquil lake. Indeed, the park provides haven for a multitude of water birds (including a flock of pelicans given by a Russian czar more than 300 years ago), office workers and civil servants. The wooden footbridge across the lake gives a superb view of Buckingham Palace. **Green Park** is a wild and rugged contrast. There are no tidy flower beds or ornate fountains – just rolling expanses of grass and woods where Charles II used to take his daily constitutional.

Westminster's grandeur: A short walk from the southeast corner of St James's Park is **Westminster**, the symbol of English government for nearly 1,000 years. Westminster is also a holy place – the burial ground of English monarchs, the site of one of the greatest monasteries of the Middle Ages and the location of the most inspiring Gothic

The 1,000-roomed Houses of Parliament.

architecture in London. The area was a marshy wasteland inhabited by lepers until the 11th-century reign of Edward the Confessor, who took a distinct liking to Westminster and built both a great church and a palace upon the reclaimed land. Edward never saw the completion of this Gothic *tour de force*; he died the day before the consecration of Westminster Abbey and was buried behind the high altar. Within days, the ill-fated Harold (soon to lose his throne to William the Conqueror) was crowned as the new king during a special ceremony in the Abbey. This set yet another precedent, for since that day in 1065, all but two English monarchs have been crowned in the church.

Little remains of Edward's Saxon Abbey; it was completely rebuilt under the invading Normans and then redesigned in flamboyant French-Gothic style 200 years later. The Abbey's top treasure is the **Henry VII Chapel**, a 16th-century masterpiece of fan-vaulted ceilings in pure white stone, decked out in the colourful medieval banners of the Knights Grand Cross of the Order of the Bath. Behind lies the Royal Air Force Chapel, with its stunning stained-glass window containing the badges of every squadron which fought in the Battle of Britain. **Poets' Corner** contains the graves of Chaucer, Tennyson and Dryden, plus monuments to Shakespeare, Milton, Keats and many others.

The Abbey also houses the **English Coronation Chair**, built in 1300 for Edward I and still used for the installation of new monarchs. Underneath the throne is the famed **Stone of Scone**, a cold block of rock that once served as the traditional coronation seat of Scottish kings – until it was stolen by the English and spirited back to London. The stone was kidnapped by Scottish Nationalists in 1950 but retrieved in time for the coronation of Elizabeth II.

East of Westminster Square rise the **Houses of Parliament**, an intrepid Gothic structure designed in the 1860s by Charles Barry and August Pugin to replace the old Westminster Palace built by Edward the Confessor. Parliament is

Left, **Whitehall from Trafalgar Square**. A turning on the right leads to **10 Downing Street**, the prime minister's residence (*below*).

one of the triumphs of Victorian England: 940 ft (280 metres) long with 2 miles (3 km) of passages and over 1,000 rooms. At the south end is **Victoria Tower**, from which a Union Jack flies whenever Parliament is in session, while on the north flank rises the majestic Clock Tower, commonly known as **Big Ben** for the massive bell, cast in 1858, that strikes the hours. The minute hands of the huge clock are as tall as a double-decker bus, and the mechanism is still wound by hand – with small adjustments made by placing or removing coins from the colossal mechanism.

Within Parliament convene the two governing bodies of Great Britain, the House of Commons and the House of Lords, which moved into Westminster after Henry VIII vacated the premises in the 16th century. The Commons, comprised of the elected representatives of various political parties, is the scene of both lively debate and loutish heckling as MPs (Members of Parliament) wage verbal battle across their wood-panelled hall. If you are accompanied by an MP,

Westminster Abbey, built in the 11th century on a marshy wasteland.

you can watch this wordy struggle from the safety of the **Visitors' Gallery** – and wonder, like so many others, how the British government ever gets anything accomplished.

The lavish State Opening of Parliament takes place in the House of Commons each autumn, as the monarch reads a proclamation from a golden throne at the head of the room. The Lord Chancellor sits upon the famous Woolsack, a symbol of the importance of wool to the English economy during medieval times. The highlight of any tour through Parliament is **Westminster Hall**, a huge 240-ft (72-metre) long room built in 1099 with a sturdy hammer-beam roof of ancient oak. The hall has witnessed some of the most dramatic and crucial moments in English history – from the tragic trial of Sir Thomas More to the investiture of Oliver Cromwell as Lord Protector – and it's one of the few relics of the old Westminster Palace to withstand a fire that occurred in 1834.

Another survivor is the **Jewel Tower**, a moated keep beside Westminster Ab-

bey that held the Crown Jewels for more than 250 years before they were moved to the Tower of London. It now houses a pottery collection and archaeological finds from the Westminster area.

Whitehall is the broad and busy avenue that runs north from Westminster Square to Trafalgar Square. Whitehall today may seem like an anachronism, since it was once the fulcrum of British colonial power. The Foreign and Commonwealth Offices, the Treasury, Admiralty and Ministry of Defence are still situated in Whitehall – as is the Prime Minister's residence at **No. 10 Downing Street** – but in fact much of the government has moved elsewhere to more modern and spacious locations.

For a startling contrast to the drab architecture of modern government take a detour into the **Banqueting House**, one of the few relics of the old Whitehall Palace and a masterpiece of the English baroque. Inigo Jones built the hall in 1622 at the request of James I. A decade later Peter Paul Rubens added the lovely allegorical ceiling. Why are those peo-

ple pushing around little carts with mirrors on the top? All the better to observe the Rubens landscape without straining their necks.

Victoria Street shoots southwest from Parliament Square as an unexpected corridor of steel and glass skyscrapers in the heart of neo-Gothic London. Almost hidden between the corporate headquarters and banking houses is the terracotta bulk of **Westminster Cathedral**, England's best-known Roman Catholic church. It arose in the 1890s in a bizarre Italo-Byzantine style, a welcome contrast to the Gothic spires of Westminster, with its lavish interior of multi-coloured marble and its exterior in alternating red and white bricks. Climb the **Campanile Tower** for a superb view of Westminster and Belgravia.

Further west is **Victoria Station**, one of London's gateways and one of Europe's largest train depots. The station is constantly awash with the ebb and flow of travellers – people heading for the Continent or just across town.

Millbank follows the gentle curve of

On-duty policemen.

the Thames to the south of Parliament Square, first passing the sylvan **Victoria Tower Gardens** (home of Rodin's *The Burghers of Calais*) before sweeping round to the grand neoclassical mansion which is the **Tate Gallery**, London's superb repository of 20th-century painting and sculpture. Take your pick from Picasso to Pollock, Matisse to Munch. But don't forget, the Tate is also the nation's showcase for 19th-century British art with a host of old masters, including Constable, Hogarth and Reynolds. However, the highlight is the new Clore Gallery, designed by James Stirling to house the extensive Turner collection. Further west along the bank, Battersea Power Station looms large on the far side of the river. Now gutted, its shell stands as impressive as ever, the vision of cathedral builder Sir Giles Gilbert Scott.

Those with enough stamina can follow the riverside path for another mile or so, as it traces a sinuous bend in the Thames. Just past Grosvenor Railway Bridge the river enters the weird and wonderful land of **Chelsea**, perhaps London's most interesting avant-garde neighbourhood. Chelsea became a popular "village" just outside the sprawl of central London in the early 19th century and among its more famous residents have been Oscar Wilde, John Singer Sargeant, Thomas Carlyle, Mark Twain and T.S. Eliot. Cheyne Walk, a row of elegant Georgian terraced houses just off the river, has long been Chelsea's most popular residential street. George Eliot, Turner and Carlyle lived there in the 19th century, and, more recently, J. Paul Getty and Mick Jagger.

The **King's Road** is Chelsea's other famous thoroughfare and one of London's most curious. It started life as a tranquil country lane but was later widened into a private carriage road from St James's Palace to Hampton Court on the order of King Charles II. Since the late 1950s, when it exploded into a trend-setting fashion centre with boutiques such as Mary Quant's Bazaar setting the style, the King's Road has continued to be a mecca for the streetwise

The Man in the Moon pub, Chelsea.

A NIGHT ON THE TOWN

"Up West" is where Londoners go for a night on the town. The West End is a mythical place, of Shaftesbury Avenue shows, Covent Garden chatter, Leicester Square picture palaces and Trafalgar Square strolls. At its heart, if it is not surrounded by renovators' boards, is the statue of Eros in Piccadilly. Many people find enough entertainment just by strolling around.

Early evenings are for late shopping in Oxford and Regent Street, for accepting an invitation to a private showing at a Cork Street art gallery, for a wander through St James's or Hyde Park, and for buying an evening paper or listings magazine to see what the night might have in store. There are plenty of pubs or wine bars to sit in and read. Most have an after-work clientele "avoiding the rush hour" before catching the train home. In the City, many establishments close down around 8pm after the last customers have left.

In summer the river opens up and people squeeze on to the licensed boats moored along the Embankment, or walk over Hungerford Bridge (remembering to have some change for the homeless) to the South Bank complex to watch jugglers and other street theatre.

There is serious eating to be done Up West. At the top end is Albert Roux's Le Gavroche in Upper Brook Street which shines with Michelin stars, while Nico Ladenis's Chez Nico in Great Portland Street is hard on its heels. Cheaper and trendier is The Ivy in Covent Garden, and people still queue for hamburgers at Piccadilly's Hard Rock Café. Every ethnic cuisine is catered for, and there is an exciting Chinatown around Soho's Gerrard Street.

The music clubs in the West End have been popular for decades. The Marquee in Wardour Street saw the young Rolling Stones, gave punk a home and is now a point of pilgrimage for heavy metal fans. The 100 Club in Oxford Street is equally ancient and majors in jazz, and Ronnie Scott has been attracting the best jazz names to his Soho club for centuries. The basement Bass Clef in Coronet Street, N1, is also popular.

Many go Up West to take in a show, many coming in by car or train from suburbia, some from further afield by coach. Tickets to the most popular shows are not usually easy to get but more than 40 percent of all seats are sold on the door on the night. A half-price ticket booth in Leicester Square has some tickets for the evening's performances.

Leicester Square is the capital's cinema centre, and the striking black Odeon holds premieres when limousines roll up with the stars. Vintage films are put on at the National Film Theatre on the South Bank. The Comedy Store, the city's main alternative cabaret venue, which has launched a number of bright stars, is also situated in Leicester Square. More risqué is Madame Jo Jo's in Soho, a remnant of the area's steamier days.

The club scene is thriving, but dress up rather than down as codes can be strict. Many clubs have "one nighters" featuring a particular style of music. To see who is going to be in tomorrow's gossip columns, head for Stringfellows in Upper St Martin's Lane or the Hippodrome in Cranbourne Street which has the latest technological tricks. Leicester Square's Empire is one of the largest discos in Europe.

London's most exclusive night club is Annabel's, where the rich and the royal hang out. The Wag in Soho is for heavy-duty dance music and the best gay club is Heaven in Villiers Street, but there are interesting night spots away from the centre: The Fridge in Brixton and Subterrania in Ladbroke Grove, the trendy place for the 1990s.

Gaming is strictly controlled. Gamblers need to apply for casino membership 48 hours before they can get in, and though there are 20 casinos in the capital it is illegal to publish a list of them.

Britain's unsympathetic licensing laws, which close pubs at 11 p.m., combined with the early departure of the last Underground trains, mean the West End begins to feel empty by midnight and only those who know the scene can keep the party going till dawn. Most clubs wind down by 3am when weary revellers head for the night buses in Trafalgar Square, or hail a cab and hope the driver won't mind a long trip. If they fail, they can go up to Frith Street and the Bar Italia and catch an early breakfast with the best cappuccino in town.

and fashion-conscious. Mods and Rockers were followed by an influx of kaftan-clad hippies, whilst the late 1970s saw the birth of the colourful, if somewhat aggressive, punks. Since then it has become famous as the domain of Sloane Rangers, the well-heeled inhabitants of mansion blocks around Sloane Square who typically wear dowdy country-style clothing. Nevertheless it still remains boldly on the map of the young and trendy.

Down on the riverfront is **Chelsea Royal Hospital**, Sir Christopher Wren's masterpiece of the English baroque style, opened as a home for invalid and veteran soldiers in 1682. More than 500 army pensioners still reside there, and they can be seen parading in their famous scarlet frockcoats on Oak Apple Day (29 May) each spring. Nearby is the **National Army Museum**, which traces the history of the British military from the 15th century. **Ranelagh Gardens** stands adjacent to the Royal Hospital, the site of the Chelsea Flower Show held each spring.

Chelsea has two other riverside gardens which also deserve a visit: **Roper's Garden** in Cheyne Walk (which used to be part of Thomas More's estate) and the strange little **Chelsea Physic Garden**, a botanical laboratory from which the first cotton seeds were taken to the American South in 1673. Walk across either Albert or Chelsea Bridges and enjoy the lush expanse of **Battersea Park** on the south bank, with its gardens designed as part of the Festival of Britain in 1951. If all this urban trekking dries you out then walk back across Battersea Bridge into Chelsea and duck into the **Frog & Firkin**, on Lots Road, one of a chain of pubs which brew their own beer on the premises. Right by the pub is the luxury Chelsea Harbour housing development.

Leave Chelsea via Sloane Square and proceed east on King's Road into the elegant district of Belgravia, where the Bellamys lived in the television series *Upstairs, Downstairs*. The area was a disease-infested swamp until Thomas Cubitt drained the site in the early 19th

Statue of Sir Thomas More, a former resident, Chelsea.

century and developed it as a town estate for aristocrats. The district retains this exclusive quality as the home of diplomats, senior civil servants, celebrities and the occasional duke or baron. Belgravia is littered with grand Regency terraces and squares, bound by cream-coloured mansions and carefully tended gardens. Behind these grand facades lie the diminutive mews, tiny cobblestoned alleys that once served as stables. In recent years they have been refurbished into quaint and extremely desirable residences. This is London's most expensive district and buying a modest flat here won't leave you much change out of £1 million.

North of Belgravia via Sloane Street is a bustling neighbourhood of luxury shops and first-class hotels known as **Knightsbridge**. This is the home of **Harrods**, London's most famous department store. As in the British Museum, you could spend days wandering the aisles of Harrods and still not see everything. But be sure to visit the food halls, which display more than 500 varieties of cheese, 140 different breads and 160 brands of whisky. The Victorian tiles underfoot are also under a preservation order, which means they cannot be removed or altered without government permission. And don't miss Harrods at night, when the light-spangled facade resembles an enormous Victorian birthday cake.

Turn left outside Harrods and follow Brompton Road west to the fashionable neighbourhood of the same name. Brompton is renowned for its **Oratory**, a majestic Roman Catholic church in the Italian Renaissance style that is rich in both mosaics and marbles.

Museums and more museums: South Kensington Tube station is the jumping-off point for Exhibition Road's cluster of fine museums. The **Victoria & Albert** is the most famous of these, housing a marvellous collection of millions of items dedicated to the fine and applied arts of all nations, eras and styles. It has been called a vast box of delights and indeed there must be something for everyone within its brick walls. The

<u>Left</u>, Albert Memorial, Kensington Gardens. <u>Below</u>, Harrods, the Knightsbridge store.

maze-like interior includes 7 miles (11 km) of galleries, with exhibits that range from furniture and paintings to textiles and armour.

Are you into pterodactyls? Try the **Natural History Museum** in Cromwell Road for one of the best dinosaur and prehistoric lizard collections anywhere. But don't stop with the dinosaurs. The museum also has fascinating exhibits on early man, Darwin's theory of evolution, human biology, birth and whales (including a life-size model of a blue whale). The adjacent **Science Museum**, a favourite with children, has items ranging from Puffing Billy (the world's first locomotive) to the Apollo 10 moon capsule and a Lunar Rover. There's even a display of Victorian toilets. The **Geology Museum** has the world's largest collection of ore samples (a rock hound's paradise), plus a special exhibition on Britain Before Man.

One of Victorian England's greatest monuments also lies within South Kensington. Queen Victoria laid the foundation stone for the **Royal Albert Hall** in 1867 in memory of her late husband, Prince Albert. The circular 6,000-seat auditorium is still one of the largest theatres in London, and hosts a varied programme from pop concerts to brass band competitions. However, the Albert Hall is most famous for the BBC-sponsored summer Promenade Concerts, a marvellous showcase of both classical and more modern music.

Across Kensington sits the **Albert Memorial**, a flamboyant Gothic monument that rises suddenly from the plane trees of Kensington Gardens and Hyde Park. Prince Albert sits under a lavish canopy, forever reading the catalogue from the 1851 Great Exhibition, which he engineered on the site. **Kensington Palace** is a short walk away through the prolific and tranquil gardens. Wren refurbished the mansion for William III in the late 17th century, and for nearly 100 years it served as the principal private royal residence in London. Queen Victoria was born within its brick walls. Today it is the London residence of Prince Charles, Princess Diana and Prin-

Below, the 6,000-seat Royal Albert Hall. **Right**, Kensington Palace Gardens.

cess Margaret. Another popular spot in the park is the **Serpentine Gallery**, a tiny art museum beside the bird-filled lake of the same name.

West of Kensington is **Earl's Court**, sometimes called the Australian ghetto of London because of its large population of transient Antipodeans. With its multitude of cheap eateries and hotels, Earl's Court is also a summertime haven for foreign students and backpacking travellers. But Londoners know the area for its huge arena – Earl's Court **Exhibition Centre** – which hosts a number of prestigious annual events including the Royal Tournament, the Ideal Home Exhibition and the National Boat Show.

Holland Park delights: Holland Park House, just west of Kensington Palace via the High Street, centres around a leafy confine of the same name. It is one of the least known but more interesting green spaces in London. The Earls of Holland built a lavish Jacobean manor upon the site and surrounded their house with 55 acres (22 hectares) of exotic gardens. Over the years they imported over 3,000 species of trees and plants from around the world, and they filled the grounds with an assortment of exotic birds – including peacocks.

Holland Park has two other great treasures. **Leighton House** is now a centre for Victorian studies, especially the work of late-19th century artists and craftsmen like the mansion's original owner, Lord Leighton. The nearby **Commonwealth Institute** marks a complete contrast in style and mood, for this futuristic building is dedicated to the resources, culture and economies of former British Empire outposts. The Institute includes a reference library, cinema and several exhibition galleries.

North of Holland Park is **Notting Hill**, one of London's most highly sought-after residential districts with its handsome white stucco Victorian terraces and villas. However, the relative calm which prevails throughout the year is shattered every August Bank Holiday when the streets explode with music and colour as the city's huge West Indian population stage the largest street

Portobello Road market, near Notting Hill Gate.

carnival in Europe. The atmosphere is electric as thousands flock to see the wild and exciting costumes of the procession which moves to the rhythmic beat of steel bands and reggae music.

The district's other famous attraction is the **Portobello Road Market**. On Saturdays the whole street becomes jammed: at the top end with tourists in search of antique treasures, whilst, at the far end, those with an eye for a bargain rummage through the second-hand clothes and bric-a-brac stalls. In the middle of it all locals battle to buy their fruit and vegetables.

East of Notting Hill and on the north side of Hyde Park is **Bayswater**, a schizophrenic district that is at the same time trendy and posh, a transport hub and a shopping mall. Bayswater stretches up to **Paddington Station**, the mainline station for trains to the west of England.

To the north of Paddington begins a network of man-made waterways that once linked north London with Oxford and the Midlands. The posh residential district of **Little Venice** now lies at the junction of the Grand Union, Regent's and Paddington Canals. Houses aren't cheap here, and the canal-side homes sell as soon as they come on the market.

From April to October, a refurbished canal barge called the Zoo Waterbus runs east from Little Venice to Regent's Park through yet another exclusive neighbourhood, **St John's Wood**. The Rolling Stones sang about it; the Beatles crossed Abbey Road in the middle of it. Now St John's Wood is populated by an offbeat collection of diplomats, record company executives, pop stars, and Porsche-driving businessmen. These new-age knights are a contrast to the gentlemen in white who frequent **Lord's Cricket Ground**, tucked away in the heart of the Wood. Lord's is the grand shrine of cricket, the best-known ground in the world and the home of the famous Middlesex and Marylebone Cricket Clubs, the governing body of the sport for more than a century. The **Cricket Museum** is filled with sporting memorabilia, stretching back to the time of Thomas Lord, the groundsman who

Lord's cricket ground, St John's Wood.

founded the original field here in 1813.

Just east of Lord's is **Regent's Park**, a massive green space with a long and chequered history. Henry VII established a royal hunting ground on what had previously been agricultural fields. Cromwell sold both the timber and deer to finance his revolution, and Charles II sold off the land to various nobles. Later, in the early 19th century, the park became part of George VI's great scheme for a huge processional thoroughfare and palace complex to stretch from Pall Mall to Primrose Hill. The Prince commissioned John Nash to design and develop the scheme, but the dream got only as far as the famed Regency terraces on the southern fringe of the park, which represent Nash at his best.

London Zoo in Regent's Park faces an uncertain future unless it attracts further funding. The zoo was founded in 1826 by Sir Stamford Raffles of Singapore fame. Many of the zoo's first animals were captured by British soldiers and diplomats in the field, then shipped back to London via men-of-war, tea clippers or whatever else they could find. Tommy, the first chimp, arrived at the front gates in a stagecoach, while the first giraffes were unloaded at London Docks and carried straight through the City, startling pedestrians and halting traffic. The most famous resident was Jumbo the Elephant, which the zoo sold to the American showman P.T. Barnum for the then phenomenal sum of US$10,000. London Zoo is also famed as a testing ground for modern zoo architecture. Among its features are the futuristic Snowdon Aviary, the nocturnal world of the Charles Clore Pavilion, and the acclaimed modernist penguin pool designed in the 1930s.

Village Hampstead: Even further north – past the green nob of Primrose Hill (one of the best lookout points in London) and up the slow gradient of Haverstock Hill – lies another London "village". For more than 300 years **Hampstead** has attracted men of arts and letters – Keats, Constable, Shelley, Dickens, Byron, Gainsborough, D.H. Lawrence and H.G. Wells all had asso-

Hampstead: a rural avenue on the Heath and (*below*) the Old Bull and Bush.

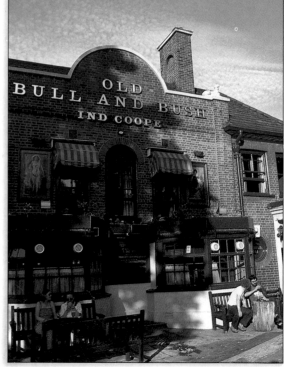

ciations with the place. Today, Hampstead is populated by a mixed bag of music, stage and cinema stars who maintain the district's trendy and transient flavour. Despite the steady encroachment of suburbia, Hampstead retains a certain village atmosphere, aided no doubt by the proximity of 790-acre (310-hectare) **Hampstead Heath**, one of the largest green spaces in London. For the visitor, Hampstead is best viewed on foot, window shopping along the **High Street**, or exploring the elegant Georgian and Regency mansions along **Church Row**, **Flask Walk**, **Downshire Hill** and **Holly Hill**.

Hampstead has a number of important dwellings, like the house called Wentworth Place where the poet is said (incorrectly) to have written *Ode to a Nightingale*, dedicated to his fiancée, Fanny Browne, who lived next door. The 17th-century **Fenton House** is now a musical instrument museum, while the 18th-century **Admiral's House** was once the home of an eccentric naval commander who had parts of the mansion reconstructed in the form of a ship's main and quarter decks. With news of a British sea victory, the mad admiral used to fire a salute from two cannons perched on top of the roof.

Hampstead Heath was once the haunt of highwaymen and outlaws, colourful characters like Sixteen String Jack and the Frenchman Claude Duval, a dashing figure who would invite female passengers to dance a minuet by moonlight after he had robbed their stagecoach. An 18th-century decree forbade building on the Heath, thus preserving a rambling tract of dark woods and lush meadows that would have otherwise have disappeared beneath houses and factories. One wooded area has now become a night-time pick-up spot for gay men.

The 18th-century **Kenwood House** is the only large structure on the Heath. It now houses the Iveagh Bequest, a rich collection of English and Dutch paintings that includes works by Rembrandt, Reynolds and Vermeer.

Adjacent to the Heath is **Highgate Cemetery**, perhaps the most famous

London's parks offer solitude in the sunshine.

burial ground in England. Chinese men in grey suits and left-wing students still bring flowers to the grave of Karl Marx. Among other famous people laid to rest here are Dickens, Wordsworth, George Eliot and Sir Ralph Richardson.

Haverstock Hill runs from Hampstead into **Camden Town**, a journey which takes you from the literary past into the rag-tag present. Camden became famous in the 1960s as a gathering place for hippies, street artists and various vagrants, who set up small shops and stalls around Camden Lock. This curious assemblage evolved into a market which is now one of the most popular London weekend attractions. Browse through the antiques, crafts, old clothes and military surplus goods, and listen to the talented buskers who gather in the cobblestone courtyard beside the Lock.

Today Camden is well served by trendy music venues, although none eclipses the legendary 1960s exploits of the Round House, a huge Victorian locomotive shed that was converted into a fringe theatre and rock venue. Today

there's the **Town and Country Club** up the road in Kentish Town, **Dingwalls** at the Lock, the **Camden Palace** and the **Electric Ballroom**.

Along the southern edge of Regent's Park sprawls **Marylebone** (pronounced *marly-bun*) district, infamous in the 18th century for its taverns, boxing matches and cockfights, but now a staid professional neighbourhood of doctors, dentists and accountants. The popular **London Planetarium** and **Madame Tussaud's Wax Museum**, neighbours on Marylebone Road, are both run by the conglomerate which also owns the *Financial Times* and long queues outside testify to their financial success. The waxworks were founded in 1802 by Marie Tussaud, a tiny woman who learned her craft in post-Revolution Paris – making wax effigies of the heads of guillotine victims. Today's effigies, which vary from the breathtakingly lifelike to the barely recognisable, cover celebrities from pop stars to popes.

Hereford House in nearby Manchester Square contains the superb **Wallace**

<u>Left</u>, Oxford Street, the shopper's delight. <u>Below</u>, Sotheby's, auctioneers.

SHOP TILL YOU DROP

One of the proud boasts by which Harrods made its name was that it could provide customers with anything they wanted. The assistant in the pet department would not flinch at a request for a pair of hippopotamuses; the manager of the jewellery department would be sympathetic towards a sudden craving for Fabergé eggs.

Of course, most desires can still be satisfied in this world-weary city, but there are also many items waiting to give shoppers a surprise. That's the fun and fascination of joining the crowds in the West End, searching out the glamour names, pursuing a collector's passion, milling around markets or simply gawping at the glitter. Britain is after all, as Napoleon said, a nation of shopkeepers, and the capital's shops are trying to catch everyone's eye.

Oxford Street is a good starting point. Between the Virgin Records Megastore in Tottenham Court Road (the hi-fi hub) and Marks & Spencer's premiere branch near Marble Arch, every British chain store gets a look-in, led by the street's stalwart Selfridges, John Lewis and Debenhams. Little enclaves lead off it, such as St Christopher's Place, which beckons to a cluster of chic boutiques.

At Oxford Circus half way along, Regent Street curves down to Piccadilly and here the old-style labels still dominate: Liberty's (the building alone is worth a visit), Dickens and Jones, the glass and china shops of Waterford, Wedgwood and Villeroy & Bosch, and Garrard's, the royal jewellers. English clothes are sold at Jaeger, Austin Reed and Aquascutum, now Japanese-owned. When these two streets show off their Christmas lights, children demand to be taken to Hamley's, one of the world's largest toy stores.

South of Oxford Street and west of Regent Street is Mayfair and the aristocrats of the retail trade. Aspreys, Tiffany and Cartier sparkle, and Valentino, Chanel and Lagerfeld tease out the latest fashion styles, which should also be checked in South Molton Street. More than 400 antique and fine art galleries flourish in this area: the auction houses of Sotheby's and Phillips hammer out the best deals for the nation's transient treasures; the galleries of Cork Street sell genuine paintings from Picasso (up or) down.

Slip between the glittering parade of little shops in Burlington Arcade to Piccadilly and St James's, a male preserve of tailors and shirt-makers, though woman are definitely allowed in to Fortnum and Mason's to buy exotic groceries and partake of afternoon tea.

Piccadilly leads west to Knightsbridge and Harrods, where again the food stall is well worth a perusal (not to mention the pet and jewellery sections, of course). From Knightsbridge the Fulham Road begins with a Golden Mile around the Conran Shop in the Art Nouveau Michelin building. Sloane Street, home to designers from Joseph to Yamamoto, runs south from Harrods to Sloane Square and King's Road, still trendy after all these years. Above Chelsea and Fulham is Kensington High Street where two indoor clothes markets cater for both nostalgic hippies and those in search of new young designers.

Meanwhile, the centre of London can still offer good bets. Young designers such as Christopher New, John Richmond and Boyd & Storey have rediscovered Soho, where Italian delicatessens are a draw. Paul Smith, Michiko Koshino and Nicole Farhi are worth searching out in Covent Garden. Hunger pangs can be checked at Neal's Yard, which has its own bakery, dairy, grocer, apothecary and wholefood warehouse.

Charing Cross Road and Cecil Court are the places to buy old and new books, and prints. Look also in Museum Street near the British Museum.

In the antiques world, the major weekly events are the Friday early-morning market at Bermondsey, where the best items change hands before 10am, and at Portobello Road on Friday and Saturday mornings when browsers crowd around the antique and junk stalls.

On Sundays, it feels as if the whole population descends on the market stalls of Camden. The streets of Greenwich fill up, too, around four street markets, while Brick Lane and Petticoat Lane in the East End are famous for clothes and bargains of dubious origin. The glorious flower market nearby in Columbia Street is a joy to behold.

Collection, a treasure chest of 17th and 18th-century art and ornaments, among which there is Sèvres porcelain, Limoges enamels and antique French furniture. On the walls hang works by Titian, Rubens and Holbein.

Shoppers' heaven: The busiest shopping street in London is **Oxford Street**, which marks the boundary between Marylebone and the exclusive district of Mayfair. This is the hub of English wealth, the home of oil barons and property giants, of landed aristocrats and self-made nabobs. Mayfair's narrow streets are abuzz by day with the flow of cash, but at night the district slides into an eerie quiet as the financial wizards and fashion models retreat into their terracotta towers. The district was once pasture and farmland outside the confines of London. The name literally derives from the medieval May Fair, which took place each spring. For two weeks, the otherwise tranquil pastures sprang to life with fire eaters and eel divers, sausage tables and hasty-pudding stands. By the mid-18th century,

the powerful Grosvenor family had purchased the land and developed Mayfair into an elegant Georgian housing estate. This enticed the wealthy of dreary inner London to move out and settle in one of the city's first suburbs.

Today, Mayfair is known for its stylish shops and lavish auction houses. The names roll off the tongue as a testament to affluence: Cartier, Rolls-Royce, Floris, Gieves & Hawkes, Yardley and Smythson's. **Bond Street** is the kind of place where you can buy something for that person who already has everything. For a quiet walk, try one of Mayfair's elegant Victorian arcades, the tiny covered streets lined with a startling array of unique and interesting shops. **Burlington Arcade** with its uniformed doormen is the most famous, only a few doors up from the **Royal Academy**. **The Royal Opera Arcade** is the oldest, but the **Piccadilly**, **Prince's** and **Royal Arcades** are just as elegant.

Mayfair antiques and art are world renowned. **Christie's** in King Street auctions off over 150,000 objects each

All but the wealthy window-shop in Bond Street.

year including furniture, armour, jewels and paintings. **Sotheby's** in New Bond Street has been the scene of some of the most important deals in art history. It is also a major innovator in the auction community, introducing features like closed circuit television, trans-Atlantic satellite transmissions and the instant computer conversion of bids into six currencies.

John Nash's curving **Regent Street** divides Mayfair from **Soho** as effectively as if there were an ocean between the two. Soho, long known for its low-life bars and sex clubs, has recently returned to being a neighbourhood of cosmopolitan foodshops and restaurants, with a population of East European émigrés, French, Italian and Greek restaurateurs and a thriving Chinese community. This multi-ethnic mix reflects the area's origins as a home to refugees – originally French Protestants who fled here after the Revocation of the Edict of Nantes (1685). The sleazy side of Soho has all but gone. Raymond's well-established Revue Bar has terribly taste-ful strip shows and a few hole-in-the-wall dens offer "live" entertainment.

Piccadilly Circus is the spiritual heart of Soho, once a roundabout and now a frenzied junction which is forever crowded with black cabs, red buses and awe-struck tourists. Eros sits atop a fountain in the middle of the mêlée, but his bronze arrows do little against the neon curtain blasting slogans upon the masses. Nearby, **Carnaby Street** was the birthplace of psychedelia, Paisley prints, mini-skirts and other manifestations of the glorious 1960s. Today it is a sort of living museum of junk culture and remains a magnet for young people from around the world.

Nearby, in the heart of Soho, is Berwick Street, the site of one of the best fruit and vegetable markets in London, excellent for both quality and price. Karl Marx used to live around the corner on Dean Street in the building now inhabited by an Italian restaurant, Leoni's Quo Vadis. John Baird succeeded in transmitting the first pictures via wireless from a workshop in nearby

The top tailors are found in Savile Row.

Frith Street in 1926. His was a new-fangled invention that would soon be known as television.

Brainy Bloomsbury: For yet another drastic change in mood, hop on the tube at Piccadilly Circus and ride three stops to Russell Square. This will deposit you in **Bloomsbury**, the intellectual and scholastic heart of the city.

Bloomsbury plays host to the **British Museum**, one of the largest and best in the world. The museum is both a price-less art collection and a monument to human civilisation, for it encompasses antiquities from almost every period and every part of the world – Egyptian, Assyrian, Greek, Roman, Indian, Chinese, Islamic and Anglo-Saxon, to name a few. Among its multiple treasures are the Rosetta Stone from Egypt, the Sutton Hoo treasures, the Nimrud friezes from Mesopotamia and the Elgin Marbles, the remarkable figures that once graced the Parthenon in Athens. Don't expect to see everything in one day; it's impossible. But do expect to visit the British Museum every time you return to London. The **British Library** is housed within the same 19th-century building. However, in the future it is due to move its collection of over nine million books – including a Gutenberg Bible, the Magna Carta and original texts by Shakespeare, Dickens and da Vinci – to a controversial new multi-million pound building near King's Cross. (You must apply for special permission to visit the domed Reading Room, once the work-shop of Marx, Trotsky and Lenin.)

Behind the museum lies the sprawl-ing campus of the **University of London**, a loose collection of colleges and institutes that comprises the third most important seat of learning in England. It was founded in 1825 – rather young compared to the heritage of Oxford or Cambridge – but London gained an in-ternational reputation in a very short time. The **Courtauld Institute**, the University's faculty of art history is the custodian of a superb art collection (now moved to new premises at Somerset House, on the Strand); the collection includes an exceptional series of Im-

The reading room at the British Library.

146

pressionist paintings with works by Van Gogh, Gauguin and Cézanne. The district's other great art collection is part of the Thomas Coram Foundation on Brunswick Square, home of the **Founding Hospital Art Treasures** and the works of Hogarth, Gainsborough and Kneller.

Bloomsbury was home to such intellectual figures as John Maynard Keynes and Virginia Woolf. But of all the writers and thinkers who have lived here one stands head and shoulders above the others: Charles Dickens. He lived with his family at **48 Doughty Street** for almost two years (1837–39), during which time he wrote parts of *Oliver Twist*, *Nicholas Nickleby* and *Barnaby Rudge*. Now the house is a small museum filled with portraits, letters, furniture and other personal effects of Victorian England's most famous novelist.

East of Bloomsbury Square is the hardworking district of **Holborn** (pronounced *ho-bun*), which centres on the busy street and Tube station of the same name. A pair of silver griffins on either

side of Holborn High Street marks the official boundary of the City of London. Nearby is **Staple Inn**, a timber-framed Elizabethan structure (the only one left in London) that once served as a hostel for wool merchants. Life in medieval Holborn focused on an open area called Smith Fields, site of the riotous St Bartholomew's Fair, London's chief place of public execution where Bloody Mary burned more than 300 of her critics.

For the past 150 years **Smithfield** has been London's primary meat market, 8 acres (3 hectares) of beef, pork and poultry housed beneath a vast canopy of steel and glass. In the mid-19th century, all the livestock was herded through the streets of north London on its way to the chopping block. Nowadays, most of the 200,000 tons of meat sold annually is moved by truck. **St Bartholomew** is the patron church of the butchers, but during its 1,000-year history the building has also served as a stable, factory, wine cellar, coal store, and even as Benjamin Franklin's London printworks.

Nearby is **St Bartholomew's Hospital**, the oldest medical facility in London, founded in 1123 but now threatened with closure. A plaque in the pathology lab commemorates the first (fictional) meeting between Sherlock Holmes and Dr Watson in 1881.

Legal London: Lying between Holborn and the Thames are the prestigious **Inns of Court** – the confluence of London's legal world since the Middle Ages. There were originally 12 inns, founded in the 14th century for the lodging and education of lawyers on "neutral" ground between the merchants of the City and the monarchs of Westminster. But today only four remain. Dr Johnson called the inns "the noblest nurseries of humanity and liberty in the Kingdom." Even today, no one can enter the legal profession in London without acceptance into one of the inns – a practice known as "passing the bar". **Gray's Inn** has a garden designed by Francis Bacon, a haven of plane trees and smooth lawns that provides a tranquil lunchtime retreat away from the hustle of the City. **Lincoln's Inn** boasts a medieval hall and a 17th-century chapel by Inigo Jones.

The Royal Courts of Justice in the Strand.

But the most fascinating of the inns is the twin complex of the Inner and Middle Temples. The name derives from the Knights Templar, a medieval religious fraternity that occupied this site until the early 14th century. The temple has changed little: it is still a precinct of vaulted chambers, hammerbeam roofs and lush wood panelling. In the 16th-century Middle Temple Hall, Shakespeare's own company once performed *Twelfth Night* for the Elizabethan court.

The 12th-century **Temple Church** is one of only four "round churches" left in England. The lawyers and judges who now inhabit the Temple may seem as anachronistic as the buildings, for they can still be seen rushing about clad in white wigs, flowing black robes and highwing collars.

Fleet Street used to be the realm of a much different power block— the national newspaper offices and press agencies of the Fourth Estate. The street takes its name from the Fleet River, which once flowed from Hampstead River into the Thames. However, the 1980s saw the decentralisation of this sector of the media to various locations scattered throughout London, a move which coincided with the introduction of computerised typesetting.

St Bride's is the official parish church of the British press, an impressive 17th-century church built by Christopher Wren. The unique three-tiered steeple was used by a local baker as the model for his wedding cakes – a design now copied all around the world.

Dr Johnson compiled his famous *Dictionary* and the *Complete Works of Shakespeare* in the attic of a house at **No. 17 Gough Square**, just off Fleet Street. Between bouts with pen and ink, Dr Johnson did his drinking at the **Old Cheshire Cheese**, a charming pub that still stands in Wine Office Court. Nearby is a leafy expanse called **Lincoln's Inn Fields**, once a notorious venue for duels and executions, now restricted to picnics and summer sunbathing. On the north side of the fields is the **Sir John Soane Museum**, an outlandish mansion which houses Soane's remarkable collection of antiquities, paintings and architectural designs. Nowhere else in London can you see such an odd assortment of artifacts under one roof. The **Old Curiosity Shop** – made famous by Charles Dickens – sits near the southeast corner of the fields.

Past St Bride's, Fleet Street sweeps into Ludgate Hill and the **City of London**, that history-packed square mile that sits atop the remains of both Roman and medieval towns. The City has long been the domain of merchants and craftsmen, a powerful coalition of men who helped force democracy upon the English monarchy and then built a mercantile empire on which the sun never set. Despite the encroachment of modern office blocks and computers, the city retains something of its medieval ways: the square mile is still governed separately from the rest of London, by the ancient City Corporation and its Court of Common Council – relics of the medieval trade and craft guilds.

Wren's masterpiece: Sitting at the top of Ludgate Hill is **St Paul's Cathedral**, dominating the skyline of the City like

St Paul's Cathedral, built between 1675 and 1710.

no other structure, the massive 365-ft (110-metre) dome punching upward through the forest of highrises that has come to surround it since the last war. After the original Norman St Paul's was destroyed in the Great Fire of 1666, the king asked Christopher Wren to design a new cathedral to befit the status of London. Wren's first plan was rejected as too radical, but he then responded with a brilliant blend of Italian baroque and Classical influences – a huge cruciform building topped by a stone cupola reminiscent of St Peter's in Rome.

St Paul's arose in 1675–1710 as the first cathedral built and dedicated to the Protestant faith, and it remains to this day the crowning achievement of Wren's career. It has played host to many important scenes of English history: Queen Victoria's Diamond Jubilee ceremonies in 1897; Winston Churchill's funeral in 1965; and the wedding of Prince Charles and Lady Diana Spencer in 1981. The cathedral miraculously survived the Blitz, though the neighbourhood around it was destroyed by German bombs and

missiles. St Paul's is also a notable burial place; among those entombed within are Wellington, Nelson, Reynolds, Turner and Wren himself. The cathedral's interior displays the work of the finest artists and craftsmen of the late 17th century: iron grillework of Tijou, wooden choir stalls by Grinling Gibbons, and the murals on the inside of the dome by Sir James Thornhill. Around the inside of the dome stretches the famous **Whispering Gallery**, so called because you can easily comprehend the voices of anyone standing on the opposite side of the void. A winding stairway leads to the outside of the dome, with its panoramic views of central London.

Sprawling north from St Paul's is the futuristic **Barbican** development, a startling contrast to the maze of twisting streets and ancient buildings that surround the cathedral. This urban renewal project arose from the rubble of an old neighbourhood that had been destroyed in the Blitz. The architecture is an ambitious example of typical post-war style, but many London residents today con-

The City, London's financial centre.

sider the 40-storey office blocks and cement plazas a scar on the face of the city. One of the Barbican's many showcases is the **Museum of London**, a superb collection devoted to the history of the city from prehistoric to modern times. There are models of old buildings, reconstructed shop fronts, audiovisual shows, a reference library, antique vehicles and a number of historic artifacts such as the Lord Mayor's State Coach. The Barbican is also home to the Guildhall School of Music and Drama, and the London base of both the Royal Shakespeare Company and the London Symphony Orchestra.

In the shadows of the Barbican's skyscrapers is the **Guildhall**, one of the few buildings to survive the Great Fire and now the home of the government of the City in the form of the Lord Mayor and the Court of Common Council. Largely restored, this ornate Gothic structure was originally built in 1411 with funds donated by various livery companies, the medieval trade and craft guilds that held sway over the City. Within the Guildhall is a 15th-century library with thousands of manuscripts and books detailing the history of London. There's also the famous **Great Hall**, decorated with the colourful banners of the 12 livery companies and the shields of all 92 guilds. The Guildhall is the scene in November of the Lord Mayor's Banquet, a flamboyant affair attended by the Prime Minister and the Archbishop of Canterbury that recalls the rowdy and raucous feasts of the Middle Ages.

A short walk east along Gresham Street brings you to the **Bank of England**, a building of powerful Classical design that befits Britain's most prestigious financial institution. The Bank still prints and mints all British money, administers to the national debt and protects the country's gold reserves. Nearby stands the old London **Stock Exchange**, founded in 1773 but now housed in a towering skyscraper at the junction of Threadneedle and Old Broad Street. The trading floor is no longer used – these days shares are traded by telephone and computer – but the building houses an

The Bank of England, right, and the Royal Exchange, left.

exhibition on the history of stocks and securities. Further east is the black silhouette of the **National Westminster Bank** building, completed in 1981 and then the tallest office block in Britain (more than 600 ft/180 metres) but not open to the general public; the NatWest tower has now been exceeded in height by the gigantic Canary Wharf in Docklands, visible for miles around and considered by some to be a blot on the landscape.

Directly opposite the Bank are the **Royal Exchange** (obviously modelled on the Parthenon) and **Mansion House**, the official residence of the Lord Mayor since the 1750s. Many of the City's treasures are housed within this Palladian-style palace: the 15th-century Mayoral Chain of Office; the 17th-century Sword of State; the 18th-century Great Mace; and an extensive collection of Corporation plates, tapestries and crystal. The Lord Mayor's Show begins at Mansion House each November, as the newly elected mayor rides through the City in a golden coach. Thousands of spectators line the route as the colourful procession winds its way to the Royal Courts of Justice in the Strand before returning to the Guildhall.

King William Street leads south from the bustling Bank intersection to London Bridge and the Thames. Just before you reach the river, a huge fluted column peers over the helter-skelter of rooftops: the 202-ft (60-metre) **Monument** – Wren's memorial to the Great Fire of 1666. Climb to the summit for a superb panorama of central London.

The torturous tower: Lower Thames Street traces the medieval banks of the river past the old Billingsgate Fish Market and the elegant Custom House. A squat stone building commands this southeast corner of the City, a pensive medieval fortress known as the **Tower of London**. The Tower has served, over the centuries, as fortress, palace, prison and museum, as well as arsenal, archive, menagerie and treasure chest. It remains the most alluring of London's many monuments – attracting millions of tourists each year; so expect queues.

The Tower of London, medieval strongbox for the Crown Jewels.

William the Conqueror built the inner keep (now called the **White Tower**) as both a military stronghold and a means of impressing his new subjects in England. It took over 20 years to construct – from 1078 to 1098 – and was the largest building in Britain at that time. The Tower served William well, for it soon evolved into a bastion of royal wealth and power but, even more importantly, a symbol of royal domination over almost everything in the realm. It remained a royal residence until the 16th century, when the court moved to more comfortable quarters in Westminster.

The Tower then became the storehouse for the Crown Jewels and the most infamous prison and execution ground in London. Only important figures were given the "privilege" of dying within the Tower, and those figures include Sir Thomas More, Anne Boleyn, Lady Jane Grey, Catherine Howard, Edward V and his younger brother, the Duke of York. The final execution took place in 1747, after which the Tower became the Royal Mint, Archive and Menagerie – until the elephants, lions and bears were moved to the new Regent's Park Zoo a century later.

The White Tower now houses an impressive array of royal arms and armour, plus the diminutive **St John's Chapel**, built in 1080 and now the oldest church in London. Beneath Waterloo Barracks is a vault containing the **Crown Jewels**, including the Imperial State Crown which sparkles with 3,000 stones and the **Royal Sceptre**, which centres around a 530-carat diamond called the Star of Africa.

Beefeaters: The Tower is protected by the famous Yeomen Wardens or Beefeaters, so-called not because of their carnivorous habits, but because they were founded in 1485 by Henry VIII as the *boufitiers* or guardians of the king's buffet. An authentic chopping block sits upon Tower Green – yes, you may place your head on it for photographs. The black birds who flock around the castle precinct are ravens, the descendants of creatures who have lived within the Tower for over 900 years. Legend says

A Beefeater, once guardian of the king's buffet.

that if the ravens ever leave, the Tower will crumble – and for nine centuries no army has taken the castle by force.

Mansell Street leads north from the Tower into the warren of narrow streets that marks the start of London's infamous **East End**. Most of the district will present scant interest to the overseas visitor; it's a massive sprawl of working-class homes and lower-class slums. But **Whitechapel** and **Spitalfields** – both at the north end of Mansell Street – are colourful and startling exceptions to the East End atmosphere. They comprise the heart of the old Jewish ghetto, where you can still stumble upon ancient synagogues and kosher delicatessens. Wander in the opposite direction down Aldgate Hill Street to the ancient **Spanish and Portuguese Synagogue**, built in 1701 and now the oldest place of Jewish worship in Britain. Or take a look in the **Whitechapel Art Gallery** which sits rather incongruously on the Whitechapel Road. This beautiful piece of *fin-de-siècle* architecture, with its large arched doorway and delicate detailing of carved stone foliage, is one of London's most exciting galleries, hosting regular exhibitions by living artists.

Petticoat Lane is the most famous East End market, thus named because it was once the domain of old clothes dealers. Today, the market stalls along Middlesex Street are a chromatic jumble of clothes, antiques, food and just about everything else manufactured by mankind. Even more interesting are the traders – a mixed bag of Cockneys, West Indians and Asians – who prove every Sunday morning that racial harmony is indeed possible. A sub-market of the Petticoat Lane complex is **Club Row**, London's venue for both domestic and exotic pets (Sunday mornings only), while the daily **Wentworth Street** market is a good place to sample West Indian or Jewish foods. Also in the East End is the little-known but excellent **Museum of Childhood** on Cambridge Heath Street in Bethnal Green.

Much further to the northeast is the **William Morris Gallery** on Forest Road in Walthamstow, the childhood home

Tower Bridge, a triumph of Victorian Gothic architecture.

of the famous 19th-century interior designer and artist, William Morris.

Dockside digression: The most spectacular of London's many spans is **Tower Bridge**, a striking Gothic profile opened in 1894. Perhaps the most infamous moment in the bridge's history came in 1954 when the warning lights failed and a double decker bus became wedged between the open spans. The inside of Tower Bridge is now open to the public. There's a museum of London bridges and superb views from the glass-enclosed catwalks.

Downstream from the bridge lie **St Katharine's Docks**; built in 1828 as a shipment point for wool and wine, the docks were renovated in the early 1980s and have become a posh residential and commercial district. The complex contains a shopping arcade, a yacht harbour, a hotel and several old warehouses (like the Ivory House) now converted as modern offices and flats. St Katharine's also has a floating ship museum including the *Discovery* (Captain Scott's famous polar exploration vessel), a re-tired lightship and venerable Thames sailing barges.

Southern ways: Across the river, on Shad Thames, is **Butler's Wharf** and the Conran Foundation **Design Museum**, whose changing exhibitions are aimed at provoking visitors into an appreciation of good commercial design. Heading upstream again, the riverside walk between Tower Bridge and London Bridge passes by the blue-grey outline of *HMS Belfast*, a Royal Navy cruiser that is now a maritime museum. The *Belfast* was commissioned in 1939 as the largest cruiser in the British Navy, and she has the distinction of having fired the first shots over Normandy on D-Day.

More renovated warehouses line the riverside up to London Bridge, some of them converted to chic apartments, some of them sheltering shopping arcades such as **Hays Galleria**. The **London Dungeon**, at 28–34 Tooley Street, is a gruesome, gory and noisy account of life in medieval London – children love it.

Beyond London Bridge rises the ma-

St Katherine's Dock by Tower Bridge, haven for old boats and tourists.

jestic **Southwark Cathedral**, the most important Gothic structure in London after Westminster Abbey. Augustinian canons erected the original church in the 13th century, but the cathedral has been rebuilt and refurbished several times over the centuries.

Londoners look at the **South Bank Complex** (alongside Waterloo Bridge, half a mile to the west) in two ways: as the greatest fine arts forum in Europe, or as an uninspired mass of concrete and steel that should be put out of its misery. The truth lies somewhere in between. The **Festival Hall** plays host to the London Symphony and Philharmonic Orchestras, a spacious arena that is famed for its acoustics and visibility. Next door are **Queen Elizabeth Hall** and the **Purcell Room**, used for a variety of events, from solo recitals and chamber music to poetry readings.

The **National Film Theatre** (members only) sits in the shadow of Waterloo Bridge, presenting an ever-changing bill of vintage and foreign-language films as well as the London Film Festi-

val each November and, year round, the superb **Museum of the Moving Image**.

The huge **National Theatre** – actually three arenas in one – is known for the high quality of its drama productions and its enthusiasm for new playwrights; its vast concrete bulk tends to attract divided critical opinion.

The **Hayward Gallery** rounds off the South Bank show. It is an art gallery that sometimes goes in for the offbeat and the bizarre in its programme of temporary exhibitions of predominantly 20th-century art.

Upriver from the South Bank Complex, beyond Westminster Bridge, is **Lambeth Palace** which has been the London residence of the Archbishop of Canterbury for more than 700 years.

Another great landmark of the south bank is the **Imperial War Museum**, situated within the remains of the "Bedlam", the old Bethlehem Hospital for lunatics. The museum, which was completely redesigned in 1989, houses weapons, vehicles, paintings, uniforms, decorations and scale models.

Lambeth Palace, on the south bank, home of the Archbishop of Canterbury.

THE THAMES BEYOND LONDON

Dr Johnson may roll over in his grave, but it is possible that a visitor will actually get tired of London. The capital's environs spread out from the centre seemingly for ever, as more than seven million people find space to live over 610 sq. miles (1,570 sq. km). Wedged among this mass of humanity are many parks, palaces and museums which offer rest and respite from the hustle and bustle of the big city. From Greenwich to Richmond, every suburb has its own personality, and they can be reached by local London transport.

Eastwards, London's Docklands have been replaced by largely uninviting developments which have turned their backs on the river. To the west, however, the river is a focus of pleasure: in summer, beside Victorian boat houses and beneath weeping willows, boat-lovers, bathers and walkers gather along its grassy banks and spill into the terraces and gardens of some fine old pubs. The M4 motorway follows the lower reaches past Heathrow to Reading, from where lesser roads trace the river northwards. Train links are via Paddington station; Windsor is served from Waterloo.

Royal Greenwich: Since Tudor times, when Bella Court Palace stood upon the riverside, **Greenwich** has been a royal retreat. Henry VIII, Elizabeth I and Mary Tudor were all born at Greenwich, and it was here that Sir Walter Raleigh performed his famous act of laying a cloak over a pool of mud so that Queen Elizabeth would not get her feet wet. James I had the old palace demolished and commissioned Inigo Jones to build a new private residence for Queen Anne.

The result was the astounding **Queen's House**, a masterpiece of the Palladian style and perhaps the finest piece of Stuart architecture in England. It's now the focus of the **National Maritime Museum**. Charles II constructed a Royal Observatory at Greenwich in 1675 in order to perfect the arts of navigation and astronomy. Since that time, the globe's longitude and time zones have

been measured from the Greenwich Meridian, which cuts right through the middle of **Flamsteed House**, now a museum of astronomical instruments and timepieces.

Greenwich has also been associated with British sea power for the past 500 years. Just downstream is the **Royal Navy Dockyard**, which flourished under Henry VIII and Elizabeth. Christopher Wren built the **Royal Hospital for Seamen** at Greenwich in the late 17th century, an elegant complex in the baroque style that now serves as the **Royal Naval College.**

Along the Greenwich waterfront are anchored two of England's most famous ships. The *Cutty Sark* was the last of the great China clippers, a speedy square-rigger that once ran tea from the Orient to Europe. It has been superbly preserved and now contains a small museum and a collection of ship figureheads. Nearby sits the tiny *Gipsy Moth IV*, the yacht in which Sir Francis Chichester sailed solo round the world in 1966. The most pleasant way to reach

Preceding pages: Windsor Castle, home to English monarchs since the 12th century. Left, Mill End Lock on the Thames. Right, all the river's swans belong to the Queen.

Greenwich is to catch one of the frequent river boats from Westminster, Charing Cross or Tower Piers. Take the river boat further downstream to catch a glimpse of the **Thames Barrier**, one of the modern wonders of the world. This great shining steel wall, which stretches 1,700 ft (520 metres) across the width of the River Thames, protects London from the danger of flooding.

Docklands: In contrast to the historic charm of Greenwich is the view across the Thames to the **Isle of Dogs**, easily reached by a foot tunnel under the Thames. Standing out like a sore thumb on the landscape is the vast tower of **Canary Wharf**, Britain's tallest building and the largest structure of its kind in Europe. This development is central to a huge construction programme begun in the early 1980s but set back by Canary Wharf's Canadian parent running out of money in 1992. The plan had been to regenerate the 8½ sq. miles (13.5 sq. km) of London's derelict dock area, once the greatest port in the world.

Rapid changes have been made to the four main dock areas of Wapping, the Isle of Dogs, Royal Docks and Surrey Docks which lie between Tower Bridge and Woolwich. In the 19th century these major dock schemes were built to cater for increased world trade as vessels poured into London laden with valuable and exotic cargoes from the colonies. Today they provide the basis for commercial trading of a different variety as big business moves in and businessmen operate where dockers once laboured.

Vast chasms and harsh contrasts are apparent here, between the new and the old, the rich and the poor. Once a working-class stronghold, the native East Ender has been gradually forced out by the upwardly mobile. Rocketing land prices and the influx of modern commercial properties have changed the character of this waterfront forever, though some developers came to grief when property prices plunged in the recession of the early 1990s.

To encourage investment this area was made into an Enterprise Zone, relatively free from architectural restric-

The *Cutty Sark*, last of the China tea clippers, at Greenwich.

tions. The result is an unrestrained post-modernist legoland. Although many of the garish buildings which have arisen cannot be taken too seriously, there are several of considerable note; the problem is the lack of any visual coherence. Road and rail facilities to this space-age city have some way to go, but the computerised **Docklands Light Railway** which hovers above the ground between Island Gardens, Tower Gateway and Stratford, gives fine views.

Although the Isle of Dogs commands the greatest attention, the other areas of Docklands should not be ignored. At the furthest point west, next to the south side of London Bridge, is **Hays Galleria**, one of several large Victorian warehouses which, like those at **Tobacco Dock** in Wapping, have become shopping centres with cafés and restaurants.

Heading east from here is **Shad Thames**, an area composed of narrrow streets of towering Victorian warehousing. Here a Dickensian atmosphere prevails even though the developers have moved in and turned the interiors of old industrial buildings, such as the Anchor Brewery, into desirable loft-style apartments. As you walk further east, you'll know you are passing Cinnamon Wharf by the scent of the spice in the air.

Further on a stark white modernist building at Butler's Wharf, the **Design Museum**, is dedicated to the history of the design of everyday items.

Over on the north bank of the Thames is **Limehouse** where a large Chinese community settled in the 19th century. It is still a good place to go to find Chinese restaurants. It is also the location of St Anne's Limehouse, Docklands' major church, which was built in 1730 by the great baroque architect, Nicholas Hawksmoor.

Docklands has its own **airport** which is located at the Royal Albert Dock and from here business travellers are carried in small planes to European capitals. The Royal Docks are also used for a variety of watersports from waterskiing to windsurfing.

To gain some insight into the historic past of Docklands, visit some of the

Docklands Light Railway rides above the new riverside city.

area's ancient pubs. The fine Dickensian riverside pubs such as The Angel at Bermondsey and the Mayflower at old Rotherhithe date back to the 17th century and have associations with smugglers and thieves, while the popular 16th-century Prospect of Whitby on Wapping Wall is considered to be London's oldest tavern.

Gardens galore: At the opposite end of London is the borough of Richmond-upon-Thames, which includes Richmond, Kew, Twickenham and Hampton. As with Greenwich, the most enjoyable way of reaching Richmond from central London is by riverboat from Westminster Pier (calling at Kew, Richmond and Hampton Court). But those with speed in mind can take the District Line Tube to Kew and Richmond, or British Rail to Richmond, Twickenham and Hampton from Waterloo Station.

Richmond retains its village atmosphere with its cluster of book and antique shops, tea salons and charming riverside pubs. The Three Pigeons and the White Cross are two of the most popular. The Victorian-style **Richmond Theatre** sits on the edge of the green and is an important showcase for big-name productions on their way to the West End. **Richmond Park** was enclosed by Charles I as a royal hunting estate and is now the only royal park that keeps a large stock of deer. On the way to the park, a walk up Richmond Hill from the centre of town leads to a magnificent view west over the Thames.

Richmond Bridge leads across to **Twickenham**, a village famous for its fabulous mansions. It's also the mecca of English rugby (international games are staged in winter at the huge Twickenham Rugby Football Ground). The 18th-century **Marble Hill House** is a Palladian-style dwelling that has long provided a retreat for the secret affairs of the Crown. Both George II and George IV kept their mistresses in this mansion. Today the house contains a fine picture gallery and a lovely garden, the scene of outdoor Shakespeare productions during the summer months.

Across the river is the flamboyant

Deer in Richmond Park, a former royal hunting estate.

17th-century **Ham House**, an annex of the Victoria and Albert Museum. Ham House contains a rich collection of period paintings (including Reynolds and Van Dyck), tapestries, furniture, carpets and clothing. Cavaliers and Roundheads do fierce battle each spring on the Ham House grounds as part of the three-week Richmond Festival. Riverside Twickenham offers a number of worthy pubs including the White Swan, the Eel Pie and the Barmy Arms.

Tropical house in Kew: Kew plays host to the Royal Botanic Gardens, often called simply **Kew Gardens**, 300 acres (120 hectares) of exotic plants from around the world. The gardens were first planted under the direction of Princess Augusta, the mother of George III, but they didn't come into full bloom until the Victorian era under the green fingers of botanist Sir Joseph Hanks and gardener William Aiten. There are special areas given over to redwoods, orchids, roses, rhododendrons, alpine and desert plants. But the most famous of Kew's nurseries is the **Palm House**, a vast pavilion of steel and glass that contains hundreds of tropical plants. Sadly, the Palm House had to be restored following damage sustained in the storms of 1987 when many of Kew's old and rare species of trees were damaged or lost. The latest addition to the greenhouses is the ecologically correct and energy-saving **Princess of Wales Conservatory**, opened in the same year. (Find the towpath along the Thames at Kew and walk the riverside to Richmond and even further.)

Farther upstream is **Hampton Court Palace**, the paragon of the Tudor style and the self-proclaimed English version of Versailles. Hampton Court was built by Cardinal Wolsey as the finest and most flamboyant residence in the realm. When Wolsey fell from grace, in a futile attempt to regain favour, he gave the palace to Henry VIII. The king fell instantly in love with it and moved there with Anne Boleyn. He ordered the construction of the Great Hall, the Clock Court and the Library, and he enlarged the gardens. It is said that Elizabeth I used Hampton Court as an illicit love nest away from the prying eyes of Westminster. She also planted the gardens with exotic trees and flowers brought to England from the New World by Drake and Raleigh.

The sumptuous **State Apartments** were designed for William and Mary, who also commissioned the famous Maze and the Tijou grillework atop the entrance gates. Today the 1,000 rooms are filled with paintings, tapestries and furnishings from the past 450 years.

Across the Thames from Kew is another famous botanical centre – **Syon Park**. The Dukes of Northumberland built a great mansion on the site in the 16th century while the lush gardens were added later by Capability Brown. Syon now offers a number of interesting attractions: the **National Gardening Centre**, the **Living Butterfly Museum**, the **Heritage Collection of British Automobiles** and **Syon House** itself, with its lavish baroque interior and vivid conservatory. To get there, take British Rail from Waterloo to Syon Lane.

A number of other interesting sights

Osterley House, an elegant suburban mansion.

are found in the western suburbs. A massive green space known as **Osterley Park** centres around a Tudor mansion by the same name, built as a country home by Sir Thomas Gresham, the wealthiest man in 16th-century England. (Take the Piccadilly Line Tube to Osterley station.) The excellent **Royal Air Force Museum** is situated at Hendon (Northern Line Tube to Colindale), while **Wimbledon** plays host to the All-England Lawn Tennis Championships each June (District Line Tube to Southfields or Wimbledon). Nearby Wimbledon Common is a great place for a quiet walk. And, of course, there's **Chiswick**, with Hogarth's House, a 17th-century mansion now filled with engravings and personal relics of one of England's most famous artists, and Chiswick House, a delightful 18th-century Palladian villa. (Take British Rail from Waterloo to Chiswick, or District Line Tube to Turnham Green).

By taking the Tube to Hammersmith and then walking to the nearby Thames towpath at Hammersmith Bridge you'll be at the starting point of another riverside walk that leads to Chiswick. If you time your stroll for "opening hours" you'll be able to try a number of popular riverside pubs on the way, such as the Dove on Upper Mall, a historic 18th-century tavern where *Rule, Britannia* is supposed to have been written.

Ancient suburb: Twenty-two miles (36 km) north of central London is the ancient and venerable city of **St Albans**, one of the most important historic sites in Britain. The town was founded by the Romans more than 2,000 years ago and called Verulamium. The modern name derives from Alban, a 3rd-century Roman soldier who was beheaded for sheltering a Christian priest, thus becoming Britain's first martyr. A huge abbey later arose atop the Roman ruins, and from the 11th to the 15th centuries the magnificent St Albans Cathedral was constructed from red brick and the remains of old Roman buildings. The first blood of the War of the Roses was shed in the narrow streets of St Albans as the forces of the Yorks and the Lancasters staged hand-to-hand combat.

Life is a bit less frenetic in St Albans today. The town was largely passed over by the Industrial Revolution, and it remains a tranquil medieval anachronism on the edge of bustling London. The cathedral is St Albans' main attraction, but just as interesting is the **Roman Archaeological Park**, with its well-stocked museum and famous mosaic floors. For a time warp into the Middle Ages, visit **French Row**, a meticulously preserved medieval street with 15th-century houses and a clock tower. For another leap in time, walk past the Georgian terraces of either **Fishpool Street** or **Holywell Hill**. Sir Francis Bacon's 16th-century manor house is 2 miles (3 km) west of St Albans. Then, when you have finished exploring, duck into **Ye Old Fighting Cocks** for a drink. This ancient tavern claims, as do many, to be the oldest in England, built originally as a fishing lodge for St Albans monks and used later for cock fights. (To reach St Albans, take a British Rail train from King's Cross/St Pancras Station, or drive north from London on the North Circular until you see a signpost for the A6.)

The Thames Valley: Winding its way across the western Home Counties of Buckinghamshire, Berkshire and Oxfordshire, the Thames above the metropolis crosses some of the gentlest and most quintessentially English of landscapes. This is an historic waterway, whose banks have seen civilizations come and go. On the twin hills of Sinodun, south of Dorchester-on-Thames, the early Britons built a major camp as early as 1500 BC. ("Dun" in Celtic means fort.) After the arrival of Caesar, the Romans did the same, and the remains of both settlements can be seen today.

The Thames is a river of plenty and has made its valley a fertile farmland. In the Middle Ages the river was so thick with salmon even the poor ate it as a staple. Great abbeys and monasteries flourished here, and kings and queens have made it their home. Yet the centre of attraction of the Thames Valley comes 62 locks upriver and 89 bridges north of the capital, when the inspired city of Oxford rises timelessly from its banks.

To fly-fishermen, the Thames Valley begins at Bell Weir Lock just a mile north of **Staines**, south of the M4 beside the orbital M25. From Bell Weir north to the river's source (a muddy patch in a field near Coates in Gloucestershire), the river is bordered almost continuously by hills. On the west side of the motorway is Egham and the riverside meadow at **Runnymede** where, on 15 June 1215, King John signed the Magna Carta. Tradition maintains that the barons encamped on one side of the Thames while the king's forces occupied the other. Magna Carta Island, the larger of the two river islands, was the neutral ground on which they met. Above is **Cooper's Hill**, which affords a panoramic view of Windsor Castle to the north. Of this hill Alexander Pope wrote:

On Cooper's Hill eternal wreaths shall grow,
While lasts the mountains or while Thames shall flow.

At the bottom of the hill lies the Magna Carta Memorial, an uninspiring structure presented by the American Bar Association. Nearby is the John F. Kennedy Memorial – three plush acres that the Queen gave to the United States in 1965 in perpetuity. Farther inland on Egham Hill stands the **Royal Holloway College** (part of the University of London). Its picture gallery has fine examples of 19th-century British painting.

A pleasant diversion from Runnymede follows the riverside road from Staines to **Datchet**. This was once the Datchet Lane mentioned in *The Merry Wives of Windsor* – the road that Falstaff was carried along in a dirty linen basket to be ducked in the Thames.

Windsor's royal castle: From Datchet across the river is England's most famous castle, **Windsor**. Since the reign of Henry I in the 12th century, Windsor has been the chief residence of English and British sovereigns. William the Conqueror founded the original structure, a wooden building that consisted most likely of a motte and two large baileys enclosed by palisades. The stone fortifications were built in the 12th and 13th centuries. Rising dramatically on a

The Thames arrives in the countryside around Sonning.

chalk cliff above the Thames, the castle you see today incorporates additions by nearly every sovereign since. In the 19th century, George IV and Queen Victoria spent almost £1 million on additions. This century has seen great restorations of the interior, in particular of **St George's Chapel**, the worst casualty of a disastrous fire in 1992.

Part of the Lower Ward, St George's Chapel is one of the finest examples of Perpendicular architecture in England (rivalled only by King's College Chapel at Cambridge and the Henry VII Chapel at Westminster). Dedicated to the patron saint of the Order of the Garter, the chapel displays in the choir stalls the swords, helmets, mantles and banners of the respective knights. Also in the choir are the tombs of Henry VIII, Jane Seymour and Charles I; Windsor is, after all, the resting place of royalty. The **Albert Memorial Chapel**, built by Henry VIII as his own mausoleum but later converted by Victoria as a monument to her husband, Prince Albert, houses more tombs of royalty.

In the Upper Ward are the **State Apartments**. These serve as accommodation for visiting foreign sovereigns and are occasionally closed to the public. Lavishly furnished, they include many important paintings from the royal collection, including works by Rubens, Van Dyck, Canaletto and Reynolds. There are also drawings by Holbein, Michelangelo, da Vinci and Raphael.

The Round Tower is what everyone thinks of as Windsor Castle. Climb the 220 steps for the wide valley view, but don't try to see the east side of the Upper Ward which houses the private apartments of the Queen. Instead, venture outside and south of the castle to the **Great Park**, more than 2,000 acres (800 hectares) of lush greenery. The **Savill and Valley Gardens** have the largest collection of rhododendrons in the world. The Changing of the Guard at 10.30am has more pizazz than at Buckingham Palace.

Eton across the river: Across the river from Windsor is **Eton College**, that most famous of English public schools,

Coach ride around Windsor Castle.

founded in 1440 by 18-year-old Henry VI. The original set of buildings included a collegiate church, an attached grammar school and an almshouse. It was Henry's intention that the church and school become a place of pilgrimage and devotion to the Virgin. The Wars of the Roses cut him short. Henry was murdered in the Tower of London and every year on the anniversary of his death an Etonian lays a wreath of lilies in the cell in which he died.

To the visitor, Eton is a cluster of redbrick Tudor buildings with little towers and hulking chimneys. The **School Yard** (the outer quadrangle), the **Long Chamber** and the **Lower School** all date from the 15th century. The chapel, in Perpendicular style, has outstanding 15th-century wall paintings depicting the miracles and legends of the Virgin. Most of the windows were damaged in World War II, but some of the modern installations are interesting. The cloisters dating from the 1440s are stunning, and beyond them stretch the fields of which the Duke of Wellington is said to have made his famous remark that Waterloo was won on the playing fields of Eton. These are also the fields which Thomas Gray (1716–71) had in mind in his *Ode on a Distant Prospect of Eton College*. Watching the young scholars romp, he fondly remarked:

Alas, regardless of their doom,
the little victims play.

Stoke Poges, north of Eton and on the far side of Slough (a town to avoid) marks another Gray memorial. Here is the inspiration for his other most famous poem, *Elegy in a Country Churchyard*. The statue erected in 1799 commemorates him with a maudlin inscription, though the sheer beauty of the churchyard – its old lychgates, its rose bushes and its garden of remembrance – are what brings visitors. The church dates from the 14th century. The 17th-century "Bicycle Window" in the cloister depicts an angel riding a hobby horse.

Valley villages: Half a dozen miles (10 km) upriver from Eton lies **Maidenhead**, the starting point of some of the most beautiful countryside in the val-

ley. Known in medieval times as "Maydenhythe", meaning maidens' landing place, in the 18th century the town became an important coaching stop between London and the fashionable spa town of Bath. Today it has the added atmosphere of a commuter town. Its bridges are its most interesting feature: the 128-ft (38-metre) arches of Brunel's railway bridge are the largest brick spans ever constructed.

From Maidenhead the A423 goes 8 miles (13 km) direct to Henley, but there are several picturesque villages and towns clustered on either side of the river nearby. **Bray**, nestled in a bend in the Thames just south of Maidenhead, has a lovely church that dates from 1293. The style is a blend of Early English and Perpendicular, with lots of restorations. The **Jesus Hospital**, founded in 1627, is also interesting, and still cares for 26 older citizens from a trust set up by its originator.

Taplow is another pretty village on the north side of the Thames opposite Maidenhead. From Taplow a road leads through Burnham to **Burnham Beeches**, a pastoral stretch of 375 wooded acres (150 hectares) under the care of the City of London.

Upstream from Maidenhead is **Cliveden Reach**, another wooded tract, this one owned by the National Trust. The house called **Cliveden**, once the home of Lord Astor, is poised dramatically above cliffs that rise to a height of 200 ft (90 metres). Before World War II Nancy Astor turned the house into a popular meeting place for politicians and celebrities. Today, Cliveden is run as a luxury hotel by the Blakerey Hotels group. The gardens are open to the public, however, and are lavishly decorated with Roman sarcophagi, fountains, temples and topiary; maps are also available at the entrance showing suggested walks through the woodland with spectacular views of the Thames.

Cookham is yet another picturesque riverside village, though it's perhaps better known as the home of the artist Stanley Spencer (1891–1959). Spencer's portrait of Cookham Bridge hangs

A dray outside Henley's brewery.

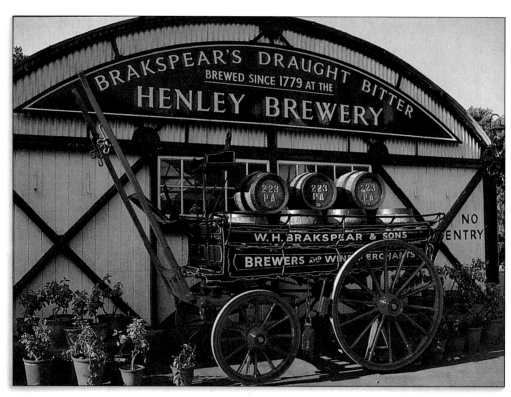

in the Tate Gallery. Cookham has a gallery dedicated to his work, housed in the King's Hall where he attended Sunday School. His painting of the *Last Supper* hangs in the church, parts of which date from the 12th century though it is mentioned in the Domesday Book. The 15th-century tower is unusual; it is one of the few church towers with both a clock and a sun dial. An attractive row of boat-houses lines the river, one of which is the office of the Keeper of the Royal Swans – almost every swan in Britain is the property of the Queen.

Six miles (9 km) upriver is **Marlow**, the town in which Mary Wollstonecraft wrote *Frankenstein*. In 1817 she lived in West Street ("Poets' Row") with her husband, the poet Shelley, while he wrote the poem *The Revolt of Islam*. Marlow goes back to Saxon times, when it was known under the name of "Merelaw" but what you see today is comparatively new, like the suspension bridge and the **All Saints Church**, which both date from the 1830s. The rustic walks along the river below Marlow Lock are re-freshing, as is **Quarry Wood**, 25,000 acres (10,000 hectares) of beechwoods on the Berkshire bank.

Just a mile upstream from Marlow, on the Berkshire side, is **Bisham**. Here the village church stands right on the river bank. **Bisham Abbey**, a well-preserved Tudor residence, is unfortunately not open to the public. Its historical significance rests in the fact, that before she became queen, Elizabeth I lived here for three years during the reign of her half-sister Mary.

Another abbey, upstream on the Buckinghamshire side, has a legacy at least as interesting. **Medmenham Abbey** is a pseudo-ruin built 300 years ago by Sir Francis Dashwood on the site of a 13th-century monastery. It was here that Dashwood founded the Hell-Fire Club, a rakish society with the motto, "*Fay ce que voudras*" (Do what you please). The society's "monks" included the satirists Charles Churchill and Paul Whitehead, and it was notorious for mock-religious orgies.

Crew capital of the world: Although it

can not compete with Medmenham in raciness, **Henley** has been known for its races since 1839, when it was host to the world's first river regatta. The four-day Henley Regatta is now held every year, usually in the first week of July, and attracts oarsmen and women from all over the globe. Just as interesting as the crews are the spectators, an audience of near-Edwardian elegance – white linen dresses, straw hats and bottles of bubbly. Henley was once, and arguably still is, a great society haunt, with seasonal balls and large parties floating downriver. Lesser known (and less celebrated) regattas are held on weekends throughout the summer. In any season, the main street of the town is elegantly wide and Georgian. Beside the Perpendicular church is the 14th-century, timber-framed **Chantry House**. The **Kenton Theatre** in New Street, built in 1805, is one of the oldest surviving theatres in Britain.

There are several stately homes around Henley, but the most exquisite is **Greys Court**. West of Henley on the road to Peppard, this well-preserved Tudor house has remains of an earlier, fortified manor house dating from the 14th century. There is a crenellated tower, a huge donkey wheel once used for drawing water and a garden maze.

Shiplake is a sprawling village notable for its church, rebuilt in 1689, but housing excellent 15th-century stained glass from the abbey church of Saint-Bertin in Saint-Omer, France. Tennyson was married here in 1850. Shiplake is best visited en route to **Sonning**, considered by many as the prettiest of Thames villages. The little islands that rise here in the river make the views especially pastoral. In Saxon times, Sonning was the centre of a large diocese, with a cathedral, a Bishop's Palace and a Deanery. Today, only parts of the Deanery garden walls remain, though the present church incorporates fragments of Saxon work. The old houses in the village are well preserved. The half-timbered **White Hart Inn** is 500 years old and has a lovely rose garden. The bridge at Sonning is one of the oldest on the river and, on the Oxfordshire side

surrounded by trees, there is a picturesque mill.

Reading is the single industrial town in the lower valley, a somewhat dreary place capitalising on the Thames Valley's aspiration to be Silicon Valley. The playwright Oscar Wilde (1854–1900) was broken by two years' hard labour in the red-brick jail.

Streatley and **Goring**, 10 miles (16 km) north of the A329 face each other on either side of the river – Streatley in Berkshire, Goring in Oxfordshire. Streatley is the prettier of the two, situated at the foot of the Berkshire Downs. Through here runs the **Ridgeway**, one of Britain's most ancient paths, still popular with visitors, going north over the Berkshire Downs to Dunstable and west through the **Vale of the White Horse** to the magic stone circles of Avebury and Stonehenge. Five miles (8 km) northwest is **Blewbury**, an ancient town with thatched cottages, watercress beds and winding lanes. A mansion here, **Hall Barb**, is said to have been one of Henry VIII's hunting lodges.

The Henley Regatta, part of the English summer season.

This is also where Kenneth Grahame, the author of the 1908 children's classic *The Wind in the Willows*, lived.

Dorchester's roman legacy: Upriver about 8 miles (13 km) is **Dorchester**, where the Thame joins the Thames. This ancient town was, at different times, a Roman fort (known then as Durocina) and a cathedral city. The abbey church was spared demolition at the Dissolution by a local resident who bought it from the Crown for £140. The stained glass in the nave dates from the 14th century. In the chancel is a Jesse Window in which Jesse, Christ's ancestor, lies on the sill with a fruit vine springing from his belly. Dorchester's High Street, which follows the line of the old Roman road to Silchester, is lined with period timber-framed buildings.

Clifton Hampden and **Sutton Courtney** are riverside villages with wide willow trees hanging low over the banks. There's good swimming here in summer. Sutton Courtney is especially interesting, with a well-preserved Norman church and a cluster of medieval houses nearby. In the graveyard is the resting place of Eric Blair (1903–50), known to most as George Orwell.

After Sutton Courtney the river takes a sharp turn north, making its way to **Abingdon** on the doorstep of Oxford. This is an old town that sprang up in the 7th century around a powerful Benedictine mitred abbey. In the 14th century the townspeople, aided by the mayor and undergraduates of Oxford, rose up against the monks, though it was not until the Dissolution that the abbey lost its stronghold.

Most of the ecclesiastical buildings were destroyed (don't be fooled by the 19th-century artificial ruins in the abbey grounds). But there are some authentic remains. These include the abbey **Gateway**, the 13th-century **Checker** (with its idiosyncratic chimney) and the 15th-century **Long Gallery**. In the **Guildhall** is a grammar school dating from 1563. All the major streets have houses from the 17th and 18th centuries. East Saint Helen's, with the church at the foot of it, is perhaps the prettiest.

Dorchester, a riverside town dating back to Roman times.

OXFORD TO STRATFORD

The triangle of Britain between Oxford, Warwick and the River Severn contains a history, culture and architectural style which seem to grow out of the ground. At its heart are the Cotswolds, part of a range of limestone hills which stretch from the Dorset coast northeast to Lincolnshire. What distinguishes them here is oolite. Oolite, called egg-stone because it looks like the roe of a fish, is the fine-grained freestone that has given a special character to the houses, barns, churches and pigsties from the hills' edge above Chipping Camden to the southern full stop at Bath. More than in any other region of Britain, the buildings here are organic, shaped by local hands. The stone takes on colours from gold to blue-grey, and responds with different hues to changing weather conditions in a quite remarkable way.

In Oxford these stones glisten wet after a noontime shower, and none of their warmth has left those that were used to build the rose-covered cottages of Stratford-upon-Avon or the castle and timbered Tudor houses beneath the castle at Warwick.

As if to reinforce the idea of a natural triangle, this area of the west Midlands is now enclosed by motorways on its three sides: the M4 from London to Bristol at its base; the M40 from London to Birmingham via Oxford and Warwick on the eastern side; the M5 from Birmingham to Bristol on the west. A good hopping-off point to the region is Oxford, which is about one hour's drive (60 miles/95 km) from both London and Birmingham. Paddington station serves the region.

City of dreaming spires: When Britain's noblest river passes through **Oxford**, it cannot be called the Thames as it is everywhere else. Instead it is called the Isis. Another river flows into it, the Cherwell (pronounced *Charwell*), and rising from the confluence of these muddy banks are the spires of that most mythologised of cities.

However you arrive, you will see them: the spire of Christ Church Cathedral, Tom Tower and Magdalen Tower. This is Oxford, the city that has given its name to many things from marmalade to movements, where undergraduates, cycling around corners, trail their gowns in the wind. But Oxford is also the site of the first Morris Motors works and since World War II it has been an industrial city as much as an academic one. Yet the twain rarely meet and, despite the arrival of both a McDonald's and a Kentucky Fried Chicken in Cornmarket Street, Oxford has weathered the late 20th century amazingly unscathed.

A tour of Oxford is essentially a tour of the colleges, and a good starting point is **Carfax**. (The name derives from the French, *Quatre Voies*, "four ways".) This is the old centre of the city, around the pedestrianised area, where the four main streets meet: Cornmarket, High Street, Queen Street and St Aldate's. The tower at the northwest corner, all that remains of St Martin's Church, dates from the 14th century, and from the top of it you take in a good view of the city. From Carfax, walk south along St Aldate's (passing the Tourist Information Office on the right) to **Christ Church**, the most grand of the colleges. But don't make the *faux pas* of calling it a college. Christ Church is "The House".

Christ Church was founded in 1525 by Cardinal Wolsey (his pointed hat is the House's insignia), on the site of an old priory. **Tom Tower** was built by Sir Christopher Wren in 1681. In it hangs the seven-ton bell, Great Tom, that sounds 101 strokes every night at 9.05 (101 strokes for the original 101 college members, and 9.05 because Oxford is 1° 15' west of Greenwich, so when the clocks of the capital show five past it is really nine at Oxford).

Tom Quad, the largest quadrangle in Oxford, has splendid grace and magnitude, and it was in the pool here, which is known as Mercury, that Anthony Blanche was dunked in Evelyn Waugh's 1945 novel *Brideshead Revisited*.

The Dean of Christ Church is a life appointment made by the Queen, and its chapel is the **Cathedral** of Oxford. The 144-ft (43-metre) spire is one of the earliest in England, dating from the 13th century. The **Picture Gallery** has fine Renaissance paintings and drawings, including works by da Vinci, Titian, Michelangelo, Rubens, Van Dyck, Gainsborough and Reynolds. Behind the college buildings, extending down to the confluence of the Thames and Cherwell, is the glorious **Meadow** where cows graze. Along the Thames are the University and college boathouses. It's here, at the end of May in Eights Week, that the summer college races take place, and somebody – usually one of the coxswains – gets dunked in the river.

College tour: From the Broadwalk, the wide path running east-west across the Meadow, there's a path cutting north to **Merton College**. Founded in 1264, Merton has some of the oldest buildings in Oxford. Its library in Mob Quad (the rear quadrangle) was built in the 1370s. The library's 16th-century bookshelves make it the first Renaissance Library in England, one where the books were set upright instead of being kept in presses.

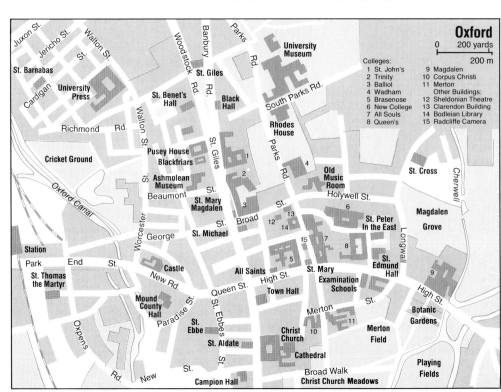

Oxford

0   200 yards
     200 m

Colleges:
1 St. John's
2 Trinity
3 Balliol
4 Wadham
5 Brasenose
6 New College
7 All Souls
8 Queen's
9 Magdalen
10 Corpus Christi
11 Merton
Other Buildings:
12 Sheldonian Theatre
13 Clarendon Building
14 Bodleian Library
15 Radcliffe Camera

One of Merton's illustrious graduates was the writer and caricaturist Max Beerbohm (1872–1956), and in Mob Quad is a set of rooms decorated with his memorabilia.

Opposite Merton are **Corpus Christi** and **Oriel**, smaller colleges both, though no less picturesque. The chapel at Corpus has an altarpiece ascribed to Rubens. Merton Street turns left at the top and takes you into the **High Street** where **Magdalen Tower** (pronounced *maudlin*) rises to the right. The Tower is just 6 inches (15 cm) higher than the Christ Church spire.

Magdalen was founded in 1458 by William of Waynflete. The chapel is a fine example of Perpendicular architecture and the cloisters are stunning. Behind them is the **Grove**, Magdalen's famous deer park, and the lovely **Water Walks**, a pastoral maze of garden and stream-side paths. Opposite the college on the other side of High Street is the **University Botanic Garden**, which has an endless variety of roses.

Walking west along High Street you

pass on the left the **Examination Schools,** an administrative building in late 19th-century English Renaissance style, and on the right **St Edmund Hall** (entrance in Queen's Lane). Also known as Teddy Hall, this was incorporated as a college in 1957. Before that, it remained the sole survivor of the once numerous residence halls of the medieval university. St Edmund Hall came into existence in the mid-13th century, and its name honours Edmund of Abingdon, who died in 1240 and was the first Oxford graduate to become Archbishop of Canterbury and be canonised.

Farther west along High Street are **University College** on the left (with a Shelley memorial) and **All Souls** on the right, the only college with no undergraduates. But a winding stroll along Queen's Lane will take you to the rear of **New College**. The chapel and cloisters of both are stunning. Queen's Lane curves and suddenly you stand beneath the Venetian bridge (built in 1903 – don't be fooled) that connects the new and old buildings of **Hertford College**.

From here there is a lovely view of the round **Radcliffe Camera** (1749) on the left and Wren's **Sheldonian Theatre** (1669) straight ahead. Dominating the scene, however, is the **Bodleian Library**. This is one of the largest libraries in the world, founded in 1602 by Sir Thomas Bodley. Currently it houses more than 5 million volumes including 50,000 of the world's most precious manuscripts. Don't expect to see any, except whatever happens to be on exhibit on the ground-floor display rooms. The Bodleian is not a lending library. Most of the books are underground beneath Broad Street in cavernous stacks to which not even the university members are permitted entry. Its reading room is on the ground floor of the Radcliffe Camera.

The best known place to actually buy books in the city is **Blackwell's** in Broad Street. Nearby, Sir Alec Guinness is the taped commentator for *The Oxford Story,* an audio-visual show. At the top of Broad Street, passing **Trinity** and **Balliol Colleges** on the right, is St Giles Street.

The church ahead is **St Mary Magdalen**, and the Gothic structure just north of it is the **Martyrs' Memorial**. Erected in 1841, the Memorial marks the spot where three Protestant bishops, Cranmer, Ridley and Latimer, were burnt at the stake in 1555 and 1556.

The **Ashmolean Museum**, the neo-classical building opposite the Martyrs' Memorial, is the oldest public museum in Britain. It houses a superb collection of Italian Renaissance, Dutch still-life and modern French painting. It also has an impressive collection of 16th and 17th-century tapestries, bronzes and silver; Greek, Roman and Egyptian sculpture; a Stradivarius, ceramics and jewellery.

North along St Giles is **St John's College**, founded in 1555. Its lovely gardens, landscaped by Capability Brown, rival those of Wadham and Trinity as the prettiest in Oxford. Behind St John's stretches Parks Road, with the **University Museum**, built in 19th-century neo-Gothic to the taste of the art critic John Ruskin (1819–1900). The

The coat of arms of Brasenose College.

museum is a storehouse of zoological, entomological, mineralogical and geological odds and ends.

Around Oxford: There are several villages worth visiting nearby. **Iffley**, southwest of the city, has a well-preserved Norman church that dates from 1170 and stands gracefully and timelessly above the river. The thatched cottage is the old church school. Some 16 miles (25 km) further southwest is the market town of **Wantage**, birthplace of King Alfred (AD 849–99), and 3 miles (5 km) further west is Uffington where the 360-ft (110-metre) **White Horse** was carved in the Iron Age at the highest point in the Berkshire Downs.

Eynsham, 8 miles (13 km) west of Oxford along the A40, is a picturesque village with the remains of a once famous abbey. Another 8 miles beyond is **Minster Lovell**, which has a 15th-century cruciform church and the romantic moated ruins of Minster Lovell Hall. The remains of this 15th-century manor house stand above the Windrush with a gloomy beauty. Francis, the 9th Baron Lovell, went into hiding here and starved to death in 1487.

Eight miles (13 km) north of Oxford on the A34 is **Blenheim Palace**, the destination not only of admirers of Sir Winston Churchill, but of those who like the natural-style gardens of Capability Brown. An afternoon stroll at Blenheim, with tea afterwards in the town of Woodstock (where the Oxfordshire County Museum is located), is a quintessentially English country excursion.

Britain's largest private house, covering 3 acres (1.2 hectares), Blenheim is the masterpiece of the playwright and architect John Vanbrugh (1664–1726). The estate was awarded by Queen Anne to John Churchill, 1st Duke of Marlborough, for his defeat of Louis XIV at Blenheim, France, in 1704. As it turned out, Parliament withheld most of the funds, and the Duke had to finance much of the construction himself. The house is open to visitors from mid-March to the end of October and is still in the family's hands. The exterior of

Blenheim Palace, the Churchill family home.

the Palace is an orgy of the baroque style, with both Doric and Corinthian columns. Inside is a maze of state apartments and, on the ground floor, the small bedroom where Winston Churchill was born in 1874. When the house is closed, there is still a 2,500-acre (1,000-hectare) park to enjoy. Originally designed in the ornate French style by Henry Wise, the landscaping was completely redone by Brown, who constructed a dam across the River Glyme and created the majestic lake which can be seen today.

The Cotswolds: Shaking off the clay of Oxford's vale, the roads west climb gradually to the heights of the edge facing the Severn and the distant mountains of Wales. Here are the Cotswold hills, broken by steep wooded valleys and rushing streams, Coln and Churn, Windrush, Dikler, Leach and Evenlode. They thrust out like fingers and detach themselves in isolated humps. Height and defensibility made their tops the towns of prehistoric man. Their sheep pastures and rivers provided subsistence in Roman times, and wealth for medieval peoples in the production of wool and cloth. Cirencester, 40 miles (65 km) west of Oxford was second only to London in size in Roman Britain, and Burford, half way between the two, had its wool-merchants' guild before the Norman Conquest. (Just south of Burford, at Filkins, is **Cotswold Woollen Weavers**, a fully working 18th-century woollen mill with a permanent exhibition of the industry.)

Thus, the architecture of Cotswold villages, churches and cathedrals was subsidised by the profits of the clothing industry. With its collapse, the Cotswolds went to sleep till pricked awake by the tourist.

Just south of Burford, **Lechlade**, 22 miles (36 km) west of Oxford on the A420/A417, on the upper Thames, makes a good starting point on the circuitous tour. Limestone-built, Cotswold-style, it has a church "whose pinnacles point from one shrine like pyramids of fire!" according to the poet Shelley, who wrote his *Stanzas in Lechlade Churchyard* here in 1815.

Below St John's Bridge cabin cruisers pass, and trout wait beside the 13th-century **Trout Inn**. No doubt William Morris, the utopian craftsman, dropped in here from his house just downstream at **Kelmscott Manor**. A typical Cotswold stonebuilt house, the manor has a roof of split stones, of which Morris said: "It gives me the same sort of pleasure in their orderly beauty as a fish's scales or a bird's feathers." Morris took the house in a joint tenancy with Dante Gabriel Rossetti, in 1871, and it became a centre for the pre-Raphaelite movement. His body was carried from here to the churchyard in 1896. Rossetti hadn't quite the same feeling for the place that Morris had. He called it "the doziest dump of old grey beehives".

Morris delighted in taking friends to his local "sight" – the tithe barn at **Great Coxwell**. This cathedral among barns owes its importance to the 13th-century monks at Beaulieu Abbey in Hampshire. The great oak timbers that support the roof rest on pillars of stone taller than a man. The nave, aisles and tran-

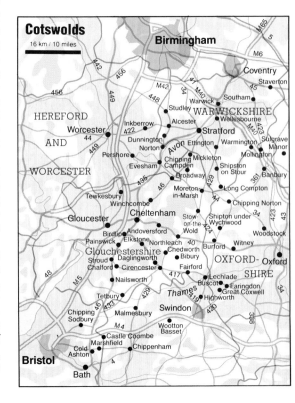

sept convey the message that this is indeed a house of God. Just across the river from Kelmscott is **Buscot Park**. Lord Farringdon enlarged the Adam-style house in the late 19th century, engaging the pre-Raphaelite Edward Burne-Jones, who was staying with Morris, to paint panels for the saloon and design the glass for the east window in the church.

Mysteries you can see through right away are rare. The windows of **Fairford** church, 5 miles (8 km) west of Lechlade, are one of them. Was this fantastic stained glass the work of Henry VIII's master glass painter, the man who worked on King's College Chapel, Cambridge? Or was it a prize taken from a captured ship? Did it come, perhaps, from the Netherlands, and did Dürer have a hand in it? Was the glass made for the church, or the church built for the glass? How did it survive the Civil War? Speculation aside, the "Last Judgment" is a masterpiece, and the red and blue devils, all with spiked teeth and yellow horns, are wonderfully frightening.

Five miles (8 km) north of Fairford, up the River Coln, is the beautiful village of **Bibury**. William Morris is credited with having discovered it, but Bibury's beauty has been there for all to see since the 17th century. **Arlington Row's** gables and high-pitched roofs are the very essence of the Cotswolds. These stone-built cottages, beside a stream from the mill, once housed weavers, who dried the cloth on Rack Isle, where a wild fowl reserve is now. The nearby 17th-century mill still has its working machinery, and has a fine display of Arts and Crafts furniture.

To the west of Bibury is the A429, the Cirencester-Northleach road, which follows the route of the original Roman road, Fosse Way. **Chedworth**, on the left 5 miles (8 km) north of Cirencester, has cottages scattered in terraces above the river and below are the woods which shelter what is probably the country's best-preserved Roman villa, dating from AD 180 and covering an area of 6½ acres (2.6 hectares). The baths are especially well preserved, and the mosaics are

made from two varieties of local Cotswold stone.

The church tower at **Northleach**, 10 miles (16 km) north of Cirencester, soars unchallenged above the town's roofs, and demonstrates at once the force of religious fervour and the high achievement of the Perpendicular style. Wool money built it, and the merchants who provided the money are remembered in the church's fine memorial brasses dating from the 15th and 16th centuries. Engraved feet rest on engraved woolsacks, and a woolman of 1485 has a left foot on a woolsack and a right foot on a sheep. A tailor's feet are parted by a pair of shears. Husbandry gets a look in at the **Cotswold Countryside Collection**, a museum of wagons and agricultural implements.

Cotswold capital: Fosse Way leads south to join two other Roman roads, Icknield Way and Ermine Street, in **Cirencester**, which some would have you say "Cissiter" and the Romans "Corinium", though locals call it Ciren. Second only in size and importance to London under the Romans, its fortunes flourished under the wool merchants, and floundered during the 19th century. Today, the medieval character of this "capital of the Cotswolds" is remarkably preserved. Unlike Northleach, Cirencester's church tower and porch err into being over-decorated and, in the case of the porch, over-large. One of the best examples of Perpendicular in the country, the porch of the church of St John the Baptist, once doubled for the town hall. Of the 12 bells in the tower, the ninth is called the "Pancake Bell", because it is always rung on Shrove Tuesday. **Cirencester Park**, home of the Earl Bathurst, shows a green wall to the town – a horseshoe hedge of a yew so high it must take a fireman's ladder to clip. The story of Roman Cirencester is compellingly told at the **Corinium Museum** and substantial remains of the town walls remain, along with a well-preserved amphitheatre.

Ermine Street is the A417 leaving the town to the northwest, where two village churches are not to be missed. First,

Millstone in the old wool town of Northleach.

is **Daglingworth** 4 miles (6 km) away, with Saxon sculptures, including a crucifixion of compelling simplicity. Then, high up, 5 miles (8 km) further on, is **Elkstone's** church, with a view to its east window under low Norman arches like a limestone cave.

Malmesbury lies 12 miles (20 km) southwest of Cirencester on the A429. Two distressing things have happened here. A woman was once killed by a tiger, and the abbey became a factory. The woman was Hannah Twynnoy, who died in 1703. As her tombstone records: "For Tyger fierce took life away ...And here she lies in bed of clay!" The tiger was from a visiting menagerie. At the Dissolution a rich clothier bought the abbey in a package deal which allowed him to convert it into a weaving-shed, and the parishioners to use the nave for services. Enough remains, especially a richly decorated porch and inner door, helped to give a good idea of the abbey's former glory.

Five miles northwest, in **Tetbury**, a fine 17th-century market hall recalls the one-time bustle of trading in wool that was conducted in the pillared open space beneath it.

West of the A46 16 miles (25 km) south of Tetbury near Chipping Sodbury, is **Dodington House,** one of England's greatest family houses, and still inhabited. The 18th-century architect James Wyatt gave it a splendid staircase, and Capability Brown a handsomely landscaped park.

For three days every year, pilgrims flock to **Badminton House**, 8 miles (13 km) southwest of Malmesbury. The occasion is the Three Day Event Horse Trials, a highlight for horse-lovers including the Queen. At other times the house, owned by the Duke of Beaufort, is interesting for its own sake; it was built in Charles II's reign and transformed into a palace by William Kent in the 18th century.

Gorgeous valley: Returning north 10 miles (16 km) beyond Tetbury the A46 arrives at Nailsworth and the start of the gorge-like valleys of Stroudwater, of wheels now still and looms long silent.

Cotswolds buildings seem to grow from the soil.

There are still one or two cloth mills here, and cottages hug the terraces above the steep streets.

At **Chalford** the descent into the **Golden Valley** begins. Curiosities are both here and upstream at **Sapperton.** One is a round house with conical roof and Gothic windows on the banks of the canal opened in 1789 to link the Thames with the Severn. At Sappeton it disappears into the hillside under a triumphal arch. From where the River Frome breaks through the western wall of the Cotswolds, **Stroud**, on its hill, looks across to the mountains of Wales. The country's cloth industry was concentrated here in the Stroudwater valley in the 16th century, and England's armies went to war in uniforms of scarlet and blue cloth from these mills.

Take to the heights to the left of the A46 Stroud-Painswick road, and you are in a "Little Switzerland" of swift-flowing streams and wooded ravines. **Slad**, on the B4070 old way to Cheltenham, is the village on which the novel *Cider With Rosie* was based. Laurie Lee's cottage and pub are still there, but the school has taught its last children.

Painswick's traditions are weaving, tomb-carving and yew-clipping. When the mills closed, weavers starved and masons put down their tools. In the churchyard are 99 yew trees – 99 and not 100 because the tradition says that one more would die. There is still more tradition at nearby **Cooper's Hill**, where seven-pound cheeses are rolled down its slope on spring Bank Holiday, with the cheese going to whoever manages to catch hold of it.

Kings, queens and tailors: The nearby county town of **Gloucester** is a cathedral city and inland port and has been a strategic centre guarding the route to Wales since Roman times. Alfred held a parliament here in AD 896, Canute signed a treaty and William the Conqueror ordered the *Domesday* survey from the Chapter House. Henry I died here of eating lampreys, Henry III was crowned and crook-backed Richard III ordered the murder of his nephews. Charles II took out his spite on the city

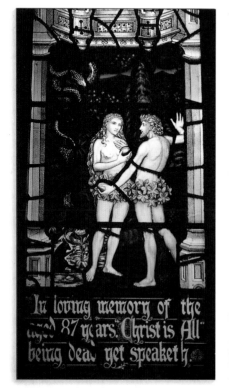

Left, stained glass from Gloucester Cathedral. **Right**, a local pub.

for opposing his father, by having its walls demolished. Queen Victoria stayed here in a pub. Of the Roman walls vestiges remain; of the medieval town very little.

The Victorian warehouses in the old docks have been renovated and include an antique centre with a street of period shops, the **National Waterways Museum** and the **Robert Opie Collection of the Museum of Advertising and Packaging**.

The cathedral remains the city's focal point. The nave is Norman, and the windows in the south transept are in earlier Perpendicular style. Fourteenth-century stained glass fills the largest east window in England and over the choir is an amazingly complicated cross-ribbed vault. Pilgrims once came to the richly ornamented tomb of Edward II, who was murdered at nearby Berkeley Castle. There is marvellous fan vaulting in the cloisters and even the Monks' Lavatory has its appeal. In the town there is a **folk museum** with a reconstructed Double Gloucester dairy. There

are Turners and Gainsboroughs in the **City Museum and Art Gallery**.

Just 8 miles (13 km) northeast is **Cheltenham**, a spa town which makes a good base for the Cotswolds. Lord Byron came here, as did George III, and Gustav Holst was born here in 1874. It was the discovery of the mineral spring in 1718 that started it, but it was the visit of George III and his queen 70 years later that made the spa fashionable as a summer resort. Like Bath, it was fortunate in its architects, J.B. Papworth and J.B. Forbes, who chose Cotswold building stone or stucco, and in the lightness and gaiety of the Greek revival style. This elegant Regency town has no burden of history, only a recent inheritance of fine building in the setting of parks and gardens.

Lansdowne Terrace, Place and **Crescent** as well as **Suffolk Square** and the **Pittville Estate** are the staged backdrop to the individual performances of the **Rotunda** and the **Pittville Pump Room** where the waters can be tasted. There is good ironwork everywhere, in

The Pittville Pump Room in the spa town of Cheltenham.

balconies, railings and verandas. For a frisson of the surreal, walk the street of statues, the caryatids of **Montpelier Walk**. The **Promenade** is a walk of a different kind, with lots of trees, shrubs, flowers and shops. Orchestras play, and so do fountains: there is a well established music festival in July.

Cotswold limits: The Cotswolds reach their western limit 10 miles (16 km) north at **Tewkesbury** where the Avon joins the Severn. Here stone gives way to attractive timbered cottages many of them serving as pubs, such as the 17th-century Bell Inn. In 1473 the Battle of Bloody Meadow, the last of the Wars of the Roses, was fought here, spilling over into the abbey itself. Even the monks took a hand. In that building there are a remarkable number of monuments, and from the 132-ft (47-metre) square tower there are views over the river valleys to the Malvern Hills and the mountains of Wales.

If ghosts walk, they walk at **Sudeley Castle** at Winchcombe 6 miles (10 km) northwest of Cheltenham on the A46.

This great, castellated house, just south of Winchcombe, saw Tudor history pass like a pageant. Katherine Parr lived there after Henry VIII's death, and was married again to Thomas Seymour. Lady Jane Grey stayed there, and Queen Elizabeth I was a frequent visitor. Carefully restored, it displays a fascinating collection of royal relics and paintings.

Two villages further along this road to Broadway are **Stanway**, with scallop shells over the rather pretentious gateway to the manor, and **Stanton**. Nearly every cottage here is built in the best period of Cotswold architecture, from the mid-16th to the mid-17th century. **Snowshill Manor**, in a valley south of Broadway, was Katherine Parr's, too. Tudor beneath the skin, it houses a magpie collection from musical instruments to toys.

Broadway is the Cotswolds' show village, and a broad street it is. Houses and cottages face one another across an expanse of green on the road from London to Worcester, all in the same style and, barring the odd exception, in the

Re-thatching at Chipping Campden.

same honey-coloured stone. The **Abbot's Grange** dates from the 14th century and the **Lygon Arms** (one of the Cotswolds' best restaurants) from the 16th. Charles I and Cromwell stayed there, but of course not at the same time. **Broadway Tower** in a country park on Broadway Hill, the second highest point in the Cotswolds, will take your breath away if you have any left after the climb.

Chipping Campden, 5 miles northeast of Broadway has a 16th-century market hall which poses for photographs in the middle of the long main street, curved like Oxford's High Street, and lined with fine stone houses dating from the years before the 17th century, when this was one of the most prosperous wool towns. Especially interesting are the almshouses and church, the town hall, and William Grevel's house. Grevel, a wool merchant, died in 1401, and his memorial brass in the church remembers him well.

On **Dover's Hill**, an open space a mile from Campden, Robert Dover first held what he described as his "Cots-wold Olympicks" in 1612. Not only did he get the king's support, but he also acquired some of his old clothes to dress up in. Events were different from today's – stick fighting, backsword play, quintain, and country dancing among them. There is little doubt that Shakespeare came down from Stratford to see them.

Turning back eastwards towards Oxford on the A44, the circuitous route reaches **Moreton-in-Marsh**, which took to linen weaving when the woollen industry failed. A mile or two west is **Sezincote**, a house in the Indian style, which gave the Prince Regent his ideas for Brighton Pavilion.

"Chipping" means market and 8 miles (13 km) further on is **Chipping Norton**. Beside many 18th-century houses is **Bliss Tweed Mill**, looking like a country mansion with a factory chimney on top. The town is handy for an excursion to the **Rollright Stones**. These are a big circle of some 70 standing stones on a hilltop, called the King's Men, a smaller group called the five Whispering Knights

Lower Slaughter.

and a menhir standing alone called the King. Like Stonehenge, their origins remain unknown, though they date certainly from the Bronze Age. According to legend, the king and his knights were turned to stone by a local witch.

Secret valleys: The hill town of **Stow-on-the-Wold** 4 miles (6 km) south of Moreton-in-Marsh, was once the scene of great sheep fairs. Daniel Defoe recorded as many as 20,000 sheep being sold on one occasion. Like sheep, 1,000 defeated Royalists were penned in the church after the last battle of the Civil War in 1646. On the west of the town are the Swells, **Upper Swell** and **Lower Swell**, villages on the River Dikler. They owe their odd name to "Our Lady's Well", but they are pure Cotswold. The Guitings, **Temple Guiting** and **Guiting Power**, in thick woods on the Windrush a few miles further west, are a little too perfect. Between them, the **Cotswold Farm Park** offers a chance to see rare but local farm animals like Cotswold lions – sheep with fleeces like lions' manes – and pigs such as Tamworth

Gingers. Downstream, **Naunton's** water meadows sport a grand hotel among dovecots with innumerable nest holes.

Over the hill, just below the Swells, are another pair of villages worth discovering – **Upper Slaughter** and **Lower Slaughter**, with fords on the tiny Slaughterbrook, dovecots and mills. Nearby is **Bourton-on-the-Water**, one of the best of the Cotswold stone villages. Set on the river Windrush, it has all the ingredients of fairyland: miniature footbridges over streams and under willow trees, sweet smells in the perfumery, a motor museum in a barley mill, a model railway, and a model village. Also nearby, the Birdland Zoo Gardens covers 4 acres (1.5 hectares) of ponds, groves and aviaries; this setting is the home to hundreds of species of exotic birds.

Burford, to the southeast, is another wool town. Here is a churchyard with tombs in the shape of wool bales. Wool merchants' houses of the 14th to 16th centuries can often be found hiding behind later fronts, and one behind the

The house where Shakespeare was born.

name "Rampant Cat". That isn't the only mystery you will leave behind on leaving the Cotswolds.

On their northern side, the Cotswolds merge into the **Vale of Evesham**, part of the Avon valley where the climate is mild and ideal for growing fruit and vegetables which have given the town of **Evesham** a prosperous air. Attractive villages in the valley lie just to the east, at **Bretforton** and the **Littletons**.

Birthplace of the Bard: Above Evesham the A439 follows the Avon for 14 miles (22 km) to **Stratford-upon-Avon**. William Shakespeare was born here in Henley Street on 23 April 1564. His father was a local farmer and wool dealer. He was christened in the local Holy Trinity Church and went to the local school; at 18 he married 16-year-old Anne Hathaway and they had three children. In 1597, after his extraordinary career as a playwright in London, he bought New Place in Chapel Street where he lived for the last half dozen years of his life. He died on his 52nd birthday and is buried at Holy Trinity.

In spite of the numbers of tourists, the town, of half-timbered buildings beside the river, still manages to evoke the atmosphere of the times of its most famous son. Men of lesser stature but of considerable literary accomplishment have added testimony to his fame in the upstairs room of the timber-framed house in which he was born. Sir Walter Scott, Thomas Carlyle and Isaac Watts inscribed the window that shed first light on the playwright at his birth. There is a bust in the 15th-century church made from his death mask by Gerard Jansseni in his London studio a yard or two from the place of his subject's triumphs, the Globe Theatre in Southwark.

His birthplace is the starting point for a tour of the town. The entrance is through the modern **Shakespeare Centre**, the headquarters of the Birthplace Trust. An exhibition of the costumes made for BBC Television's complete cycle of Shakespeare's plays, and displays on the life and work of the dramatist, occupy visitors while they queue up

Stratford's typical Tudor style.

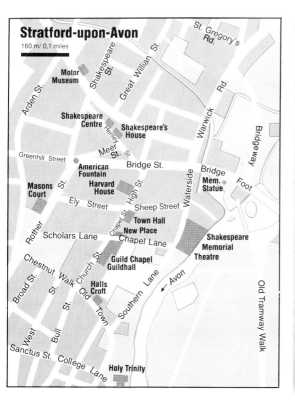

to enter the birthplace itself. Shakespeare's granddaughter married Thomas Nash and they lived in **Nash's House**, which is now a museum of the town. Nash's House was next door to New Place, of which only the foundations remain, preserved in a garden. The living legacy of the playwright can be found at the **Swan Theatre**, home of the **Royal Shakespeare Company** from March to September. There is a collection of RSC theatre items and backstage tours can be arranged.

Between Shakespeare's birthplace and Nash's House is **Harvard House** which has transatlantic connections. Built in 1596, this was the home of Katherine Rogers whose son, John Harvard, founded the US university.

In **Shottery**, a mile or so to the west of the town, is **Anne Hathaway's Cottage**. The daughter of a farmer, she lived in this timber-framed, thatched and much-restored cottage during the 16 years Shakespeare was in London. Their life together resumed when he returned to settle down in New Place.

Not surprisingly, Stratford tends to fill up in summer, but there are other towns nearby which can form good touring bases. **Leamington Spa**, a spacious Regency and Victorian spa town, is just 8 miles (13 km) northeast on the A46, which continues another 8 miles to **Coventry**. This is a car manufacturing town terribly bombed during World War II, when all but the steeple of its cathedral was demolished. The **New Cathedral**, by Sir Basil Spence, was completed in 1962 and is highly imaginative with immense stained-glass windows and a richly coloured interior. On even-numbered years the cathedral ruins provide the stage for the city's medieval **Mystery Plays** on the first two weeks of August.

West of Stratford and 12 miles (20 km) north of Tewkesbury is **Great Malvern** on the slopes of the **Malvern Hills**, from which there are magnificent views over 10 counties. This is another health resort and the hills are the source of bottled mineral water.

A most princely seat: Eight miles (13

Coventry's re-built cathedral.

km) north is the county town of **Warwick**, which grew up around its castle. Despite a serious fire in 1694, many of the buildings from the Tudor period remain standing.

First fortified in 914 by Ethelfleda, the daughter of Alfred the Great, **Warwick Castle** has had a long and rich history. Although only a mound of earth remains of the original Saxon structure, the 14th-century towers standing today are the proud features of what is regarded as England's finest medieval castle. For hundreds of years England's most powerful families lived at Warwick. It was Fulke Greville, in the early 17th century, who set about making the castle's interiors "the most princely seat within the midland parts of the realm". His success cannot be disputed. A collection of paintings, including portraits by Rubens, Van Dyck and Holbein, is complemented by a collection of arms and armour. The graffiti in the dungeon and torture chamber is attributed to Royalist soldiers from the Civil War.

Bordering the River Avon, the castle's 60-acre (25-hectare) gardens landscaped by Capability Brown are impeccably maintained. The footbridge across the Avon to the River Island offers a rear view of the castle that really brings home its size. Madame Tussaud's wax figures portray a garden party tableau. The castle is the most visited stately home in Great Britain. Outdoor events include afternoon musical performances, dancing and knights in armour on horseback explaining the finer points of medieval jousting.

The nave and the tower of **St Mary's Church** (between Jury Street and the Butts) were built after the 1694 fire. In keeping with the high state of preservation of the castle, the **Beauchamp Chapel** houses one of the most perfect medieval tombs known.

Lord Leycester's Hospital by the West Gate was originally founded as a guildhall in 1383. In 1571, Robert Dudley, Earl of Leicester, had the buildings renovated as almshouses. Today the hospital is a museum and the home of ex-servicemen.

A dignatory of Warwick is immortalised in front of Lord Leycester's Hospital.

CAMBRIDGE AND EAST ANGLIA

East Anglia, the four counties of Norfolk, Suffolk, Cambridgeshire and Essex, bulging into the North Sea between the Thames estuary and the Wash has the least annual rainfall in all of Britain. You would not know this, however, since it is also a region of fens and great rivers, of lakes, called meres or broads, and bird-filled coastal marshes. The beauty of East Anglia is not a typical one. Few places rise higher than 300 ft (90 metres) above sea level. Charles Dickens' young hero, David Copperfield, noticed this upon his first visit to Yarmouth: "It looked rather spongy and soppy... and I could not help wondering, if the world were really as round as my geography book said, how any of it could be so flat."

No one passes through East Anglia; nowhere lies on the other side. Road and rail connections with the rest of the country are poor. To East Anglians, emigration means moving 5 miles down the road. To the south the A12 (junction 28 on the orbital M25) leads west from London to Colchester, famed for its oysters, and on to Ipswich before heading up to the seaside towns of Lowestoft and Great Yarmouth. From East London the M11 (junction 27 on the M25) runs up to Cambridge 53 miles (85 km) directly north, from where the A11 goes northeast to Norwich and the A10 continues to King's Lynn and the fenlands around the Wash. The main rail routes run from London's Liverpool Street.

At the time of the *Domesday Book*, the four counties of East Anglia were some of the richest and most highly populated in the country. Today, with a population density less than half the national average, East Anglia resolutely refuses to follow the nation's trends.

In the Middle Ages, a huge forest in the south (a fraction of which remains today as Epping Forest) and a strip of uncrossable marshlands in the north (the

Preceding pages: *The Hay Wain* by Suffolk's John Constable. **Left**, Fens wildfowler.

Fens) separated East Anglia from the rest of the country. The region became a sanctuary from the power struggles that wracked the rest of the emerging kingdom, and it was to East Anglia that many religious orders fled for peace. Their legacy is in the form of churches, cathedrals and abbeys. In Norfolk alone there are 600 medieval churches.

East Anglia was also a region of gentry, whose houses still mark the landscape much as the churches. **Audley End**, in the medieval town of Saffron Walden 15 miles (24 km) south of Cambridge, was built for a Lord Treasurer and said by James I to be "too large for a king". As it stands today the house is large, but it is only a fraction of the original; much of it was demolished in 1721. The interior decoration, by Robert Adam, and the immaculate gardens, landscaped by Capability Brown, are classics of English country design.

Sandringham in Norfolk, on the other hand, was embellished by a king and is still used as a royal country retreat. Edward VII, when Prince of Wales,

bought Sandringham in 1861, but it is decorated in styles ranging from Jacobean to Regency. The house, 8 miles (13 km) north of King's Lynn, is closed when a member of the royal family is in residence, but the 7,000-acre (2,800-hectare) parklands are kept open. The long drive is particularly impressive.

Despite the backwater quality about East Anglia, it is still a region of wealth. Farmers here drive luxury cars, and the modern gentry, dressed casually but rich nonetheless, host grouse shoots for their southern cousins who cannot spare the time to go to Scotland. University brainpower has been harnessed in the hi-tech industries of Cambridge's science parks. But what the visitor feels most in East Anglia is the sense of isolation. It has changed little since the 11th century.

Undisturbed by both the sooty touch of the Industrial Revolution and the bombs of World War II, many villages and towns remain unspoiled, apart from noise pollution around the airforce bases at Mildenhall and Lakenheath. In the Suffolk village of **Lavenham**, 20 miles

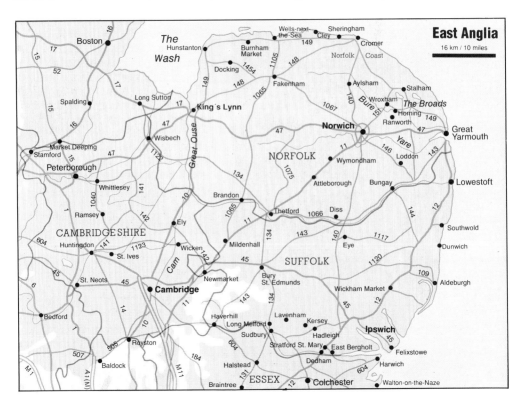

(32 km) west of Ipswich, almost all the houses are at least 400 years old. The townspeople have removed the telegraph poles and buried the wires underground to preserve the village's Tudor appearance. The only element that destroys East Anglia is the sea, which is devouring the eastern shores. The ancient capital of **Dunwich**, 15 miles (24 km) south of Lowestoft, at one time had eight churches; now the sea has swept the town away. All that remains is one gravestone that has not yet crumbled into the waves, though residents claim they hear the bells of drowned churches ringing at low tide.

East Anglia harbours myriad landscapes that range from the flat wilds of north Norfolk to the rolling green tranquillity of south Suffolk, an inch of land for every mile of sky. Gainsborough and Constable both declared that the beauty of Suffolk landscape – its winding lanes, sloping fields and still waters – was what spurred them to paint.

University town: An Elizabethan historian once described the fen dwellers as "brutish, uncivilised and ignorant". Today's Oxford undergraduates invoke this claim when they scornfully refer to the university at **Cambridge** as the "Fenland Polytechnic", but some of the world's finest thinkers, artists and architects matured in this fenland town.

Cambridge was founded in the 12th century by a settlement of Franciscans, Dominicans and Carmelites. In 1209, a handful of scholars hurriedly fled Oxford after a disagreement with the town authorities and settled in Cambridge. It was this – and the founding in 1281 of the first college, Peterhouse, by Hugh de Balsam, Bishop of Ely – that established the university.

Other colleges were soon founded under the patronage of local gentry and a succession of monarchs. In 1441 Henry VI founded **King's College**, central to the University on King's Parade. Five years later, **King's College Chapel** – considered the glory of Cambridge and the finest Gothic building in Europe – began construction, which took nearly 70 years. Chapel services are open to

Trinity College, Cambridge.

visitors, and it is worth standing in the ancient pews alongside Rubens' *Adoration of the Magi*, listening to the voices of the choir float up along the curves of the magnificent fan-vaulting and gazing at the series of 25 16th-century stained-glass windows, which portray the story of the New Testament. The choir is arguably the best in the country, and its annual carol service reaches audiences in all corners of the world; it has even been listened to in a tent at the foot of Mount Everest.

From the top of **Great St Mary's Church** opposite King's Chapel (whose clock tower chimes are the same as those of Big Ben) visitors can see the whole of Cambridge, including the distant gaunt tower of the **University Library.** Like the Bodleian at Oxford, the University Library at Cambridge by law receives a copy of every book published in the United Kingdom. Opposite St Mary's is the dignified **Senate House** – the university parliament, built by James Gibbs between 1722 and 1730.

The beauty of Cambridge is its compactness; a few steps in any direction will take you past a piece of history, whether it be the Anglo-Saxon tower of the tiny church of St Benét's (eclipsed by the college buildings, but 250 years older) or the Cavendish Laboratory, the site of the first splitting of the atom.

In the gardens of **Christ's College** the tree supposedly planted by the poet John Milton (1608–74) still stands. It was while at Christ's that Milton composed the *Hymn of Christ's Nativity* as a college exercise. The Great Court at **Trinity** is the largest university quadrangle in the world, but look closely at the figure of its founder, Henry VIII, above the Trinity gateway: instead of a sceptre he holds a chair leg. Trinity's library, seen from the riverfront, was built by Sir Christopher Wren. Further north is **St John's**, founded in 1511 by Lady Margaret Beaufort. Its three-storey gatehouse, decorated with carvings of heraldic beasts, is magnificent. Behind it, along the river, is the **Bridge of Sighs** (1831), modelled on its more famous namesake in Venice. Across Bridge

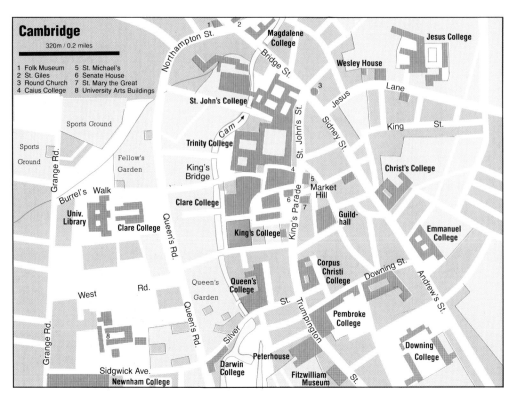

Cambridge
320m / 0.2 miles

1 Folk Museum   5 St. Michael's
2 St. Giles   6 Senate House
3 Round Church   7 St. Mary the Great
4 Caius College   8 University Arts Buildings

Street from St John's is the **Holy Sepulchre Round Church**, one of only four round churches in England. This one was founded in 1130 by the Knights Templar and was connected with the Crusades. The shape is based on that of the Holy Sepulchre in Jerusalem.

Queen's College, hidden behind St Catharine's, has an unusual and seemingly rickety half-timbered President's Lodge, but its **Mathematicians' Bridge**, also of wood and originally built in 1749 without a single nail, is amazingly sturdy. A curious Victorian took it apart in 1867 and was unable to put it back together without iron bolts.

A little beyond the town centre along Trumpington Road stands **Peterhouse**, the oldest and most traditional of the colleges. Portraits of the college benefactors stare down from the walls of the dark and rich hall at the necks of today's undergraduates seated at the original 17th-century tables. Next door is the **Fitzwilliam Museum**, a spectacular collection including works by Turner, Titian and Rembrandt and a fine selection of manuscripts, including Blake's original poems. Beyond the Fitzwilliam the **Botanical Gardens** make a haven for tired tourists and students alike. In Castle Street is a delightful **Folk Museum**, and around the corner, the **Kettle's Yard Art Gallery** has an eclectic collection of modern works.

The best way to see many colleges is to hire a punt from **Scudamore's Boatyard** at the end of Mill Lane. Drift down the "Backs" (only undergraduates try to speed) from Charles Darwin's House to the Bridge of Sighs, gliding between the willows at the backs of the best-known colleges.

The wetlands: Flat, spongy and soppy the Yarmouth area may have seemed to young Copperfield, but the **fenland** is flatter, spongier and soppier still. The village names – Landbeach, Waterbeach, Gedney Marsh and Dry Drayton – all tell the same story. Never marry a fenland woman, runs the saying, because on the wedding night you may discover she has webbed feet. For centuries no one tried to cross the marshes,

Below, *Adoration of the Magi* by Rubens in King's College. **Right,** Henry VIII looks down over Trinity Gate.

let alone build on them, yet today the black fenland soil is some of the most productive land in the country.

The Romans were the first to try to drain the 2,000-sq.-mile (5,200-sq.-km) marsh that stretched from Cambridge to Lincoln, but success came only during the reign of Charles I, when the Dutch engineer Vermuyden (1595–1683) cut rivers through the marshes. Even he, however, was not prepared for the dramatic land-shrinking that resulted. Today's fields are often 10 ft (3 metres) below the rivers that were cut to drain them. Vermuyden used 700 windmills to pump up the water.

Today only one remains undrained; at **Wicken Fen** (signposted off the A10, 17 miles/27 km north of Cambridge) the windmill works to keep 600 acres (240 hectares) of marshland wet, preserved by the National Trust as a corner of the fens as it once was.

Where the A10 approaches Ely, 16 miles (25 km) north of Cambridge, the everlastingly flat skyline is broken. **Ely Cathedral** (completed in 1351) domi-nates the fens from its perch on the top of what used to be called the Isle of Eels – after the staple diet of the villagers. Eels no longer appear on the menu of the Old Fire Engine House restaurant in Ely, but you can still get local specialities, such as smoked pike soufflé and asparagus and marsh samphire.

The Isle, a knoll of dry land, was selected as a cathedral site by St Etheldreda in AD 673. Four hundred years later it made an ideal refuge for Hereward the Wake from the pursuit of William the Conqueror. Hereward seemed unreachable on Ely (then an island), but eventually the monks tired of the siege and showed the conqueror's men the secret pathway through the marshes, giving Hereward away.

The splendour of Ely Cathedral lies in its unusual situation and in its unique lantern. In the evening, the lantern – an octagon of wood and glass built high on the back of the nave in an extraordinary feat of engineering – reflects the rays of the dying sun. By night its glass gleams with the light within.

The unique lantern in Ely Cathedral.

The A1101 on the left, 5 miles (8 km) north of Ely, crosses the unimaginatively named Hundred Foot Drain and passes between the rows of marching crops to **Wisbech**, a market town that styles itself as the capital of the fens. The two imposing Georgian streets (Southbrink and Northbrink) illustrate the prosperity fen drainage brought, and Market Square is full of the produce it provided in abundance. In the eccentric **Fenland Museum** are pictures of Wisbech in its heyday and the complete furnishings of a Victorian post office.

While Wisbech has been preserved by a lack of economic development, **King's Lynn**, 12 miles (20 km) northeast along the coast, has marched on. Much of the town has been rebuilt since the late 1950s, and the grand Tuesday and Saturday market places are now (during the rest of the week) car-parks. Several areas present a sombre face, and its sometimes Germanic look is taken from the Hansa cities that were once its trade links. In 1600, King's Lynn was the third major port in England; today

Norwich Castle Museum.

its town centre is a featureless shopping mall. Many of the buildings worth seeing lie in the streets bordering the River Ouse with **King Street** marking the heart of the old town. The flint-fronted **Guildhall** claims to be the last surviving building in Britain where Shakespeare appeared in one of his plays. The **King's Lynn Festival** is held in the Guildhall in the last week of July. **St Margaret's Church** (which, in 1977, had 8 tons of pigeon manure removed from its roof) is located next to the marketplace. Dating from the 13th century, the high-water levels etched outside the west door are a reminder of East Anglia's vulnerability to flooding. The **Customhouse**, designed by Henry Bell in 1683, and the contemporary and highly imaginative **Femoy Arts Centre** are also worth the visit.

City of spires: A city that retains its sense of history alongside economic success is a rare place, yet **Norwich** manages to do both. The city has a church for every week of the year and a pub for every day, they say, and every vista of this surprisingly hilly town confirms it. Within the city walls 32 medieval churches still stand, though some now have secular purposes. **St James'** is a puppet theatre; the imaginative **Elizabethan Theatre** at the Maddermarket is a combination of chapel and warehouse; and **St Peter Hungate** at the top of Elm Hill is a museum of ecclesiastical treasures.

There are 119 Saxon flint round towers in Norfolk, but the local stone was undramatic; stone for **Norwich Cathedral** had to be brought from Normandy up the river Wensum so that the Cathedral's spire could rival that at Salisbury. Besides the Cathedral and its fine **Cloisters**, the **Cathedral Houses** in the Close and **Pull's Ferry** (last used as a river-crossing in 1939) are worth seeing. The appropriately named Tombland Square, just outside the Cathedral gates, in fact derives its name from the Anglo-Saxon "toom", an open market-place.

With no source of fuel readily available to drive machines, Norwich, once the third richest town in England, was left behind by the Industrial Revolution.

The city became self-sufficient and to-day continues to prosper, with a relatively low percentage of unemployment compared with other areas of the country. Retailing became the profession of the prosperous, and it was a succession of wealthy grocers who, century by century, added to **Strangers' Hall**. The result today is a charming museum with 23 rooms designed in a bewildering variety of styles. The earliest parts of the house date from 1320.

Today's wealthy grocers are no less munificent: the **Sainsbury Arts Centre** at the university, founded by the High Street supermarket family and designed by Norman Foster, has won several architectural awards (closed: Mon). Its wide collection does not house the works of the Dutch-inspired impressionist Norwich School, however, which hang in the imaginatively converted keep in the 12th-century **castle**.

In the 18th century, when weaving was at its height, there were 30,000 weavers in Norwich. But Norwich today is an excellent shopping centre.

Lavish antique shops line **Elm Hill** and in **Colman's Mustard Shop** in Bridewell Alley customers can still buy mustard for their bathwater. Elm Hill's impression of antiquity is slightly misleading, for all but the Briton's Arms was destroyed in a fire in the 18th century, and it has since been rebuilt. More recently, the tree that gave the street its name contracted Dutch Elm disease and has been replaced by a plane tree.

Birds, boats and Broads: Northeast of Norwich, the A1161 turns off to the little village of **Woodbastwick**. As you approach it, the buzz of distant tractors fade, and is replaced by a pastoral silence. In winter, drizzle may drip into the peat-dark waters of Bure marshes, and somewhere a coot grates its voice in alarm as the white triangle of the sail of a late-season yachtsman slides slowly through the brown sedge. Heeding the alarm, a cormorant splashes across the water's surface and labours into the heavy air before watchful ornithologists. The **Norfolk Broads** have begun.

For the bird-watcher, winter is a grip-

Sailing
through
Suffolk, near
Southwold.

ping time on the Broads, but most visitors to this chain of lakes – thought to be medieval peat-diggings which have flooded over the centuries – come with the summer sun.

Hiring a boat is undoubtedly the best way of enjoying the Broads, since they are largely inaccessible by road. There are some 10,000 craft on the 200 miles (320 km) of navigable waterways, though fortunately not everyone goes afloat at the same time. The best places for boat hire are either **Wroxham** or **Horning** (both on the River Bure near Woodbastwick, off the A1151). The former, with 20 boatyards, may be the capital of the Broads, but the latter, with its Venetian-style inlets to private houses and the thatched houses which line its main street, is the more attractive. Yachtsmen come from miles around to tie up alongside the local pub public-house for a quiet evening drink.

From the water the landscape is one of church towers, windmills, reeds and sails cutting through fields, all of which would be missed from the land. The village staithes (a local word for jetty) date from the time when most supplies came by water. Until the early part of this century sailing wherries laden with cargo used to navigate the River Yare from Norwich to the sea; one such vessel is preserved at Horning.

At **Ranworth**, the home of the Broadlands Conservation Centre, the tower of **St Helen's Church** provides a magnificent view of the network of waterways. A little farther down the River Bure stand the ruins of **St Benet's Abbey**, first built in AD 870 but now oddly misshapen thanks to the stump of a windmill (now disused) that was added to the ruins 200 years ago.

In some places the Broads are tidal, and the slightly brackish water attracts unusual wildlife. Coots, heron, bittern and the nation's largest butterfly, the swallowtail, live in the reeds. So does the coypu, which escaped from a nearby fur farm, and is now regarded as a major pest by preservationists. But more disturbing is the disappearance of the plant life from the waters of all but a few

Broadlands
Conservation
Centre at
Ranworth.

Broads over the last decades. Some blame the farmers' fertilisers for increasing the level of nitrates in the water. The cause remains unknown.

Seaside towns: The sea giveth and the sea taketh away – or so the waves seem to clamour on the shingle and hiss of the sands of East Anglia. On the north Norfolk coast **Cley** and **Wells-next-the-Sea** are now more than a mile from the shore. On the Suffolk coast **Dunwich**, once the seat of a bishop and a town with churches, monasteries and hospitals, has disappeared altogether. In 1326 one storm alone swept away 400 houses, and year by year the last gravestone in the All Saints' churchyard edges closer to the crumbling cliff.

In the 1880s the Great Eastern Railway Company published *Holiday Haunts in East Anglia*. The new railway network opened up a dozen resorts on the sunny coastline. But today, with many routes no longer in service and with travel abroad easier than ever, few holidaymakers come to the East Anglian coast. Some of the smaller beachside resorts have been all but forgotten, thus preserving their Victorian atmosphere. Two such spots are **Sheringham** and **Cromer** in north Norfolk, a coastline lashed by winter storms. In 1855–56 there were 500 wrecks off this shore. Even today almost every village has its own lifeboat. The one at Cromer is famous. Henry Blogg, a crew member for 53 years, helped save 873 lives. Meanwhile, at Sheringham, fishermen haul their boats up to the top of the cliff with tractors.

Midway around the coast, **Great Yarmouth** has kept its popularity with the tourists. Once the scene of great activity with the arrival of herring (and with it the Scottish herring-girls who had followed the shoal southwards to clean and pack the fish) its harbour is now full of support vessels for the offshore oil industry. In the 11th century fishermen paid their taxes in herring, but the industry finally died in the 1930s, and Yarmouth sold itself to the tourists. Today it is a tacky place, its visitors white-skinned and fleshy. In the market

Bowling at Great Yarmouth.

204

the fish-and-chip stalls no longer bother to sell fish, only chips, and the golden sands of the beach are hidden behind the spires of the helter-skelters and the walls of the roller-coaster.

So changed is Yarmouth that the 1969 film of *David Copperfield* had to be shot in the resort of **Southwold**, 20 miles (32 km) south. This town has a dignity and refinement that Yarmouth lacks. Its manicured appearance is due partly to a fire in 1659 which destroyed much of the fishing village and allowed careful planning in reconstruction.

Southwold is the home of Adnams, traditional brewers of strong, knee-bending and mind-boggling real ales. The brewery's horse-and-cart still makes local deliveries. In the magnificent Perpendicular church, Southwold Jack, a figure in armour, rings in the services by striking a bell with his sword.

Despite the dominance of tourism, Southwold has one of the few estuary ports still used by fishermen. It also has what must be the cheapest passenger ferry in the country which sails across to **Walberswick**, an attractive village frequented by painters.

Artists' inspiration: Across the Blythe estuary from Walberswick to **Aldeburgh** is a rewarding, though long, walk. Benjamin Britten (1913–76) made the fishing village his home and in 1948 started the prestigious annual music festival that runs for two weeks every June. Since then, Aldeburgh has become fashionable indeed. The village was also the birthplace of George Crabbe (1754–1832), whose poetry inspired Britten. Crabbe hated the rough nature of life in the fishing community, and it is ironic that it is indirectly through Crabbe and through the Aldeburgh festival that the town has become so refined – 150 years too late for the poet to enjoy.

Some 25 miles (40 km) southwest of Aldeburgh is the Suffolk county town of **Ipswich**, once described as a load of old bricks that fell off a lorry between Norwich and London. It has little to recommend it apart from an atmospheric Victorian dockland, complete with lightship and sailing barges, on the River

Fashionable Aldeburgh in Suffolk.

Orwell. The author of *1984* took his pen name from the Orwell, but the Stour, which meets the Orwell at its mouth around the North Sea passenger and cargo ports of **Harwich** and **Felixstowe**, is the more famous of the two rivers, thanks to the work of a much-loved British artist.

Constable country, as the Suffolk countryside alongside the Stour is called, is exactly that. John Constable (1776–1837) painted the river, the trees and the villages with a love that has made this landscape familiar even to those who have never been there. The artist was born in the grand village of **East Bergholt** (just off the A12 between Ipswich and Colchester), where the bells of the church tower, never finished, are housed in a shed in the graveyard. His father was the mill owner at **Flatford**, just down the hill. The setting had great sentiment for Constable, and when he recreated it in the painting *The Hay Wain*, he postponed his marriage for a month simply to finish the work. The water mills of nearby **Stratford St Mary**

were another favourite subject. In fact, all along the river Stour is Constable's element. He wrote: "The sound of water escaping from mill dams, willows, old rotten planks, slung posts and brickwork…these scenes made me a painter."

The village of **Dedham**, only a few miles up the banks of the Stour from Flatford and best approached that way, has changed little. The row of neoclassical houses that faces the church is pristine. And yet Dedham is not entirely unmodern; inside the timeless church one of the pews is decorated with medallions from the first moon landing.

Woollen finery: Unspoilt as Dedham may seem, the villages inland are even more so. In **Kersey, Hadleigh** and **Lavenham**, many of the timbered houses that lean over the streets date from the early 16th century. This is wool country, and these villages were well known and wealthy for 700 years after the Norman Conquest (Kersey cloth is mentioned by Shakespeare). The rich mill owners lived in grand halls and worshipped in magnificent

East Bergholt where John Constable was born.

churches, all built with their profits. Fine examples of both of these are at **Long Melford** (north of Sudbury). The village's Tudor houses present a pleasing visage of turrets and moats; the two best examples are Melford Hall and Kentwell Hall.

Timber-framed houses give the villages their beauty, but flint and brick dominates at **Bury St Edmunds**, the cathedral city of the area, midway between Ipswich and Cambridge on the A45. Thomas Carlyle called this a "prosperous brick town beautifully diversifying, with its clear brick houses and ancient clean streets, the general face of it looking out pleasantly towards the rising sun". But the city is no backwater, and the narrow streets around the **Buttermarket** are jammed with people, as is the **Nutshell**, said to be the smallest pub in England.

The **Moyse's Hall Museum**, built in the 12th century, is considered the oldest Norman house in East Anglia. It is also said to have been the house of a Jewish merchant, or even a synagogue, but with no evidence to support the claims. Inside are Bronze Age and Saxon artefacts found in the area, plus relics of the grisly Red Barn murder. At the centre of the town is the beautiful Robert Adam **Market Cross Gallery** housing temporary exhibitions.

The gem of Bury is the ancient **Abbey** and **Cathedral**. The beautiful grounds, laid out as formal gardens, are twice the size of the city centre, and the surrounding walls exclude the noise of the town. Below the Cathedral, built in the 12th century, lie the remains of the Abbey swathed in grass. Originally founded in the 7th century, it was an important place of pilgrimage after the body of Edmund, last king of the East Angles who was killed by the Danes, was placed there in about 900. In 1214 a group of barons swore before the altar to raise arms against King John if he refused to set his seal to the Magna Carta. He did, unwillingly, a year later, and today Bury still celebrates this – and Edmund's burial – in its motto: Shrine of a King, Cradle of the Law.

Bury St Edmunds where King Edmund was buried.

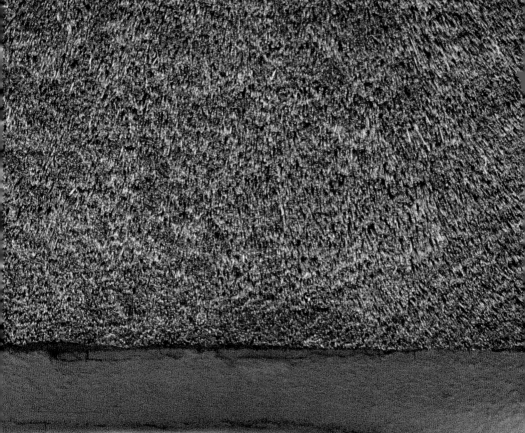

THE SOUTHEAST

The counties of **Kent** and **Sussex** in the southeast corner of England lie south of the Thames estuary, between London and the Channel, no more than 70 miles (115 km) away. Any part of them can therefore be seen on a day trip from the capital, particularly their historic centres such as Canterbury, Rye, Brighton and Chichester which are best explored on foot. From London's orbital M25 motorway the M23 leads south to Brighton, principal resort of Sussex, while the M2 and M20 head for the Channel ports of Folkestone and Dover in Kent. Victoria and Charing Cross stations provide the rail links.

The Kent coast is 21 miles (34 km) from France, and in 1875 the two countries were proved to be within swimming distance by Captain Matthew Webb (it took him 21 hours and 45 minutes). As the nearest point of the country to the Continent, this is the way invaders came: Romans, Angles, Saxons and Britain's last conquerors, the Normans, who scorched the date of 1066 into the history books with their triumph at the Battle of Hastings. Towers, castles and moated mansions were built to withstand later invasion attempts by France, Spain and, in the 20th century, Germany, while cathedrals rose at Chichester and Canterbury, the Church of England's spiritual home and the focus of centuries of pilgrims.

The counties have a common geology in which all the strata run east to west. Kent's North Downs mirror the Sussex South Downs and the filling in this cake is Greensand, Weald Clay and Sandstone, repeated in reverse order. All contribute to a rich variety of landscape in a relatively small space. Some is spectacular, like the White Cliffs of Dover and Beachy Head near Eastbourne, and some unique like the South Downs themselves, hailed somewhat exaggeratedly by the eminent 18th-century naturalist Gilbert White as "a chain of majestic mountains".

The Downs have long supported sheep. The Weald is excellent for fruit growing, particularly apples, and in recent years grapes for white English wines (the chalk Downs are the same geological strata that runs through Champagne in France). Hops grown for beer were once picked by London's East Enders in a holiday mood but barely 50 hop farms remain, though their stems decorate many pubs.

Sussex, with its bandstands, beaches, Victorian piers and promenades is rightly famous for its sea. "Kent, Sir!" as Dickens's Mr Jingle exclaimed. "Everybody knows Kent. Apples, cherries, hops and women." Together they offer the hedonist a deckchair on a sunny beach, the delights of rolling countryside, the thrill of walking in high places, and the discovery of churches and rambling country houses.

Canute's shore: To the west lies the county town of **Chichester** where the cathedral spire rises like a beckoning finger above this typical English rural town of notable Georgian houses. The **South Downs** provide a backdrop and

Preceding pages: typical Devon thatched roof. **Left**, chalk cliffs of the South Downs at Beachy Head. **Right**, Sussex thatcher.

the creeks and marshes of its harbour nearly lap its walls. The 227-ft (70-metre) 14th-century spire, the only one in the country visible from the sea, was rebuilt in 1861 after a storm had brought it down. Inside, the modern altar tapestry by John Piper (born 1903) is a dramatic surprise. Among many fine carvings and relief work the most remarkable is the 12th-century Raising of Lazarus which can be found in the south side of the choir.

The 15th-century **Market Cross** is one of the finest in the country. Good local pubs with accommodation include the 15th-century Dolphin and Anchor in West Street and The Ship in North Street. To the north of the town in Oakland's Park is **The Festival Theatre** where Laurence Olivier was the first director. It is a theatre in the round, and no seats are more than a cricket pitch's length from the stage.

Little of Chichester's Roman walls remain but at **Fishbourne**, a mile to the west, Britain's largest Roman palace was uncovered in 1960 and it is worth seeing for its well preserved mosaics as well as to appreciate its formidable scale and size. The estuary it stood beside has receded and Chichester's harbour now has myriad muddy inlets (harbour tours from **Itchenor**), the most attractive being at **Bosham**. From his seaside residence, Canute (994–1035) confounded his grovelling court by proving even he, King of England, Denmark and Norway, was unable to halt the waves. His daughter is buried in the delightful nearby church which is depicted in the Bayeux tapestry.

In the South Downs up behind Chichester is **Goodwood**, site of a racecourse and country house. At the summit is the hill fort of the Trundle, giving wonderful views before dropping down to **Singleton** and the **Weald and Downland Museum.** For this ambitious open-air project, buildings from throughout the ages have been collected from the region and reassembled for visitors to wander round.

Continuing north for 6 miles (9 km) the A286 arrives at the elderly market

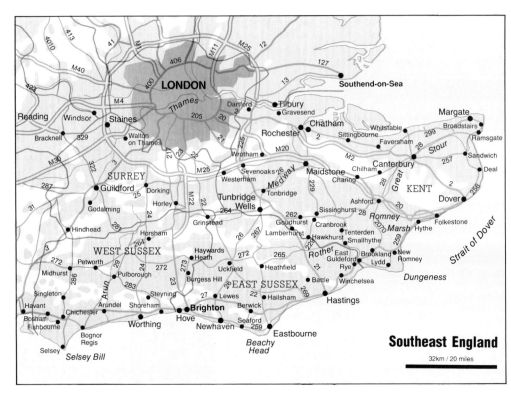

Southeast England

32km / 20 miles

town of **Midhurst**, where a right turn on to the A272 leads another 6 miles to **Petworth**. Here narrow streets are twisted and turned by the walls of the great 17th-century **Petworth House**, seat of the Percys, Earls of Northumberland. It has a deer park landscaped by Capability Brown and an exceptional art collection. J.M.W. Turner painted here in 1810 and 1830. It also features an astounding wood carving by Grinling Gibbons.

Follow the Rother downstream to join the Arun and below is **Pulborough**. This is the fishing capital of Sussex, famed for Arundel mullet and Amberley trout. **Amberley**, 5 miles (8 km) to the south has a castle rescued from a farm which overlooks the pristine village of whitewashed cottages and thatch. Just to the east lies **Parham**, a remote and carefully restored Tudor house. It has a delightful 4-acre walled garden and there is a small family church in the grounds.

The lord lays an egg: The Arun finally emerges from the South Downs around **Arundel**, commanded by the imposing castle of the Dukes of Norfolk, Earls Marshal of England, organisers of the pomp of state processions. More French than English, the competing views of the castle and churches (both Anglican and Catholic) dominate the skyline. Unfortunately much reconstruction through the 19th century has made the castle a sham, but it's a sham carried off with a flourish. Owls once inhabited the keep, and some were known by the names of prominent people. "Please, Your Grace, Lord Thurlow has laid an egg." Lord Thurlow, the owl, died in 1859. There are splendid views of the castle from Swanborne lake in the grounds and an adjacent wildfowl trust was set up by Sir Peter Scott.

Earlier peoples clung to the heights around here and the Downs behind are littered with hill forts, flint mines, burial mounds and tracks used 2,000 years before the Romans came. There is a **Chalk Pits Museum** at Houghton Bridge, Amberley, and 10 miles (15 km) east are two hills worth a climb,

Arundel Castle, West Sussex.

Cissbury and **Chanctonbury** which has a crown of beeches. These are all along the **South Downs Way**, an 80-mile (130-km) footpath running from the coast at **Eastbourne** to **Petersfield** in Hampshire.

Brighton Rock: The history of **Brighton** is the history of a poor fishing town that became the country's best-known seaside resort through the rec-ommendation of a local doctor, Richard Russell, who prescribed sea bathing for his patients. With the patronage of George IV (then Prince of Wales) he opened an establishment with attend-ants called "bathers" for men and "dip-pers" for women. London society fol-lowed. In 1785 the prince stayed in a villa on the old Steine, which was later redesigned by John Nash, Indian in style outside, oriental within, as the **Royal Pavilion**, which was completed in 1822. One of the decorative wonders of the world, with a fascinating kitchen, it is open all year and frequently has exhibitions and concerts.

The narrow **Lanes** nearby invite browsers and are among the best-known haunts of antique collectors in the south of England. Old pubs, wine bars and inexpensive restaurants, such as Food for Friends in Prince Albert Street, are easily found and are popular with language and university students in the town. Stuccoed squares, terraces and crescents spread into redbrick Hove and eastwards into Kemp Town.

Beyond **Brighton Marina**, the white cliffs rise and fall to the gap that leads inland to the pond and green of **Rottingdean**, a village colonised by writers and painters of the 1890s. Among them were Edward Burne-Jones and Rudyard Kipling, though Kipling is mainly associated with Bateman's some 30 miles (48 km) northeast near Burwash, where con-certs are occasionally performed in summer.

Lewes, capital of East Sussex, lies to the north east of Brighton. Its hills have been the scene of battles since Saxon times and it seems almost overburdened with history. From the Barbican en-

Brighton Pavilion, East Sussex.

trance and the Norman castle to the Regency Court Hall and Victorian Town Hall, the High Street drops steeply to the river. At **Bull House**, Thomas Paine, author of *The Rights of Man*, lived from 1768 to 1774. In the same High Street, 10 men and women were burned at the stake during times of religious intolerance.

From Lewes the A27 to Eastbourne passes near **Glyndebourne**, Mr John Christie's celebrated opera house, where it is fashionable to go during the summer season. On this road look out for the **English Farm Cider Centre** which has 100 varieties, and a large selection of farm produce with tastings of more than 30 cheeses.

The area on the opposite, southern side of the highway could be described as rural Bloomsbury. At **Rodmell** Leonard and Virginia Woolf lived in Monk's House from 1919. In 1941 she left her life in the nearby river Ouse; he died here in 1969. Her sister Vanessa Bell lived with Duncan Grant a few miles away at **Charleston**, a mellow farmhouse they enhanced with murals and a brimming garden. The couple also painted the interior of the church nearby at **Berwick**.

From Berwick the River Cuckmere runs south to **Alfriston**. Next to the church is the thatched Old Clergy House and in the village are former smuggling inns. Chalk cliffs, called "the Seven Sisters", lead to **Beachy Head**, at 530 ft (160 metres) the highest cliff on the coast, and to Eastbourne.

Conqueror's country: In the levels to the east, **Pevensey** has the most considerable Roman monument in Sussex, but the Roman fort was incomplete and could not withstand the landing of William, Duke of Normandy, in 1066. The Conqueror did not meet up with Harold of England until some 10 miles (16 km) inland; the spot where Harold fell, his eye pierced through by an arrow, was marked by William who built upon it the high altar of the abbey church at **Battle** as a thanksgiving. An imposing 14th-century gatehouse leads to the grounds and ruins of the abbey. In

Beside the seaside, Eastbourne.

the town, look out for **Buckleys Museum of Shops**.

The place where William prepared for battle and which lent the encounter its name is 6 miles (9 km) southeast of Battle. **Hastings'** hilltop Norman castle, above a warren of caves where smugglers' adventures are re-enacted, is now a ruin, though a siege tent inside re-tells the battle story on which the town has thrived. For centuries, however, it had been little more than a fishing village until it was rescued by the vogue for sea bathing in the 18th century. On the Stade tall, tarred and weatherboarded sheds used by the fishermen for storing nets are architectural fantasies.

To the east is **Winchelsea**, which Edward I began as a new town in 1283 to help the wine trade with Bordeaux. Like neighbouring **Rye**, it has suffered from floods and the French and now lies high and dry. Edward III (1327–77) gave Rye its walls and gates. The **Landgate** and **Ypres Tower** survive, as well as much half-timbering in the old street below the church which has the oldest clock in an English church. In Mermaid Street the **Mermaid Inn**, dating from 1500, is so untouched by time that you might think Elizabeth I was still on the throne. The American writer Henry James lived here in **Lamb House**. Today Rye is a pottery town and there is an active artists' colony whose work can be seen at the Stormont Studio in East Street and the Easton Rooms in High Street.

From Rye the land lies flat across the great expanse of **Romney Marsh**, a strange, haunted area of a special breed of sheep, of water weeds and wading birds such as the Kentish plover. Along its coast runs a small light railway from **Hythe** to near the power station at **Dungeness**, and small passenger aircraft at **Lydd** airport can reach Le Touquet in France in just 12 minutes.

The Weald: But before continuing in this direction, a detour back up from Rye on the B2082 to the white weatherboard town of **Tenterden**, home of another small historic railway, leads to-

A colourful corner in the old Channel port of Rye.

216

wards the **High Weald**. On the right just before the town is **Smallhythe**, once on a tidal river, there is a 16th-century half-timbered yeoman's house where the English actress Ellen Terry (1847–1928) lived and it now houses her many mementoes.

The region to the west of here was made rich by Flemish weavers, notably around **Cranbrook**, dominated by a white windmill and St Dunstan's church, known as the "Cathedral of the Weald". Daniel Defoe wrote *Robinson Crusoe* here (1719). Some 50 years later, during the Seven Years' War, 23-year-old Edward Gibbon, who wrote *The Decline and Fall of the Roman Empire*, was guarding French prisoners held in **Sissinghurst Castle,** 2 miles (3 km) to the east. The 16th-century castle was in ruins when it was bought by Vita Sackville-West (1892–1962), poet, novelist and gardener extraordinary and her politician husband Harold Nicolson in 1930. The beautiful garden which they created is among the most visited in Britain, though belated revelations about Vita's love life no doubt has helped to bring the curious.

Eight miles west is **Goudhurst**, peaceful enough now, but in 1747 the villagers locked themselves in the church while a gang of smugglers from nearby **Hawkhurst** fought the local militia in the churchyard. From this half-timbered town there are wonderful views south over hop and fruit country and there are several places nearby worth visiting. **Bodiam Castle**, to the south beyond Hawkhurst, is a classical fort set in a 3-acre moat, while **Scotney Castle** 5 miles (8 km) southwest, has been described as one of the loveliest surviving landscapes in the 18th-century pictorial tradition.

Beyond the castle is the village of **Lamberhurst**, on the main A21, which in Elizabethan times was the centre of the Wealdon iron industry. The railings for St Paul's in London were made here and it is rumoured that cannons used against the English by ships of the Spanish Armada were cast in this corner of the country. One of Britain's foremost

An idyll in the Sussex countryside.

modern vineyards is at Ridge Farm and winery and cellar tours take place from May to October.

Taking the waters: North of the village of Lamberhurst, half way down the A21 between London and Hastings, lies **Royal Tunbridge Wells**, a place supposedly full of blimpish retired colonels who write letters to *The Times* and sign themselves "Disgusted". Lord North, father of the British prime minister, founded the spot when he unexpectedly discovered a spring on the common in 1606. Court and fashion followed, and the waters, rich in iron salts, were, and still are, taken at the **Pantiles**. This terraced walk, with shops behind a colonnade, is named from the original tiles laid in 1638, some of which are still there. When Henrietta Maria, wife of Charles I, came here after the birth of Prince Charles eight years earlier, she had to camp in a tent on the common. The former home of the novelist William Thackeray in London Road is now a restaurant with a good reputation. There are a number of good second-hand bookshops in the old part of town.

Nearby stone outcrops, **Toad Rock** and **High Rocks**, attract romantics and climbers. **Penshurst Place**, just to the northwest of the town is one of Kent's finest mansions, dating from 1340. Home of the Viscount De L'Isle, it was for two centuries the seat of the Sidney family, notably Sir Philip Sidney, the Elizabethan soldier and poet.

A few miles to the west lies **Hever Castle**. Henry VIII, who first met Anne Boleyn in this, her father's house, seized Hever after her execution and murdered her brother. William Waldorf Astor (1848–1919) applied his American millions to make massive and sympathetic improvements to the moated castle, 35-acre (15-hectare) lake and gardens where flower beds are laid out exactly as they were 400 years ago in Tudor times.

Some 10 miles (16 km) to the north on the B2026 is **Westerham**, a town that commemorates General James Wolfe, who decisively drove the French from Canada when he stormed Quebec in 1759. His statue shares the limelight on the village green with one of Winston Churchill and down the hill is the mansion where he lived his first 11 years, **Quebec House.** There are more mementoes of Wolfe at **Squerryes Court**, a 17th-century mansion just outside the village. Churchill's connection with the village is **Chartwell**, just to the south, his home from 1924 until his death in 1965. There is often quite a queue to see his home, left much as it was – particularly his studio where there are many of his paintings.

Sevenoaks is the town 5 miles (8 km) to the east on the far side of the A21 and on its outskirts is **Knole**, one of the largest private houses in the country. It was the Archbishop of Canterbury's residence until confiscated by Henry VIII, and Elizabeth I gave it to Thomas Sackville who greatly extended it. It has 365 rooms, 52 stairways and seven courtyards. There are exceptionally fine portraits of the Sackville family by Gainsborough and Van Dyck, as well as some rare furniture. In the 1,000-acre (400-hectare) deer park is a fascinating

The Pantiles in Tunbridge Wells.

Gothic folly birdhouse. **Long Barn** 2 miles (3 km) south, on the other side of the A21, dates from the 14th century and is reputed to be the birthplace of William Caxton (1422–91) who introduced printing to Britain. It was also the early home of Sir Harold Nicolson and Vita Sackville West before they moved to Sissinghurst.

Six miles (10 km) east of Sevenoaks on the A25 at Ivy Hatch is **Ightham Mote**, one of the most complete examples of a medieval moated manor house. But Kent's pride and joy lies to the east, six miles (10 km) beyond the county town of **Maidstone**. **Leeds Castle**, the castle of the queens of medieval England, is a fairytale place built on islands in a lake. It has 500 acres (200 hectares) of parkland and is a popular day out. In summer there are concerts.

Dickens country: Maidstone lies on the River Medway which empties into the Thames estuary between **Rochester** and **Chatham** 10 miles (16 km) to the north. Charles Dickens lived at 11 Ordnance Terrace in Chatham as a boy, when his father worked for the navy. A Norman castle and keep stand above the river at Rochester, which holds an annual Dickens festival. The writer is remembered in the Bull & Royal Victoria Hotel ("a good house – nice beds," *Pickwick Papers*) and at **Eastgate House**, where his chalet from Gad's Hill where he lived from 1857 to his death in 1871, has been re-erected.

Chatham's tradition as one of Britain's foremost dockyards has now passed into the hands of the heritage industry, but the forts, defences, yards and rope lofts are still impressive to see. From Chatham the A2 goes east between the North Downs and the sandy shore, to **Sittingbourne** and **Faversham**, an attractive town opposite the Isle of Sheppey. In centuries gone by these were roads of pilgrimage, of Chaucer's tell-tale band who set out from the Tabbard Inn in Southwark to walk to **Canterbury**.

Pilgrims' promise: Canterbury is the cradle of English Christianity. The Conqueror's Castle, the cathedral and

The Ballroom at Knole, one of Britain's largest private houses.

its Thomas Becket Shrine were a magnet for pilgrims for centuries, and in St Margaret's Street the **Canterbury Pilgrims' Way** promises a "medieval adventure" with the sights, sounds and even the smells of the journey made by five of Chaucer's characters.

Despite German aerial bomb attacks in 1942, much of the town's medieval character remains, and there are a number of good pubs in its narrow streets. The cathedral itself is a hodgepodge of styles. The oldest part is the crypt, which dates from 1100 but there are traces of still earlier work. The first church on the site was established in AD 597 by St Augustine who had been sent by Gregory the Great to convert the heathen English, and it became a great focus of attention when Archbishop Thomas Becket was canonised after being slain here in 1170. The glorious, soaring nave was rebuilt in 1400 and the main **Bell Harry Tower** was added a century later. The stunning stained glass rivals the best in France.

Canterbury's other delights include the remains of the original Roman wall which once enclosed it. When the Romans established themselves in Canterbury in AD 43, it became a trading centre on the central route between London and the Continent. Standing on flat land between the North Sea and the Channel, the city was always vulnerable to raiders. It fell to the Vikings in 851 and to the Danes in 1011. When the Normans arrived they fortified the city, but only about a mile of the medieval wall remains.

Worth visiting are the excavated ruins of **St Augustine's Abbey** near the grounds of **St Augustine's College** where Anglican clergy are trained. Farther east along Longport is **St Martin's Church** which was used for Christian services even before the arrival of Augustine. In the 4th century this area was the selected by rich Romans for their villas, and there are still remains to be seen.

The only surviving gate, **Westgate**, now stands across the busy London road. Since the River Stour formed a

Canterbury: journey's end for thousands of pilgrims.

natural barrier, there was no need for a wall here. The Westgate had a drawbridge as an added means of defence. For many years the Westgate was used as a prison but since 1906 it has been used as a museum. Today the town's main, **Heritage Museum** is located in Stour Street.

Daytrip towns: Britain's first passenger railway line was opened in 1839 between Canterbury and **Whitstable** 6 miles (10 km) to the north. Romans from Canterbury used to venture out to Whitstable for their oysters, which have been famous for 2,000 years. Here, on the north Kent coast, weatherboarded pubs serve the succulent bivalve, and Somerset Maugham (1874–1975) lived with his uncle, the vicar, while attending King's School in Canterbury.

Further east lies **Margate**, which the railway opened up to East Enders as one of the capital's most popular seaside resorts. Bathing machines were invented here by a local Quaker and it still has a breezy holiday air. A couple of miles away is **North Foreland**, the tip of the duck's tail of Kent and Britain's most easterly spot. Immediately below is **Broadstairs**, a more up-market resort which has a sandy bay and landscaped cliffs, which Dickens described as being "left high and dry by the tide of years". When he knew it, the clifftop **Bleak House** was called Fort House. He spent his summer holidays there in the 1850s and 1860s.

Ramsgate, one of the smaller Continental ferry ports, borders Broadstairs to the south. Near here the Anglo-Saxons under Hengist and Horsa landed in AD 499. Ramsgate took over from **Sandwich** 7 miles (11 km) south when it became another of those ports left high and dry by the fickle sea and is now surrounded by a 500-acre (200-hectare) coastal bird sanctuary. It was also one of the original Cinque Ports, a string of safe harbours from here to Hastings which were specially fortified against invaders. **Walmer Castle** in **Deal** is still the official residence of the Lord Warden of the Cinque Ports. On the beaches of this small resort Julius Caesar landed in 55 BC. The latest attack on the town came not from the sea but from an IRA bomb smuggled into an army barracks in 1989. By the shingle beach, from which there is good fishing, is a plaque commemorating Julius Caesar's landing here in 55 BC.

Sandwich, Deal and Dover are now billed as "**White Cliffs Country**", and at Dover, Britain's busiest passenger port, the chalk massif of the South Downs dramatically drops into the sea. On these cliffs the Romans built a lighthouse, the Normans a castle, and from here Calais can be seen. But it is near the neighbouring Channel port of **Folkestone** that the Continent is coming more sharply into view. Here dried dogfish is called "Folkestone beef" and the town has a good market on Sundays.

But it has become more famous for its nearby tunnel, broken through at the end of 1990 and destined to connect England to France, with fast trains running between the two countries. Once traffic begins to roll freely back and forth, all the coast's castles, towers and parapets will look more ancient still.

Whitstable has always been the place to go for oysters.

HARDY COUNTRY

Preceding
pages:
Salisbury's
spire and
sunny
meadows.
Left, thatched
cottages in
Milton Abbas.
Below, the
soaring nave
of Winchester
Cathedral.

No literary works bear the impress of place so strongly as the novels of Thomas Hardy (1840–1928) and no place has had its character and the character of its people revealed as Wessex has by Dorset's most famous son. Wessex is in fact an ancient kingdom, rather larger than the one in which the novelist's trail winds. This was the kingdom of the West Saxons, who had supremacy in England from 802 to AD 1013. It extended across the modern counties of Hampshire, Wiltshire, Dorset and Somerset and even for a short while included Devon and Cornwall which were conquered from the Welsh.

The M3 motorway west of London leads to the ancient capital of Winchester in little more than an hour, and beyond it the urban sprawl of Southampton, the once-glorious transatlantic liner port. Skirting it, the A31 continues through the New Forest to the smart seaside town of Bournemouth and then to Dorchester, centre of the Hardy tours. To the north, the A303 leaves the M3 at junction 8 and heads for Salisbury Plain and Devon. Trains to London arrive at Waterloo.

From the springboard of Winchester you move out of the magnetic field of London to walk in the freedom of space before the pull of the West Country makes itself felt. Wessex is a wild country of forest and chase, of sea coasts, great cliffs and shifting, shingle banks, of thrusting headlands and hills where people lived, fought and died thousands of years before the Normans arrived.

There is no hurry about Wessex. The pace of life here is dictated by the cattle on its farms and the slow cycle of its growing crops. Its economy is largely agricultural and industry, where it does raise its head, is discreet. Wessex is for wandering. Roads are generally minor and invariably go the long way round. Great architecture may be lacking, but there are plenty of ruins, among them Corfe Castle, about which the painter Paul Nash wrote: "No mood of nature or human intrusion can affect that terrific personality." Maiden Castle's vast earthwork is another such "personality". Dorset provides most of the coastline. To be lulled, go to Lyme Regis or Weymouth; to be threatened, go to Chesil Beach or Portland; to be overawed, go to the cliffs of Lulworth and Purbeck. Wessex seaside, like the country that lies behind, puts on a great show.

The second capital: Winchester was England's other capital, as well as capital of Wessex, until all decision-making was moved to London in the time of Charles II. William the Conqueror had to be crowned in both places, though whether he had tea at the Old Norman Palace Tea Rooms is not so certain. Beneath the medieval and modern city is a Roman town, and a Norman **cathedral** replaced the Saxon. Older than Canterbury and the longest in Europe, its Norman transepts and tower survive, but nave and choir were modernised by William of Wykeham in Perpendicular style towards the end of the 14th century. The organ's first notes were heard at the Crystal Palace in London's Hyde Park in 1851. The palace, cloisters, colleges and mill are all breathtaking. The Great Hall near Westgate is all that is left of Henry III's castle and it is one of the finest in the country. Sir Walter Raleigh was condemned to death here in 1685 and it is still the county court.

The A272 road west drops suddenly to the broad main street of **Stockbridge**, on the River Test, a delightful stop before the 15-mile (24-km) haul across the barren plain to Salisbury. The old coaching inn in the High Street, the White Heart, has plenty of atmosphere. **Salisbury** ("Melchester" in the Hardy novels) wasn't always where it is now. It used to be at Old Sarum, over a mile away on a hill, until, in the 13th century, Bishop Roger Poore quarrelled with the captain of the castle there and founded the breakaway cathedral we see now. The townsfolk followed, and it became New Sarum. There was a water shortage at Old Sarum, anyway. The new cathedral was built between 1220 and 1258, with "as many windows as days in the year, as many pillars as hours, and as many gates as moons". The spire took even longer to complete. It is the loftiest in England and the inspiration of one of Constable's most famous paintings. **The Close**, a green space fringed with fine houses (mostly Georgian), distances the confusion of the modern city.

Stonehenge mystery: About 8 miles (13 km) north of Salisbury on the A345 is Amesbury and from there the A303 leads to that infamous collection of standing stones, **Stonehenge**. On first view, it may seem disappointing; Emerson the American poet, thought it "looked like a group of brown dwarfs on the wide expanse". Get closer and you will see its beauty – despite the throbbing crowds of tourists. Its pattern consists of an outer ring and inner horseshoe of sarsen stone brought from the Marlborough Downs. (Originally, there seem to have been two rings and two horseshoes, the remains of which still stand). The blue stones are of a kind quarried in the Preseli Hills in Pembrokeshire – in Wales.

The largest standing trilithon is 21 ft (6 metres) high and extends more than 8 ft (2.5 metres) below ground. The purpose of the circle remains unknown, but many believe it was a temple to the sun. On Midsummer Day, the sun rises over the Hele Stone, on the axis of the avenue. On that day Druids celebrated their rites until the mid-1980s; now all Midsummer festivities have been banned because of the large convoys of hippies who were using the verge as a

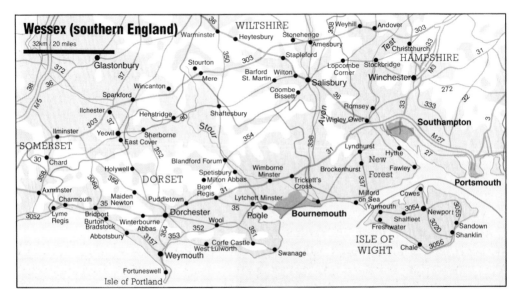

campsite and causing considerable damage. Druids in hooded white robes with mistletoe in hand and brandishing banners used to sing and chant before dawn. The numerous tumuli around the site hint, perhaps, at some ancient funerary significance. Some scholars even believe the stones were used to predict astronomical occurrences.

Just west of Salisbury, the great house of **Wilton**, the seat of the Earls of Pembroke, is splendidly framed in the entrance arch which prepares us for the sweetness and strength of Inigo Jones's rooms within. Here are the miscellaneous delights of a lock of Queen Elizabeth I's hair, Napoleon's despatch case, and some Rembrandts and Van Dycks. In the park, the Palladian bridge of 1737 over the River Nadder fuses function with great elegance.

Spiritual journey: Leaving Wilton, the A30 bounds the wilderness of the old hunting forest of **Cranbourne Chase** and then climbs to one of England's few hill towns, **Shaftesbury**. Hardy renamed it "Shaston" in *Jude the Obscure*. Walk the town walls above the steep drop to the horse-and-hound country of Blackmore Vale, and put the clock back centuries with a climb up the cobbled **Gold Hill** – like pilgrims to St Edward the Martyr's resting place.

In the village of Stourton, 8 miles (13 km) north of Shaftesbury near Mere, is the mansion at **Stourhead**, built for Henry Hoare, a banker, in 1720–24. The magnificent gardens are landscaped around the lake. There is an atmosphere of sweet melancholy about these classic temples. Gothic cottages and towers reflected in the lake's dark waters, best seen in the half light of the flint and pebble-lined grotto.

Further south, 16 miles (25 km) west of Shaftesbury, is **Sherborne**. Once the capital of Wessex and the burial place of two Saxon kings, it retains a medieval flavour. You almost expect old conflicts between townsfolk and monks to flare again or to come upon Sir Walter Raleigh and his wife in their seats in the abbey chapel. In the airy conservatories at **Compton House**, butterflies fly free

Shaftesbury's famously quaint Gold Hill.

in what, for want of a better word, is called a farm, and caterpillars produce the thread for silk. At Yeovil 5 miles (8 km) west you stray into Somerset for a visit to **Montacute**, an Elizabethan house begun by the lawyer who opened the prosecution at the trial of Guy Fawkes. In golden Ham Hill stone, the ornamental gazebos or lookouts at the corners of the forecourt are exquisite mansions in miniature with latticed windows.

In the church at **East Coker**, 3 miles (5 km) to the south, are the ashes of T.S. Eliot (1888–1965). The poet's ancestors emigrated from here to America. "In my beginning is my end," he wrote in the poem named after the village. There's also a memorial to William Dampier (1652–1715), the pirate who developed a taste for exploration and inspired Defoe's *Robinson Crusoe*.

There is a warm briny wind at **Lyme Regis**, just east of the Devon border. This old fishing town was once as fashionable a resort as Bath, and it was popular 100 years before Bournemouth was even thought of. Regency bow windows and trellised verandas on Victorian villas line the **Parade** on the way to the tiny harbour and its curved protecting arm, the **Cobb**, where the Duke of Monmouth landed in 1685, aspiring to the crown. Its sea-lashed walls were a supporting role for Meryl Streep in *The French Lieutenant's Woman*. "Granny's Teeth", its stone steps, are described by Jane Austen in *Persuasion*, and it was here that Louisa Musgrove tumbled. The story goes that when the poet Tennyson was shown the exact spot where the Duke landed, he said: "Don't talk to me of Monmouth, show me the exact spot where Louisa Musgrove fell!" Austen's house, **Bay Cottage**, is near the harbour end of the Parade, and she wrote much of her book here. Charles II's illegitimate son, Monmouth, stayed at the George, in the town, and his blue ensign flew in the market place.

The road that hugs the sea to the east has a precarious footing above the landslips, descending to Charmouth and Jane

Lyme Regis, a fishing village that found early fame.

228

Austen's "happiest spot for watching the flow of the tide". Hereabouts the cliffs reveal the existence of earlier visitors, like the elephant and rhinoceros, not in zoos, but in fossils. Ichthyosaurus turned up here in 1811. **Bridport** ("Port Bredy" to Hardy) is 2 miles (3 km) from the sea, yet there is no denying its marine character. Rope and cordage, nets and tackle, this was the stuff of Bridport's prosperity. Long, narrow gardens behind the handsome, red-brick houses were once ropewalks, and flax for ropemaking was the local crop. To be "stabbed with a Bridport dagger" was to be hanged.

West Bay is Bridport's improbable harbour. A narrow channel dug in the shingle bank and flanked by two high piers only feet apart offers a needle-threading operation for the small craft that lie uneasily in the little basin. In the old days coasters had to be hauled in with Bridport ropes. Visit on a Saturday and enjoy the outdoor market.

Shingle finger: The next town east, nearby **Burton Bradstock**, is warmly summed up in thatch and smoky stone, flowers everywhere and a stream that trickles to the sea below Burton Cliff. It turned the wheel of the last flax mills which ceased operation in 1930.

The dreaded Chesil Bank begins here, curving away eastwards to where it becomes the slender link that makes the **Isle of Portland** only a courtesy title. It is in fact, only a peninsula. The pebbles of the steeply shelving bank increase the size towards Portland, and at night, local fisherman docking at any point on the 16-mile (25-km) ridge can tell exactly where they are from the size of the pebbles. The bank has no mercy. To drive a boat in here spells almost certain disaster. **St Catherine's Chapel**, on a green hill above the bank at Abbotsbury, leads a double life. A place of prayer for 500 years, it is also maintained as a mark for seamen. On the land side it overlooks the most fascinating miscellany of monastic ruin, a swannery and sub-tropical gardens. During the Civil War the Benedictine abbey was used to store gunpowder, and the explosion

St Catherine's Chapel, a landmark for mariners.

which reduced most of its buildings to ruins provided the whole neighbourhood with material for new houses. The vicarage, farm and countless cottages in the village have the tell-tale white stones in their walls. The 15th-century abbey barn is impressive for its sheer size. Bigger and more splendid than many a parish church, it was built as a wheat store. Further along the same road, by the salt water of Fleet, is the swan sanctuary founded in the 14th century, and in the sheltered lee of Chesil Beach, are the gardens.

George III did **Weymouth** a good turn when he went there in 1789 for his convalescence after a serious illness. The grateful citizens responded by erecting the eye-stopping, highly coloured statue that ends, on a frivolous note, the half-mile esplanade. The king bathed from his "machine" to the music of his own anthem. Fanny Burney records the occasion in the diary she kept while Second Mistress of the Robes to Queen Charlotte. George can be seen in chalk outline on a neighbouring hillside astride a horse. There is much of the character of the 18th-century watering place about Weymouth today. Stuccoed terraces still front the esplanade, the sands are golden and the sea is blue. There are museums of sea life, diving and shipwrecks. From Weymouth's jetty, ferries maintain a regular service to the Channel Isles.

Hardy's heartlands: To the south of Weymouth a narrow strip of land carries the road to the "island" of **Portland**. Thomas Hardy observed that the people who lived on what he called "the Gibraltar of Wessex" had manners and customs of their own. The sheer structure of Portland makes it a place apart. Everything is stone: buildings, walls, quarries – heaps of it everywhere. This is the stuff of which most of London's best loved buildings are made: Portland Stone. The lighthouse on the island's south tip overlooks the broken water of the notorious Portland Race, which yachtsmen avoid even in good weather.

The green of the high hills inland of Weymouth comes as a welcome relief. **Dorchester**, 8 miles (13 km) north, is

Punch and Judy show on Weymouth beach.

best approached from the great hill of **Maiden Castle**, *Mai Dun* (great hill) just before the town on the left. Probably the largest earthwork in the world, the ramparts and ditches of this prehistoric hill fort extend for 900 by 400 yards (820 by 360 metres). The entrance is concealed in a clever maze. These "walls", in places 60 ft (18 metres) high, were created with the most primitive hand tools. Excavations have shown that the hill was occupied in 2000 BC.

Dorchester, Dorset's county town, is well aware of its past, and the pace of life here, beyond the fast motorways, is noticeably slower. Thomas Hardy, Judge Jeffries and the Tolpuddle Martyrs all try to catch the visitor's eye. Hardy's statue commands his "Casterbridge" from the top of the High Street. The judge of the 1685 Bloody Assize which dealt so harshly with the followers of Monmouth's rebellion invites visitors to drink tea where he lodged, and the men of Dorset, sentenced to transportation here in 1834 for asking for a wage increase, left a courtroom in the **Shire Hall** remarkably unchanged since. Hardy's is perhaps the most potent influence. He was apprenticed to an architect at 39 South Street, and after he left the practice in 1885, he used his knowledge to design his own house, **Max Gate**, on the Wareham Road, where he died in 1928. There is a memorial collection devoted to Hardy in the **Dorset County Museum** which is a cast-iron building of 1880, all columns and arches, delightfully decorated in bright primary colours. Stunning finds from Maiden Castle are here, too.

Dorchester has yet another literary connection, the poet William Barnes (1800–86), who is also honoured with a statue. Barnes's Dorset lingers in his dialect verse: "Where elems lofty heads do show Their sheades vor hay-makers below." Thomas Hardy was actually born in the cottage his great-grandfather built at **Higher Bockhampton**, just north of Dorchester in 1840. *Far From the Madding Crowd* and *Under the Greenwood Tree* were written here.

The village of **Milton Abbas** off the

Thomas Hardy's study in the museum, Dorchester.

A354, 12 miles (20 km) to the northeast, annoyed Viscount Milton. It interfered with the view from his rebuilt mansion, **Milton Abbey**, so he moved the village as well, half a mile away, sticking to the rustic tradition of cob and thatch. Nobody has any idea how much the re-housed villagers appreciated their new homes, but it is known that theirs were the first semi-detached dwellings, and they look surprisingly modern for 1752.

The 30-mile (48-km) coast from Weymouth east to Swanage, below Poole Harbour, is strictly for walking, army operations permitting, but approachable by car at Lulworth, Kimmeridge and Worth Matravers. A geologist's paradise, it is full of surprises – like the tiny circular bay between steep cliffs at **Lulworth Cove**, and the neighbouring **Stair Hole**, the oozing black layers of shale at **Kimmeridge** (long a source of oil) and the great cliff at **Worbarrow**.

Towards the east, the chalk hills around the **Isle of Purbeck** break at **Corfe Castle**, a too-picturesque ruin haunted by treachery, cruelty and murder. Here King Edward was murdered by his stepmother in AD 978, French prisoners were starved to death in the dungeons by King John, and the castle was traitorously handed over to the Roundheads in 1646 who pulled a large part of it down.

Swanage ("Knollsea" to Thomas Hardy) "was a seaside village, lying snugly within two headlands as between a finger and a thumb." To this we can add the attraction of the world, a stone globe, 10 ft (3 metres) in diameter, weighing 40 tons, and flanked by panels lettered with sobering information on the nature of the universe. **Old Swanage**, sitting on the hilltop, traps between its stone houses a millpond.

Around Poole Harbour's creeks, mud flats and islands is **Poole** itself, most beautiful on the quay and overlooking ships and shipyards, yachts and chandler's stores. Curving steps meet under the portico of the **Custom House** with its coat of arms representing an authority the Dorset smuggler never acknowledged. The town is also famous for its

The cliffs at Durdle Door near Lulworth.

pottery. Here's a tongue-twister: "If Poole was a fish-pool, and the men of Poole fish, There'd be a pool for the devil, and fish for his dish."

Hampshire hunts: Beyond Poole are the hotels and elegant terraces of **Bournemouth**, the sedate and salubrious resort built at the end of the 19th century. To the northwest lies **Wimborne** where the church has a fine 13th-century clock. It has no hands, but rather the planets revolve with winged angels in attendance. To the east is **Christchurch** on the mouth of the Avon, which goes back more than 100 years. There is a turret at the **Priory** with a deliciously interlaced pattern of Norman arches that strongly recalls Pisa's leaning tower.

These rivers and harbours are all popular yachting country. **Lymington** is the next safe port of call and on the River Beaulieu (pronounced *Bew-lee*) 6 miles (10 km) beyond, **Buckler's Hard** was famous for shipbuilding from the mid-18th century. Many of Nelson's warships took to the water here, launched between the two rows of shipwrights'

Corfe Castle, a ruin with a murderous history.

cottages. At the end of the Napoleonic wars it all came to an abrupt end, but the **Maritime Museum** captures the flavour of the good old days. Beaulieu's church is unique; the monks' dining room was transformed into a pulpit. Lord Montagu runs Britain's best-known Motor Museum here, and the local wine should be sampled.

To describe the wild, dense 100 sq. mile (260 sq. km) woodland of the **New Forest**, which lies behind this coast, as "new" would seem to support the traditional belief that William the Conqueror had a hand in its creation. But this was always forest. What William did was to enforce measures to protect his deer. There is no evidence to suggest he destroyed villages and churches to achieve his objective, although there are few of either in the area.

The best-known history-book story concerns William II, called "Rufus" for his red hair, who was killed by an arrow while hunting. Sir Walter Tyrell, also in the party, had quarrelled with William the night before, but maintained the

shooting was an accident. His flight to France immediately afterwards confirmed his guilt to many, though he seems to have had a legitimate reason for leaving. An iron monument, called the **Rufus Stone**, marks the spot in the forest where murder, or accident, struck in the summer of 1100. When driving through, remember the wild ponies have priority. Alice Lydell, Lewis Carroll's real Alice, is buried at **Lyndhurst**, the forest's capital, 8 miles (13 km) north of Lymington.

Miniature England: From Lymington a regular ferry crosses to the **Isle of Wight** in 30 minutes. The 147 sq. mile (380 sq. km) island is shaped like a kite, with the capital, **Newport**, just about where you might attach a string. Close by is **Carisbrooke Castle**, built by Elizabeth I as a defence against the Spanish Armada and remembered chiefly as the prison of Charles I. He was taken back to trial and execution from here, having made the mistake of thinking he would get protection from the local governor. No such luck – the governor's father-in-

law was one of Cromwell's close allies. Tragically, Charles's daughter, 15-year-old Princess Elizabeth, died here in captivity and is commemorated by a monument in Newport church. **Cowes**, at the mouth of the Medina River, lives once a year (every August) for Cowes Week – the yachtsman's Ascot.

Osborne House is highest Victorian, Queen Victoria's favourite residence, and left very much as it was in her lifetime. The **Durbar Room** was designed by Rudyard Kipling's father. The chalk cliffs of the island shatter spectacularly in the Needles at the eastern end. Tucked behind them is **Alum Bay**, where sands come in all the colours of the rainbow, and are carried away in bottles as souvenirs. Tennyson took walks on the chalk downs above Freshwater, where he lived for 30 years, and declared the air "worth 6d a pint". That was Champagne money. Keats took inspiration from the woods at **Shanklin**, and countless holidaymakers take to Sandown's pier. Pretty bays, thatched villages, roses and honeysuckle – England in miniature.

The best way back from Cowes is up the long arm of Southampton Water to **Southampton**. The armies that won the battles of Crécy and Agincourt embarked from here, the tiny *Mayflower* sailed for America, and many great ocean liners have followed since. The image was blemished by the bombing of World War II, but the phoenix city rose again, and there is vivid history all around in the surviving Norman walls, gates and houses.

Ferries also cross the Solent from the Isle of Wight to "Pompey", the major naval base of **Portsmouth**. This, too, was heavily bombed in the war, but the naval tradition could never be destroyed. The Royal Navy's museum is here, at the Naval Base, but most visitors head first to Admiral Lord Nelson's flagship *Victory* on which he died at the Battle of Trafalgar in 1805, and to the skeleton of *Mary Rose*, Henry VIII's "favourite warship", dredged up in 1982. Charles Dickens was born here in Commercial Road in 1812, but of Thomas Hardy there is no longer any sign.

Left, The Needles Lighthouse off the Isle of Wight. **Right**, the River Fleet, Hampshire.

THE WEST COUNTRY

The mystique of the West Country transcends its reputation as Britain's most popular holiday region. Beneath the Bristol Channel and Wales and on the edge of the moderating Atlantic, the peninsula is made up of Somerset, Devon and Cornwall, rural counties tucked away with hidden fishing hamlets and Britain's warmest winter weather.

The West Country is also steeped in legend. This is the land of King Arthur, Camelot and the Holy Grail; the land of Jack the Giant Killer and the myth of an ancient Druid who gave weary travellers sips of water from a golden cup. History here takes on a romantic, elusive quality, with facts obscured by time and fictions embellished with tales of piracy, smuggling and shipwrecks. The West Country folk have always considered themselves special, celebrating their Celtic origins and taking pride in their self-reliance. There's a certain island

mentality here – in fact Cornwall itself is almost an island. The River Tamar flows along all but 5 miles of the Devon border. Old traditions flourish, like the Helston Furry Dance in early May when people fill the town with flowers and dance in the streets.

Historically, the West Country has been cut off from the mainstream of British culture both by geography and choice. Unlike the rest of England, the peninsula was settled by hard-working Celts from Brittany and Ireland who scraped a living off the essentials of the land. They dug tin and copper, grazed their sheep and cattle on windswept moors, and braved treacherous currents to take fish from the sea. Like their fabulous landscape, the people of Cornwall, Devon and Somerset are a blend of rugged power and muted tranquillity – and this sets them apart from many other peoples of Britain.

The tip of the peninsula, **Land's End**, is 290 miles (465 km) from London. The main artery into the region is the M5 which comes down from Birmingham, meeting the M4 from London at Bristol, and continuing down to Exeter. On a good day the 175-mile (282-km) drive from London to Somerset will take three hours. Tourist routes are well signposted and walkers can make the most of the 500-mile (800-km) footpath which encircles the region, from Minehead in north Devon to Poole in Dorset. The region is served from Paddington station in London.

Points of departure: A jumping-off point into the region could be the old Atlantic port of **Bristol**, much of it now in the hands of the heritage industry. John Cabot set off for Newfoundland from here in 1497. Greatly rebuilt after World War II, the city manages to keep some interest around its port, such as the 17th-century Llandoger Trow pub in King Street which Robert Louis Stevenson supposedly used as a model for the inn favoured by Long John Silver in *Treasure Island*. Opposite is the Bristol Old Vic's **Theatre Royal** (1766), while the **Arnolfini Gallery** has also been making its name as an arts venue in this lively university city. Britain's most

Left, an abandoned shaft, North Penwith tin mine. Below, the Wills Tower, Bristol University.

famous engineer is celebrated here: Isambard Kingdom Brunel (1806–59) designed the world's first ocean-going propeller ship, **SS Great Britain**, and she can be seen in her original dock. Brunel was also responsible for the superb **Clifton Suspension Bridge** which majestically spans the Avon gorge.

Another jumping-off point for the West Country is 10 miles (16 km) southeast, at the more leisurely and salubrious **Bath**, Britain's most celebrated spa town. It owes its good looks to Bath stone and the genius of two men, the elder and younger John Wood, who in the 18th century gave its streets, squares and crescents a harmony that recent development has done its best to disturb. The limestone they used is well suited to their neo-Grecian style.

Prince Bladud, father of King Lear, started it all back in the mists of time. The mud bath cured his pigs, and him, of scrofula. The Romans came, enjoyed the waters and went. King Offa founded the abbey some 200 years before King Edgar was crowned King of All England there in 973. But the baths were forgotten until the 18th century when the business of bathing became fashionable. The season was presided over by the dandy Beau Nash, who regulated the bathing, gambling and sedan-chair carrying and hosted lavish balls.

The town maintains a good cultural tradition: the 18th-century Theatre Royal has recently been restored and there is a prestigious arts festival in May. Among the many things that must be seen, viewed preferably from the **Parade Gardens**, is **Robert Adams' Pulteney Bridge** which has houses on it like old London Bridge. John Wood junior designed the **Royal Crescent** from where the playwright Sheridan eloped with Elizabeth Linley.

The Circus, at the town's centre, **Assembly Rooms**, **Queen Square** and **Cross Bath** must also be seen. But the steamy core of it all are the **Roman Baths**, at basement level to the modern city, and the **Pump Room** where the hot springs erupt and where the water, good for rheumatism, can be drunk.

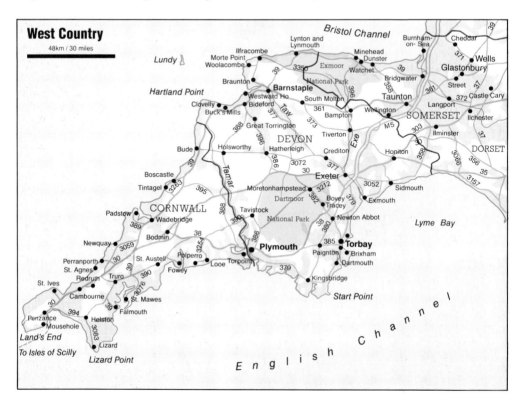

Americans can feel at home at **Claverton Manor**, high above the Avon valley, 4 miles (6 km) south of Bath. This houses the **American Museum in Britain**, with folk art and period furnished rooms.

The Mendip Hills, just east of the coast and south of Bristol, mark an abrupt end to the flat, cultured landscape of the Avon Valley and the start of the wild, robust expanses of the West Country. Across the crest of the hills runs the **West Mendip Way**, a popular hiking trail that twists from Wells, 20 miles (32 km) southwest to Bath, to the Bristol Channel and offers superb views of the countryside on all sides.

Much of the natural scenery here is simply breathtaking; **Cheddar Gorge** 12 miles (20 km) northwest of Wells, is carved by a river that now runs underground. The sheer limestone cliffs, 450 ft (135 metres) above the Cheddar village below, cut through the Mendips for more than a mile.

In the village itself you can see the entrances to vast underground caverns.

South of Cheddar along the A371 (towards Wells) is the **Ebbor Gorge**. Formed 270 million years ago by enormous pressure from inside the earth's crust, this is the most beautiful and most unspoiled gorge of the Mendips. Here you'll find a lush and glorious mix of elms, oaks and ash trees, mosses, fungi and ferns, and even enchanter's nightshade. Stone Age caves, dating from 3000 BC, are here too, and with them the remains of another time: pots, axes and reindeer.

On the Holy Grail trail: The pride and joy of **Wells**, at the southern tip of the Mendip Hills is the **Cathedral**, a massive Gothic shrine started in about 1185 and finished four centuries later. Unlike other English cathedrals, the two main towers were built outside the church proper, thus extending the western facade into a massive gallery for 400 individual statues. More than 25 percent of the sculpture has been destroyed (most by rampaging Puritans in the 17th century) but the remaining group is a comprehensive array of bishops and

Wells's pride and joy is its magnificent cathedral.

kings, saints and prophets, angels and apostles, all gazing down upon the green. The interior is no less spectacular, especially the "hour-glass" arches at the junction of the nave and transept. These were constructed in the 14th century after the cathedral threatened to collapse under the weight of a new central tower. Above the north transept is a marvellous 14th-century astronomic clock. Every quarter hour, four knights on horseback do battle outside the clock; and one of them is always unseated before the group returns to its stable behind the face.

Outside the cathedral, the **Vicar's Close** beckons to a row of 14th-century buildings (the only complete medieval street remaining in Britain). The exteriors have changed little from their original design. The communal dining hall above the Chain Gate has much of its original furniture. The 15th-century **St Cuthbert's Church** has an imposing tower. But the **Bishop's Palace**, south of the cathedral, is outstanding. One of the oldest inhabited houses in England,

the Palace is home to the Bishop of Bath and Wells. The high wall surrounding it dates from the beginning of the 13th century. Swans glide across the broad moat and, since Victorian times, they have been trained to ring a bell for their food. By the Cathedral Green the **Wells Museum** houses plaster casts of the statues on the cathedral.

It's a pity that the abbey at **Glastonbury**, 6 miles (10 km) southwest, has not been preserved in the same way, for it was once the richest and most beautiful in England. Little remains of the great complex – a few ruined pillars and walls. But these remain an impressive monument to the power of the Roman Catholic church in England before Henry VIII's dissolution of the monasteries.

Like much of West Country history, the origins of Glastonbury Abbey are shrouded in myth and legend. One story claims that St Patrick founded the original abbey and that St George killed the famous dragon nearby. The most popular legend says that Joseph of Arimathea, the man who gave his tomb to Christ,

Glastonbury Abbey where King Arthur and Guinevere are said to be buried.

sailed from the Holy Land to Britain to convert the heathens in AD 60. Joseph was leaning on his staff on Wearyall Hill, when it magically rooted and flowered. To Joseph, this was an omen that he should settle and found the abbey. Joseph brought with him the chalice from the Last Supper, the so-called Holy Grail. In the 6th century King Arthur came to Glastonbury in search of the Holy Grail, and tradition says Arthur and Guinevere were buried under the abbey floor.

A short walk to the steep, conical hill called **Glastonbury Tor**, which rises up from the flat Somerset plain, is a worthwhile excursion. The view from the top (all that remains from the 15th-century St Michael's Church) is terrific. At the foot of the tor lies the **Chalice Wall**, where, according to legend, Joseph buried the Holy Grail.

The boundary between Somerset and Devon falls within the confines of **Exmoor National Park**, a 265 sq. miles (690 sq. km) wilderness filled with the sights and sounds of Richard Doddridge Blackmore's novel, *Lorna Doone*, the story of a 17th-century family of outlaws. Exmoor ponies, direct descendants of the prehistoric horse, are the most ubiquitous inhabitants, but the moor is also populated by red deer, sheep and Devon Red cattle. The landscape of the park transforms itself from windswept ridges covered with bracken and heather, to forested ravines carved out by white-water streams.

The undulating Somerset and Devon Coast Path, stretching more than 30 miles (48 km) along the shore, north of the A39, is the most fascinating of Exmoor's many hiking trails. Hugging tightly to cliffs and coves, it offers splendid views of the Bristol Channel and the far-off Atlantic.

Snatches of sandy beaches, like **Morte Pointe** northwest of **Barnstaple** (as the name implies, not for swimming) and **Porlock Bay**, 6 miles (10 km) west of Minehead, are good for birdwatching. Just east of Minehead the village of **Dunster** is a pleasant stopping-place. Dunster has been a fortress site since

Dunster, a village owned by one family for 600 years.

Saxon times, but the present castle dates from the 13th century. Most of the original structure was destroyed after Charles I's execution in 1649 – it smacked too much of royalism. The graceful turrets and towers seen today are the work of Anthony Salvin, a 19th-century architect. The village itself is considered a perfect replica of feudal times, largely because one family, the Luttrells, owned it for 600 years until 1950. The parish church of warm pink sandstone is one of the West Country's finest.

King Arthur's country: Where Devon turns to Cornwall, a chain of fishing villages and hidden beauties lie beside the A39 running down to Tintagel. **Westward Ho!**, by Bideford, is a popular seaside resort named after the novel by Charles Kingsley (1819–75). It boasts 3 miles (5 km) of sandy beach. **Buck's Mills** is an unspoiled village of thatched cottages nestling at the bottom of a wooded valley. **Clovelly** is probably the most well known of these hamlets in Bideford Bay. Cars are banned from the village and donkeys carry visitors' luggage. The steep cobbled street descends 400 ft (120 metres) to the sea in a series of steps. A romantic 2-mile (3-km) walk west from the harbour leads to a magnificent range of cliffs.

Farther south and into Cornwall, the rolling waves at **Bude** have long attracted surfers. For those who prefer calmer swimming, **Summerleaze Beach** is a good spot, a sheltered sandy expanse north of the River Neet.

The legend of King Arthur comes alive at **Tintagel**, a wild and romantic castle on the north Cornwall coast about 18 miles (29 km) south of Bude. Tradition claims that Arthur was born or washed ashore at Tintagel, where he built a sturdy castle for Guinevere and the Knights of the Round Table. Merlin the Magician is said to have lived in a cave below the castle. There is no archaeological evidence to support the Arthurian claim. In fact, all that remains at Tintagel are the ruins of a 6th-century Celtic monastery and a 12th-century bastion, most of it washed away by the sea. In the town itself, the old slate-built

Tintagel Post Office, a 14th-century manor house.

post office is interesting. This 14th-century manor house is now owned by the National Trust.

Some 20 miles (32 km) south on the A39 and then west along the A389, is **Padstow**, the only safe harbour in north Cornwall and an important port for more than 1,000 years. The town is named after St Petroc, the Celtic missionary who landed here in the 6th century as the first of numerous Irish and Welsh priests who came to covert the heathen Cornish. The Vikings sacked Padstow in AD 981, but it later grew into a fishing centre and mineral port. The primary industry these days is tourism, especially during the summer, when Padstow overflows with families and young couples attracted by Cornwall's abundant sunshine.

Clustered around the picturesque harbour are the historic **Abbey House**, **St Petroc Church**, the **Harbour Master's Office** and **Raleigh Cottage**, where Sir Walter collected port dues as the Royal Warden of Cornwall. Every May Day the town fills up when a bizarre Hobby Horse festival creates a carnival atmosphere.

Continuing south along the coast, **Newquay** is Cornwall's Malibu – the beach where Britain's surfers cruise the waves. Famous in the 18th and 19th centuries as a pilchard port, Newquay exported dried fish to Spain and Italy. A sharp-eyed look-out called the "huar" used to sit in a hut atop a nearby cliff and scan the Bristol Channel for a school of pilchard. The huar would blow a signal on his might horn when the fish entered Newquay Bay, and the fishermen would scurry out on the attack. You can visit the **Huar's Hut**, but little remains of bygone fishing days. Newquay also has Cornwall's only zoo, in **Trenance Park.**

Worthwhile excursions south of Newquay include the ancient Norman church at **Crantock**, a village once notorious for its involvement in contraband. Crantock Beach is lovely, too. Still further south is **Cubert**, which features a church tower shaped curiously like a bishop's mitre. The interior of the church preserves fine Norman

and 14th-century carvings and a font.

The corridor between the neighbouring towns of Redruth and Camborne, 18 miles (29 km) southwest and inland, was the fulcrum of Cornish tin mining for more than 200 years. Little active mining remains, but you can get some idea of what tin meant to the region's economy by visiting the **Camborne Museum**. It also has exhibits relating to Richard Trevithick, the "Father of the Locomotive", who manufactured the first high-pressure steam engine in 1797. Four years later he attached his engine to a four-wheeled carriage and drove 10 friends up Beacon Hill in Cambourne; they were the first people ever transported by steam power.

Truro, 10 miles (16 km) east, is the cathedral city of Cornwall and the county's unofficial capital. In the 18th century it was both a centre for tin smelting and a society haunt that rivalled Bath. **Lenion Street**, laid out around 1795, features fine Georgian architecture and is complemented by **Walsingham Place**, an early 19th-century crescent off Victoria Place. One of Cornwall's oldest and most famous potteries, **Lakes**, still operates in Chapel Street, and is open to visitors. Edward VII, then Prince of Wales, laid the cathedral's foundation stone in 1880; it stands on the site of the 16th-century **Church of St Mary**.

Out to the coast again on the A390, **St Agnes Beacon**, outside the village of St Agnes, offers a view of 32 church towers and 23 miles (40 km) of coast from 628 ft (190 metres) above. Now owned by the National Trust, much of the surrounding area was once mining land. Today the old buildings and scars of industry give the area a melancholy beauty. One of the last ports of call on this north coast is **St Ives**, a classic Cornish fishing village populated mainly by artists who have been coming here since the end of the 19th century. Among them was the sculptor Barbara Hepworth who lived and worked here from 1949 to 1975. Her home and sub-tropical gardens are now a museum.

Britain's toe: **Penwith** is the name given to the barren and windswept knob that

St Agnes Beach, north Cornwall.

marks the end of Cornwall. This is a land of bleak hills and wide open spaces, surrounded by deep blue sea and thick Atlantic fog. The Cornwall Coastal Path traces the entire shore of Penwith, passing submerged reefs and wave-eroded cliffs, sheltered coves and weird-shaped rocks with strange Celtic names like The Carracks, Pendeen Watch and Gwennap Head. **Land's End**, the most westerly point on mainland Britain, is an eerie but beautiful place almost constantly swept by North Atlantic storms and swirling underwater currents.

At **Sennen Cove** there's a tiny pub and a Royal Naval Lifeguard Station constantly on alert for a shipwreck or yachting disaster. Tin mines at **Geevor** have tunnels that extend 250 fathoms below the sea floor. There's a mining museum with tours of the treatment plant, magnetic separators and tunnels.

The fog-shrouded, ship-eating **Isles of Scilly** (pronounced *silly*) lie 28 miles (45 km) west of Land's End. Phoenician traders landed upon the islands before the birth of Christ in search of Cornish tin, copper and other precious metals. The isles became the haunt of pirates, smugglers and shipwreck scavengers during the Middle Ages, and at one point the Prince of Wales (the future King Charles II) took refuge in Scilly after a temporary royalist defeat. Five of the islands are now inhabited and all but one, **Tresco**, is part of the Duchy of Cornwall, under the control of the present Prince of Wales. Frequent ferry and helicopter services link the isles with Penzance. Among the worthy sights are the **Abbey Gardens** and the **Valhalla Maritime Museum** on Tresco, and the **Scilly Museum** and summer racing off St Mary's of six-oar gigs.

Two picturesque villages sit on the south shore of Penwith. **Mousehole** (pronounced *maus-ill*) is as tiny as the name suggests, a minuscule cluster of granite cottages and half-timbered pubs. The village is named after an old smugglers' cave called the Mouse Hole. Take a pint at the **Ship**, a friendly pub which serves good crab sandwiches, or take a walk to majestic **Merlin** and **Battery Rocks**.

Pleasure boats on St Ives beach.

Nearby lies **Newlyn**, one of the few true fishing villages left in Cornwall. There are daily catches of lobster, mackerel, whitefish and crab, much of which is canned locally or shipped off to market in London.

Pleasures of Penzance: Penzance has long been the premier town of western Cornwall thanks to its commanding site of **Mount's Bay**. The town has served a number of important functions over the centuries: tin shipping port for the Roman Empire and medieval Europe, passenger terminal for emigrants bound for the New World, fresh-flower and fish-despatch point for London and the Midlands and, most recently, a highly popular holiday and tourist town.

Within the town lies the **Barbican**, an 18th-century fish market transformed into a lively arts and crafts centre. The **Western Promenade** is lined with 18th and 19th-century town houses, many in the regal Regency style. But the intriguing heart of Penzance lies at the junction of Chapel Street and Market Jew, an ancient cobblestoned quarter that re-tains much of the flavour of the seafaring past. There are a number of historic buildings, such as the 18th-century **Union Hotel** (from which the first news of Nelson's victory and death at Trafalgar was announced), the **Victorian Market House** and the **Penlee House Museum**. The **Movab Gardens** store a variety of exotic plants. Even better for the botanically inclined is the National Trust's **Trengwainton Garden** 2 miles (3 km) inland. It was here that magnolias first bloomed in Britain.

St Michael's Mount, a huge medieval castle and abbey, dominates a hunk of granite in Mount's bay. At low tide you can reach the island along a sandy causeway, but at other times you must take the short ferry ride from the mainland. The origins of the Mount are obscure. It may have been the ancient Isle of Ictis, where Phoenician traders came in the 4th century BC. According to local legend, the abbey was founded in the 5th century AD after a fisherman saw St Michael standing on the granite outcrop. A legend still more outlandish

A ferry bound for St Michael's Mount.

says that the castle was built by a black-bearded giant called Cormoran who stole sheep and cattle from the mainland until he was killed by a local farm boy called Jack. Historians place the founding of the monastery in the 8th century, about the same time as Celtic monks founded a similar structure at Mont St Michel in Brittany.

To the east, beyond the treacherous Lizard Point and the attractive Helford river, lies **Falmouth**, a name steeped in the tradition and history of the seas. As a famous port and fishing centre for more than 300 years, it is one of the most interesting towns in Cornwall. Falmouth was a tiny hamlet until 1699 when it became the most westerly Mail Packet station in England. Regular ships from America, the West Indies and the Mediterranean called at Falmouth to transfer their mail into quick stagecoaches bound for London. **Pendennis Castle** guarded Falmouth for three centuries against Spanish and French raids and also against Cromwell's troops during a 23-week siege in the Civil War. **King's Pipe** is a

brick chimney once used to burn contraband tobacco. Nearby is the 17th-century **Pandora Inn**, a white-washed and thatch-roofed tavern that makes a great spot for lunch. There are fine Georgian houses along Boscamen and Lemon Streets, plus the 18th-century Cornwall County Library.

Fowey (pronounced *foy*), on the A3082 off the A390, 25 miles (40 km) further up the coast, is covered in a mantle of fine white dust, testament to its position as Cornwall's greatest china-clay shipping port. With the decline of Cornwall's other important minerals, china clay has become its primary economic product and export item, supplying more than 80 percent of the world's raw material for porcelain. The harbour is dominated by the great bulk carriers and machinery that move clay out of the port. But Fowey is also a snug harbour for numerous pleasure craft and fishing boats. The ancient town centre remains intact (visit the 18th-century Town Hall and 14th-century Toll Bar House) and is still recognisably a Cornish "village."

Drake territory: Plymouth, on the Devon-Cornwall border, is a relic of the Age of Exploration, the city of Drake, Raleigh and the Pilgrim Fathers, a town where young Englishmen have long gone in search of seafaring adventure. But today's Plymouth is more than a history book, for it's still a thriving port, industrial centre, market town and cultural mecca, the metropolis of the West Country and the largest city west of Bristol. Plymouth is at its best on Sunday morning, when the office workers still lie snug in their beds, the shops are closed and the streets are all but empty. Only then does the town recover its purely nautical self with the sun rising over Plymouth Sound and the waves splashing in well-timed rhythm against the foreshore rocks. You can feel the fresh salt air fill your lungs, and you can hear gulls squawking over a morsel of fish. Stand atop that famous green lump called the **Hoe**, 120 ft (37 metres) above the sea, and gaze into the wide Sound, dreaming of all the seafaring history that has passed this way.

Drake has long been Plymouth's favourite son. He sailed from the port in 1577 on his renowned global circumnavigation, and upon his return the citizens of Plymouth elected him as mayor. Drake established himself as a naval commander against the mighty Spanish Armada in 1588. As he was bowling upon the Hoe, he got word of the approach of the enemy fleet. Legend says that he insisted on finishing the game before doing battle, but history records that in fact he had to wait for the outgoing tides.

The Pilgrims sailed from Plymouth's West Pier in 1620 aboard the fragile *Mayflower* to the New World. (They originally launched from Southampton, but bad weather damaged their ship and they called at Plymouth for repairs). While at Plymouth, the Pilgrims took shelter in the wine cellers of the firm of James Hawker, which still carries on business today.

The Hoe still dominates Plymouth as it did in Drake's day. **Smeaton's Tower** is a red-and-white striped lighthouse

Sir Francis Drake, Plymouth's most famous son.

248

that offers excellent views of the Sound. Nearby is the **Royal Citadel**, a chunky fortress built in the 17th century by Charles II to stall any Republican comeback. Down by the port is an Elizabethan quarter known as the **Barbican**, a mixture of cobblestoned streets, medieval houses and bustling piers where the **Armada Experience** recreates bygone swashbuckling days.

The 16th-century **Island House** is where the Pilgrims spent their last night in England, while nearby New Street boasts the authentic **Elizabethan House**. There's a fish market each morning, and plenty of cafés, shops, taverns and art studios to keep visitors occupied for the rest of the day.

A walk in the wilderness: Directly inland from Plymouth is **Dartmoor National Park**, an expansive 365 sq. miles (915 sq. km) of forest and moorland that protects the largest of the West Country's wilderness areas. Beneath all that heather and bracken is a solid core of stone, one of five granite masses that form the geological heart of the West Country. There are hundreds of miles of public footpaths and hiking trails across the moor, walked by an estimated 8 million people each year. The visitors tend to overwhelm Dartmoor's indigenous population, the 30,000 people who live in and around the park. But the villagers still have grazing rights to the open grasslands on the moor, and they can also collect peat, stone and thatching for their homes. The largest land owner is Prince Charles, who, as the Duke of Cornwall, controls more than 70,000 acres (28,000 hectares) of the park. Otherwise, Dartmoor remains much as it has been for 1,000 years: a harsh landscape of open moors, rocky outcrops, wooded vales and muddy bogs broken only occasionally by a village or farm. The famous Dartmoor ponies are related to Stone Age horses who have lived on this land for millions of years. The Galloway and Highland cattle and black-faced sheep are later imports.

Dartmouth, directly east of Plymouth, is yet another of the West Country's famous ports. It gained notoriety in

Ponies on Dartmoor's wild National Park.

the 12th century as the sailing point for both the Second and Third Crusades. It was back in the headlines more than 900 years later as one of the major Allied staging points for the invasion of Normandy. The town retains much of its seafaring heritage in the form of **Britannia College**, which has trained such officers as Prince Charles and the Duke of Edinburgh for the Royal Navy. (Even Chaucer's pilgrim Shipman was a Dartmouth man.) Dartmouth Harbour is lined with 16th-century merchant's houses and half-timbered taverns. **Pannier Market** still sells fresh fruit and vegetables on Friday mornings, but the rest of the week it becomes a cluster of art and craft stalls.

Just a stone's throw up the coast lies **Torbay**, a conurbation of Torquay, Paignton and Brixham which likes to bill itself as the English Riviera because of its mild climate, lengthy beaches and scattered palms. **Brixham**, reachable by ferry, is the only one that maintains something of its fishing village ambience. William of Orange landed here in 1688 to begin the Glorious Revolution, glorious because not a drop of blood was spilled in unseating James II from the throne and establishing the constitutional monarchy upon which British government is still based.

West of Torbay (and within walking distance) is **Cockington**, a pretty thatched-cottage village. Three miles (5 km) on is **Marldon**, with a lovely old church, and still one mile farther is **Compton Castle**. This manor house, still the seat of the Gilbert family, was originally built in 1320. Sir Humphrey Gilbert (1539–83) was the founder of Newfoundland, the first British colony in North America, and the half-brother of Sir Walter Raleigh.

Cathedral city: Exeter is many things to many people: a university town in the mould of Oxford and Cambridge, the cathedral city of Devon, and still the most important city in the West Country after Plymouth. The immense **cathedral** dominates the skyline and is the finest structure in all Devon, built from the 11th to 14th centuries in Norman Gothic style. The exterior displays a remarkable collection of stone statues, the largest surviving group of 14th-century sculpture in England. The lavish interior is dominated by a striking vaulted ceiling carved to resemble the radiating branches of a palm tree. Among the church's treasures are the 14th-century Bishop's Throne and the *Exeter Book of Old English Verse*, compiled between AD 950 and 1000.

Outside the cathedral, much of Exeter pales in comparison. But the **Maritime Museum** comprises more than 100 historic vessels displayed in two warehouses and along both banks of the River Exe, ranging from Arabian dhows and Polynesian dugouts to Chinese sampans and Peruvian reed rafts. A 17th-century building on the quay displays work by Devon's craftsmen, with regular demonstrations. Also interesting are the 11th to 16th-century rooms of **St Nicholas Priory**, **Rougemont Museum** and the castle ruins. Exeter is a market town in the middle of properous dairy country, and an ideal place to sample Devon's famous cream teas.

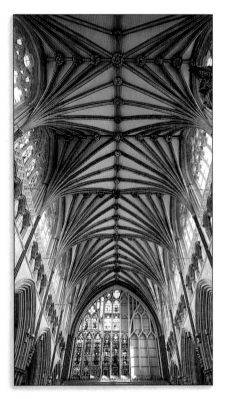

Left, the palm-tree vaulted ceiling of Exeter Cathedral. **Right**, serried ranks of slate-roofed houses.

Wales

Irish Sea

Carmel Head

Holyhead

Isle of
Anglesey

Amlwch

Llandudno   Colwyn
                 Bay   Prestatyn
Llangefni   Beaumaris   Rhyl
             Conwy   Holywell   Liverpool
Menai   Bangor   Abergele   St. Asaph
Bridge
        Bethesda   Denbigh   Mold   Chester
Caernarfon   Llanrwst
        Llanberis   Ruthin
Pen-y-groes   CLWYD
Nefyn   GWYNEDD Betws-y-coed

Lleyn Peninsula   Criccieth
                  Beddgelert Blaenau   Llangollen   Ruabon
        Porthmadog   Ffestiniog   Corwen   Withchurch
Pwllheli
                  Harlech Trawsfynydd   Bala
Abersoch   Snowdonia
                        National   Oswestry
Bardsey Island   Park
                  Barmouth Dolgellau   Llanfyllin
                                                     Shrewsbury
                          Dinas Mawddwy
                                       Vyrnwy
        Tywyn   Machynlleth   Lydham
        Aberdyfi   W A L E S
Cardigan   Caersws   Newtown
                Talybont
Bay   Ponterwyd Llanidloes
        Aberystwyth   44 Llangurig
                  Devil's   POWYS   Knighton   Ludlow
                  Bridge   Rhayader
Aberaeron   Elan   New Radnor Presteigne
                        Valley   Llandrindod   44
                  Tregaron   Wells   Kington
        Lampeter Teifi
Cardigan   Llanwrtyd
        Llandyssul   Wells   Hereford
Fishguard Newcastle
        Emlyn   Llandovery   Hay-on-Wye
St.   DYFED   Brecon
David's   Carmarthen   Brecon Beacons
Head   Treffgarne   Tywi   Llandeilo National Park   Crickhowell
Milford Haven Narberth St. Clears   Craig-y-   Brynmawr Abergavenny
        Laugharne   nos Tredegar
                        WEST   Abercraf Merthyr   Raglan
Pembroke Saundersfoot   GLAMORGAN Tydfil Ebbw Vale   Usk Tintern
        Tenby   Pontardulais Pontardawe Aberdare Rhymney Abertillery   Parva
                Llanelli Neath   Moutain Ash GWENT Cwmbran Chepstow
St. Govan's Llangennith Swansea   MID   Pontypridd
Head   Killay   Aberavon GLAMORGAN   Caerphilly   Newport
        Rhossili   The   Llantrisant   Blacktown
                  Mumbles   SOUTH   Cardiff
                        Porthcawl   GLAMORGAN Penarth
Wales

48km / 30 miles   Bristol Channel   Barry

THE WYE VALLEY
AND SOUTH WALES

The principality of Wales, the mountainous land in the lap of Great Britain which points to the Irish Sea, is little more than 135 miles (216 km) long and at one part less than 35 miles (56 km) wide. The border runs from the mouth of the Dee in Liverpool Bay in the north to the mouth of the Wye on the Severn estuary in the south. It roughly follows the lines of the dyke built to contain the Celts by Offa, Anglo-Saxon king of Mercia from 757 to 796 and the most powerful ruler in Britain until then.

This 168-mile (269-km) frontier earthwork provides walkers with an introduction to the country (a good place to start is Knighton, at about the halfway mark). Some 300 years after Offa, the Normans drove the Welsh further into the hills, establishing the Marches and the powerful Marcher Lordships along the border.

Traditionally, this is a melodic land of green hills and welcoming valleys, of Welshcakes, crumbling castles, poets and song. It has sweeping sandy beaches and dramatic coves, sheep for shawls, lamb for the pot and ponies for trekking over hills. It is less populous than England, though its accessibility from southern, central and northern parts of the country make it a popular summer holiday haunt. Britain's manufacturing heartlands of the west Midlands, less economically buoyant these days, are centred on the UK's second largest city, **Birmingham**, to the east.

From London the M4, skirting Bristol, crosses the Severn Bridge and plunges immediately into Wales, following the industrial south coast, past Newport, the capital at Cardiff, and Swansea towards the cliffs and beaches of Pembroke. Halfway up the M5 between Bristol and Birmingham, at junction 8, the M50 leads west towards the pretty town of Ross-on-Wye, where it meets the A40 from Gloucester, crosses the border at Monmouth and dives between the Black Mountains and Brecon Beacons before heading back down to the Pembroke coast. Mid Wales can be approached from here or from the M54 which leaves the M6 at junction 10ᴀ just north of Birmingham. The A5 takes the road on to Shrewsbury, crosses the border at Welshpool and makes its way down to Aberystwyth, the town of the University of Wales in the middle of Cardigan Bay.

The Wye Valley: Commanding the mouth of the Wye, where it empties into the River Severn near the suspension bridge, is the fortress town of **Chepstow**. The castle's Norman keep, set on a high rock, stands out against the limestone cliffs. The old town wall, which in some places is 7 ft (2 metres) thick, was originally designed as an extension of the castle.

Wordsworth did not exaggerate when he wrote his eulogy of **Tintern Abbey**, 6 miles (10 km) north of Chepstow on the A466. It is an extraordinarily lovely spot. Built by Cistercian monks in 1131, it is the most handsome and most complete of Britain's ruined monasteries. Outside it is The Anchor Inn which was

probably the abbey's watergate; an arch dating from the 13th century links it with the slipway.

Some 10 miles (16 km) further north on the A466 is **Monmouth**, a market town on the confluence of the Wye and Monnow rivers. At one time a Roman settlement, it became home to Breton lords. Henry V, who spent several years of his reign putting down the Welsh revolt of Owain Glyndwr, was born here in 1387. The 11th-century castle has magnificent decorative ceilings. **Raglan Castle** is 7 miles (11 km) southwest of Monmouth on the A40. During the Wars of the Roses it was used as a fortress and it later became the home of the Earls of Worcester. Now mostly a ruin, it retains an elegant hexagonal moated keep.

A few miles east of Monmouth is **Coleford** in the **Forest of Dean**. In the 17th-century Speech House, now a hotel, Verderers, keepers of the forest, conduct their business as they have always done. This former royal hunting ground of some 40 sq. miles (105 sq. km) is mostly of oak and beech and there are some good views from the trails. A **Museum of Forest Life** is sited on the northeast side of the forest at **Camp Mill** near **Cinderford**, where there are the last vestiges of a coal and iron industry.

Just to the north is **Symond's Yat**, a dramatic outcrop 400 ft (122 metres) over a great loop in the Wye valley. The river twists along to the east of the A40 for another 8 miles (13 km) until it reaches **Ross-on-Wye**, a town whose situation and quaintness ensures it is full of visitors in summer. A market town, it is centred on an attractive arcaded hall, although the whole place was townscaped by a local man, John Kyrle (1637–1724), whom the contemporary poet Alexander Pope immortalised as "The Man of Ross".

Black-and-white, half-timbered Tudor buildings are a speciality of these Welsh border towns. Above Ross are **Ledbury**, which has a renowned herring-bone patterned Market House, and **Hereford**, 10 miles (16 km) distant.

Left, Ross-on-Wye. **Below**, Raglan Castle cat.

The **cathedral** in the county town of Hereford was founded by King Offa, and its greatest treasure is the *Mappa Mundi*, one of the first maps of the world, dating from around 1300. The city is also centre of a cider making industry and the **Cider Museum** in Whitecross Road tells the story.

While in Hereford the chance should not be missed of visiting **Kilpeck**, 8 miles (13 km) southwest on the A465 Abergavenny road. This is the most wonderfully ornate Norman church in Britain, built around 1140. The River Wye heads west from Hereford, up towards the Cambrian mountains in the heart of Wales.

Just off the A438, 23 miles (38 km) west of Hereford, is **Hay-on-Wye**, known to all book collectors, for this is where they come to buy and browse among the second-hand emporiums. Richard Booth, who was responsible for setting up the world's largest collection of bookstores here, went on to declare Hay-on-Wye an independent country, with himself as monarch. Most

of the town is in Wales. William de Braose, a Marcher Lord, built a castle here to replace the one burned down by King John. Owain Glyndwr was the subsequent destroyer in the 15th century, though a gateway, the keep and part of the wall remain.

Beckoning hills: The next major town on the Wye is **Builth Wells**, 20 miles (32 km) west. This is pony trekking, walking and fishing country, among the rapids that crash down into the river. The Royal Welsh Show, the principal agricultural event, is held here in July. Seven miles (10 km) to the north is **Llandrindod Wells**, a spa town which in its Victorian heyday attracted some 80,000 visitors a year. Its wide streets have Georgian houses and a number of hotels. The land has risen to some 1,000 ft (305 metres) above sea level.

To the west, near now to the source of the Wye, lies the little tourist town of **Rhayader**, where many Welsh crafts are on sale. Beyond it is the **Elan Valley**, dubbed the Lake District of Wales. This is the heart of the Cambrian moun-

tains and the valley's wild and remote course has enchanted poets such as Shelley. The landscape was changed dramatically towards the end of the last century when the Corporation of Birmingham decided that the valley should be the centre of a reservoir system. The result was a scenic success and a complex of lakes now enhances the already beautiful scenery.

On the south side of Hay-on-Wye is the 2,220-ft (677-metre) **Hay Bluff** which heralds the **Black Mountains** which rise to 2,660 ft (810 metres) at **Waun Fach** 6 miles (10 km) beyond. To the south, the Black Mountains are cut off from the neighbouring Brecon Beacons by the **Usk Valley** which the A40 follows between Abergavenny and Brecon (15 miles/24 km southwest of Hay). **Crickhowell**, 6 miles west of Abergavenny, is a good base for the Black Mountains. It has some elegant Georgian houses and a 15th-century gatehouse, Prthmawr, which led to a manor house long vanished. Just over 2 miles (3 km) to the southwest is **Agen Allwedd Cave**, at 14 miles (22 km) one of the longest in Britain. **Dan-yr-Ogof**, a few miles southwest of Brecon, is a maze of limestone caverns, and nearby **Ogof Fynnon Ddu** has stalactites, stalagmites, grotesque rock forms and subterranean lakes.

The Brecon Beacons, which cover 529 sq. miles (1,370 sq. km) and stretch 20 miles (32 km) south to Merthyr Tydfil, have become a national park. These old red sandstone mountains are the highest in south Wales, rising to 2,906 ft (885 metres) at **Pen-y-fan** (meaning "the top of the place"), and they take their name from their use as locations for signal fires. The landscape bears the marks of long glacial history: sheer precipices hang like waves about to break over huge, semicircular valleys gouged out by the ice.

Brecon, though not actually in the mountains that bear its name, is an old market town of narrow streets at the confluence of the Usk and the Honddu. Its cathedral has only been such since 1923, though a church of some kind has occupied the site since the 12th century.

Much of the present building bears the stamp of 19th-century restoration. The **Brecon Beacons National Park Information Centre** is in the town. There is also a **Mountain Centre** just off the A470 at **Libanus** 4 miles (6 km) south of Brecon. They are both good sources of information about the area's many activities, including climbing, pony trekking and reservoir sailing.

King coal: Between the mountains and the industrial south coast run the valleys whose names – Ebbw Vale, Merthyr, Rhondda, Neath – were once synonymous with mining, making **Cardiff** the world's greatest coal port. But by the beginning of the 1990s only a handful of deep mines remained and other industries have had to take their place. Cardiff is the capital of Wales and its administrative centre, with a population of 280,000. **Cardiff Castle** brings together all the strands of the city's history. The outer walls contain Roman stonework and the Norman keep, built by Robert Fitzhamon at the end of the 11th century, still stands tall. At the

The elaborate interior of Cardiff Castle.

CROESO I CYMRU

"Welcome to Wales: *Croeso i Cymru*," the sign says in two languages, as has been the rule everywhere in the principality since 1973. It is the first visible evidence that the visitor is in a different country, a part of Britain where a culture has remained outside the dominant whole.

Wales, the smallest of the three constituent parts of Great Britain, is the only one with an active language of its own. Overall only around 20 percent of the 2.8 million who live there speak it, and it is patchy, from around 2 percent in Gwent, near Bristol in England, rising to 61 percent in the distant northwest. Famously, the poet Dylan Thomas did not speak the language (though his parents did). The actor Richard Burton, also from the valleys, spoke it. Tom Jones can sing a few songs in Welsh but isn't fluent.

The point is not perhaps how the language has declined, but how it has survived so long at all, because English had been the official language ever since the the Act of Union in 1536. From then on, Welsh was seen by London as a hinderance to administration and education, and it was not encouraged at all. It has had periods of popularity, encouraged by poets and politicians, by Methodist preachers and by the Romantic revival of the Eisteddfodau literary and music festivals. But since the end of World War II the language has declined some 50 percent.

This decline was helped in part by people moving away to find work, leaving their houses prey to the English who were on the lookout for a cheap second home, or even to new settlers seeking an alternative rural way of life. The second-home buyers were particularly resented locally, especially in parts of the north where, in the 1960s, there were an increasing number of arson attacks on their unoccupied cottages.

Growing resentment of English "colonialisation" produced Cymdeithas yr Iaith Gymraeg, the Welsh Language Society, whose militant members were prepared to be imprisoned – and frequently were – for bringing attention to their beliefs. They were not just a handful of troublemakers. In 1966, Gwynfor Evans became the first Plaid Cymru (Welsh Nationalist) member of parliament and finally, in 1973, Westminster passed the Welsh Language Act, giving the language equal status with English.

There is no doubt that this new open duality, combined with television and radio broadcasts in Welsh, is helping to keep the language from further decline. An increase in the number of bilingual primary schools means that the language might now even be on the increase. A Welsh television channel, SC4, has helped to spread the culture, providing an outlet for actors, writers and producers in Welsh. It may also turn out that increasing tourism proves to be an ally rather than an enemy. Many of the new tourist attractions strongly emphasise the language and its place in Wales's cultural identity. There is little danger now of encountering a repetition of the infamous index entry which was published in the *Encyclopaedia Britannica:* "For Wales, see England".

Cymru is the name the Welsh have for themselves, and it means "comrade". Welsh is a Germanic name meaning "stranger", and it is used in various forms for several peoples in Europe (Vlachs, Walloons). The language is based on Brythonic Celtic, as is Cornish, which died out in the 18th century. It is different from Scottish Gaelic and a speaker of one cannot understand a speaker of the other. There are regional variations and the dialect of north Wales sounds as different from that of the south as does Yorkshire from London in England. Welsh, which has six letters fewer than English (J, K, Q, V, X and Z are missing), is basically a phonetic language. Y, meaning "the" is pronounced "*uh*", w is pronounced "*oo*" and both are treated as vowels. *Bore da* means good morning, *Dydd da* good day (dd is pronouced th). *Sut mae?* is how are you?, *diolch* is thanks and *lachd da!* means good health!

Some place names are recognisable in Welsh – Caernarvon becomes Caernarfon – and some are quite different: Swansea (becomes Abertawe), Newport (Casnewydd) and Abergavenny (Y Fenni). Deciphering road signs is the visitor's first lesson in one of Europe's oldest languages.

height of Cardiff's prosperity, between 1867 and 1872, the Marquis of Bute (responsible for building much of the docks) added to the castle, with a clock tower and many elaborately decorated banqueting halls. Most of the work was executed by William Burges whose speciality was the revival of medieval tiles. The rooms are still used for functions and even for boisterous medieval banquets. The Marquis was also responsible for **Castell Coch** (Red Castle) 5 miles (8 km) north of the city. This folly-cum-hunting lodge above the River Taff looks like the home of Sleeping Beauty.

The **National Museum of Wales** has much evidence of the principality's history and its **Art Gallery** has an Impressionist collection as well as works from both English and Welsh painters. But for those who really want to know about Wales **St Fagan's National Folk Museum**, 4 miles (6 km) west of the city, is a must. Set in some 100 acres (40 hectares) of grounds around the Tudor **St Fagan's Castle**, it has brought together buildings of interest from all over the country – cottages, a toll gate, chapel, cock pit – and there are demonstrations by craftsmen, all giving a flavour of rural Wales.

Caerphilly, 5 miles (8 km) north of Cardiff, is where the famous white cheese comes from and it also has the remains of one of the most extensive castles in Britain, covering 30 acres (12 hectares). To the east of Cardiff is the industrial town of **Newport** on the mouth of the Usk where the exceptional tide has caused the bridges to be built high in the air. The main A48, more attractive than the M4, here follows the old Roman road towards Chepstow, arriving, after some 10 miles (16 km) at the Roman walled town of **Venta Silurum**, near **Caerwent**. Some of its remains are among the important collection in the Newport **archaeology museum**, while just outside the town, up the Usk Valley at **Caerleon** is the remains of a fortress, Isca Silurum, and the most complete surviving Roman amphitheatre in Britain.

Cardiff's Bute Street in 1925.

The Gower Peninsula: The second largest city in Wales is **Swansea**, 40 miles (64 km) west of Cardiff, lying on the mouth of the Tawe, which gives it its Welsh name, Abertawe. It has been scarred by World War II bombs and subsequent industrialisation, and Dylan Thomas (1914–53), Wales's most famous poet, called it "an ugly, lovely town... jerry villa'd and smug suburbaned by the site of a long and splendid curving shore". He was born here at 5 Cwmdonkin Drive, close to Uplands. He also called the **Royal Institute of South Wales** a "museum which should be in a museum" because of its striking Greek revival architecture. The city has some 50 parks, which make it colourful in spring, but its main attraction is its regular **market**, the largest in Wales, where such traditional local food as cockles and laverbread (a delicacy made with seaweed and eaten fried with bacon) can be bought.

On the southern edge of Swansea Bay is **The Mumbles** where there are good boating and water skiing facilities. The town claims to have inaugurated the world's first passenger-carrying railway when in 1807 it ran a horse-drawn tramway into Swansea. Thomas Bowdler (1754–1825), who cleaned up Shakespeare's texts for family reading and thus brought the word "Bowdlerise" into the English language, is buried in the churchyard.

The Mumbles is the start of the Gower peninsula, a small finger of land 20 miles by 5 (32 by 8 km) which juts out into Carmarthen Bay. This area has some of Wales's best scenery and it contrasts starkly with industrial Swansea. There are good surfing beaches on its southern coast, much of which is given over to a nature reserve. Five miles (8 km) west of The Mumbles on the A4118 is **Parkmill** where sand dunes are reputed to have buried two churches and are threatening to do the same to the ruins of **Pennard Castle**. At the west end of the peninsula is the gracious 3-mile (5-km) sweep of **Rhosilli beach** and above it **Llangenith** where traces of antiquity are sited on

Mumbles Head, start of the scenic Gower Peninsula.

slopes looking out towards the Atlantic Ocean. In the 6th century St Cenydd built a monastery here and Norman monks adopted it as their home 600 years later. **Llanmadoc Hill**, just north of Llangennith, is topped by a hill fort which is the best viewpoint at this end of the peninsula.

On the mainland behind the peninsula, the River Tywi forces the road inland to **Carmarthen** and, 9 miles (15 km) beyond, skirts the River Taf on which **Laugharne** lies. Anyone who has read or heard *Under Milk Wood*, his memorable play, may feel themselves to be in familiar territory, though Dylan Thomas, who lived here from 1949, probably based his play on New Quay on the Cardigan Bay Coast. The young, drunken, bad-boy, poet-angel has left his mark on this cockle-fishing village. The boat-house on the "heron-priested shore" where he lived and worked is now a museum. He was not the only literary luminary attracted to the calm of Laugharne: his friend Richard Hughes (1900–76), the author of *A High Wind in Jamaica*, lived in the castle nearby.

The Pembroke Coast: Carmarthen is the county town of Dyfed which has engulfed the region of **Pembrokeshire** in the extreme south west. Called "Little England beyond Wales" because of the numbers of English who have settled here, it is renowned for its rugged coastline. The 180-mile (288-km) **Pembrokeshire Coast National Park**, rarely wider than 5 miles (8 km), stretches from Armoth in Carmarthen Bay around St David's Head and up to Cardigan in Cardigan Bay. This is one of the best walking paths in Britain and it provides endless opportunities for watching gannets, fulmars, puffins, cormorants and other wildlife which thrives in the region.

Tenby is the first major resort on this coast. In Welsh the town is **Dinbychypysgod**, which means "Tenby, little fort of the fished" and it has retained its town walls as well as the remains of a castle among its narrow streets. Its 15th-century prosperity shows in the **Tudor**

Dylan Thomas's study in Laugharne.

Merchant's Hall and in St Mary's Church, the largest parish church in Wales. Boats leave here for **Caldy Island** 2½ miles (4 km) offshore, where monks in the Cistercian abbey produce scent from flowers.

The coast around **St Govan's Head**, 12 miles (20 km) west of Tenby, is one of the most popular sections of the park. Just inland is **Bosherston**, famous for its waterlily ponds and mere from which, some believe, came King Arthur's sword, Excalibur (Merlin, the Welsh wizard of Arthur's court, is said to have originally come from Carmarthen). **Pembroke** is a few miles north at the head of an estuary in the large natural harbour of **Milford Haven**, a major oil terminal. There are many boating facilities in the area, particularly around **Dale** near the sea.

Pembroke is dominated by its castle, the birthplace of the wise and thrifty Henry VII, son of Owen Tudor and England's first Tudor monarch. An inspiring castle, it has a fine circular stone keep, which was harder to undermine than the old square towers. Beneath the Great Hall is a cave, called The Wogan, which leads to the harbour.

The House of David: A toll bridge leads over Milford Haven, otherwise the road around the valley via the market town of **Haverfordwest** is circuitous. The coast west of here is drawn in to sandy **St Bride's Bay** with St Ann's Head and the bird sanctuary islands of Skomer and Skokholm in the south, and Ramsey Island and St David's Head, Wales's western extremity, in the north.

St David is the patron saint of Wales and the cathedral built to him in the small town of **St David's** has a mysterious sanctity. Together with the **Bishop's Palace**, it was built in **Glyn Rhosyn** (Valley of Roses) half a mile from the sea to keep it out of sight of marauders, and only when approaching it through the south gate does the full majesty of the principality's greatest church become apparent. At one time two pilgrimages to St David's were worth one to Rome.

Fears of attack on this coast were not

Tenby, "little fort of the fished".

ill-founded: the last foreign invasion was in 1797 when the French landed at **Fishguard** 16 miles (25 km) further north, though they were tricked into surrendering by the townswomen. **Lower Fishguard**, which has a charming harbour, was used for the setting of the 1971 film version of Dylan Thomas's *Under Milk Wood*, starring that other famous son of South Wales, Richard Burton.

The A487 continues 18 miles (28 km) to **Cardigan**, a lively market town which has given its name to the great bay that sweeps down Wales's west coast. Upstream from Cardigan is some of the best fishing in Wales. At **Cenarth** and **Cilgerran** a few coracle licences for netting are still allowed.

The coracle (*cwrwgl* in Welsh) is an ancient boat made of intertwined laths of willow and hazel and covered with hide, in a design that has hardly changed since the Iron Age. The great virtue of this boat is that it is light enough to be carried on a fisherman's back. Today they are confined to the River Teifi here

above Cardigan, and to the Tywi above Carmarthen in south Wales. The Teifi coracle is pinched amidships, while the one which is used on the Tywi is oval and more suitable for calm waters. It is a fine sight to see local fishermen handle the sturdier Teifi coracle below Cenarth Falls.

From Cardigan the A487 traces the coast north past unexpected little inlets and coves such as **Tresaith** and **Llanrannog** before arriving 19 miles (34 km) later at the small seaside resort of **New Quay**. Just beyond, among rocky headlands, is the port of **Aberaeron** and these small fishing villages continue 16 miles (25 km) to **Aberystwyth**.

The sweep of the promenade at Aberystwyth, with its Georgian frontages, makes as fine a place as could be wished for to watch the sun set towards Ireland. The town is a resort, university and market town built on two levels. The **University of Wales** campus looks down on the grey buildings huddled round on the beach and the **National Library of Wales** has a similarly elevated position and a splendid view of Cardigan Bay. On a fine Saturday evening stirring hymn singing can be heard from the castle. The beach is of shingle, gravel and sand – don't forget to kick the last bar of the promenade outside Alexandra Hall for good luck (an old student tradition).

One of those "great little trains of Wales" leaves the Alexandra Road station to follow the **Vale of Rheidol Narrow Gauge Railway** 12 miles (20 km) inland to **Devil's Bridge**. This picturesque Wales at its most dramatic, combining spectacle with rumour from the Celtic twilight. Where the rivers Mynach and Rheidol meet there is a series of steep falls tumbling 300 ft (90 metres). There are three bridges, built one over the other, the lowest reputedly the devil's and built for the monks of **Strata Florida Abbey**, 7 miles (11 km) south. Now a ruin, in the 13th century this Cistercian establishment was the cultural centre of Wales. East of Devil's Bridge the B4574 leads back to the lakes and high lands of the Elan Valley.

Left, a tower on the University of Wales, Aberystwyth. **Right**, a fisherman with a traditional coracle made of hide.

THE MERSEY AND NORTH WALES

Manchester is the capital of northern England. A Victorian bastion, it was in the vanguard of the industrial revolution and it prospered greatly when machinery and products from its cotton mills were transported down the 35-mile (48-km) Manchester Ship Canal to Liverpool for export. Today, it is still a relatively prosperous city, with a population of around 500,000.

In spite of its industrial reputation, it has, within easy striking distance of its centre, rolling green countryside. And not far away are the city's favourite holiday coasts of Lancashire and North Wales. London is 188 miles (303 km) to the south via the M6 and M1 motorways and Inter-City trains to Euston station take three hours. Its airport is 10 miles (16 km) south of the city centre, reached from junction 5 on the M56.

A lively city, Manchester has a number of night spots, such as the Hacienda, which made a name for itself in the 1980s. On a night out, many people eat Chinese: **Chinatown** is not only renowned, it is also well signposted by a huge, ornate archway. The city is proud to have what it calls Britain's "first Urban Heritage Park" at Castleford. This part of town is designed for family entertainment. The **Science and Industry Museum,** winner of awards, is located here, and there is a chance to walk down television's long-running Coronation Street or drop in on Sherlock Holmes's Baker Street home in **Granada TV's studios**.

To the west of the City is the working-class district of Salford where the **Lowry Heritage Centre** has a good collection of the paintings of L. S. Lowry (1887–1976).

The worst excess of Heritage-mania is at **Wigan**, between Manchester and Liverpool, which is doubtless trying to make up for the image it was given by George Orwell in his 1937 book about working conditions in the north, *The Road to Wigan Pier*. Now the town trades on nostalgia, putting a romantic gloss on those grisly times with a reconstructed shop, schoolroom, pub, cottage and even a coal mine from around 1900.

Greater Manchester is encircled by motorways. The M6 flies past it towards the Lake District and Scotland and crossing it, at junction 21A, is the M62 bound for **Liverpool**. The shipping industry upon which Liverpool prospered has now all but deserted the Merseyside port, which suffered heavy unemployment through the 1970s and 80s. Nevertheless, some rejuvenation has taken place, notably in the **King Albert Dock**. The warehousing area has become a complex of small shops and it includes a **Maritime Museum**, a sister gallery to the **Tate** in London and, inevitably, **The Beatles Story**, an "experience" of the city's illustrious sons (The Cavern, Penny Lane... all are included on guided tours) which is naturally open "eight days a week".

The city's architecture is on a grand scale and includes the imposing 295-ft (90-metre) **Royal Liver Building** by the docks, and two new churches – the

circular **Roman Catholic Cathedral**, designed by Sir Edwin Lutyens and Sir Frederick W. Gibberd, consecrated in 1967, and the **Anglican Cathedral**, Britain's largest, by Giles Gilbert Scott, completed in 1978. The Liverpool **Museum** and the **Walker Art Gallery**, both in William Brown Street, are worth a visit. There is also a good pre-Raphaelite collection at the **Lady Lever Art Gallery**.

This is an excuse to take the much sung-about ferry across the Mersey to the Wirrall peninsula which protrudes between this estuary and that of the Dee to the south. Alternatively, you can drive through the Mersey Tunnel to emerge on the Wirrall at Birkenhead. The gallery is nearby in **Port Sunlight**, a model workers' village founded by Lord Leverhulme (1851–1928) for his soap empire. From the Wirrall there are good views across the Dee estuary to the enticing hills of North Wales.

North of Liverpool are Lancashire's sandy resorts of **Southport**, **Lytham St Anne's** and **Blackpool**, Britain's most popular seaside resort. Up to 6 million people come here each year, their numbers swelled by trades union and political party conferences. The promenade, all 7 miles (11 km) of it, centred on a 518-ft (160-metre) Eiffel-style tower, is lit up in the autumn and these "illuminations" are an event in themselves. In fact **Morecambe**, a resort in the bay of the same name to the north, claims to have started this idea as a way of extending its summer season. Be sure anyway to try some Morecambe Bay shrimps, gathered in nets taken across the sandy beaches by horse and cart. The beaches all down this coast are wide and long, and sand yachting is popular at the more up-market resort of Lytham St Anne's.

Border towns: South of Liverpool, at the head of the Wirrall peninsula and at the end of the 40-mile (64-km) M56 from Manchester, is **Chester**, the most northerly and the most exciting of the timbered Tudor towns of the Welsh Marches, the hilly country bordering Wales. Its particular architectural character can be seen by walking down

Chester, a border town with its own special style.

Eastgate, Watergate or Bridge Street with their **Rows**, double tiers of shops and covered walkways, one on top of the other. The oldest dates from 1486, and most of them were built in the following century.

In Roman times Chester was an important stronghold called Deva and part of an **amphitheatre** can be seen just outside the city walls by St John's Street. The **Grosvenor Museum** records the Roman legacy with models of the fortress city. Under the Normans Chester was a near-independent state governed by a succession of earls. The tidal estuary of the Dee allowed the city to flourish as a port up until the 15th century when it began to silt up and after that shipping was transferred to the large natural port of Liverpool.

The 2-mile (3-km) round trip of the **city walls** helps orientation. This is one of the few British cities with its medieval walls still intact, those on the north and east sides following the original Roman plan. The **Cathedral**, off St Werburg Street, was a Benedictine Ab-

bey until the Dissolution. Unusually squat, it has a short nave and a massive south transept featuring a grand, Victorian stained-glass window.

Two miles (4 km) north of the city is **Chester Zoo**, the largest outside London. South of the city the A483 heads for **Wrexham**, where Elihu Yale, founder of Yale University in America is buried.

To the west is **Llangollen**, venue for the **International Eisteddfod** (meeting) held every July, which has given this small town the reputation of being the centre of Welsh culture and music. Its two most famous residents were eccentric gossips, Lady Eleanor Butler and the Hon Sarah Ponsonby, the "Llangollen Ladies", who from 1780 lived at **Plas Newydd** cottage at the end of Castle Street and entertained anyone passing through on the A5 road to Dublin via the Holyhead ferry. The Duke of Wellington was a guest, as were Lord Byron and Sir Walter Scott, though a sonnet offered by William Wordsworth was ill received by the ladies who in-

The station at Llangollen, home of the annual Eisteddfod.

sisted on gifts of carved wood from their guests.

To the south of Wrexham is the 13th-century Marcher fortress of Chirk Castle. From the attractive town of **Oswestry** the A483 continues 18 miles (28 km) to **Welshpool**, county town of Powys. There are unexpected red-brick Georgian houses here, but there are also ancient, timbered, lopsided hotels and pubs which give a rare feeling of domesticity. Opposite the porch of the parish church of St Mary is the Maen Llog, once a Druid altar. A mile south of the town is **Powis Castle**, an imposing building and one of the most important in Wales. Built by Welsh princes around 1300, the castle is used to display treasures collected by the 1st Lord Clive ("Clive of India") and the 17th-century terraced garden is arguably the most dramatic in the country.

Following the Shropshire-Union Canal, the road continues 14 miles (22 km) south to Newtown, which despite its name was first settled in 1280. It has, however, been important in recent years as the focus on the New Town Development Corporation, highlighting the fact that rural depopulation has taken a severe toll on this part of Wales. This used to be an important weaving and textile district and it is still a busy centre, having attracted, among others, the Laura Ashley fashion and fabrics company here. The town's best-known son was Robert Owen (1771–1858), a pioneer of socialism and the co-operative movement, who is commemorated in a small museum in the library.

The A5 southeast of Oswestry leads 18 miles (28 km) to **Shrewsbury**. Beautifully situated on a meander in the River Severn, crossed by the English bridge and the Welsh bridge, it has houses dating back to the 15th century. The pink sandstone **castle**, near the station, was converted into a house by the 18th-century engineer Thomas Telford.

But **Telford** has been awarded a larger memorial, a whole new town named after him a dozen miles east of Shrewsbury, at the end of the M54 from Birmingham. Begun only in the 1960s,

Brecon churchyard carpeted with beech leaves.

272

the ambitious project takes in Coalbrookdale, where coke was first used to smelt iron, and Ironbridge on the River Severn, where the world's first iron bridge was built by Telford in 1773. The **Ironbridge Gorge Museum**, open all year, has Darby's original furnace, as well as the warehouses and other industrial heritage.

Shrewsbury is the county town of Shropshire, the home of the poet A.E. Housman (1859–1936) who eulogised the dreamy slopes of this agricultural land in *A Shropshire Lad*. Writing of **Wenlock Edge**, a ridge of hills between Shrewsbury and Ludlow 29 miles (46 km) south, and of the duality of these Welsh Marches, he says:

> *The flag of morn in conqueror's state*
> *Enters at the English gate*
> *The vanquished Eve, as night prevails,*
> *Bleeds upon the road to Wales.*

These lands of the Marcher lords, captured vividly in the novels of Raymond Williams (1921–88), have been the scene of many a carnage and

Conwy Castle, part of Edward I frontline defences against the Welsh.

have a flavour unlike anywhere else in Wales. It was in this area that the native culture mingled most thoroughly with that of the Roman and Norman invaders, giving rise to a fascinating blend of Celtic and foreign culture. All down the border the hills, as well as the accents, roll softly towards England.

Perhaps the loveliest of these border towns is **Ludlow**, where Housman's ashes lie. The centre of the town is remarkably consistent architecturally, with 13th-century taverns and Tudor market buildings. It was at **Ludlow castle**, the former seat of the presidents of the council of the Marches, that John Milton's masque *Comus* was first performed in 1634. It is still easy to imagine how it looked then. Sixteen miles (25 km) west of Ludlow is **Knighton**, the centre for exploring Offa's Dyke.

Wales's north coast: From Chester the Dee estuary, followed by the A548, leads out to the sandy resorts of north Wales, starting with **Prestatyn** 28 miles (45 km) west. Adjoining it is **Rhyl** which has a 3-mile (5-km) promenade but the largest and most pleasant of these resorts is **Llandudno**, 15 miles (24 km) further on. Behind the town on the 678-ft (265-metre) summit of Great Orme there are spectacular views of the north Wales coast. All these resorts are within easy reach of northern England and within touring distance of the national park of Snowdonia.

Opposite Llandudno, on the far side of Thomas Telford's pedestrian-only suspension bridge (a new tunnel takes care of the traffic), lies **Conwy**. Residents of this ancient town never feared attacks from the sea, ensconced as they were inside its stunning walls. The **castle** was built under the orders of Edward I and was one of four (the others are Beaumaris, Caernarfon and Harlech) built by his Master of Works in Wales, James St George, cousin of the Count of Savoy. From these northern bastions Edward sallied forth to defeat the Welsh during the conquest of 1277–84.

Mother island: Bangor, a university town, is 20 miles (32 km) west and from here another Telford bridge crosses the **Menai Straits** to reach the 276 sq. mile

(715 sq. km) island of **Anglesey**. This ancient Celtic island was called Mona by the Romans who rounded up Druids and brought them here to be massacred. The Welsh call it *Mon, man Cymru*, Anglesey, mother of Wales, because her grain used to feed the rest of the country.

The suspension bridge was built in 1826 and was the first of its kind and the most difficult feat in the great Holyhead Road scheme which Telford engineered to link Dublin to London. Ferries still go to Ireland from **Holyhead**, a small island just off the west coast and on a clear day from the 710-ft Holyhead Mountain there is a view of Ireland, the Isle of Man way to the north, and south to Wales's highest mountain, **Snowdon**.

A drive across Anglesey, through its small lanes and winding roads, can be frustrating for anyone in a hurry to catch the ferry, but it is a good way to see some of the farming way of life and the small, lime-washed cottages with slurried roofs. A warning of the island's eccentricities comes just after crossing the

Straits when the A5 passes the village of **Llanfairpwllgwyngyllgogerychwyrndrobwllllantysiliogogogoch**, which is an accurate description of the place: "St Mary's Church by the white aspens over the whirlpool and St Tysilio's Church by the red cave".

Beaumaris is towards the eastern end of the island, while **Caernarfon**, the largest town in the area, is at the opposite end of the straits on the mainland. With its city walls and towers intact, this handsome town is a fine resort, popular with yachtsmen. Only the shell of Edward's moated castle remains, but it still looked impressive in July 1969 when Prince Charles was invested as Prince of Wales, an office conferred on Britain's heir apparent since 1282. Its strategic position meant Caernarfon was an important settlement long before the present castle was built. The Romans arrived in AD 78 and built a fortress, Segontium, and some excavated remains of it can be seen.

Mountain scenery: Immediately behind these coastal resorts is Eryri, the

Caernarfon Castle where Prince Charles was made Prince of Wales.

land of the eagles. This is **Snowdonia**, Wales's most mountainous region. Fourteen summits are above 3,000 ft (1,000 metres) and Snowdon itself, 11 miles (18 km) as the eagle flies due south of Bangor, is the highest at 3,560 ft (1,070 metres). Although these mountains, formed by centuries of glacial activity, cannot be compared with the Alps or the Pyrenees, generations of climbers and visitors have agreed that they are some of the most beautiful in the world.

Rolling green foothills rise into sheer crags, and stone sheepfolds cling impossibly to high slopes. Simply driving around Snowdonia is an exhilarating experience and it can be difficult to concentrate on the road. Mountain passes such as **Llanberis**, a dozen miles (20 km) inland from Caernarfon on the A4086, and **Aberglaslyn**, 14 miles (22 km) south of Caernarfon on the A4085, offer breathtaking views of the whole of Snowdonia, which is studded with brilliant mountain lakes.

A mile north of the Aberglaslyn Pass is **Beddgelert**, a tiny, compact village nestled in the middle of beautiful scenery. The name means "the grave of Gerlert". According to legend, Gerlert was a loyal dog mistakenly killed by Prince Llewellyn after it had rescued his son from a wolf.

Purists insist that, like the poet William Wordsworth, visitors should climb Snowdon in order to see the dawn. The easiest path to the summit starts on its northern side at **Llanberis** and is 3½ miles (5.5 km) long. For the less energetic, there is the option of the **Snowdon Mountain Railway**, a slow rack-and-pinion railway which has three stops on the way.

Slate quarrying was once the most important industry of northwest Wales, and the huge heaps of slate spoil which overshadow quarrying villages such as **Bethesda**, 4 miles (7 km) south of Bangor, and **Blaenau Ffestiniog**, southeast of Snowdon on the A470, become eerily beautiful when wetted by the rain which falls so plentifully there. On the north side of Blaenau Ffestiniog is **Llech-**

The road to Dolgellau, the heart of Welsh-speaking Wales.

wedd quarry, mostly underground, which is open to the public: the sight of workmen splitting and dressing slate is guaranteed to make any idle onlooker feel clumsy.

Ten miles (16 km) north of Blaenau Ffestiniog on the A470 is **Betws-y-Coed**, which is less interesting as a village than as the meeting point of three valleys, Lledr, Llugwy and Conwy. In the Wybrnant valley 3.5 miles (5 km) southwest, is a small cottage called **Ty Mawr Wybrnant** which was the birthplace of Bishop William Morgan (1545–1604) who first translated the Bible into Welsh. The National Trust runs nature trails from here in summer.

Two miles (3 km) west of Betws-y-Coed are the famous **Swallow Falls** and, close by, **Conwy Falls**, some of the most spectacular in the country. A salmon leap has been built to help fish negotiate the formidable Conwy Falls.

The old lady's arm: Wales is sometimes depicted as an old lady throwing a ball out to sea. Her head is Anglesey, her leg Pembroke and the **Lleyn Peninsula** is her arm. Caernarfon lies on her shoulder and from **Aberdaron**, at the tip of the peninsula, Bardsley Island, her ball, can be reached, although the crossing is often difficult. In the 7th century monks came to settle on the island. Whether or not 20,000 saints are buried there, as the story goes, the island does feel like a holy place.

Around the peninsula are tiny coastal harbours such as **Porthdinllain** and **Nefyn**, unforgettably situated between the sea and Snowdonia and constantly altering their aspect under the shifting light. Travelling north of Nefyn on the B4417, the 1,850-ft (560-metre) mountain **Yr Eifl**, appears large on the left. On its eastern peak is the site of **Tre'r Ceiri**, one of the oldest Iron-Age forts in Britain. There are 200 circular stone huts clustered within the fortress's double defensive wall and the peak offers magnificent views over the whole peninsula.

In the southeast corner of the peninsula is **Porthmadog**, the creation of

Snowdonia railway takes the mountain strain.

William Maddocks (1773–1828), a local mill owner and parliamentarian. Maddocks constructed the mile-long embankment, called the Cobb, across the river mouth which reclaimed 7,000 acres (2,800 hectares) and gave rise to the lovely town. A Tremadog, at the back of Porthmadog, the poet Shelley rented a house where in 1888 T.E. Lawrence (of Arabia) was born.

A ride on the **Ffestiniog Narrow Gauge Railway** is a must. It starts at Porthmadog and chugs its way high up into the hills of the Vale of Ffestiniog, giving wonderful views over Snowdonia National Park. The architect Sir Clough William Ellis had an even more vivid imagination than Maddocks when, in 1926, he decided to build an Italianate village beside Porthmadog in the Dwyryd estuary. He called this elaborate folly **Portmeirion** and many millions of people know it as the village where "No. 6" was kept in the cult television series, *The Prisoner*. On a summer evening it can be disorientating to look at these pastel-coloured buildings and hear Welsh voices all around.

A short distance beyond the far side of the estuary lies **Harlech**, the perfect place from which to view the Lleyn Peninsula, Cardigan Bay and the Cadair Idris mountains to the south in one breathtaking gaze. The castle, perched dramatically on a promontory looking out to sea, was defended for eight years (1460–68) by the Lancastrian Dafydd ab Ifan during the Wars of the Roses, a feat commemorated in the stirring song, *Men of Harlech*. Eleven miles (18 km) south of Harlech is the holiday resort of **Barmouth**, attractively built up against towering cliffs. Houses seem to perch wherever they can find a foothold.

From here the road turns inland up the Mawddach Valley to **Dolgellau**, a town people apparently either love or hate. Either way, it is an excellent place to explore the Cadair Idris range in the south of the Snowdonia National Park. A neat, stone-built town, it is very Welsh in speech and custom and is in many ways the epitome of the plain, sturdy, close-knit Welsh community.

Harlech Castle, cue for a rousing song.

AROUND THE PEAK DISTRICT

In a region littered with the relics of ancient wars, no sign remains of some comparatively recent hand-to-hand combat. Unless, that is, you count the sign that reads: "Public access to this private land has been granted by agreement with the owners". Blood bought this access when, in the 1930s, hikers from the depressed industrial cities of Manchester and Sheffield sought to walk for weekend recreation. They were met by owners' gamekeepers armed with clubs and guns.

Today the major threat is from the capricious weather. The rights of ramblers are protected within the **Peak District National Park**, and the popularity of the long-distance footpaths disproves the image of the British as a nation of armchair sportsmen and video addicts. The longest footpath, the **Pennine Way**, winds along England's backbone for 250 miles (400 km), starting in the Peak District, crossing Yorkshire and Northumbria, and finishing north of the border with Scotland. It is a very serious walk, crossing remote, exposed terrain, and few people are ambitious enough to attempt the entire course which would take at least two weeks. But, since it opened in 1965, this "everyman's Everest" has become remarkably popular. Human feet have reduced some stretches of peat to the consistency of thick porridge, and conservationists are beginning to wish the gamekeepers had won.

The Peak District is like a massive English rockery garden, 30 miles long and 20 miles at its widest point (48 km by 32 km). To the west the M6 motorway heads up to Manchester; to the east the M1 runs north towards Leeds. The park begins in Derbyshire, extends north into Yorkshire, and offers airy adventures to the inhabitants of half a dozen adjacent cities.

Cutlery and crockery: The north's largest city, Manchester, is to the northwest; Yorkshire's largest city, Sheffield, lies to the northeast. **Sheffield** prospered at the foot of the Pennines, using the cascading water to drive grindstones manufactured from their millstone grit. Its reputation as a cutlery-making town reaches back to Chaucer and the *Canterbury Tales*, in which a miller carried a Sheffield knife in his stocking. But in 1760 another writer, Horace Walpole, described Sheffield as "one of the foulest towns in England in the most charming situation".

Efforts during the 20th century to tame the furnaces have worked: the depth of dust on one nearby golf course measures less than 1 percent of what it did 30 years ago, and it now claims to be the cleanest industrial city in the world. But there were also many factory closures during the 1970s and '80s: Sheffield steel may still be best but Korean cutlery costs less.

Today's shopping centre is emphatically modern, neat suburbs cling to steep gradients, and the **Crucible Theatre** has a national reputation. The **Central Library and Art Gallery** has a good collection of British and French

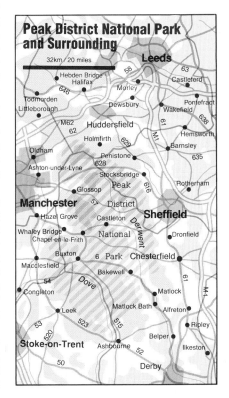

Peak District National Park and Surrounding

32km / 20 miles

Leeds, Hebden Bridge, Halifax, Castleford, Todmorden, Littleborough, Morley, Dewsbury, Wakefield, Pontefract, Hemsworth, Huddersfield, Holmfirth, Barnsley, Oldham, Penistone, Ashton-under-Lyne, Stocksbridge, Glossop, Peak, Rotherham, Manchester, District, Sheffield, Hazel Grove, Castleton, Dronfield, Whaley Bridge, National, Chapel-en-le-Frith, Buxton, Park, Chesterfield, Macclesfield, Bakewell, Congleton, Dove, Matlock, Leek, Matlock Bath, Alfreton, Derwent, Belper, Ripley, Stoke-on-Trent, Ashbourne, Ilkeston, Derby

painters from the 18th century to today. Silverware is on show in the appropriate setting of the 17th-century **Cutlers' Hall** opposite the **Cathedral**.

To the south of the Park lies the town of **Stoke-on-Trent**, main town of The Potteries, the region that has supplied Britain with its finest china since the 17th century. Royal Doulton, Royal Grafton, Coalport, Minton, Spode… all the well-known porcelain and china factories are here and may be visited. A good starting point is the **Potteries Centre** by the station, where the products of two dozen local manufacturers are on display.

Three miles (5 km) north of the town is the **Chatterley Whitfield Mining Museum** which offers trips down the mines in rattling cages, pit ponies and a 1930s pit canteen. It's an excursion especially popular with children.

Derby and Nottingham to the southeast are also coal mining areas. **Nottingham** is where D.H. Lawrence (1885–1930) grew up and where the sheriff used to be continually outwitted by the legendary outlaw Robin Hood. The sheriff's castle is no longer intact, but a statue of *Robin and his Merry Men* is by the old walls and a new building houses the **Museum and Art Gallery**. **Sherwood Forest** is nearby.

Motorists approaching the Peak District National Park from the south will probably leave the M1 motorway at junction 24 and pass through **Derby**, 116 miles (187 km) northwest of London (trains from the capital leave from St Pancras). This ancient county town on the River Derwent has Britain's first real factory, a five-storey silk mill built in 1718. In the 19th century railway engineering became the main employer. Rolls-Royce cars have been made here since 1908.

Further east lie the cathedral cities of **Leicester** and **Lincoln** in the low-lying wolds which reach the North Sea on the Lincolnshire coast. Resorts include **Cleethorpes**, **Mablethorpe** and **Skegness**, the latter known from an early advertising campaign to be "so bracing" – a euphemism for downright windy.

Stained glass in Sheffield's cathedral.

Southern approach: Some of the summits in the Peak District National Park rise to 2,000 ft (660 metres), attracting hang-gliders and providing rock climbing opportunities to suit novices and satisfy experts. Pot-holers, too, are drawn here. Sir Arthur Conan Doyle (1859–1930), creator of Sherlock Holmes, wrote: "All this country is hollow. Could you strike it with some gigantic hammer, it would boom like a drum or possibly cave in altogether."

In some parts the Peak District is a turf-covered, undulating plateau, broken by narrow ravines. In others it is a rugged, heath-clad moor, broken by wooded dales, with loose stone walls creating a chequerboard of fields. It is a place for soporific pleasures as well as activity. As a National Park guide advises: "Kill nothing but time; take nothing but photographs; leave nothing but footprints."

From Derby the A52 approaches the park through **Ashbourne**, 12 miles (20 km) west. Its fine main thoroughfare, Church Street, contains a 16th-century school, 17th-century almshouse and 20th-century traffic jams. Cars aside, it is said to look much the same as when Charles I attended a service in St Oswald's church after being defeated at the Battle of Naseby in 1645. George Eliot (1819–80) set her novel *Adam Bede* in nearby Ellastone and she described the church (substantially 13th and 14th-century) as "the finest mere parish church in the kingdom".

Each Shrove Tuesday, Ashbourne hosts a no-holds-barred football match in which up to 300 players a side try to score goals by touching the walls of Sturston Mill and Clifton Mill, 3 miles (5 km) apart. The game can last well into Ash Wednesday, by which time not all limbs are intact.

From Ashbourne, take the A515 north into the Park, taking the left turn down the quiet lane that twists through **Dovedale**, a gentle limestone glen fancifully dubbed "little Switzerland". Dr Johnson was moved to compare it favourably with Scotland. In the best unsolicited testimonial the local tourist

Winnatts Pass, near Castletown.

Peak District 283

board could wish for, he wrote: "He who has seen Dovedale has no need to visit the Highlands".

Sheep densely populate these dales and sheepdog trials are popular summer distractions. Black-and-white collie dogs, obeying a farmer's every whistle, round up the hardy, black-faced sheep, expertly guiding them into pens. Top trials are televised nationwide.

A few miles further along the A515 – or, for the adventurous, after a delightful mystery tour through unclassified country lanes – **Buxton** is a resort whose thermal springs made it a kind of English Lourdes in medieval times. Today it markets the product of its nine springs by claiming that it doesn't have the disagreeable smell and taste of some spa waters. You can swim in an indoor spa-water pool at the Pavilion Gardens.

Between 1570 and 1583, Mary Queen of Scots sought treatment in Buxton for her rheumatism, a complaint doubtless aggravated by her imprisonment in a succession of draughty establishments. The ravine of the **Wye** provides a beautiful limestone route for walkers, but the town itself never succeeded in outshining Bath, as the fifth Duke of Devonshire intended when, at the end of the 18th century, he planned and built his grand crescent.

The fourth Duke did better with nearby **Chatsworth House**, "the Palace of the Peak," a vast Palladian mansion built between 1687 and 1707 and set in a spacious deer park with gardens landscaped by Capability Brown. It houses priceless collections of books and furniture, as well as fine paintings by Rembrandt and Reynolds. Chatsworth boosts business by staging an angling fair, a brass band festival, show-jumping and horse trials. Half-a-million people visit it every year; the current duchess calls it "a town".

Chapel-en-le-Frith, on the A625, is a small market town. "Frith" means "forest," but little of that is left today. Nearby, north of the A625, is **Edale**, a tidy cul-de-sac village huddling at the foot of the **Kinder Scout** peak, marking the start of the Pennine Way. "The

Chatsworth, "the Palace of the Peak".

Way" doesn't go in for many signposts or way-markings; embark on it without a good map and you'll probably be lost within 2 miles.

Further along the A625, **Castleton** is a centre for subterranean exploration. **Speedwell Mine** has a pothole so deep and high that rockets have gone up 450 ft (138 metres) without hitting the roof. A secret passage connects **Devil's Cavern** with **Peveril Castle**, high above the village, where Sir Walter Scott set *Peveril of the Peak*. The blackened ceilings of some caves date back centuries to the fires of villages who, forewarned of raiding parties, took refuge in them for long periods.

Hathersage, on the same road, is the hillside village that inspired "Morton" in Charlotte Brontë's *Jane Eyre*. Little John, lieutenant of the outlaw Robin Hood, is a native and he is supposed to be buried in a 14-ft (5-metre) grave in the churchyard.

A diversion south along the B6001 leads to **Eyam** (pronounced *Eem*), a pretty village remarkable for the action of its villagers in 1665. Finding that plague germs had arrived in a box of cloth sent from London to the local tailor, they completely sealed off the village to confine the disease; within a year, three-quarters of the 350 inhabitants were dead.

Eyam is one of several villages staging well-dressing ceremonies each August, when the wells are garlanded with elaborate tableaux of flower petals. Some believe the original purpose was part of a prayer for purity in the water during the Black Death; but the ceremony probably has pagan roots.

The A6 trunk road, en route back to Derby, passes through **Bakewell**, a stone-built agricultural town with two medieval bridges over the Wye. Two miles (4 km) to the southeast, **Haddon Hall** is one of Britain's best preserved and most atmospheric old houses, dating in parts from the 12th century. Nikolaus Pevsner, chronicler of architectural excellence, called it "a large, safe, grey, lovable house of knights and their ladies".

Hathersage, "Morton" in Jane Eyre.

YORK AND
THE NORTHEAST

The feet that preceded Sunday afternoon strollers across the Pennine millstone grit and mountain limestone in northern England were the feet of armies. Power in Britain has long centred in London, but the identity of those who have exercised it has very often been determined in the north. The region's history is as turbulent as the sudden storms that rage on the North Yorkshire Moors; no other part of the country has more fortresses and fortifications.

In AD 122, the Roman emperor Hadrian built a fortified wall for 73 miles (117 km) across the country from sea to sea to keep back barbarian Scots. The Borders region, known as the "Debatable Lands" from the Middle Ages to Elizabethan times, was in a state of constant feuding. The Wars of the Roses, from 1455 to 1485, saw the Houses of Lancaster (red rose) and York (white rose) locked in a struggle to win control of the throne. The Civil War in the 17th century divided local allegiances between king and parliament.

Other revolutions took place here, too. The seed of Christianity in Britain was planted in AD 634 on Lindisfarne, off the coast of Northumbria, and in Jarrow on Tyneside the Venerable Bede first wrote down the history of England. These lands of the northeast, the Yorkshire Dales and the sweeping Northumbrian moors, are wild, wide-open spaces. At the southern extremity, on the edge of the industrial north which spreads out from Greater Manchester, is Leeds, 190 miles (305 km) from London. York is 196 miles (315 km) and Newcastle 275 miles (440 km), 46 miles (75 km) short of the Scottish border. The A1(M) motorway goes to Leeds and on to Newcastle where the A1 takes over up the coast to Edinburgh. Fast InterCity trains run to Leeds, York and Newcastle from King's Cross in London.

Although most of the north's industries have been in upheaval, traditional life goes on. At **Huddersfield**, to the north of the Peak District and 15 miles

(24 km) south of Leeds, the famous choral society has performed Handel's *Messiah* every year since 1836. In the ranks of the Black Dyke Mills Band, Britain's most celebrated brass band, are weavers, shotfirers and furnacemen.

Victorian thrift is alive and well in local towns, made manifest by the numerous building societies, which borrow money from small savers in order to lend to house buyers. Few of the societies actually build anything these days – except for increasingly mammoth headquarters to accommodate clerks and computers. The "world's largest building society", the Halifax, takes its name from the town 10 miles (16 km) northwest of Huddersfield and boasts assets of £20 billion.

Halifax's gift to the world's motorists was the reflecting "cat's eyes," invented in 1934 by Percy Shaw. But the town earned its wealth from textiles, as did neighbouring **Bradford**. The 19th-century textile barons built solid dependability and vigour into every brick of Bradford's Italianate Town Hall and

its Gothic Wool Exchange. One of the richest, Titus Salt, enshrined his ideals in a model village near the town, providing it with mill, hospital, school, library, church and almshouses, but religiously excluding pubs. He called it **Saltaire**. (These days, alcohol *is* on sale.)

More recently, many immigrants have been attracted by the wool trade, which is still important. Asians make up 20 percent of Bradford's old city and it is to their Muslim leaders that the media turns when wanting vox pop quotes about the Middle East.

Bradford's tourism promoters, who call themselves "The Myth-breakers", have opened a **J.B. Priestley trail**, tracing the early life of the novelist and playwright who was born in the town in 1894 and immortalised it as "Bruddesford" in *The Good Companions*. Festivals feature the music of Frederick Delius (1862–1934), also a native. Other famous sons are the contemporary playwright Alan Bennett and the artist David Hockney, whose work can be seen at Saltaire.

The **National Museum of Photography, Film and Television** has a screen five storeys high by 96 ft (30 metres) wide, as well as the Kodak Museum's collection of cameras and pictures. Although the mills have been eclipsed, 50 mill shops strenuously promote their wares to visitors. **Leeds**, the town's larger next-door neighbour and Yorkshire's main city, has developed into a world centre for ready-made clothing.

The Brontë bonanza: Presented with the matchless raw material of the Brontës, Yorkshire's tragic literary family, the engine of tourism has shifted into overdrive. The steep cobbled street of **Haworth**, a hill village of grey stone houses 14 miles (22 km) west of Bradford on the B6144, are tramped by 700,000 visitors a year. A babble of nationalities queue in the peculiarly penetrating rain to file through the parsonage, now a museum, where Charlotte, Emily, Anne and Branwell grew up. Various relics and clothes are on display, rather too many only "*believed* to have been" owned by the Brontës. Visitors gazing at a boot are unanimous

in their conclusion that the author of *Jane Eyre* must have had exceptionally small feet.

The church where the Brontës' father was parson scarcely exists; it was rebuilt by his successor in 1879. But the congestion of old tombstones in the burial ground recalls mid-19th-century conditions here, when the average life expectancy was 28. Few pilgrims today, passing Ye Shoppe of Haworth or the Buckle 'n' Hide boutique, can visualise the insanitary town racked with typhus and cholera.

The moors, an unchanging backdrop, retain their grandeur, though the spirits of Heathcliff and Cathy can't hope for much rest as visitors trek in search of **Ponden Kirk**, the outcrop said to have inspired "Penistone Crag" in Charlotte Brontë's *Wuthering Heights*.

Haworth station is the headquarters of the **Keighley and Worth Valley Railway Preservation Society**, which runs steam locomotives on a 5-mile (8-km) track between **Keighley** and **Oxenhope**. Three other steam railways

290

operate in Yorkshire: the **Middleton Line** in Leeds; the **Dales Railway** near Skipton; and the **North York Moors Railway** from Pickering to Grosmont.

A dozen miles north of Haworth, **Ilkley**, a Victorian inland spa for the prosperous burghers of Leeds and Bradford, has immortalised its rugged climate in the Yorkshire anthem *On Ilkla Moor baht 'at* which, translated, means that it is not prudent to venture forth on Ilkley Moor without a hat.

On the A65 between Ilkley and Leeds, you can dine at the world's biggest fish and chip shop, **Harry Ramsden's.** It has chandeliers, plush decor, parking for 400 cars, plus a coach park, and is as commercial as it sounds.

The undespoiled Dales: To the north of Ilkley lies the expanse of the **Yorkshire Dales**, characterised by their dry-stone walls, flourishing hedgerows, bustling market towns, lonely farmhouses, cathedral-like caverns and ancient lead mines. You stumble across prehistoric man everywhere here. Many dales – such as **Rosedale**, **Farndale** and **Bilsdale** – are little known, and the motorist can do worse than abandon a fixed itinerary and explore at will. Most Dalesmen, though conservative and taciturn by nature, prove hospitable, even if some persist in branding as a failure any farmer who dabbles in tourism to make an extra penny or two. "Dales for the Dalesmen" has been a familiar cry.

Try to attend a sheep sale and see if you can comprehend a single word the auctioneer utters. Watch a village cricket match – the game is a Yorkshire passion – and you'll never again think of cricket as sedate.

The easiest excursion from Ilkley takes you into surrounding **Wharfedale**, an alluring cocktail of water, wood, crag and castle. **Bolton Abbey**, 5 miles (8 km) northwest of Ilkley, a beautiful ruin reminiscent of Tintern Abbey in Wales, dates to the 12th century; you can reach it by stepping stones across the river Wharfe.

Further north, **Wensleydale** is broad and wooded, and seems serene until your eye catches the forbidding **Bolton**

Barden Moorland in the moody Yorkshire Dales.

Castle perched on a hillside. Tradition has it that the mortar was mixed with oxblood to strengthen the building. Because little attempt has been made to tackle the castle's current disrepair, you can, by wandering through the stables area, into the open courtyard which once was the Great Hall, readily imagine yourself transported back to 1568, when Mary Queen of Scots was imprisoned here. One wing has been opened as a restaurant and you are invited to "dine where a Queen once dined". It is popular with wedding parties.

Middleham Castle, on the A6108 due north of Ilkley, is a massive, brooding ruin, owned briefly by Richard III; its substantial remains include a 12th-century keep, 13th-century chapel, 14th-century gatehouse and two 14th-century chapels.

Hawes, at the heart of the North Yorkshire Dales National Park, 16 miles (25 km) due west on the A684, has a park and folk museum, and is famous for the manufacture of Wensleydale cheese. (Try buying it fresh from farmhouses.)

The 19th-century railway builders were tested in this terrain; the foundations of the **Ribblehead viaduct**, which strides across **Batty Moss**, were stabilised on thousands of sheep fleeces.

Buttertubs Pass, 1,726 ft (575 metres) high, links Wensleydale with **Swaledale to** the northeast ("buttertubs" are deep limestone shafts). Swaledale is a steep and rocky dale, and has the mighty ruins of a castle at **Richmond**, a market town with a capacious cobbled square. **Friar's Wynd** is its splendidly restored Georgian theatre.

Splendour and sulphur: There are other ways to leave Leeds than via Ilkley. Strike north on the A61 and, after 9 miles (14 km), you reach the ornate **Harewood House** (interiors by Robert Adam, furniture by Thomas Chippendale), set in landscaped gardens laid out by Capability Brown and featuring a remarkable bird park. Now the home of the Earl and Countess of Harewood, it was built in the 1760s by Edwin Lascelles. He represented the authentic Yorkshire spirit, demanding the best

Swaledale's great empty landscape.

materials and labour at the cheapest possible price and assuring his workers: "He who will do it most reasonably, and at the same time well, shall always be employed by me."

Eight miles (13 km) further along the A61 is **Harrogate**, an inland spa whose snobbery was once as strong as the sulphur which made it the world's biggest hydrotherapy centre and whose seaside ambience, though bogus, is strong enough to fool seagulls. Harrogate, say some Yorkshiremen, can take credit for one great invention: respectability. It has lavish lawns, abundant flowers, and the Harrogate Centre, a fortress-like brick conference complex whose construction budget ballooned from £750,000 to £30 million as civic visions grew more grandiose.

Four miles (6.5 km) to the north, **Ripley** is a village conceived in the style of Alsace; the town hall is labelled Hôtel de Ville. Bullet holes in the walls of the parish church mark the passage of Cromwell in the Civil War. **Ripley Castle** has good collections of armour and paintings; it has been the home of the Ingleby family for 600 years, though the current Inglebys complain ruefully about the crippling cost of insurance and central heating.

Ripon, further along the A61, developed around the sombre Saxon cathedral founded by St Wilfrid in the 7th century. Three miles (5 km) to the southwest are the atmospheric remains of **Fountains Abbey**, once British's richest Cistercian monastery. Kitchens and dormitories survive, a tribute to old craftsmanship, giving today's visitor an unusually clear idea of medieval monastic life.

To the northeast, across the A1 artery, **Thirsk**, a thriving market town, is fast creating a new literary trail. It is the "Darrowby" of James Herriot's vet books, which have been translated into such successful television series as *All Creatures Great and Small*.

The heritage of York: To the east of Harrogate is the jewel that, as the traffic congestion testifies, must not be missed: **York**. It's easier, and more appropriate,

The old shopping lanes of York.

to travel there by train, for York became the 19th-century hub of Britain's railway system and today it houses the **National Railway Museum**; its diverse fascinations range from Queen Victoria's sumptuous carriage to the latest tilting-train technology. Entry is free.

The Romans set up a base here in AD 71. Eight centuries later, the Vikings came, naming the settlement Jorvik. A routine archaeological dig in 1976 turned up a treasure chest of 15,000 artefacts, now the core of an inspired museum project, the **Jorvik Viking Centre**. Lines, serenaded by buskers, form outside long before the 9am opening time. Visitors descend into a basement below a new shopping precinct and ride in electric buggies down a "time tunnel" into an authentically reconstructed 10th-century Viking village, complete with everyday sights, sounds and smells (often unpleasant ones, too). The buggies then pass through the actual excavation site. Happily, there's not a trace of Disney-like condescension, and intelligent commentaries spell out the realities of life as it was lived 1,000 years ago, intestinal worms and all.

Above ground again, you can wander through mazes of ancient alleyways, such as the **Shambles**, the former butchers' quarter. Now antiques and souvenirs clog the shop windows instead of carcasses. Some alleys are so narrow that the overhanging upper storeys of buildings on opposite sides almost touch. You can walk on top of the city walls, wide enough for horses to pass – though it can take two hours to complete the circuit on foot. Medieval timber-framed buildings, such as **Merchant Adventurers' Hall**, abound. So do antiquarian bookshops. Further out is one of the North's top racecourses.

But it is the **Minster**, Britain's largest cathedral, that dominates York. It seems to float above the city. It was built, the saying goes, over a period of 250 years, as "an act of prayer by the most practical people in the world," and costs £2 a minute to maintain. In its display of medieval stained glass, it is the equal of Chartres. When lightning struck the

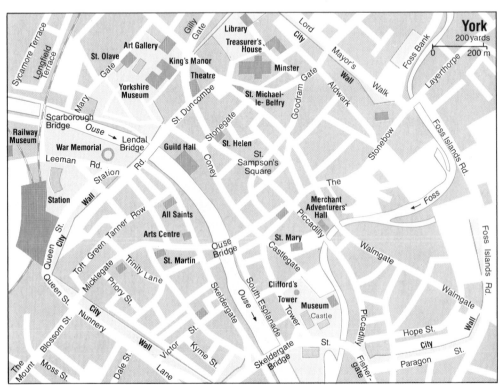

south transept in 1984, the day after a controversial bishop had been consecrated in the Minster, the devout saw the fire that followed as a divine judgment. The more practical-minded embarked on the most ambitious medieval jigsaw puzzle in the world: restoring the 8,000 pieces of 12th-century glass in the Rose Window which the fire had fractured into 40,000 fragments.

The **Yorkshire Museum** has a permanent gallery depicting Roman life in Britain. It, the Minster and the city all repay unhurried study. King George VI summed it up. "The history of York," he said, "is the history of England."

For an insight into the 18th-century at its most magnificent, drive 15 miles (24 km) northeast from York on the A64, into the Howardian Hills, to **Castle Howard**, one of the grandest houses in England. This treasure-filled creation of Sir John Vanbrugh (1664–1726) provided an opulent location for the television version of Evelyn Waugh's *Brideshead Revisited*.

Due north, on the B1363 through lanes criss-crossing high moors, woods and pastureland, are the breathtaking ruins, near **Helmsley**, of **Rievaulx Abbey**, an extensive Cistercian monastery founded in the 12th century. Ten thousand burial mounds dot the area, marking Bronze and Iron-Age graves.

The Yorkshire Riviera: Like York, the coast of the northeast reflects the history of England. Here are the distractions of Victorian watering holes and modern family resorts, and the crumbling ruins of ancient defences against invasion from Europe. Advertising copywriters foolishly dubbed the coastline "the Yorkshire Riviera" and a palm tree was ceremonially planted at the resort of Scarborough; but it soon succumbed, unlamented by locals, to salt and cold.

Nerve-centre for the "cod wars" of the 1970s, in which English and foreign trawler fleets clashed over fishing rights, was **Hull** (properly Kingston upon Hull), 38 miles (60 km) to the southeast of York. But the fishing industry is now just a part of the city's "maritime herit-

York Minster, Britain's largest cathedral.

age" to be sought out among quayside shopping malls. Rebuilding after World War II bombing has placed some striking new architecture alongside such historic buildings as **Trinity House** (1753), home of the 600-year-old Guild of Seafarers. The anti-slavery campaigner, William Wilberforce (1759–1833), a son of Hull, is commemorated.

In 1981 the surrounding area of **Humberside** was linked to the south by the world's longest single-span (4,600 ft/ 1,410 metres) suspension bridge across the Humber estuary. Yet another ferry became redundant.

By the sea to the north of Hull are lined up a series of cheap and cheerful resorts, all trying to adapt to an age in which a package tour to a Spanish *costa* can cost less than a holiday on the English coast. The first, **Hornsea**, is a small bathing resort with a neat museum, a large freshwater lake (fishing and sailing) and a popular leisure complex, **Hornsea Pottery**, with craft shops, amusements, and a bird sanctuary.

Fifteen miles (24 km) up the coast,

Bridlington is more boisterous, offering up-to-date discotheques as well as 14th-century buildings. Off the dramatic 400-ft (130-metre) cliff at nearby **Flamborough Head**, John Paul Jones won a sea battle with two English men-of-war in 1779. **Filey** offers unpretentious delights to day trippers and marks the beginning of the unsightly caravanpark pollution that disfigures many of the finer bays on the northeast coast.

Bigger still is **Scarborough**, whose eclipse as a posh watering hole is exemplified by the fate of the **Grand Hotel**, among the handsomest in Europe when it opened in 1867. Having suffered through salesmen's conventions and political party conferences, it is now run by the redcoated cheerleaders of Butlin's, a holiday camp operator. The 12th-century castle is worth seeing, though, and Anne Brontë – who, like so many invalids, came for the bracing air – is buried in the graveyard of **St Mary's Church**.

To the north, seekers after solitude can divert 5 miles (8 km) from the

Robin Hood's Bay, an old smugglers' haunt.

coastal road to find **Ravenscar**, "the resort that never was"; it has fine walks, but never developed economically beyond one rather imposing clifftop hotel. **Robin Hood's Bay**, close by, once offered sanctuary to the benign outlaw and was a haunt of smugglers. To the west, on **Fylingdales Moor**, the incongruous glass fibre domes of an early-warning station rise up, a reminder of 20th-century nuclear insecurities.

Whitby is a picturesque fishing port with little of the vulgarity of its southern neighbours. On **East Cliff** are the 13th-century remains of **Whitby Abbey**, on which site a 7th-century monk wrote the *Song* considered to mark the start of English literature. The Antarctic explorer Captain Cook (1728–79) lived in this former whaling port; his house in Grape Street is a point on a heritage trail tracing his life throughout the region. Bram Stoker's Count Dracula, "the filthy leech", came ashore at Whitby from a derelict cruiser, disguised as a monstrous black dog.

For those with less rarefied tastes than the Count, Whitby crab and kippers are worth sampling. This coastline is noted for its seafood: Bridlington for prawns, Scarborough for plaice.

Too many cars clog up Whitby during the summer. Most surrounding villages, sensibly, operate "pay and display" car parks on their fringes; keep a generous supply of 10p and 50p coins handy for visiting haunts such as **Runswick Bay**, a self-consciously pretty assortment of fishermen's cottages, and **Staithes**, where the young Cook was briefly and unhappily apprenticed to a grocer.

Across the border from north Yorkshire, in Northumbria, the lively sandy-beached resort of **Redcar** is a playground for the decaying industrial centres of **Middlesbrough, Stockton-on-Tees** and **Darlington**. The region was a Klondike in the 19th-century, as coal and iron were discovered and the railways pioneered an undreamed-of prosperity. George Stephenson's Locomotion No. 1 (1825) is displayed at Darlington's **Railway Museum**.

Sixteen miles (25 km) to the west, just

Pickering Steam Fair, near York.

southwest of the old market town of **Barnard Castle** ("Barney" to locals), the school at **Bowes** was used as a model by Dickens for the cruel Dotheboys Hall in *Nicholas Nickleby*. The château-like **Bowes Museum** has a superb collection of exhibits and paintings; artists include El Greco and Goya.

Near **Staindrop**, on the A688 to the northeast, is the commanding nine-towered **Raby Castle**, set in a 250-acre (100-hectare) deer park. To the northwest, off the B6277 near **Middleton in Teesdale**, is the impressive **High Force** waterfall, where the river Tees, bottlenecked, crashes down 70 ft (23 metres). There are reservoirs which one can sail on; otherwise, **Teesdale** has been described as an area of outstanding natural bleakness.

Nineteen miles (30 km) north of Darlington, **Durham** is a university city maintaining a scholarly, almost medieval, air. It has a very fine Romanesque cathedral and the only castle in the north never to fall to the marauding Scots. Until 1836, the militant prince-bishops of Durham were granted complete sovereignty within their diocese, holding their own parliaments and minting their own coins.

A few miles farther north, heavy industry abruptly changes the landscape. **Sunderland** is a grimy shipbuilding town, though it has sandy beaches too. Most American visitors head 5 miles (8 km) westwards to **Washington** and the Old Hall, ancestral home of the USA's first president; a collection of family relics is on show.

Dominating the area is one of Britain's workshops, **Newcastle upon Tyne**. It is a sprawling shipbuilding city, celebrated for its resilient natives ("Geordies"), whose dialect borders on impenetrability, and for its potent brew, Newcastle Brown (pronounced *Broon*) Ale. Just as a true Cockney must be born within sound of Bow Bells, so the true Geordie must be born within sound of Armstrong's factory horn.

No town prospered more from the Industrial Revolution – its streets were the first in Europe to be lit by electricity

Bamburgh Castle on Northumberland's dramatic coast.

– and few have suffered more in recent years. Too many drab old dwellings remain, but spanking new high-rise offices have also sprung up, and Newcastle likes to remind visitors that it is the third home (after Stratford and London) of the Royal Shakespeare Company.

Its castle, begun by Henry II in 1172, testifies to the strategic importance of the site. This was first recognised by the Romans who founded the city as a minor fort and bridge on **Hadrians's Wall**. The Roman fort of **Arbeia** has been excavated at nearby **South Shields**.

Fearing that such ancient attractions would be insufficient bait for modern tourists, the South Shields city fathers have created "Catherine Cookson Country"; one problem is that many of the slums she graphically describes in her novels have been pulled down.

Hadrian's Wall itself, 15 ft high and 7½ ft thick (5 metres by 2.5 metres), snakes westwards across the Border country for 73 miles (117 km). It has several easy points of access from the A69. Just above Hexham **Chesters** is a beautiful site, occupied by a military bath-house and headquarters building. A few miles further west **Housesteads** (Vercovicium) is a well-preserved fort and nearby **Vindolanda** has been extensively excavated.

The fortified town of **Alnwick**, 34 miles (54 km) to the north of Newcastle, has one of Britain's best examples of a medieval fortress on an extremely large scale. The castle, though none too sensitively restored with an Italian Renaissance interior, radiates power and enabled the Percy family to exercise it over northeast England for 600 years.

Also stunning, **Bamburgh Castle** sits inviolably on a clifftop 16 miles (25 km) to the north. It has a good weapons collection and tapestries. From here, on a clear day, you can see the **Farne Islands**, 4½ miles (7 km) offshore. Monks from Iona settled on **Lindisfarne** (also known as Holy Island) in the 7th century, turning it into a centre of scholarship renowned throughout Europe. The island, which can be reached at low tide by a 3-mile (5-km) causeway, has a small fairy-like castle dating

from 1550. Birdwatchers also flock to see the islands' breeding grounds.

On the border between England and Scotland, the old seaport and fishing town of **Berwick upon Tweed** is no longer a shuttlecock between the two nations. From 1147 to 1482 alone, it changed hands 13 times. On the 2-mile (3.5 km) walk along the top of the best-preserved example of Elizabethan ramparts, among the first in Europe designed to incorporate cannons, you can gaze down into its twisting cobbled streets and out towards the salmon fisheries and shore-line.

History suffuses the stone of Berwick. The trouble is that the stones had to be reassembled after each successive border war had scattered them. As a result, few really old buildings survive in this, the most northerly town in England. As if in sympathy with its blood-stained history, the surrounding landscape seems uncommonly brooding. Heathcliff, somebody once suggested, would have taken a break here when Wuthering Heights got too summery.

Lindisfarne Castle can be reached only at low tide.

THE LAKE DISTRICT

The Lake District in northeast England covers a small area, measuring scarcely more than 30 miles (48 km) from north to south and 20 miles (32 km) east to west. But the poet William Wordsworth, who was born here at Cockermouth in 1770 and spent most of his life in the region, rightly remarked: "I do not know any tract of country in which, within so narrow a compass, may be found an equal variety in the influences of light and shadow upon the sublime or beautiful features of landscape." The landscape is indeed beautiful, with the varied treasures of soft hills and woodland, the lengthy panoramas of the great lakes, the unexpected discoveries of the smaller waters or tarns, the bare contours of the fells and high ground and the awe-inspiring power of the more remote mountains and mountain passes.

The Lake District is 250 miles (400 km) from London and 75 miles (120 km) north of Manchester and it is more frequently visited by day tourists and holidaymakers than any other region of outstanding natural beauty in the British Isles. Fortunately it has proven remarkably able to cope with the vastly increased numbers that have visited it since the motorway system reached it in the early 1970s.

The two routes which were popularised by the first tourists in the 1760s and 1770s still carry the greatest share of summer traffic. One is from Penrith to Ambleside by the west shore of Ullswater (scene of Wordsworth's poem *The Daffodils*) and over the Kirkstone Pass, now the A592; the other is from Keswick to Windermere by the side of Thirlmere, Grasmere, Rydal Water and Lake Windermere, now the A591.

Away from these it remains possible to find areas of great beauty. Here you can experience for a time the sense of aloneness with nature which the first visitors and the poets of the early 19th-century Romantic period (Wordsworth and Samuel Taylor Coleridge) valued so highly.

Sheep and shopping: The central area of mountains was never much affected by industry or quarrying, and the 19th-century developments in shipbuilding, iron manufacturing, coal mining and lesser trades that once flourished by the Cumberland coast have now almost entirely disappeared. Sheep farming was the traditional way of life of the hill folk, and it continues today throughout the area covered by the Lake District National Park, often on farms owned and leased by the National Trust. The wool of the Herdwick and Swaledale sheep, the most popular breeds kept on these farms, provides the material for many of the most attractive garments on sale in the gift shops of the area.

From the time of the first Lake District guidebook, Thomas West's *Guide to the Lakes* of 1778, the pleasures of the area have remained those of the eye; the landscape is what matters most. In the early 19th century, visitors began to walk the high paths over the fells, and after about 1860 they started to climb the more difficult rock faces. Climbers

Preceding pages: old-fashioned boating on Lake Windermere. The Lake District's incomparable countryside (below) gives pleasure to thousands every year.

still congregate in **Great Langdale**, **Borrowdale** and **Wasdale** to tackle the central heights of the **Langdales**, **Scafell Crags**, **Great Gable**, **Steeple** and **Pillar**. There are hundreds of miles of paths to tempt the walker. Paths over the high fells must be tackled with respect for the region's notoriously rapid changes of weather, and with the proper equipment, but there are innumerable easy walks by the lakesides or along the streams which anyone can enjoy. Walking is the best way to witness the constant change of scene which is so characteristic of this small but endlessly varied district.

In recent years the Lake District has developed a greater range of places of interest for visitors. Most of these are museums, preserving the history of the area, but they vary from permanent displays and houses to working mills and steam railways.

Approaching the Lake District from the south by means of the M6, a turn off at junction 35 just above Lancaster for **Carnforth** leads to **Steamtown** with its preserved locomotives and railway relics. A little further north on the A6 lie two country houses. **Levens Hall**, a largely 16th-century house with a famous topiary garden, is little changed since its trees were first shaped in the 17th century. **Sizergh Castle** shows its origins as a medieval defensive structure even more clearly.

Kendal, a good centre for the Lakes, is approached from junction 36 on the M6. The Lake District poet Norman Nicholson describes it as "the best example in the Lakes of a town which has held on to its true character and refused to decline into a mere holiday centre." It is, indeed, still a working town, all the more fascinating for carrying on in the midst of fine 17th and 18th-century buildings. Among these buildings are old coaching inns and a horn shop which sells locally manufactured items in this ancient material. The church is a fine, unusually broad Perpendicular building. Beside it stands **Abbot Hall**, a mid-17th-century house which now displays a remarkable collection of furniture, china and paintings by local artists, in

particular George Romney. There is also a room filled with watercolours by John Ruskin which may be unrivalled. Abbot Hall also houses the **Museum of Lakeland Life and Industry**, which has a room devoted to the *Swallows and Amazons* author Arthur Ransom (1884–1967). Kendal has still another gallery to offer: the exhibition gallery at the **Brewery Arts Centre** where concerts and plays also take place.

Home of the Wordsworths: The A591 runs from Kendal to **Windermere**. Below the town lies **Bowness**, with a pretty village centre unfortunately almost always too crowded for comfort. At Bowness, boats depart for **Belle Isle**, with the handsome late 18th-century circular house of the same name. Also at Bowness is the car ferry to **Beatrix Potter's House** at Sawrey, a fine example of a traditional Lakeland farmhouse.

In Main Street in nearby **Hawkshead** is the **Beatrix Potter Gallery** in the former office of her husband, a solicitor. It has displays of many of the original drawings from her famous children's

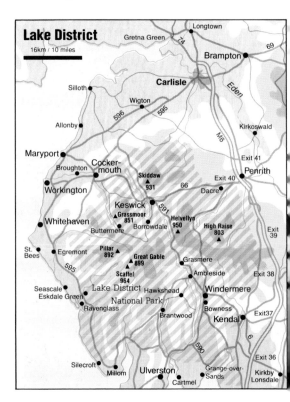

books. Wordsworth studied at the ancient grammar school at Hawkshead and lodged with an elderly lady in the village. Later, he lodged at nearby **Colthouse**, close to the bare but imposing late 17th-century Quaker meeting house, which still stands.

The old grammar school at Hawkshead is now a museum. Downstairs, it suggests little of the excellence of its teaching in the 1780s when Wordsworth and his brothers studied there. But upstairs is a superb library with books dating back to the foundation of the school by Archbishop Sandys in Elizabeth I's reign. The church preserves wall paintings of scriptural texts. From beneath its east window you can take in the view of this tiny, whitewashed town with its close-packed lanes and the occasional house still keeping the spinning gallery where the women would sit to work.

South of Hawkshead lies **Esthwaite Lake**, which Wordsworth would walk round in the mornings before classes began. Close to Hawkshead stands the medieval arched **Courthouse**, a relic of the times when the Cistercian monks from Cartmel ruled much of the southern part of the area.

Whether you continue towards the head of Lake Windermere on this west side, or take the eastern road from Windermere to Ambleside, you will eventually follow the Keswick road to Rydal Water. **Rydal Hall** was famous in the early days of tourism for its waterfalls, painted by Joseph Wright and John Constable, among others. Across the road lies **Rydal Mount**, home of the Wordsworths from 1813 until William died in 1850. The house contains portraits and family mementoes; the grounds are laid out in their original form and the views from their higher reaches are fine. **Rydal Chapel** contains memorials to the family of Dr Arnold, who built a summer home nearby.

Two miles (3 km) north lies **Grasmere Lake**. The southernmost part of the village, **Town End,** is where the poet and his sister Dorothy first settled in 1799. The white cottage is movingly

Lake Windermere, 10 miles long, is the main tourist centre.

simple in its furnishings, but it takes the display of manuscripts and portraits of the poet's family and friends in the nearby **Grasmere and Wordsworth Museum** to bring home the magnitude of the poetry which was written here and the importance which Wordsworth and Coleridge held in the cultural life of their day.

Grasmere Church is a plain, roughly built structure with a remarkable and much-altered ancient timber roof. The Wordsworth family graves and that of Coleridge's son Hartley lie behind it. All about are the paths, streams and hills which Dorothy Wordworth described along with the daily life of **Dove Cottage** (included with a visit to the museum), in her 1800–02 *Journal*. Behind the old **Swan Inn**, where the road through the village joins the way to Keswick, lies **Greenhead Ghyll**, the sombre valley that is the setting of Wordsworth's poem *Michael*.

Pencils for poets: The 17-miles (28-km) A591 to Keswick passes **Thirlmere**, a lake often compared with those in Switzerland. It is, in fact, largely man-made, the result of the building of a dam in the 1880s to provide additional water for Manchester and the great cities of the northwest. The coniferous trees that were then planted have now matured to present a handsome but not very Lakeland scene. **Helvellyn**, the third highest mountain in England (3,118 ft/950 metres), snowcapped for much of the year, lies to the right.

Close to Keswick you may turn off to **Castlerigg Stone Circle**, an ancient monument commanding tremendous views, which the early tourists associated with the Druids. Recent writers think the stones may have been intended as a giant calendar to show by its shadows the return of the seasons for planting and reaping. There are similar monuments at **Great Salkeld**, near Penrith (known as "Long Meg and her Daughters") and at **Swinside**, near Broughton-in Furness.

Keswick, a Victorian town with an older centre, has been popular with visitors since the 1760s, when the poet

Castlerigg Stone Circle, near Keswick.

Thomas Gray stayed there to explore its lake, **Derwentwater.** With fear and trembling, Gray ventured to the mouth of mountain-surrounded **Borrowdale,** just past the southern end of the lake, which early visitors associated with the sublimity and terror of Salvator Rosa's paintings. Even today one might fear that the tottering pinnacles will detach themselves and fall upon one's head. A favourite excursion since Gray's time is the **Powder Stone,** a little way up the valley. The giant stone still stands balanced on the side of the hill, although there is no longer an old lady selling refreshments. But the stone and the other early attraction, the waterfall at **Lodore,** near the head of Derwentwater, are still worth seeing.

Borrowdale was famed among the early tourists for the "wad" or black lead mine which enabled the manufacture of pencils in Keswick where there is a **Pencil Museum.** But Keswick is now best known for its association with writers rather than the means of writing. The **Fitz Park Museum** has mementoes of Coleridge, Robert Southey and Hugh Walpole, who lived nearby, and whose "Rogue Herries" novels are set in and around the area.

Coleridge settled at **Greta Hall** on the outskirts of Keswick in 1800 and persuaded his brother-in-law Southey to join him there. Coleridge soon left the area, but his family stayed on, along with the Southeys, for many years. **Crossthwaite Church,** which stands about half-a-mile beyond Greta Hall, has memorials to Southey and members of his family. Thomas Gray described the view from outside the parsonage as one which, if it could be captured "in all the softness of its living colours, would fairly sell for a thousand pounds." Northwards, the churchyard looks towards **Bassenthwaite Lake,** the eastern side of which is dominated by Skiddaw (3,054 ft/917 metres).

Beneath the mountain lies **Mirehouse,** the 18th-century home of the Spedding family. James Spedding was a friend of the prolific 19th-century poet, Alfred Tennyson, who visited the house and

Below, Wordsworth's Dove Cottage. Right, Dalemain Castle.

incorporated its view of the lake into his poem *Morte D'Arthur*.

Castles 'gainst the Scot: A 15-mile (24-km) drive eastwards from Keswick on the A66 to the interesting old town of **Penrith** can incorporate a visit to **Dacre**, a few miles before the town on the right. It has a largely Norman church, even earlier carvings and views of 14th-century **Dacre Castle**. Nearby is **Dalemain,** an old house last altered in 1750 that offers fine interiors (including a Chinese drawing room with original mid-18th-century wallpaper), paintings and a pleasant garden.

In the other direction the A66 westward from Keswick leads after 15 miles (24 km) to **Cockermouth** and a smaller house of the same elegant period, the **Wordsworth House** in Main Street, where William and Dorothy spent their earliest years. The furniture and pictures are not those of the time when the poet's lawyer father lived in it, but they are well chosen and the total effect is handsome. The garden, with its terrace walk looking over the beautiful river Derwent (recollected in *The Prelude*), should also be visited.

Cockermouth is an old-fashioned stone-built town stretching along a lengthy main street, very like the towns on the opposite side of the Scottish border. The road south runs through Lorton Vale to two more of the lakes, **Crummock Water** and **Buttermere**. The southeasterly road rises over the Whinlatter Pass and crosses Thornthwaite Forest back to Keswick. Both roads afford fine views of the bleak, high fells.

Before leaving northern Lakeland two other places of interest must be mentioned. **Brougham Castle**, just southeast of Penrith, is a Norman castle built on the foundations of a Roman fort. It was one of the strongholds of the famous Clifford family, one of whose members, the Lady Ann Clifford, made remarkable restorations on her various homes in the region in the mid-17th century. The ruins here are impressive: the top gallery of the keep has fine views and is worth the effort of climbing.

Green pastures near Lake Bassenthwaite.

Carlisle also deserves an excursion. The **Castle** here obtained its unusual outline when its roof was strengthened to carry early cannons. Inside, its prison cells have wall carvings cut by their inmates in the 16th and 17th centuries. The **Castle Museum and Art Gallery** houses an important collection of Roman materials connected with Hadrian's Wall, while later exhibits include paintings by Edward Burne-Jones and other pre-Raphaelites. The **Cathedral**, with its curiously shortened Norman nave, has old woodwork in the chancel along with interesting monuments.

Roman hairpins: Southwest Lakeland is rich in interest. One of the most dramatic sites of all is best approached on the Windermere-based "Mountain Goat" mini-coach service by anyone lacking both an extremely agile car and nerves of steel. The road over the Wrynose and Hardknott passes, 10 miles (16 km) west of Ambleside, was improved by the Romans, but they probably intended their narrow road with its hairpin bends and sheer drops for pedestrians only. In summer traffic conditions it can now be somewhat hazardous. But the situation of **Hardknott Roman Fort**, high above **Eskdale**, with its view of the highest peaks and the distant sea, is unforgettable. Eskdale's mines and quarries were the reason for the construction of the **Ravenglass and Eskdale Railway**, a narrow-gauge line which now delights summer tourists with its beautifully maintained miniature steam engines. The line runs for about 18 miles (28 km) through lush scenery. From **Eskdale Green** a road runs over Birker Fell to the **Duddon Valley**, still relatively unknown to visitors and an area of great natural beauty. It was Wordsworth's favourite valley.

Ravenglass, on the coast, lies close to **Muncaster Water Mill**, a restored water-driven corn mill, in which the visitor can watch the production of stoneground flour. Nearby is **Muncaster Castle**, home of the Pennington family since 1325, when a new tower was built on the foundations of a Roman watchtower commanding extensive views of

Below, Ravenglass and Eskdale Railway. Left, two happy tourists.

the fells and Eskdale. Henry VI sought refuge here and is said to have given his drinking bowl, the "Luck of Muncaster", to his host, Sir John Pennington. The bowl is still in the house which, in the course of 18th and 19th-century alterations, has grown from a medieval tower into an attractive mansion. The furnishings are, not surprisingly, good. The castle is now the centre of the British "owl release scheme", but the chief glory is the garden with its quarter-mile long terrace overlooking the valley and its vast expanse of azaleas, camelias and rhododendrons.

Abbey lands: The southern tip of Lakeland, once part of Lancashire, was in medieval days the heart of the great Cistercian estate farmed by the monks of **Furness Abbey**. The abbey was the second richest Cistercian establishment in England at the time of its suppression in 1537. Its buildings date from the 12th and 15th centuries and the impressive ruins in the Vale of the Deadly Nightshade, on the northside of the shipbuilding town of Barrow-in-Furness, lie in a

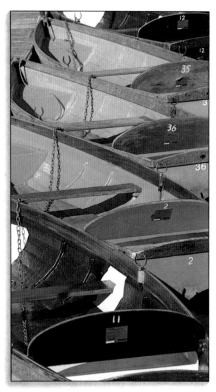

setting of great loveliness. To the east is **Cartmel Priory**, near the resort of Grange-over-Sands on a finger of land pointing down into Morecambe Bay. It was founded in 1188 by the Baron of Cartmel and it was saved at the time of the dissolution of the monasteries by the quick-wittedness of local people who claimed that it was, in fact, their parish church. The tower is unusual; the upper part is set diagonally across the lower stage. Inside there is good medieval carving and old glass. The village setting is attractive

Returning northward, the visitor approaches Windermere and, to the west, **Coniston Water**. Between the two lies **Grizedale Forest Park**, a large tract of land the Forestry Commission has imaginatively given over to nature trails, jolly modern sculptures and a 23-seat theatre. Coniston was made famous by the world water speed record attempts of Donald Campbell, who died in the last of them in 1967. Earlier, Coniston was famous for the residence of John Ruskin (1819–1900), the great art historian and writer on social and economic themes of Victorian times. At **Brantwood**, on the northeast shore, many of Ruskin's own paintings are preserved, and the house remains much as he left it. The grounds, with their dramatic views of lake and fell, have recently been improved and developed. On the lake, the Victorian steam yacht *Gondola* operates once again, with all the elegance of a Tissot painting, after lying for nearly 40 years in shallow water close to the shore.

Other mementoes from the age of steam are at the **Windermere Steamboat Museum** in Bowness-on-Windermere (including the steam-launch *Dolly* of 1850, supposed to be the oldest mechanically powered boat in the world) and on the **Haverthwaite and Lakeside Steam Railway**, which runs in season from the foot of the lake.

The **Tarns** is considered by many to be the prettiest in the Lake District. Only a half-mile long, the lake (originally three smaller lakes but joined as the result of the construction of a dam) is 2 miles (3 km) above Coniston.

Left, lake transport. **Right,** Cartmel Priory, Ulverston.

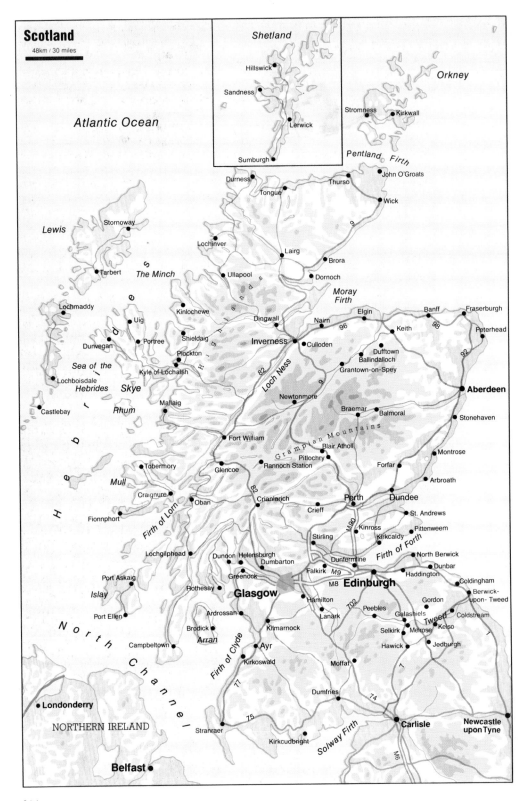

Scotland

48km / 30 miles

Shetland

Orkney

Atlantic Ocean

Hillswick
Sandness
Lerwick
Sumburgh
Stromness
Kirkwall

Pentland Firth

Durness
Tongue
Thurso
John O'Groats
Wick

Lewis
Stornoway

The Minch
Tarbert

Lochinver
Lairg
Brora
Ullapool
Dornoch

Moray Firth

Lochmaddy
Uig
Kinlochewe
Dingwall
Nairn
Elgin
Banff
Fraserburgh

Dunvegan
Portree
Shieldaig
Plockton
Inverness
Culloden
Keith
Peterhead

Sea of the
Hebrides
Lochboisdale
Kyle of Lochalsh
Skye

Dufftown
Ballindalloch
Grantown-on-Spey

Castlebay
Rhum
Mallaig
Loch Ness
Newtonmore

Aberdeen

Fort William
Braemar
Balmoral
Stonehaven

Tobermory
Glencoe
Grampian Mountains
Blair Atholl
Montrose

Mull
Craignure
Oban
Rannoch Station
Pitlochry
Forfar
Arbroath

Fionnphort
Firth of Lorn
Crianlarich
Crieff
Perth
Dundee

Lochgilphead
Dunoon Helensburgh
Dumbarton
Stirling
Kinross
Kirkcaldy
St. Andrews
Pittenweem

Port Askaig
Rothesay
Greenock
Dunfermline
Falkirk
Firth of Forth
North Berwick
Dunbar

Islay
Glasgow
Hamilton
Edinburgh
Haddington
Coldingham
Berwick-upon-Tweed

Port Ellen
Ardrossan
Lanark
Peebles
Gordon
Coldstream
Tweed

Arran
Brodick
Kilmarnock
Selkirk
Galashiels
Melrose
Kelso

Campbeltown
Ayr
Kirkoswald
Moffat
Hawick
Jedburgh

North Channel

Firth of Clyde

Londonderry
NORTHERN IRELAND
Stranraer
Kirkcudbright
Dumfries
Solway Firth
Carlisle
Newcastle upon Tyne

Belfast

THE SCOTTISH LOWLANDS

Scotland is a separate experience. The Scots themselves have a sense of identity, of different values, and of their own history and traditions unparalleled in Great Britain. Even though they relinquished their independence to England in 1707, they have maintained their own legal and educational systems, which are widely regarded as superior to those in England, and they still print their own design of bank notes – often the first clue to visitors that they are in a different part of Britain.

The region occupies the north of the country, starting just past the border established by the Roman emperor Hadrian in AD 122–6 when he built his wall to keep out the painted Celtic warriors, the Picts and Scots. At 30,405 sq. miles (78,749 sq. metres) it makes up about one-third of Great Britain, yet its population is less than one-tenth, of which more than 30 percent live in or around the three most populous cities, Glasgow, Edinburgh and Aberdeen.

Aberdeen, on the northeast coast, boomed in the 1970s with the discovery of North Sea oil. Glasgow and Edinburgh, stimulating but quite different cities, lie only 45 miles (70 km) apart at opposite sides of the Lowlands, hidden from England by the rolling Cheviot Hills and a breather before the dramatic hurdles of the Highlands. Both cities are about 380 miles (610 km) from London. Trains from London start from Euston and King's Cross, taking under five hours, and a "shuttle" air service from Heathrow airport is used by some businessmen like a commuter train.

Scotland's capital city: Edinburgh, on the south bank of the Firth (estuary) of Forth, did not become the capital of Scotland until the reign of David I (1124–53). Previously the capital had been further north on the edge of the Highlands, at Scone near Perth, where Scottish kings were crowned, seated on the Stone of Destiny (now in Westminster Abbey) and latterly at Dunfermline just the other side of the Forth in Fife.

There is evidence of an Iron-Age settlement on Arthur's Seat, the rocky outcrop behind the royal Palace of Holyroodhouse, and there was a Pictish stronghold as early as the 5th century on the rock on which Edinburgh Castle now stands.

Between the hills and the sea, Edinburgh has one of the most beautiful settings in the world. Whichever way you arrive – emerging from the tunnelled cavern of Waverley Station, driving in from the airport or motoring up from the English border through the rich farmlands and windswept golf courses of East Lothian – you end up in **Princes Street**, the heart of the city and one of the most dramatic thoroughfares in Europe.

Southward, across the gardens which were once the Nor' Loch, rises the basalt ridge of rock on which medieval Edinburgh is built. The **Castle** rides in the sky, often against a background of torn cloud, and the spires and turrets and crenellations of the Old Town spike the skyline from the Castle battlements to

the hidden Palace of Holyroodhouse below the green hill of Arthur's Seat.

In the Castle is Edinburgh's oldest building, the tiny **Queen Margaret's Chapel**, built for the saintly wife of King Malcolm Canmore by her son, David. There is also the Scottish crown, sceptre and sword of state, the oldest royal regalia in Europe. The imposing **Great Hall** is still used for banquets and has one of the finest hammerbeam ceilings in Britain. You can also visit the tiny room where in 1566 Mary Queen of Scots gave birth to James VI of Scotland, who, as James I, was the first Stuart king of England.

The Royal Mile that runs from the vast esplanade in front of the Castle (where the spectacular Tattoo is held during the Edinburgh Festival in August) was the mainstream of Edinburgh life until the end of the 18th century and is still lively today. Along its descending route are some of the finest surviving examples of 16th and 17th-century houses in Britain, courtier's houses for the most part, leading to the Royal Palace of Holyroodhouse at the foot. On the way there is much to look out for: **Parliament House**, now the law courts; **Mowbray House**, dating from the 15th century and probably the oldest inhabited house in the city; the great crown-steepled **High Kirk of St Giles**; the **house of John Knox**, the ruthless Protestant reformer who debated theology and the place of women in society with the young and spirited Mary Queen of Scots, at Holyrood; the 16th-century **Canongate Tolbooth** and the fine 17th-century **Canongate Kirk**. In the graveyard of this church are buried many notable Edinburgh folk, among them Nancie Maclehose (1749–1857), the "passionate friend" of the no doubt equally passionate Robert Burns, and the founder of the science of political economy, Adam Smith (1723–90), the author of *The Wealth of Nations*.

At the bottom of the Royal Mile lies the **Palace of Holyroodhouse** the official residence of Her Majesty the Queen when she is in Scotland. Begun in 1498 by James IV, it was enlarged in the

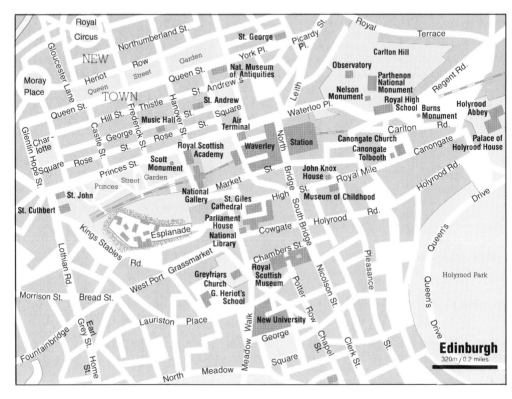

following century by James V and later by Charles II. Mary Queen of Scots lived here for six years, and in one of the still-existing rooms in the Palace her Italian secretary, David Rizzio, was murdered on 9 March 1566 in a conspiracy which was led by the Queen's husband, Lord Darnley. Darnley himself died a few months later in a mysterious explosion at a house barely a mile away.

Bonnie Prince Charlie held a ball in the palace when his troops occupied the city during the Jacobite Rebellion of 1745. He was the last of the Stuarts to live there. For years Holyroodhouse was neglected but it returned to royal favour when George IV held a lêvée there while visiting Scotland in 1822. The state apartments have some fine French and Flemish tapestries and 18th-century furniture. The Throne Room is still used by the Queen for investitures.

Narrow *wynds* (alleys) twist downwards off the Royal Mile throughout its length, like ribs off a spine. Through them, framed between the high buildings, are glimpses of the Pentland Hills to the south, the North Sea to the east and the dark silver estuary of the River Forth and the green hills of Fife across the **New Town** to the north.

New Town is a graceful complex of streets, squares and crescents north of Princes Street, on the far side of the valley below the Castle. This is a splendid 18th-century example of town planning, described by the *Pelican History of Arts* as "the most extensive example of a Romantic Classical city in the world". The elegant Georgian facades are a pleasure, an ordered rapture which is in marked contrast to the medieval chaos of the Old Town on the volcanic ridge. This intriguing architectural juxtaposition is matched by no other city in Europe. At **The Georgian House**, 7 Charlotte Square, the National Trust for Scotland has reconstructed, in part, how the first residents of these houses must have lived.

Edinburgh is the gastronomic as well as the administrative capital of Scotland. Several lively pubs in the Royal

Edinburgh Castle, looking out across the city to the Firth of Forth.

Mile and in the Grassmarket, the vast ancient square 500 ft (150 metres) below the Castle to the south, provide cheerful drinking, some with music. Robert Burns and William Wordsworth stayed at **The White Hart Inn** in the Grassmarket on their visits to Edinburgh. **Deacon Brodie's Tavern**, on the corner of the Royal Mile and The Mound, commemorates one of Edinburgh's most notorious characters, a respected cabinetmaker and town councillor by day and a burglar by night, on whom Robert Louis Stevenson based *Dr Jekyll and Mr Hyde*.

Rose Street, the lane between Princes Street and George Street, could at one time boast it had 22 pubs, but in recent years they have been slowly replaced by boutiques. The feat of drinking a pint in each of them, which was once a ritual for many rugby fans after international matches at Murrayfield, still takes a bit of doing. The prettiest and one of the best pubs is the **Abbotsford** at the east end, with its fine carved-oak bar. Edinburgh's *jeunesse*

dorée drink at **The Tilted Wig** in Cumberland Street in the New Town, which is open all day.

Edinburgh has more restaurants listed in the food guides per head of population (480,000) than any other city in Britain, and there is a wide choice of international cuisine. There is good Scots food at **Martin's** in Rose Street North Lane (imaginative use of local ingredients); **Mackintosh's,** in Stafford Street, (Charles Rennie Mackintosh decor); **Jackson's** in Jackson's Close is handy when shopping in the Royal Mile; the **Magnum** on the corner of Albany Street and Dublin Street heading north from Princes Street; **The Witchery** by the castle is fun.

It is tempting to linger in this city of particular and original enchantment and to explore all its museums and art galleries (including the **National Gallery of Scotland** in The Mound), antique shops and sporting facilities (28 golf courses within the city boundaries alone). And of course anyone coming in late August and early September will

Edinburgh's granite streetscape.

have one of the world's greatest arts festivals for entertainment.

South to the Borders: Beyond the Pentlands, the Moorfoots and the Lammermuir Hills, which ring Edinburgh to the south, lie the **Borders.** This is Scotland along the frontier with England, north of the Cheviot Hills and the Rivers Esk and Tweed, the first part of the land to encounter the Romans, the Angles and the English on their fruitless thrusts into the north. Today, it is gentle pastoral country with rolling green hills and bright clear streams where the industries are still farming, knitwear and tweed, and the passions are for trout and salmon fishing and rugby football, of which the Border towns are the great Scottish stronghold.

Sir Walter Scott (1771–1832) settled in a handsome house overlooking the River Tweed at **Abbotsford** outside Galashiels, 36 miles (44 km) south of Edinburgh on the A7. His family were Border people, and his romantic imagination was first stirred by the derring-do of his ancestors defending their land against England, the Auld Enemy, and the minstrelsy and ballads which they inspired. Abbotsford, still owned by one of Scott's descendants, is full of memorials of the author. It also has a handsome collection of historical relics, armour and weapons, among them Rob Roy's gun and Montrose's sword and a *quaich* (drinking bowl) which belonged to Bonnie Prince Charlie.

Two miles (3 km) past Abbotsford on the A68 is the charming town of **Melrose**, set beneath the triple mounds of the Eildon Hills, the haunt of the poet and seer Thomas the Rhymer (c1220–97) and the Queen of Elfland. On the easternmost of its breast-shaped summits is a Roman fort. From the highest hill is a breathtaking view of the Cheviots and the hills running westward towards Galloway. In the town itself lie the impressive ruins of the 12th-century **Melrose Abbey,** despite its final sacking by the English in 1544, still an architectural poem in red sandstone. Melrose is an agreeable little town from which to take walks on the Eildon Hills,

Fly fishing in the Borders.

to fish or explore the Borders. A more modern fame is that its rugby club invented the game of seven-a-side rugby, contested all over the world but nowhere with more enthusiasm than in this clutch of Border towns: Melrose, Galashiels, Hawick and Selkirk. There are fine medieval abbeys nearby at **Dryburgh,** 4 miles (6 km) beyond Melrose, where Scott is buried, at **Kelso**, 10 miles (16 km) east on the A699, and at **Jedburgh** 8 miles (13 km) south of Dryburgh on the A68.

There are also several impressive stately homes, such as **Floors Castle,** the seat of the Duke of Roxburgh, just outside Kelso. One of the Duke of Buccleuch's houses, **Bowhill,** is near Selkirk, and the Adam house of **Mellerstain** is on the A6089 Kelso to Gordon road. All three have outstanding collections of paintings and furniture and Mellerstain has some of the finest Adam ceilings in Britain. At Coldstream, Scottish and English armies once forded the Tweed. The town lent its name to the Coldstream Guards raised for Cromwell's army and a crack regiment today.

The Borders has plenty of small hotels offering solid comfort and plain, well-cooked food. One which climbs firmly above this category is **Cringletie House Hotel**, a few miles north of **Peebles** off the A703. Run by the McGuires for more than 20 years, it is a luxurious mansion house with exceptionally high standards of cuisine.

The Firth of Forth: On the coast of the **Lothians** east of Edinburgh, the country is different once again, with wide lush farmland beyond the Lammermuir Hills and some of the finest golf courses in Britain – Muirfield, North Berwick, Longkniddry, Luffness, the three Gullane courses, Kilspindie and Dunbar. In **Gullane**, 15 miles (24 km) east of the city along the coastal A198, is one of Scotland's best restaurants, **La Potiniére**, tiny but worth the trouble to book reservations (tel: 0620 843214). In the lovely Edwin Lutyens house at nearby **Greywalls,** right on the ninth fairway of Muirfield, is a sumptuously

A game of rugby beside Jedburgh Abbey.

comfortable and elegant hotel with a fine restaurant.

There is good bird-watching just to the southwest, at **Aberlady Bay**, with splendid dune-backed long sweeps of sandy beach to stroll, and lots of castles to explore, like **Tantallon**, an imposing ruin on a rocky headland above the North Sea off the A198 between North Berwick and Dunbar. **Dirleton Castle** is on the same road in the delightful village of that name between Gullane and North Berwick.

Six miles (10 km) inland near **Haddington** is **Lennoxlove,** the seat of the Duke of Hamilton. Haddington, with its carefully restored 17th and 18th-century houses, is worth a visit, and there is a signposted walk through the town. Just outside East Linton, 7 miles (11 km) east on the A1, is **Preston Mill**, which dates from the 16th century and is the oldest mechanically working, water-driven meal mill in Scotland.

St Abb's Head, above Eyemouth some 20 miles (32 km) southeast on the A1, is an impressive headland jutting into the North Sea with 300-ft (90-metre) cliffs, and there is a bird sanctuary. Colonies of kittiwakes, guillemots, shags, fulmars, herring gulls and razorbills nest here. Offshore at St Abb's is a marine nature reserve with some of the best scuba-diving water on the Scottish coast. Divers must get a permit from the Ranger.

Across the wide, pewter-coloured estuary of the Firth of Forth lies **Fife**, or "the kingdom of Fife" as it is still so arrogantly known from its days of insistent independence. "It taks a lang spoon tae sup with a Fifer," they say, giving the Fifer the same canny accolade as the Devil. Coal mines and industry are ubiquitous here and, although the countryside is not dramatic in structure, it has its own character and charm and even a few surprises. On its western fringes along the north bank of the Forth, upriver towards Stirling, lies the village of **Culross**. This is an ancient royal burgh which traded in coal, salt and griddle pans for making scones. Today it has some of the best-preserved

Pittenweem on Fife's easternmost promontory.

and most picturesque small-town buildings from the 16th and 17th centuries in Scotland.

To the east is **Dunfermline**, the ancient Scottish capital with its splendid 12th-century abbey in which Scotland's liberator, King Robert the Bruce, was buried in 1329. Also in Dunfermline is the museum of the birthplace of Andrew Carnegie (1835–1918), the poor weaver's son who became America's greatest steel baron and one of the world's great philanthropists. On the south coast of the Neuk of Fife, the easternmost promontory, are the picturesque fishing ports of **Earlsferry, St Monance, Pittenweem, Anstruther** and **Crail**. These are harbours still bobbing with the swaying masts of boats trawling what's left of the riches of the North Sea, hugged by quaint old fishermen's houses.

Inland is **Falkland Palace**, the hunting lodge of the Stuarts from James IV to Mary Queen of Scots; the elegant **House of Tarvit** with its fine collection of furniture, tapestries and paintings;

and the 14th-century **Kellie Castle**. But certainly the most famous town in Fife is **St Andrews**. This is the home of golf and the famous Old Course on which the game has been played for around 800 years. It is also the site of one of the oldest universities in Britain (founded in 1412) and the imposing grey town has many fine buildings. St Andrews was once the ecclesiastical capital of Scotland and John Knox preached his first sermon here. Its ruined castle is on a rock looking out to sea.

Glasgow's miles better: The Scottish **Lowlands** is divided into west and east almost as rigorously by character as by geography. Easterners regard themselves as people of taste and refinement, appropriately reflected in the ordered glory of Georgian Edinburgh. The westerners of Glasgow consider themselves warm-hearted, less pretentious and more realistic than what they call the "east-windy, west-endy" scions of the Scottish capital.

Like most long-cherished generalities, such definitions, through a haze of

St Andrew's, Britain's premier golf course.

good-natured local patriotism, do contain a grain of truth. There is something austere in Edinburgh's beauty and this, at times, is reflected in its citizens who are unlike the Glaswegian as portrayed by the comedian Billy Connolly.

Glasgow straddles the River Clyde 14 miles (22 km) from the estuary. It grew rich on shipbuilding and heavy engineering and by the end of the 19th century was Britain's second largest city, with a population of more than a million. But the solid, working-class manufacturing base on which the city was founded was whipped from under it during the recession of the 1970s. Although unemployment rose distressingly, and the population has declined to less than 700,000, an extraordinary renaissance has occurred and in 1990 Glasgow was named City of Culture by the European Community. The place once famous for its drunks and disturbances is now a firm fixture on the aesthete's Grand Tour.

Glasgow's culture is not all newly created. Its 12th-century **Cathedral** in the Old Town is the only Scottish medieval cathedral to escape the destruction of the Reformation. In Castle Street opposite is the three-storey **Provand's Lordship**, the city's oldest house dating from 1471, and now a museum. Just over half a mile (1 km) east, in Garnethill, is a home from more recent times.

The **Tenement House Museum** at 145 Buccleuch Street is a reminder that this kind of housing, in which 20 percent of the people still live, was the backbone of the city for a century or more. This was the home of Miss Agnes Toward from 1911 to 1965 and it is gaslit, just as she left it.

Two streets away is Renfrew Street and the **Glasgow School of Art** which has a wing built by Glasgow's most influential artist, Charles Rennie Mackintosh (1868–1928), wellspring of the Glasgow Art Nouveau style. Past the 1930s **Glasgow Film Theatre** and the important contemporary **McLellan Galleries**, is Sauchiehall Street and the **Willow Tearoom**, in an immaculate Mackintosh setting. You can eat in style

The sun sets on Glasgow's shipbuilding industry.

A NIGHT WITH ROBERT BURNS

Few English people know the day on which William Shakespeare was born (23 April), but every Scot is aware that 25 January is the birthday of the country's most celebrated poet, Robert Burns. Indeed on that day it is surprising how many people around the world suddenly recall the few drops of Scottish blood they have lurking in their veins.

Babbity Bowster's, a pub and hotel in a Robert Adam house in Blackfriars Street, Glasgow, has a reputation for its Burns Nights. Throughout the year its upstairs restaurant serves Scottish fare such as cullen skink (smoked haddock and potato soup), stovies (potatos cooked with onion), Loch Etive mussels and hot goat's cheese on wholemeal toast.

On Burns Night it is equally traditional. Just after 7.30pm, a kilted piper pipes in the first course of haggis, bashed neaps and tatties. (Haggis is made with sheep's or calf's offal, oatmeal, suet, onions and seasoning boiled in the skin of an animal's stomach, although the restaurant has a vegetarian alternative; bashed neaps are mashed turnips; tatties are potatoes). Next comes a main course of perhaps venison in port, or beef marinaded in whisky. A chocolate pudding may round off the meal. And

all this, of course, is washed down with usquebaugh, the water of life. In this case the whisky will be single malt (unblended and the product of one distillery). Meanwhile, guests read poems from Burns's works, starting with *Address to the Haggis*, and the evening ends after midnight as everyone crosses arms, holds hands and sings a rousing, fond chorus of *Auld Lang Syne*.

This song was just one of some 200 ballads Burns collected, developed or re-cast for The Scots Musical Museum. Though the current tune may have been added later, when Burns first came across it he sent it to his publishers, explaining: "It has never been in print nor even in manuscript until I took it down from an old man singing."

Burns, the "heaven-taught ploughman" was a well-educated farmer's son, born in 1759 in Alloway in Ayrshire, south of Glasgow. Needless to say, there is a Burns Heritage Trail there now, which takes in most of the two dozen museums, mausoleum, inns and houses associated with the 37 years of his life. He was 26 when *Poems, chiefly in the Scottish Dialect* was published with such success that all Edinburgh society fell at his feet.

Burns could write perfectly good English and the fact that some of the Scottish dialect he chose to write in was just as unintelligible to its audience then as it is to us now did not matter. It was Scottish, and something to be proud of, for this was the beginning of the Romantic Age and soon Sir Walter Scott would also be looking to the kingdom's past to rekindle its pride. Although it is unlikely the two men met, Scott was educated in Edinburgh where he was called to the bar in 1792 when Burns was 33 and a figure of enormous literary influence.

The Romantic Age was stirring not just Scotland and Britain, but all Europe. Burns supported the French Revolution and his lines on liberty and justice have touched a chord in peoples and movements in many nations. In *Awa, Whigs*, he wrote:

Grim vengeance lang has ta'en a nap,
But we may see him wauken;
Gude help the day when royal heads
Are hunted like a maukin! (a hare)

But most of all Burns is celebrated for his carousing, his love of drink and good company and his lack of domestic responsiblity. These lines are from his last major poem, *Tam O'Shanter* ("bousing at the nappy" means drinking strong ale):

While we sit bousing at the nappy,
An' getting fou and unco happy,
We think na on the lang Scots miles
The mosses, waters, slaps and styles,
That lie between us and our hame,
Where sits our sulky sullen dame,
Gathering her brows like gathering storm,
Nursing her wrath to keep it warm.

No wonder women were, for so long, excluded from Burns Nights. Even today they are liable to be a minority of the 100,000 who belong to Burns clubs in more than 20 countries, from the Pacific Rim to Russia where the "Ploughman Poet", champion of the workers, is particularly revered.

in Glasgow: in Art Deco surroundings at Rogano's famous fish establishment in Exchange Place; at the modern October in Drymen Road; or at the Robert Adam townhouse, Babbity Bowster in Blackfriars Street, a pub and hotel with Scottish food on the menu in the restaurant upstairs. Good local food is also served at the Ubiquitous Chip in Ashton Lane, a former mews to the grand houses in Byres Road.

To the west of Sauchiehall Street is the University area in Kelvingrove Park where the **Art Gallery and Museum** is a must. Second only to London's Tate Gallery in numbers of visitors, it has an impressive collection of paintings, including works from the *fin-de-siècle* Glasgow Boys and the Scottish Colourists of the post-war years.

In 1983, the art world became rather excited by **The Burrell Gallery** where a bequest of the shipowner Sir William Burrell (1861–1958) finally came to rest. There are some good pieces among the eclectic collection, but the gallery itself, in Pollock Country Park in the southwest of the city, is part of the show. Also in the park is the 18th-century **Pollock House**, which has a strong Spanish collection including works by Goya, El Greco and Murillo.

Robert Burns country: It has been unkindly said that Glasgow is a great city to get out of; it is certainly an easy one. A motorway runs right through the centre of the city and across the River Clyde down through Renfrewshire past Glasgow's airport at Abbotsinch and into Ayrshire. This is the land of Scotland's greatest poet, Robert Burns, and of the seaside resorts of **Largs, Troon, Prestwick** and **Girvan**. From Weymss Bay on this coast, there are ferries to the islands of **Bute** and **Millport**. From Ardrossan there are ferries to **Arran**, Glasgow's favourite holiday playground isle. At 166 sq. miles (430 sq. km), this mountainous and dramatic island is the biggest in the Clyde estuary. In **Brodick Castle**, parts of which date from the 14th century and have associations with Robert the Bruce, at the foot of the almost 3,000-ft (900-metre)

Cattle auction at Newton Stewart.

Goatfell, is a treasure house of pictures, porcelain, sporting prints and silver that belonged to the Hamilton family. It is now in the care of the National Trust of Scotland.

The Ayrshire coast opposite Arran has some of the finest golf courses in Scotland. Among them are three venues for the Open Championship: Turnberry, Royal Troon and Prestwick, where it all began in 1860. To the south of Ardrossan is **Ayr** itself, 35 miles (56 km) southwest of Glasgow, and on the edge of the town at **Alloway** is **Burns Cottage**, the "auld clay biggin" where the poet was born.

At **Kirkoswald** 12 miles (20 km) south on the A77 is **Souter Johnnie's House**, the home of the "ancient, trusty, druthy crony" featured in his great narrative poem, *Tam O'Shanter*, and now a museum.

On the coast next to Kirkoswald is the magnificent **Culzean Castle**, one of the greatest achievements of the 18th-century Scots architect, Robert Adam. A suite on the top floor was given as a

life tenure to General Eisenhower, a tribute from the Scottish people. Besides a fine collection of paintings, weapons, furniture and porcelain, there is a museum commemorating the US president's achievements.

South of Ayrshire in the southwesternmost corner of Scotland lie Dumfries and Galloway, pretty towns and villages along the **Solway Firth** and wild moorland country in the interior. This culminates in the hammerhead peninsula of the **Mull of Galloway.** Behind the top part of its head is **Loch Ryan**, famous for its oysters, at the end of which is **Stranraer**, the principal departure port from Scotland to Ireland. The Firth narrows near Southerness, one of Scotland's many "unknown" great golf courses, and nearby **Kirkbean** was the birthplace of John Paul Jones, founder of the US navy.

Five miles (8 km) north, towards Dumfries, lies an impressive ruin, the red sandstone **Sweetheart Abbey** built by Devorgilla, great-great-granddaughter of David I. She was the wife of John Balliol, founder of Balliol College in Oxford (1263) and the mother of the "Toom Tabard" (Empty Coat), the other John Balliol, the puppet king appointed to rule Scotland by Edward I of England.

Dumfries, nearby on the River Nith, where you can see salmon fishermen up to their waists in water, is the largest town in southwest Scotland. Burns died here in 1796, and the house where he lived is preserved as a museum. There is also a fine statue to him in the High Street, and in the nearby **Globe Inn**, one of his favourite taverns, the chair he usually occupied is preserved. In an upper room there are two verses that he supposedly scratched on a pane of glass with a diamond.

On the shores of the Solway Firth, 8 miles (12 km) southeast of Dumfries off the B725, are the ruins of the moated triangular-shaped fortress, **Caerlaverock Castle**, a the great Border strongholds. In the 17th century the Earl of Nithsdale built a classical mansion inside the ruins, creating one of the oddest architectural additions in Scotland.

Left, holiday treats on the Clyde resort of Largs. **Right**, Culzean Castle, General Eisenhower's Scottish retreat.

THE SCOTTISH HIGHLANDS

The Highlands of Scotland form one of the last great wildernesses of Europe – mile after mile of wild country, mountains, glens and moorlands probed by the long fingers of sea lochs. The southern edge of the Highland line runs across the country diagonally from the Mull of Kintyre, the long spit of land stretching southwards from Argyll on the western edge of the Firth of Clyde, right up to a point southwest of Aberdeen near Stonehaven. More than half of Scotland lies to the north of this line, most of it mountainous, with just a few fertile glens where crops can be grown and cattle reared. The population is sparse in the northwest – in Sutherland it is as low as 6 people per sq. mile (2.4 people per sq. km), compared to the national average of 955 (369).

Off the west coast lie several hundred islands, and these have the highest density of the 80,000 Gaelic speakers left in Scotland. The southernmost group comprises Gigha, Islay, Jura and Colonsay. Farther north there are the large islands of Mull and Skye and the Inner Hebrides of Iona, Staffa, Tiree, Coll, Muck, Eigg, Rum and Canna; and the Outer Hebrides group of Lewis, Harris, North Uist, Benbecula, South Uist, Eriskay and Barra.

To the north of the Scottish mainland are the Orkney and Shetland groups. You can reach some of the Scottish offshore islands by air – there are services to Islay, Benbecula, Lewis, Orkney, Shetland and Fair Isle. Ferries link the other inhabited islands to the mainland.

There is so much to see in the Highlands, such an enormous variation in the scenery of mountain, moorland, loch and glen, that anyone could spend a lifetime exploring it – and many Scots from the cities and towns do just that on weekends.

The westerly A82 out of Glasgow leads almost immediately to the Highlands, turning north after Dumbarton, along the Bonnie Bonnie Banks of

Loch Lomond, the largest freshwater lake in Britain, 23 miles (37 km) long and 5 miles (8 km) across at its widest point. The great hills dominate the landscape. Across the loch is **Ben Lomond**, first of the "Munros", Scotland's 277 mountains which rise to more than 3,000 ft (900 metres) and offer a perennial challenge to climbers from all over the country.

Scenic rail route: The A82 continues up to **Fort William**, a journey which can also be made by the scenic West Highland Line railway. Leaving Glasgow, it follows the banks of the Clyde to **Helensburgh**, the small resort town where the television pioneer John Logie Baird was born in 1888. This is also where the influential Glasgow Modern Movement architect Charles Rennie Mackintosh built the finest extant example of his domestic style, **Hill House**.

The line follows the shores of Loch Long and Loch Lomond, through the narrow valley of Glen Falloch between bronze, green and heather-purple hills

Preceding pages: absolute solitude in one of the Europe's last wildernesses, near Glencoe. **Left,** herd of elusive reindeer. **Right,** piper.

to **Crianlarich**, where the line to Oban branches off.

Crianlarich to the south and Fort William to the north are both good entry points for one of the most popular "corners" of the Scottish Highlands: **Glencoe**. This deep mountain valley stretches more than 7 miles (11 km) from Loch Leven to Rannoch Moor through magnificent scenery. The often mist-shrouded peaks of the Glen are firm favourites among experienced rock climbers, although even the most experienced have fatal accidents here, particularly in bad weather. For those who prefer a less exhilarating and slightly safer terrain, there are some beautiful trails that bypass the summits; they include the **Hidden Valley** and the **Old Military Road**.

Reminders of the Glencoe massacre of 1692 are everywhere; to it the valley owes its name, the Glen of Weeping. By order of the English King William III, more than 200 troops loyal to the English Crown, and commanded by Robert Campbell, turned on the MacDonald clan, who had been their hosts for 12 days. Men, women and children were slaughtered in an act that was supposedly a punishment for the tardiness of the chief of the MacDonald clan in giving allegiance to the English king. There is a memorial to the MacDonalds near the old Invercoe Road. Another reminder is the Signal Rock near the Clachaig Inn, said to be the place from which a signal was sent to the Campbells to go ahead with the massacre.

The West Highland Line train allows the best opportunity for witnessing the bleak splendour of **Rannoch Moor**, 60 sq. miles (155 sq. km) of peat bog, lochs and winding streams through which no road runs (one goes as far as Rannoch Station). Lying to the east of Glencoe, Rannoch is a great empty moor ringed by mountains, on which lie the two loneliest railway stations in Britain, Rannoch and Corrour, 1,365 ft (410 metres) above sea level. The moor's inhabitants are waterbirds, plovers, skylarks, eagles, herds of red deer and

Glencoe, a name forever associated with the massacre.

the succulent brown trout inhabiting peat-brown lakelets called lochans; three or four lonely households manage to exist on its surface.

At the northern edge of the moor, the line swings west again, past the deep cleft cut by the River Spean in Monessie Gorge, to Fort William at the head of Loch Linnhe and the foot of **Ben Nevis**, Britain's highest mountain, 4,406 ft (1,343 metres) and 24 miles (39 km) around. From here there are impressive views down the sea loch and over the mountain ranges of Ardgour and Moydart. The Highland rail tour can be continued by changing to the train to Mallaig, a fishing port opposite the Isle of Skye. From Fort William, Ben Nevis is not much more than a stiff walk, but proper clothes and boots are essential because the weather on mountain tops in Scotland can be treacherous even in high summer.

Fort William itself is almost enough to persuade a visitor to give Ben Nevis a miss. The fort has all but vanished; what has replaced it represents the worst in tourist overkill in a part of Britain whose magnificence hardly needs advertising. The original fortification was constructed in the 17th century to keep out "savage clans" and sundry other undesirables. During the early 19th-century Clearances, Fort William was a transit point for forced emigrants. Today the town is subjected, much by its own making, to hordes of immigrants in the form of the annual tourist season. But that shouldn't put anyone off climbing Ben Nevis – it really is worth the effort. And Fort William is at something of a crossroads in the Scottish Highlands so that the area yields much to the more intrepid explorer. A bus trip, for example, up to **Loch Ness**, 30 miles (48 km) to the northeast may just result in a sighting of the famous monster.

The train to **Mallaig** follows the A830 west through Bonnie Prince Charlie country, beginning with the stunning view from the viaduct at Glenfinnan down **Loch Shiel**, and over the monument on the shore that marks

Loch Lomond from Ben Lomond.

the spot where the Young Pretender himself raised the Stuart standard. Here the clans gathered around him to begin the Jacobite Rebellion of 1745. It was in this country, too, that he hid with a price of £30,000 on his head after the defeat at Culloden.

Beyond Lochailort there is a view seawards over the bright water and rocky islets of **Loch nan Uamh**, where the Bonnie Prince landed in 1745 with only nine men and from where he left 14 months later, despite all the pleadings of the haunting Jacobite songs, never to return. The pebbly beaches of Loch nan Uamh give way to the silver sands of Morar and Arisaig, shining like snow on the edge of the steel-blue sea. Inland are the mountains looking over the dark waters of **Loch Morar**, the deepest lake in Britain at over 1,000 ft (300 metres), which is reputed to house a monster no less mysterious than the more famous one in Loch Ness.

Over the sea: Mallaig is just a fishing port with not much to recommend it. It is, however, one of the ferry departure points for the **Isle of Skye** (the principal crossing is from Kyle of Lochalsh, further north). From the fjord-like sea lochs of the west, across to the sheer Cuillin Mountains in the south, and to the craggy northern tip of the Trotternish Peninsula, Skye epitomises Scotland's wild Celtic appeal. The 19th-century Clearances saw whole glens emptied of their ancient settlements; since then, the population of Skye has steadily decreased and it is now around 12,000.

Tourism has replaced the crofters' farms as the major source of income and has produced something of a "pre-packaged" feel in some of the main centres. But a day's hike or cycle ride around the 50-mile (80-km) long island will still set you squarely in the wilderness.

The **Cuillin Mountains** are a 6-mile (10-km) arc of peaks, 15 of which exceed 3,000 ft (900 metres). If the summits seem forbidding, take the walk down Glen Sligachan into the heart of these mountains and through to the other side 8 miles (13 km) due south to

Craggy Skye, an island with Celtic appeal.

the beach of Camasunary in Loch Scavaig. On the southern tip of Skye is **Armadale Castle**, now the site of the Clan MacDonald Centre. The main attraction of north-western Skye is **Dunvegan Castle**, claimed to be the oldest continuously inhabited castle in Scotland. Dunvegan offers abundant insights into the clan spirit of Scotland in its paintings and relics from the Macleod clan.

On the west side of the Trotternish Peninsula, **Uig** is an attractive village that encircles a bay from where ferries depart for the outer isles. This northern arm of Skye has been less altered by tourism than any part of the island.

Skye's easternmost town, **Kyleakin**, is the departure point for the short ferry crossing back to the mainland at **Kyle of Lochalsh**, which is also the terminus of the second part of the West Highland Line from Inverness. There is an excellent stopping place for the night in the **Lochalsh Hotel**, just by the ferry landing, where seafood has that special taste from having just that morning come out

of the sea. The train to Inverness, the capital of the Highlands, runs along the shores of **Loch Carron**, past the pretty village of **Plockton** on its islanded bay, with splendid views to the north of the mountains of Applecross and Wester Ross, then up Glen Carron through dramatic wild country, populated by little more than deer and eagles, wildcats and buzzards on its high tops and a few sheep and cattle among the narrow glens.

As the train heads further east, so the ruggedness of the Highland landscape begins to fade. The change is first noticeable at **Garve**, where the landscape begins to melt into the civilisation of the rich farmland around the Moray Firth on the east coast. Inverness appears on the shoreline and beyond it the Monadliath mountains loom over Loch Ness.

An alternative route out from Kyle of Lochalsh is to head north by road on either the A890 through **Glen Carron** or the A896 via **Shieldaig**. Both roads intersect with the A832 which goes west down Glen Docherty to **Loch**

Maree, one of the prettiest Lochs in Scotland, and beyond to the extraordinary gardens at **Inverewe** on Loch Ewe. This is a blaze of exotic semi-tropical colour on the same northern latitude as Labrador and St Petersburg, made possible by the protective mildness of the Gulf Stream and generations of dedicated gardeners.

From Inverewe the road heads first north and then winds back to the east, giving at many points a view of the true beauty of Scotland's west coast. The road arrives at the A835, which heads north to **Ullapool**, a fishing town on Loch Broom. The further north you go past Ullapool (until you reach Scotland's "scalp" on the north coast between Durness and John O'Groats) the more the landscape takes on an eerie yet beautiful mooniness, which is strictly for wilderness lovers. In the opposite direction to Ullapool, the A835 is the road to Inverness.

There is little reason to spend time in **Inverness**, even though it is the administrative centre of the Highlands. Disillusion awaits those who remember this city as the home of Shakespeare's Macbeth. But with the mouth of **Loch Ness** only 5 miles (8 km) from town, it is a good starting point for seeking out one of the world's greatest amphibian celebrities. If the serpentine configurations don't appear on the surface of the Loch as you make your way south down the A82, then stop at the ruins of **Urquhart Castle**, which was one of the largest in Scotland until 1692 when it was blown up to prevent the Jacobites from using it. Most photos of Nessie have been taken at this spot. The **Loch Ness Monster Information Centre**, replete with a scale replica of the wee beastie, is nearby.

The far, far north: Inverness is also a good starting point for a journey up to the northernmost fringes of Britain. The A9 follows the coast to Wick or Thurso, from where a ferry sails for **Stromness,** the **Orkney Islands'** second largest town on Mainland, the largest of some 70 islands. Orkney, invaded by Norsemen in the 11th century, did not pass

Urquhart Castle, lookout point for the Loch Ness monster.

into British hands until late in the 16th century. Ruins from the Norse era are everywhere and, to impress upon the visitor the mixed Orcadian heritage, shops sell Nordic-style sweaters instead of the usual tartans.

Everywhere in the Orkneys the feeling is one of being wide open to the sky, of great cliffs and rocky sea pinnacles. North of Stromness the coast offers one of the most dramatic cliff walks in Britain, from Black Craig north to the Bay of Skaill. Another excursion for wilderness lovers is the ferry to Moaness Pier on the Isle of Hoy.

Kirkwall, 10 miles (16 km) east of Stromness, is the largest town in the Orkneys. It is largely uninspiring except for the **Bishop's Palace** (a 12th-century ruin with a round tower added in the 16th century); **St Magnus' Cathedral**, built in 1137 and dedicated to a Viking saint; and the **Earl's Palace**, one of the finest examples of Renaissance architecture in Scotland.

Sites of antiquity grace the Orkney countryside. Best known perhaps is the wonderfully preserved Neolithic settlement at **Skara Brae**, dating from around 3000 BC, and the huge burial mound **Maes Howe**, a chambered tomb from 2700 BC with fine, runic graffiti left by 12th-century Norse plunderers. On Papa Westray, one of the smaller of the islands, is the oldest extant house in Europe.

Britain's most northerly group of islands are the **Shetlands**, 48 miles (78 km) north of the Orkneys. Lerwick is the archipelago's only town and there is a small airport on the main island served from most Scottish airports, a frequency maintained because of the Shetlands' significant oil installations. Ferries sail from Lerwick to Aberdeen. The land here is less dramatic than the Orkneys, neither are the Shetlands as rich in buildings such as St Magnus. Yet the same kind of beyond-the-world Nordic atmosphere is pervasive. Shetland, nearer to the Arctic circle than to London, was given to Scotland in 1469 as the dowry of Margaret of Denmark who married James III. Five centuries later,

Stone-Age settlement at Skara Brae, Orkney Islands.

natives of the Shetlands continue to speak a form of English full of bewildering Norse words.

In recent years the discovery of oil in the North Sea left noticeably less room for tourism, though the oil boom has quieted down now and the Shetlands' antiquity once again attracts. The tiny island of **Mousa**, off the east coast, is the site of the world's best-preserved Iron Age *broch* tower, a fortress that is just about intact after more than 1,000 years of battering from Arctic storms. **Muness Castle** on **Unst**, the most northerly of the dozen inhabited islands, and the ruins of **Scalloway Castle**, 6 miles (10 km) to the west of Lerwick, are also worth visiting.

At the southern tip of the mainland, next door to Sumburgh Airport, is **Jarlshof**, a remarkable "layer-cake" of an archaeological site. Bronze Age dune dwellers, broch builders, Vikings and more recent medieval inhabitants have all left their marks.

South from Inverness: The A9 south from Inverness leads back towards Edinburgh and Glagow, through impressive scenery in the high glens of the **Grampians** with the massive range of the Cairngorms towering over the ski and sports resort of **Aviemore**. It also passes the pretty town of **Pitlochry**, a quaint hillside town that plays patient host to an endless stream of tourist-laden vehicles. The Pitlochry Festival Theatre, over the Aldour Bridge from town, runs from April to October and draws first-class performers from all over the world. Eight miles (13 km) north of Pitlochry is **Blair Castle**, dating from the 12th century and the seat of the Duke of Atholl, the last noble in Britain licensed to have a private army. **Perth,** generally considered the gateway to the Highlands (the first line of high hills rise over the horizon), has little of interest to the visitor.

A fitting endpiece to the southerly hike down the A9 is a visit to **Stirling**. Equidistant from Edinburgh and Glasgow, this city still considers itself the rightful capital of Scotland. Stirling seems to have escaped the worst ex-

The High Street, Pitlochry, a useful base for the Highlands.

cesses of the Victorian Age; winding streets and medieval cobblestones are everywhere in evidence. Throughout history Stirling has paid the price for its strategic position; the nearby battlefields of Stirling Bridge (1297), Bannockburn (1314) and Sauchiburn (1488) are reminders of Scotland's past struggle for liberation from the English. **Stirling Castle** seems to have grown out of the 150-ft (77-metre) crag on which it was built. It featured prominently in the Scottish wars of succession during the 13th and 14th centuries, passing back and forth between the English and the Scots until the Scots finally won it for keeps in 1342. The castle was the home of the Stuart kings between 1370 and 1603; it was they who shaped it into what it is today. Mary Queen of Scots and James VI of Scotland (who became James I of England) also spent several years there.

A multi-screen presentation, at the **Landmark Visitor Centre**, traces the history of Stirling, bringing to life such events as the Battle of Bannockburn.

The Centre also has an exhibition of life in Stirling during the 19th century, along with a shop selling an undistinguished collection of Celtic paraphernalia. Worth visiting are two religious sites: the **Church of the Holy Rude** and the **Cambuskenneth Abbey**. The former is a 15th-century building with an unusual open timber roof and a five-sided apse in the choir. The 90-ft (28-metre) tower shows the scars of hostilities which may have occurred during the Jacobite Rebellion. Mary Queen of Scots was crowned here as a child and, following her abdication, it was the scene of the coronation of her son James VI of Scotland. The Abbey, founded in the 11th century, is by the River Forth east of the town. In 1326 it was the scene of Robert the Bruce's first Scottish parliament.

Scotch on the rocks: A few miles east from Inverness, the B9006 runs across **Culloden Moor** where Jacobite forces under Bonnie Prince Charlie were routed in 1746. The defeat of his men (the last battle fought on the soil of the

One of half a dozen whisky distilleries on the island of Islay.

United Kingdom) by the Hannoverian army, led by the Duke of Cumberland, represented the end of the struggle for power by the Stuart line. The savagery on the battlefield earned the Duke the sobriquet (among Scotsmen) of "Butcher" Cumberland. On either side of the road running across the moor are scattered stones marking the graves of the Highlanders. The battle is said to have centred around **Old Leanach Farmhouse**, a building which still stands and now houses a museum. **Culloden House**, where the Prince slept on the eve of the battle, is now a fine and friendly hotel.

Along the Spey from the rich farmlands of the Laigh of Moray is distillery country where most of the famous malt whiskies are made. There are distilleries on the route down the beautiful **Spey Valley** which welcome visitors to watch the process of making the *uisgebeatha*, the Gaelic "water of life," and even offer you a dram at the end of your tour. Follow the signs marked **"Whisky Trail"** from **Keith** to **Duff-town,** 17 miles (28 km) south on the A941, and along the A95 southwest.

Aberdeen, the granite city on the east coast of the Grampian region, 54 miles (87 km) east of Inverness on the A96, is the oil capital of Britain, bustling with oil-related shipping in its busy harbour, set between the Rivers Don and Dee. Aberdeen's importance has always come from its seagoing connections. As far back as the 13th century it was the main seaport in the north of Scotland. Its shipping trade grew gradually and by the mid-19th century the Aberdeen clippers which raced to China for their cargoes of tea had established their speedy reputations.

Once you leave the main thoroughfare of Union Street, you'll sense much of the city's old seaport atmosphere along the narrow cobblestone streets. Aberdeen has a widely respected university, of which the finest building is the 16th-century **King's College**, begun in 1500 and hailed as an outstanding example of Scottish Gothic style.

The **Art Gallery**, Schoolhill, has a

Left, a spectator at the Highland Games, Braemar. **Below**, Dunnottar Castle above Stonehaven.

wide range of English, French and Scottish paintings, with an especially fine 20th-century British collection. There is also the 14th-century **St Machar's Cathedral** and a **Maritime Museum** housed in the 16th-century Provost Ross's house in Shiprow leading down to the quays.

Inland from Aberdeen the A93 runs up Royal Deeside to **Balmoral**, where the royal family spends most of the summer amid some of the most beautiful scenery in the land, a unique combination of the tumbling river, the ordered trees, the palatial houses and the wild hills beyond.

Along the way is a cluster of superb castles: **Drum**, **Crathes Castle**, **Fraser** (to the north, off the A944), and, by the A980, the fairy-tale **Craigievar**. All have a special distinction of style and furnishings, superb plaster ceilings, beautiful panelling, valuable paintings and artefacts. All are in the care of the National Trust for Scotland.

The Balmoral estate, 50 miles (80 km) west of Aberdeen, dates from the 15th century but didn't come into the hands of the royal family until 1848 when the owner, Sir Robert Gordon, died and it was bought by Prince Albert. The castle is not open to the public, though the grounds can be visited when the royal family is not in residence.

Further north, but still in the Grampian region (of which Aberdeen is the administrative capital), is **Haddo House**, an 18th-century palatial mansion. It was designed by William Adam as the seat of the Earls of Aberdeen, one of whom became Queen Victoria's prime minister, and it is full of treasures. Still further north is **Leith Hall**, a handsome laird's house on a more modern scale, and **Brodie Castle**, just east of Nairn, more of a house than a fortress, belonging to the family which still lives there.

The A92 coast road south of Aberdeen goes through the North Sea ports of **Montrose** and **Arbroath**. At Arbroath are the ruins of a 12th-century abbey, the scene of Scotland's noble Declaration of Independence in 1320

that said: "For it is not for riches, nor for honours or glory that we fight but for liberty alone, which no true man lays down but with his life."

Next comes **Dundee**, the town of jam, jute and journalism (the three Js) looking across the estuary of the river Tay at the north coast of Fife. The three Js still play their part in the life of the city. D.C. Thomson produces local newspapers and weeklies that are read all over Scotland and the largest collection of children's comics in Britain. *The Discovery*, the ship Captain Scott took to the Antarctic in 1910, was built here and has now returned to find a final resting place. Dundee is one of the largest cities in Scotland; but with acres of dockland and industry it is also understandably one of the least visited.

And Dundee has at least one other claim to fame: its celebrated citizen William McGonagall (1830–1902) is The Best Bad Poet of All Time. These lines on his poem about Dundee make the point:

Oh, Bonnie Dundee, I will sing in thy praise
A few but true simple lays
Regarding some of your beauties of the present day –
And virtually speaking, there's none can them gainsay;
There's no other town I know of with which you can compare
For spinning mills and lassies fair
And for stately buildings there's none can excel
The beautiful Albert Institute or the Queen's Hotel
For it is most handsome to be seen
Where accommodation can be had for Duke, Lord or Queen

And so across "the Silvery Tay", as the Bard of Dundee referred to it in so many of his poems, to Fife and an hour and a half's run back to Edinburgh.

There is more to see in Scotland than described here – more mountains, more lochs, rivers, monuments, battlefields and more people. Such is Scotland's individuality that it is encapsulated in no one place, but perhaps it is enough to provoke a positive response to the old Gaelic greeting, "Haste ye back".

INSIGHT GUIDES
Travel Tips

TRAVEL TIPS

GETTING THERE

ENGLAND

Although your most likely destination when flying to Britain will be one of London's five airports, the regional airports of Birmingham, Manchester, Glasgow, Prestwick and Cardiff also receive international flights. Many have been expanded in recent years to cater for a greater amount of international traffic, offering alternative and often more leisurely gateways to Britain in contrast to the bustling congestion of London.

London is served by the large major international airports of Heathrow, 15 miles (24 km) to the west receiving mainly scheduled flights, and Gatwick, 28 miles (45 km) to the south, receiving a mixture of scheduked and charter flights. North of London, Stansted Airport, designed by Richard Rogers and opened in 1991, is now London's third major airport. Luton airport is also to the north whilst tiny London City Airport caters for business travellers in Docklands, to the east of the financial district.

From **Heathrow** the easiest way to reach central London is the 45-minute Tube journey on the Underground's Piccadilly Line, costing about £3 (depending on destination). By coach you can take the London Regional Transport red double-decker Airbus (A1 to Victoria or A2 to Euston) which picks up from all terminals at half-hourly intervals between 6.30am and 10.15pm. It stops off at major hotels en route and costs £5 one-way, £8 return. For 24-hour Airbus information, tel: 081-668 7261. Alternatively, Green Line provides the more comfortable Flightline 767 coach service to Victoria with on-board washrooms and a luggage loading service for the same price. A ride in a black cab will cost upwards of £20 to central London.

Gatwick Airport is served by the main-line Gatwick Express train service and also by regular coach services, both running to and from Victoria. The train leaves every 15 minutes between 5.30am and 10pm, and there is an hourly service during the night. Taking just half an hour, it costs £7.50 one-way. Flightline 777 coaches leave from both the North and South terminals and take about 70 minutes to reach Victoria. A single fare is £6 (US and Canadian dollars accepted), £8 return.

Luton Airport, 35 miles (56 km) northwest of

London is served with a regular train service to St Pancras station, taking 45 minutes, and the Green Line 757 coach service to Victoria taking 70 minutes.

From **Stansted Airport**, 37 miles (60 km) northeast of central London, there is a train service running every half hour from within the new terminal to Liverpool Street station. Taking 40 minutes, it connects with the Victoria Underground line at Tottenham Hale. Alternatively, there is a regular coach service to Victoria.

National Express runs a coach service connecting Heathrow, Gatwick, Stansted and Luton airports with each other and Victoria railway station. Enquiries and credit card bookings, tel: 071-730 0202.

For those heading elsewhere in Britain other than London, there are regular Railair bus links to nearby British Rail stations.

London City Airport caters for business travellers with small 46-seater planes flying to European capitals, most frequently Paris. It is badly served by transport despite its close proximity (6 miles/10 km) to London's financial district, "the City", with the options of a taxi, the Green Line 787 coach to Victoria or a main-line train from Silvertown station (5 minutes' walk) which connects with the Underground rail network at Stratford or West Ham. Alternatively, there is the more interesting choice of the London City Airport Express Service Boat (tel: 071-474 5555) which runs from Canary Wharf from around 7.30am to 6.30pm, taking 40 minutes to reach Charing Cross Pier (does not operate at weekends). Cost £2.80. (A free shuttle bus runs from the airport to Canary Wharf.)

Manchester International Airport is situated 10 miles (16 km) south of the city and caters for flights to 160 destinations around the world. There is a regular shuttle bus service running at half hourly intervals to Manchester Piccadilly and Victoria main-line stations and to Chorlton Street coach station. The airport is currently being expanded to include a rail link to the city centre.

Birmingham International Airport has over 100 international airlines operating services worldwide and is also being expanded to include a new passenger terminal. Trains run every 15 minutes from the airport's station to Birmingham New Street station 9 miles (14 km) away.

SCOTLAND

As a result of recent changes in UK air regulations, airports at Edinburgh, Glasgow and Prestwick all now receive transatlantic charter flights. Before these changes, all scheduled international flights to Scotland landed at Prestwick only.

Glasgow Airport is currently being extended to cope with this increased traffic. Situated 8 miles (13 km) west of the city, it is connected to the city centre by a coach service running to Anderston and

THE NOBLE TIME

JUVENIA
—— 1860 ——

Golden Age ®
COLLECTION

STEEL - STEEL/GOLD - 18KT GOLD AND WITH PRECIOUS STONES

Worldwide list of JUVENIA Agents available on request

JUVENIA MONTRES SA - 2304 LA CHAUX-DE-FONDS - SWITZERLAND
Tel. 41/39 26 04 65 Fax 41/39 26 68 00

Put on the Cutter®
...because it's a
jungle out there.

Cutter® Insect Repellent. Effective, long-lasting protection.
So no matter how delicious you look, mosquitoes will know
it's look, but don't touch. Protect yourself with Cutter®

Buchanan Bus stations. Leaving at half-hourly intervals during the day, the coaches take about 25 minutes.

Prestwick Airport is about 40 minutes south of Glasgow on the west coast of Scotland. There is a free shuttle service to nearby Prestwick railway station from where you can take a 45-minute train ride to Glasgow's Central Station. Alternatively, Scottish Citylink run a regular bus service to Glasgow (tel: 041-332 7133) and Edinburgh (tel: 031-556 8464).

Edinburgh Airport lies 8 miles (13 km) west of the city. Airlink runs a bus service to the city which takes about 30 minutes.

WALES

Cardiff-Wales Airport is located 12 miles (19 km) west of the city centre to which it is linked by a bus service. It has scheduled flights to England and Amsterdam only, and charter flights to North America, Canada and Europe.
Airport Information:
Birmingham, tel: 021-767 5511
Gatwick Airport, tel: 0293-535353
Heathrow Airport, tel: 081-759 4321
London City Airport, tel: 071-474 5555
Luton Airport, tel: 0582-405100
Manchester, tel: 061-489 3000
Stansted Airport, tel: 0279-502380
Edinburgh, tel: 031-344 3136, 333 1000
Glasgow, tel: 041-887 1111
Prestwick, tel: 0292-794822
Cardiff, tel: 0446-711111

BY SEA

Britain is well served with frequent ferry links to Ireland and many European ports. The quickest and busiest route from the Continent to Britain is between Calais and Dover which takes just 1½ hours by ferry and only 35 minutes by hovercraft (Hoverspeed, tel: 0304-240241). In an attempt to compete with the Channel Tunnel, Hoverspeed introduced in 1991 the impressive new SeaCat service which can travel at speeds of over 40 knots. It is the world's first car carrying catamaran and is capable of carrying 80 cars and 450 passengers. This service travels between Dover and Calais/Boulogne. Other popular routes from **France** are Boulogne to Dover/Folkestone, Dieppe to Newhaven, and Le Havre or Cherbourg to Portsmouth.

From **Belgium** ferries leave from Ostend and Zeebrugge for Dover and Felixstowe and from the **Netherlands** they travel between the Hook of Holland and Harwich. There are also ferry links from Bergen in **Norway** and Göteborg in **Sweden** to Newcastle. Britain's two major ferry lines are P&O (tel: 0304-203388) and Sealink (tel: 071-834 8122).

Both also provide ferry services between Britain and **Ireland,** running from Fishguard and Holyhead in Wales to Rosslare and Dun Laoghaire and from Stranraer and Cairnryan in **Scotland** to Larne (tel: 0233-647047).

If you plan to bring a vehicle over by ferry it is advisable to book in advance, particularly during peak holiday periods. If travelling by night on a long journey it is recommended also that you book a sleeping cabin in advance.

From **North America** you could arrive in style on the Cunard Steamship Company's *Queen Elizabeth II* luxury cruiser, the world's only superliner. Operating between April and December, she takes five days to cross the Atlantic. For further information, tel: 071-491 3930.

TRAVEL ESSENTIALS

VISAS & PASSPORTS

Passport holders of most European countries, North America, South Africa, Japan and many Commonwealth countries do not generally require a visa to enter the UK for a short stay. If in doubt check with the British Embassy in your home country before leaving home.

CUSTOMS

If you enter the UK directly from another European Community country, you need make no declaration to Customs for goods brought in for personal use. However, if you're found bringing in more than 800 cigarettes or 10 litres of spirits or 110 litres of beer, you may be asked to prove that they're for personal use (e.g. you're a hopeless addict or there's a family wedding coming up). Cars, boats and planes do attract duties.

On entering the UK from non-EC countries, those carrying goods within two categories of duty-free allowances may pass through the **nothing to declare** channel (green) where there are spot checks. Those with goods over the limits should go through the **goods to declare** (red) channel.
(a) Goods which have been obtained outside the EC or duty and tax free within the EC:
200 cigarettes/or 100 cigarillos/or 50 cigars/or 250g of tobacco; 2 litres still table wine; 1 litre spirits (over 22 percent by volume)/or 2 litres fortified or sparkling wine/or a further 2 litres still table wine; 60 cc/ml of perfume; 250 cc/ml of toilet water; £32 worth of gifts, souvenirs or other goods.

(b) Goods obtained duty and tax paid in the EC: 300 cigarettes/or 150 cigarillos/or 75 cigars/ or 400g of tobacco; 5 litres still table wine; 1.5 litres spirits/or 3 litres fortified or sparkling wine/or an additional 3 litres still table wine; 90 cc/ml perfume; 375 cc/ml toilet water; £265 worth of gifts, souvenirs or any other goods.

It is illegal to bring animals, plants, perishable foods, certain drugs, firearms and obscene material into the country without prior arrangement. But any amount of currency can be brought in.

For further information contact **HM Customs and Excise**, Dorset House, Stamford Street, London SE1 9PS, tel: 071-620 1313.

EXPORT PROCEDURES

VAT (value added tax) is a standard sales tax of 17.5 percent which is added to all goods except food and books. Most large department stores and smaller gift shops operate a scheme to refund this tax to visitors, but often require that more than a minimum amount (usually £50) is spent. To get a refund you will need to fill in a form from the store, have it stamped by customs when you leave the country and then post it back to the store. Provided you leave the country with the goods within three weeks of purchase you will be refunded the tax less an administration fee.

CURRENCY & EXCHANGE

The British pound sterling (£) is a decimal currency divided into 100 pence (p). Coins come in the following denominations: 1p, 2p, 5p, 10p, 20p and £1. Notes come in £5, £10, £20 and £50. Scotland issues its own notes, which are not technically legal tender in England and Wales, though some shopkeepers will accept them. English notes, however, can be used anywhere in Scotland.

General banking hours are between 9.30am and 3.30pm Monday to Friday. A few banks are open until 4.30pm and on Saturday mornings. In rural Scottish areas banks may close for lunch. Branches of the major national banks – Lloyds, Barclays, Midland, National Westminster, Royal Bank of Scotland and the Bank of Scotland – can be found on most high streets and tend to offer similar currency exchange rates. They charge no commission on travellers' cheques presented in sterling or for changing a cheque in another currency if the bank is affiliated with your own back home. However, there will be a charge for changing cash into another currency or for giving cash against a credit card. Proof of identity is usually required. Most banks have automatic machines where appropriate international credit or cashpoint cards can be used in conjunction with a personal number to withdraw cash.

Money may also be changed by travel agents, such as Thomas Cook, and at some large department stores and hotels, but bear in mind that banks tend to offer the best rates. There are numerous bureaux de change throughout towns and cities in Britain, but you should be wary of changing money at these as they may offer low rates and charge high commissions. Look out for the British Tourist Authority's (BTA) code of conduct sticker.

International credit cards are widely accepted in shops, hotels and restaurants, although there are a few exceptions. Eurocheques are also widely accepted.

GETTING ACQUAINTED

GOVERNMENT & THE MONARCHY

Britain is a constitutional monarchy reigned over, not ruled over, by **Queen Elizabeth II**, and Britons are "subjects" rather than citizens. Although the Queen is Head of State for Britain and the Commonwealth countries, head of the judiciary and commander-in-chief of the armed forces, she must follow the advice of her government which operates from the Houses of Parliament in Westminster. The continuity of the monarchy, which has had only a few changes in the direct line of succession in the past 1,000 years, has been broken only once when, between 1649 and 1660, a republic was established.

Britain is therefore governed centrally from Parliament at Westminster in London (although certain administrative differences exist for Scotland, and to a lesser extent for Wales). Parliament consists of two bodies, the **House of Commons** and the **House of Lords**, each with its own chamber. The House of Lords has over 1,000 members consisting of Lords Spiritual (church leaders) and Lords Temporal (peers, peeresses and law lords). This body has limited powers, but it acts as a watchdog over the Commons and can amend or delay legislation.

The powerful body is the House of Commons which has supreme control of national policy, finance and legislation. It consists of 650 elected Members of Parliament (MPs) with 523 from England, 38 from Wales and 72 from Scotland. The remainder are from Northern Ireland. The political party with the majority of MPs, and consequently the Prime Minister, sits on one side of the House of Commons, whilst the Opposition, elected MPs from all other parties, sits facing the Government.

The **Prime Minister** is the leader of the political party with the majority of MPs and he appoints a **Cabinet** of 20 ministers who take on the main

K P M

KÖNIGLICHE
PORZELLAN
MANUFAKTUR
Berlin

BERLIN MASTERPIECES

ROCAILLE,
Breslauer Stadtschloß
The unusual reliefs and
opulent embellishments
of this rococo design
places extremely high
demands on the artistic
abilities of the craftsmen.

SCHINKEL Basket
Design: app. 1820
by Karl Friedrich Schinkel.

KURLAND, *pattern 73*
The first classicistic service
made by KPM was created
around 1790 by order of
the Duke of Kurland.

KPM BERLIN · Wegelystraße 1 · Kurfürstendamm 26a · Postal address: Postfach 12 21 07, D-10591 Berlin · Phone
(030) 390 09 - 226 · Fax (030) 390 09 - 279 · U.K. AGENCY · Exclusif Presentations, Ltd. · 20 Vancouver Road
Edgware, Middx. HA8 5DA · Phone (081) 952 46 79 · Fax (081) 951 09 39 · JAPAN AGENCY · Hayashitok Co., Ltd.
Nakano-Cho. Ogawa. Marutamachi · Nakagyo-Ku. Kyoto 604 · Phone (075) 222 02 31 / 231 22 22 · Fax (075) 256 45 54

BREAK THE LANGUAGE BARRIER!

If you travel internationally, for business or pleasure - or if you are learning a foreign language - TI's electronic language -products can make communication a lot easier.

The **PS-5800** is a versatile 3-language dictionary with 30,000 entry words in each language. Available in English/German/French or English/Italian/French, it includes, travel sentences, business words, memory space to build and store your own vocabulary, currency and metric conversions, and more.

The **PS-5400** is a powerful 5-language translator fea-

turing up to 5,000 words and 1,000 structured sentences in English, German, French, Italian, and Spanish. Travel-related sentences, conveniently grouped by category, facilitate conversation in the language of your choice. To keep you on time and on top, there's also world time, alarm reminders, calculator, and metric conversions.

The **PS-5800** and **PS-5400**. Two pocket-sized ways to break the language barrier!

For more information, fax your request to:
Texas Instruments France, (33) 39 22 21 01

TEXAS INSTRUMENTS

governmental positions such as the Chancellor of the Exchequer, who deals with financial policy. The leader of the major opposing party, or **Shadow Government**, also appoints a shadow cabinet which makes its contribution to the ruling of the country through constructive criticism. The leaders and cabinet of both sides sit on the front benches, and their supporters, back benchers, sit behind them.

Governments can stay in power for a maximum term of five years, but they usually opt for a general election before the end of this period when they feel they are in a favourable position to regain control of government.

The main two political parties are the **Conservative Party** (Tories), which dates back to the 18th century, and the **Labour Party**, which was formed at the end of the 19th century. Since 1945 the Conservatives and Labour parties have taken it in turn to govern the country and they face little opposition from the **Social and Liberal Democratic Party**. There are also two nationalist parties, **Plaid Cymru** in Wales and the **Scottish National Party**. The **Green Party** has had limited success.

The Houses of Parliament were rebuilt between 1835 and 1857 after having been destroyed by fire and were designed by Sir Charles Barry on a classical plan with Gothic detailing by Augustus Welby Pugin. The public are admitted to the Stranger's Galleries in the House of Lords (2.30pm Mon, Tues and Wed, 3pm Thur, 11am Fri) and the House of Commons (4.30pm Mon–Thur, 9.30am Fri).

GEOGRAPHY & POPULATION

The name **Great Britain** refers to the union of England, Scotland and Wales which officially came into being in 1603 when King James VI of Scotland succeeded to the English throne as James I. England itself was made a unified state by King Egbert in the 9th century whilst the principality of Wales was annexed to England in the 13th century. The term United Kingdom encompasses Great Britain and Northern Ireland.

England, Scotland and Wales are each divided into districts called counties. There are 46 in England, 8 in Wales and 34 in Scotland with their capitals of London, Cardiff and Edinburgh respectively. England, one of the world's most densely populated countries, covers 50,056 sq. miles (129,645 sq. km), Scotland has 29,794 sq. miles (77,177 sq. km) and Wales only 7,967 sq. miles (20,635 sq. km). The total population of Great Britain is 55.5 million, of which only 5 million live in Scotland and just 2.87 million live in Wales. Some 7 million live in Greater London.

From the furthest point south in England to the furthest point north in Scotland it is 600 miles (966 km) as the crow flies and it is 300 miles (500 km) at the widest point.

Highest mountains are Scafell in England; Mount Snowdon in Wales and Ben Nevis in Scotland.

CLIMATE

The climate in Britain is temperate, generally mild and always unpredictable. Renowned for its rainfall, it is unusual for any area in the British Isles to have a dry spell for more than two or three weeks, even in the summer months from June to September. However, it rains most frequently in the mountainous areas of north and west Britain where temperatures are also cooler than in the south. On the bright side, extremes in weather are rare.

In summer the southern areas of England experience average maximum temperatures in the 70s Fahrenheit (23–25°C) although temperatures can reach above 80°F (27°C), whilst in Scotland temperatures tend to stay within the mid-60s Fahrenheit (17–19°C). In the winter months from November to February the majority of Britain, with the exception of mountainous regions in the north, tend mostly to be cold and damp rather than snowy and icy.

Be warned, temperatures can fluctuate considerably from day to day so come prepared with suitable warm and wet-weather clothing whatever the season. Generally, short sleeves and a jacket are fine for summer but a warm coat and woollens are recommended for winter. For recorded weather information, tel: 0898-141214.

CLOTHING

On the whole the British tend to dress casually and with a few exceptions, such as society balls and the Royal Opera House, formal evening dress is not essential, although a jacket and tie will be required by smart hotels, restaurants and clubs.

The young are particularly style-conscious and as a consequence there is a strong presence of *trendy* street fashion in Britain's cities. At the other end of the scale the British reputation for conservative and traditional clothing such as Burberry raincoats, tweeds, woollen jumpers and brogue shoes is still evident, especially in provincial and rural areas.

WEIGHTS & MEASURES

The British are reluctant to relinquish the Imperial system and consequently this is still used alongside Metric. For example, petrol is still widely priced by the gallon as well as by the litre, and fabric by the yard or metre. The mile is still the favoured form of measuring distance and the British refuse to drink their beer in anything other than pints.

Length: 1 inch = 2.54 centimetres
1 foot = 30.5 centimetres
1 yard = 0.914 metres
1 mile = 1.6 kilometres
Weight: 1 ounce = 28.3 grams
1 pound = 454 grams
1 ton = 1.02 metric tonnes

Capacity: 1 fl.ounce = 28.4 millilitres
1 pint = 0.568 litres
1 gallon = 4.55 litres (1.2 US gallons)

ELECTRICITY

The electrical current in the UK is 240 volts, 50 cycle AC. Sockets accept plugs with three square pins, so appliances with two-pin plugs need an adaptor.

TIME

British time is governed by Greenwich Mean Time (GMT). Zones west of the Greenwich Meridian (located in southeast London) are ahead in time and those to the east are behind. British Summer Time (BST) begins in March when the nation puts its clocks forward one hour and ends in October when clocks go back to GMT. Most of Europe is one hour ahead of Britain.

Some time differences:
Athens (+2), Brasilia (−3), Buenos Aires (−3), Canberra (+10), Hong Kong (+8), Jerusalem (+2), Los Angeles (−8), Moscow (+3), New Delhi (+2), New York (−5), Pretoria (+2), Rio de Janeiro (−2), Singapore (+8), Sydney (+10), Tokyo (+9), Washington DC (−5), Wellington (+12)

LANGUAGE

The English language contains many different dialects and accents which vary from region to region, so much so that even the British themselves have trouble at times understanding what their fellow countrymen are saying. Indeed, although Britain is a relatively small country, it is possible to pinpoint from a person's accent the exact region in which he or she has been brought up.

Having miraculously survived the onslaught of the English over the past four centuries, the **Celtic** language, one of the oldest in Europe and once spoken throughout Britain, is still widely spoken in Wales, particularly in the rural north and west. Today, one in five of the population of Wales speaks Welsh, and there is a sense of nationalism in the region. All signs and public notices appear in both Welsh and English, there is a separate television channel broadcasting programmes in Welsh only and the language is increasingly being taught in schools. There is also a great interest in the many Eisteddfodau (festivals dedicated to the literature and music in the Welsh language) which are held throughout Wales each year.

In Scotland, particularly in the Highlands and Western Isles, **Gaelic** is still spoken by older generations, although everyone also speaks English. Gaelic is not to be confused with the **Scots** (or Lallans) language which is derived from the Northumbrian dialect of Old English and which has been spoken in the lowlands for centuries.

BUSINESS HOURS

Normal banking hours are 9.30am–3.30pm Monday–Friday, though some banks open until 4.30pm and on Saturday mornings.

Shops open 9am–5.30pm Monday–Saturday, although smaller shops may close for lunch. Many small towns and villages have a half-day closing one day in the week and some shopping centres in towns and cities may have one evening of late-night shopping. In London, shops in Oxford Street stay open as late as 8pm on Thursdays, and until 7pm in Knightsbridge and Kensington on Wednesdays. Very few shops are open on Sundays apart from newsagents, small grocery shops and large hardware stores. Throughout Britain local corner shops and off-licences may stay open until 10pm.

Offices usually operate 9 am.–5.30pm Monday–Friday with an hour for lunch between 1 and 2pm.

British pubs are permitted by law to open between 11am–11pm Monday–Saturday and from 12pm–3pm and 7pm–10.30pm on Sundays. However, some may close for periods during the day.

PUBLIC HOLIDAYS

1 January: New Year's Day
2 January: Bank Holiday (Scotland only)
March/April: Good Friday
Easter Monday (not Scotland)
May (first Monday): May Day Bank Holiday
May (last Monday): Spring Bank Holiday
August (first Monday): Bank Holiday (Scotland only)
August (last Monday): Summer Bank Holiday (not Scotland)
25 December: Christmas Day
26 December: Boxing Day

TIPPING

Good service in restaurants and hotels and from cab drivers, hairdressers and sightseeing guides should be rewarded with a tip of not less than 10 percent. Porters will not welcome anything less than 50p. Tipping any other service has to be gauged carefully as in some cases it may offend. It is not customary to tip in bars and pubs, theatres and cinemas. Hotels and restaurants may add a 10–15 percent service charge to your bill which should be specified on the tariff or menu. If, however, you have justifiable reason to be dissatisfied, you may deduct this.

1993
spring-summer
COLLECTION

PART OF
THE ART

swatch⊞
automatic

swatch⊞
SCUBA 200

POP
swatch

swatch⊞
C·H·R·O·N·O

swatch⊞

SWISS
made

THE WORLD IS FLAT

MCI
123 456 7890 1111
A.R. SMITH

Its configuration may not be to Columbus' liking but to every other traveller the MCI Card is an easier, more convenient, more cost-efficient route to circle the globe.

The MCI Card offers two international services—MCI World Reach and MCI CALL USA—which let you call from country-to-country as well as back to the States, all via an English-speaking operator.

There are no delays. No hassles with foreign languages and foreign currencies. No foreign exchange rates to figure out. And no outrageous hotel surcharges.

If you don't possess the MCI Card, please call the access number of the country you're in and ask for customer service.

The MCI Card. It makes a world of difference. **MCI**

COMMUNICATIONS

POSTAL SERVICES

Post offices are open 9am–5pm Monday–Friday, 9 am.–12 noon Saturday. London's main post office, located behind the east side of Trafalgar Square, has extended hours, opening 8am–8pm Monday–Saturday. Stamps are available from post offices, newsagents, some supermarkets and from vending machines near post boxes. Mail can be forwarded to you at any post office in Britain if it is addressed c/o Poste Restante.

TELEPHONE & FAX

Recent years have seen considerable changes to Britain's public telephones with the sad replacement of the traditional red call box by modern glass and stainless steel booths. There are now two separate telephone companies: **British Telecom** (BT) and **Mercury**. BT public telephones are more plentiful and make no charge for service calls made from public telephones. However, Mercury is reputedly cheaper for international calls, but their striking blue and grey booths are at present few and far between. In addition to coin call boxes, which are becoming increasingly scarce as a result of vandalism, both companies provide telephones that only accept plastic phone cards (resembling credit cards). Phonecards can be purchased from post offices, newsagents and corner shops for varying amounts between £1 and £20. Mercury phones accept also credit cards for which there is a minimum charge of 50p, a service which BT too is introducing.

Before using a phone in your hotel room it is advisable to check the rates first as some hotels make unreasonable charges for the convenience.

In Britain the most expensive time to use the telephone is 9am–1pm weekdays, whilst the cheapest period is after 6pm on weekdays and all weekend. **International calls:** You can telephone abroad by dialling 010 (00 after April 1995) followed by the country and area codes and then the number. Codes can be obtained from the International Operator by dialling 155. Also dial 155 to make a collect call (reverse charge) or to make a call using a telephone credit card. You will be charged extra for operator-assisted calls. International Directory Enquiries is on 154. To send a telegram dial 193. When telephoning Britain from abroad, dial the country code 44 and omit the first 0 from the area code. **Note:** On 16 April 1995, all UK codes will change, with a 1 being inserted after the initial 0.

USEFUL NUMBERS

Emergency: police, fire and ambulance, tel: 999.
Operator: (for difficulties in getting through or line faults), tel: 100.
Directory Enquiries: (for UK numbers outside London), tel: 192.
London Directory Enquiries: tel: 142.
Fax Directory: tel: 153.
Speaking Clock: tel: 123 (add prefix 9801 if calling from outside London).

THE MEDIA

Newspapers: With around 130 daily and Sunday newspapers published nationwide, the British public reads more newspapers than virtually any other country in the world. Free from state control and censorship, and financially independent of political parties, many do, however, have particularly pronounced political leanings, largely dictated by their proprietors. Ownership of the major national papers is concentrated in the hands of a small number of independent publishing corporations. One of the largest and most powerful of these is Rupert Murdoch's News International which owns five national papers and is involved in other media activities such as satellite television.

The quality daily newspapers are *The Times* and *The Daily Telegraph* (right bias), *The Guardian* (left bias) and *The Independent* (in the middle). There is also the specialist *Financial Times*. Tabloids such as *The Sun, The Star* and *Daily Mirror* are smaller with news issues swamped by pages of scandal and showbiz gossip. More up-market, but still gossipy are the *Daily Mail, Daily Express* and *Today* newspapers. Most of these papers publish a weekend edition with a colour supplement.

Scotland's own quality daily is *The Scotsman,* and the *Daily Record* is the most popular Scottish tabloid. On Sundays there are *Scotland on Sunday* and *The Sunday Post.* Wales, too, has its own newspapers: the *Western Mail,* the *Daily Post* and *Wales On Sunday.*

For information on news, events and small ads in specific regions consult local evening papers published in towns and cities throughout Britain. For what's going on in London, consult the magazines, *Time Out* or *City Limits* which are published weekly. Other cities may have their own equivalents such as *What's On* in Birmingham.

Foreign newspapers and magazines can usually be found in large newsagents nationwide.
Radio: Despite the growth in local independent radio stations, funded by advertising, the BBC still continues to dominate the airwaves with its six national stations:

Radio 1 - mainstream pop music.
Radio 2 - the nation's favourite playing middle-of-the-road music, light chat shows.
Radio 3 - classical music, serious drama.
Radio 4 - heavyweight discussions, news, current affairs and plays.
Radio 5 - a mixture of light entertainment, education and sport.
BBC World Service - broadcasts international news worldwide.

A network of local stations throughout Britain are run by both the BBC and independent companies.

Television: Britain has a reputation for broadcasting some of the finest television in the world. There are four national channels, BBC1, BBC2, ITV and Channel 4 (C4). Both the BBC (British Broadcasting Corporation) and ITV (Independent Television) have regional stations throughout the country which broadcast local news and varying programme schedules in between links with the national networks based in London. The state-run BBC is financed by compulsory annual television licences (anyone with a TV set must buy one) and therefore does not rely on commercials for funding. The independent channels, ITV and C4, are funded entirely by advertising.

BBC1 and ITV broadcast programmes aimed at mainstream audiences; BBC2 and C4 cater for arts, cultural and minority interests. However, with the advent of satellite and independent franchising, things are forecast to change in the future as stations become more commercially motivated and biased towards gaining high audience ratings, with programmes such as soap operas, game shows and situation comedies.

EMERGENCIES

EMERGENCY NUMBERS

Only in an absolute emergency call **999** for fire, ambulance or police. Otherwise, in the case of a minor accident or illness, take a taxi to the nearest casualty department of a hospital. If you need the police, call Directory Enquiries on 192 and ask for the number of the nearest police station. They will also be able to give you the telephone number of your country's embassy or consulate.

HEALTH

Unless you are employed in the UK, come from an EC country, or your country has reciprocal arrangements with this one (including Australia, Hong Kong, New Zealand, USSR, Norway, Sweden, Finland and Iceland) you will be liable for the cost of medical and dental treatment and should therefore have adequate health insurance before you arrive. No one is liable to be charged by the **National Health Service** for treatment in an accident, emergency or for an infectious disease. The National Health Service, a victim of its own popularity, has suffered from underfunding in recent decades, as a result of which many better-off people have been turning to private medical health care.

For **emergency dental care** go to the nearest hospital casualty ward. Otherwise, call Directory Enquiries (192) or consult the *Yellow Pages* telephone directory for the names and numbers of dentists in your area.

LOST CREDIT CARDS

These should be reported immediately:
Access/MasterCard: Southend-on-Sea, tel: 0702-352255.
American Express: Brighton, tel: 0273-696933.
Diners Club: Farnborough, tel: 0252-516261.
Visa: Northampton, tel: 0604-230230.

LOST PROPERTY

For property lost on a **British Rail** train you must contact the station where the train on which you were travelling ended its journey. The same applies should you leave something on a coach.

For property lost in **London** on the buses or the Tube, contact London Transport Lost Property Office, 200 Baker Street, NW1 (tel: 071-486 2496) between 9.30am–2pm Monday–Friday. If you left something in a black cab, the Taxi Lost Property office is at 15 Penton Street, N1 (tel: 071-833 0996).

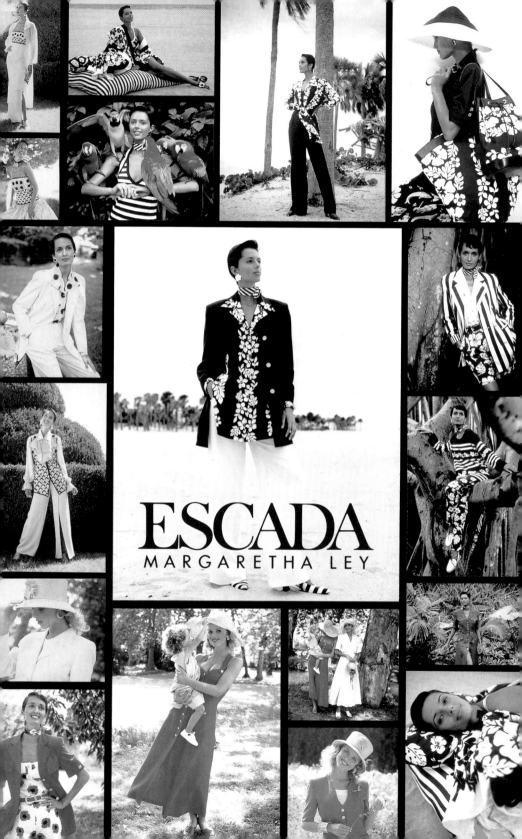

ESCADA

MARGARETHA LEY

INSIGHT GUIDES

COLORSET NUMBERS

▶ *What is the
significance
of the number
that appears
in a triangle
on the spine
of each
Insight Guide?
Each number,
in fact, is a
color code
identifying the
background
color of the
spine. Line up
all titles from
No. 100 to
300 for a
full set of
Insight Guides
and your
book-shelves
will radiate a
dazzling
rainbow of
world travel.*

GETTING AROUND

DOMESTIC AIR TRAVEL

From the major international airports there are frequent shuttle services to the many domestic airports throughout the country giving quick and easy access to many cities and difficult to reach places such as the Scottish Islands. Airlines providing domestic services in the UK are:

British Airways, Heathrow & GB flight info, tel: 081-759 2525. Reservations, tel: 081-897 4000.
British Midland Airways, tel: 081-745 4110.
Aer Lingus, tel: 081-569 5555.
Air UK, tel: 0345-666777.
Loganair, tel: 041-889 1311.

British Airways operates the Rover Ticket, for those who want to explore the inaccessible areas of Scotland at a faster pace. The ticket can be purchased abroad or in Britain but must be booked at least a week in advance. It entitles you to a maximum of 8 flights over a period of 8 to 21 days between the following airports: Aberdeen, Benbecula, Edinburgh, Glasgow, Inverness, Kirkwall, Shetland, Stornaway, Wick.

Major domestic airports:
Aberdeen, tel: 0224-722331.
Bristol, tel: 027-587 4441.
East Midlands, tel: 0332-810621.
Leeds, tel: 0532-509696.
Liverpool, tel: 051-486 8877.
Newcastle upon Tyne, tel: 091-286 0966.
Norwich, tel: 0603-411923.
Plymouth, tel: 0752-707023.
Southampton, tel: 0703-629600.
Southend, tel: 0702-340201.
Teesside, tel: 0325-332811.

BY RAIL

British Rail, known as **ScotRail** in Scotland, is the state railway. Expensive and infamous for its inefficiency, the service is however gradually improving and a journey on a speedy 125 InterCity train can be a great way to see some of Britain's wonderful scenery. British Rail offers the following special reduced rate fares for travellers:

Cheap Day Returns are reduced priced tickets to or from London on almost any train provided you leave from and return to your base on the same day.

Network AwayBreak allows you to stay away for up to five days and travel at any time except before 9.30am Monday–Friday.

The **Saver** ticket gives you a month to make your return journey but you cannot travel out at peak times from Monday–Friday (before 9.30am and between 4.15–6.15pm).

The **SuperSaver** ticket is cheaper still but the same conditions apply as for the Saver, and in addition you cannot travel on Fridays and certain Saturdays in the summer.

The **Rover** ticket allows travel on all lines for a 7-day or 14-day period. Alternatively, there are regional tickets allowing travel within a certain area for 7-day periods between March and October.

The **Britrail** ticket is similar to the Eurorail ticket on the Continent in that it allows unlimited travel in Great Britain for specific periods of time. It must be purchased before you arrive in England and can be obtained from European travel agents, main railway stations, or British Rail Travel Offices in Europe or North America.

These offers do not apply to first-class travel. If travelling long distances overnight, it is worth considering booking an InterCity sleeper which are modern and air-conditioned.

In **Scotland** you can buy a **Freedom of Scotland Travelpass** which entitles you to unlimited travel within the Highlands and Islands, for periods of 1–2 weeks, on Scotrail trains, Caledonian MacBrayne's ferries to the islands off the west coast and P&O's ferry service to Orkney. It also entitles you to a third discount on bus fares on Travelpass valid routes. For further information, tel: 0349-63434.

To see the beauty of Scotland in the luxury and style of a bygone age, take a trip on the famous **Royal Scotsman,** Scotland's answer to the Orient Express. Operated by Abercrombie and Kent there is a choice of 3, 4 and 6-day itineraries from April to November each year. This company also operates the **Great Wales Express** (5 days) and the **Great Britain Express** (6 days) luxury tours, travelling first class on scheduled train services. For further information, tel: 071-730 9600.

British Rail run a programme throughout the year of luxury **Special Train Journeys** in first-class Pullman coaches which leave from mainline London stations. Each journey is different, sometimes coinciding with festivals and events in an area, varying from day trips to the heart of Wales to long weekend Land Cruises to the Scottish Highlands and Islands. For example, the Orcadian is a three-night weekend trip to the far north of Scotland and the Orkneys with accommodation in first-class sleeping compartments and meals on board. For further information, tel: 071-388 0519 or write to Intercity Land Cruises, 104 Birmingham Road, Lichfield, Staffordshire.

Steam trains are still going strong in the Scottish Highlands where the West Highland, Strathspey, West Buchan and other lines operate along scenic routes. There are a dozen narrow-gauge railways in Wales, now restored and used for pleasure rides, but originally built to take slate from the mountains to the sea. The best known is the Ffestiniog railway, which runs 14 miles from Portmadog through the Snowdonia National Park to Blaenau Ffestiniog.

In England steam enthusiasts have kept going or resuscitated many lines, from the picturesque 72-mile Settle–Carlisle railway in the northwest to the 14-mile Romney, Hythe and Dymchurch railway in the southeast, the world's only miniature railway with locomotives one-third the normal size.

British Rail Travel Centres are located at major rail terminals and are also located at the following addresses in London: 87 King William Street, EC1; 14 Kingsgate Parade, Victoria Street, SW1; 12 Regent Street, Piccadilly, SW1.

RAIL ENQUIRIES (24 HOURS)

LONDON

Services to Europe, tel: 071-834 2345.
King's Cross, tel: 071-278 2477. Services to West Yorkshire, North East and Scotland.
St Pancras, tel: 071-387 7070. Services to East Midlands and South Yorkshire.
Euston, tel: 071-387 7070. Services to the Midlands, North Wales, North West and Scotland.
Paddington, tel: 071-262 6767: Services to the west of England, West Midlands and South Wales.
Waterloo/Victoria/Charing Cross, tel: 071-928 5100: Services to the south and south east of England.
Liverpool Street/Fenchurch Street, tel: 071-928 5100: Services to Essex and East Anglia.

SOME MAIN STATIONS OUTSIDE LONDON

Aberdeen, tel: 0224-594222.
Birmingham, tel: 021-643 2711.
Bristol, tel: 0272-294255.
Cardiff, tel: 0222-228000.
Edinburgh, tel: 031-556 2451.
Glasgow, tel: 041-204 2844.
Inverness, tel: 0463-238924.
Liverpool, tel: 051-709 9696.
Manchester, tel: 061-832 8353.
Newcastle, tel: 0632-326262.
Perth, tel: 0738-37117.

COACH

National Express and **Caledonian Express** operate a comprehensive network of coach services throughout the country with fast and comfortable *Rapide* coaches running on long journeys, equipped with washrooms, videos and stewardesses. Fares are considerably cheaper than the equivalent journey by train although it is advisable to book a ticket in advance to be assured of a seat. If you want to save extra money you can buy a standby ticket and take the risk that a seat might not be available at the time you wish to travel.

Tickets can be purchased from coach stations or from over 3,000 agents nationwide but they cannot be bought from the driver. The coach station at Victoria in London is the country's largest where credit-card bookings can be made by telephone (tel: 071-730 3499) up to 2 hours before departure.

For overseas visitors there are two special travel offers:

The **Britexpress Card** gives 30 percent discount on any amount of journeys made within a 30-day period. It costs £12 and can be purchased from travel agents before arrival in Britain or in the UK itself if proof of national identity is shown.

The **Tourist Trail Pass** allows unlimited travel on all services in England, Scotland and Wales for periods of 5, 8, 15, 22 or 30 days and costs between £56 and £160 for adults (reductions for children and pensioners). This pass is also available to UK citizens, but at a higher price.

For further information contact National Express and Caledonian Express:
London, tel: 071-730 0202
Birmingham, tel: 021-622 4373
Bristol, tel: 0272-541022
Manchester, tel: 061-228 3881
Edinburgh, tel: 031-452 8777
Glasgow, tel: 041-332 4100
Aberdeen, tel: 0224-580275
Cardiff, tel: 0222-344751

National Express and **Green Line** (tel: 081-668 7261) provide a service of scheduled day trips from London to tourist sights around the country such as Hampton Court Palace, Bath and Stratford-upon-Avon.

Towns and rural communities are generally well served by buses, often owned by private companies.

TAXIS

Outside of London and large cities and away from taxi ranks at stations, ports and airports you will usually have to telephone for a cab rather than expect to hail one in the street. By law cabs must be licensed and display charges on a meter. Add at least 10 percent for a tip.

London black cab drivers are famous for their extensive knowledge of the city's complex network of streets and one-way systems, having had to complete a rigorous study, called "The Knowledge", before being able to take to the road. Minicabs, however, are not allowed to compete with black cabs on the street and have to be hired by telephone or from a kiosk. If hiring a minicab make sure you agree a fee beforehand and, unlike black cabs, don't expect them to know precise destinations.

LONDON REGIONAL TRANSPORT (LRT)

The Underground (also known as the **Tube**) is the quickest, but not always the easiest, way to get across London. Although it is one of the most comprehensive systems of its kind in the world, it is also the oldest, having been in operation since 1863 – when the first trains puffed their way through smoke-filled tunnels between Paddington and Farringdon – and has become noticeably creaky. Apart from some central stations which have been revamped in recent years, many remain unchanged since the 1930s when the system was given its original corporate identity.

The Tube service starts at 5.30am and runs until the last trains start their final journeys at around midnight. Most Londoners and commuters use it and consequently it gets packed in the rush hours (8–9.30am and 5–6.30pm). Make sure that you have a valid ticket while in the system as it is illegal to travel without one. Smoking is prohibited. Fares are based upon a zone system with a flat fare (currently 90p) in the central zone.

A ride on the **Docklands Light Railway** is an excellent and cheap way to see the modern re-development of London's old dock area. This fully automated system, opened in 1987, currently has two branches. One starts from Tower Gateway and the other from Stratford and both finish at Island Gardens near the Greenwich Foot Tunnel on the Isle of Dogs. It connects up with the Underground network at Tower Hill and Stratford and operates in the same way as the Tube, with similar fares. Initially too light to cope with the heavy demands of the Docklands Development, the line is being expanded and connected to Bank Underground station. For further information, tel: 071-538 0311.

London buses provide a comprehensive service throughout Greater London and have their route and number clearly displayed on the front. Unlike the Underground, buses carry on running hourly throughout the night on certain routes, centring on Trafalgar Square. Smoking is prohibited on buses.

TRAVEL PASSES

The **Travelcard** is a one-day pass that allows unlimited travel on the Tube, buses, Docklands Light Railway and British Rail's Network SouthEast (tel: 071-928 5100) services to stations in Greater London. It can be used after 9.30am on weekdays and all day Saturday, Sunday and bank holidays, but not on night buses, and is available from all Underground and Network SouthEast stations. It costs £2.60 for zones 1 and 2, £3.10 for zones 1, 2, 3 and 4, and £3.50 for all zones.

Travel passes are valid for a week or a month and can be used at any time of the day. To buy a Pass you will need to supply a passport-sized photograph.

London Transport Information (24-hour), tel: 071-222 1234.

If you are staying in London for a while it is worth investing in an **A-Z Map** which gives detailed information of the capital's confusing complex of streets and post codes and is certain to save you a lot of trouble in getting about.

WATERWAYS

Britain has over 2,000 miles of rivers and canals, the latter a great legacy of the Industrial Revolution. There is a wide choice of boating on these inland waterways and a large number of places from which to hire vessels. Possibilities include exploring Britain's many canals, from the Grand Union in the Midlands to the Caledonian Canal which stretches from coast to coast in Scotland, taking a pleasure cruiser along Britain's major rivers such as the Thames, Avon or the Severn, sailing along the Norfolk Broads, or there's the romance of punting in the university towns of Oxford and Cambridge.

Things to note on Britain's waterways are that you should keep your vessel on the right-hand side of the channel when approaching another and that all pleasure boats must be licensed. Should you wish to fish you will need a licence from the local water authority. For further information, contact:

British Waterways Board, Melbury House, Melbury Terrace, London NW1 6JX. Tel: 071-262 6711.

British Waterways Board Craft Licensing Officer and Fisheries Officer, Willow Grange, Church Road, Watford, WD1 3QA. Tel: 0923 26422.

The Inland Waterways Association is a voluntary body which has fought since 1946 for the restoration and maintenance of Britain's inland waterway network. Relying totally on the help of members and volunteers, the Association has saved many of Britain's waterways which would otherwise have disappeared. It is also concerned with other waterway interests such as angling, nature conservation, walking and industrial architecture. Should you be interested in joining, or want a copy of the *Inland Waterways Handbook*, you can contact the Association at: 114 Regent's Park Road, London NW1 8UQ. Tel: 071-586 2556.

Scottish ferries: Ferry services between the 23 islands and the mainland of the northwest coast of Scotland have been monopolised by Caledonian MacBrayne. Their ferries largely cater for the needs of the islanders, delivering mail and groceries, and tourists should therefore state in advance if they wish to disembark at a particular port. The Island Hopscotch ticket is good value, allowing unlimited travel for a two-week period on most routes for car, driver and passenger. For further information, tel: 0475-33755.

Ferries to Orkney and Shetland are operated by P&O, tel: 0224-572 615.

On the Thames in London: Thames Passenger Services Federation (TPSF) run a riverboat service between Hampton Court (up-river) and the Thames Barrier (down-river) which is an excellent way to see many of London's sights. Services vary from summer to winter, with down-river services tending to run all year round, whilst most up river services run only between April and October. There are piers at Richmond, Kew, Putney, Westminster, Charing Cross, London Bridge, The Tower and Greenwich.

TPSF runs several special services from Westminster Pier, including the Circular Cruise (1-hour round trip), Floodlight and Supper cruise and the Luncheon Cruise. For more information, tel: 071-930 2062. Catamaran Cruisers, tel: 071-839 3572, also offers a variety of cruises on the Thames.

BY CAR

In the UK drive on the left-hand-side of the road and observe the speed limits: 30 mph (50 kph) in urban areas (unless otherwise indicated), 60 mph (96 kph) on two-way roads away from built-up areas, and 70 mph (112 kph) on motorways and dual-carriageways. Camping vans or cars towing a caravan are restricted to 50 mph (80 kph) on normal roads and 60 mph (96 kph) on dual-carriageways. It is strictly illegal to drink and drive; penalties are severe. The law states that both drivers and passengers must wear seat belts. Cars should give way to pedestrians at zebra crossings.

If you are bringing your own car into Britain you will need a valid driving licence or International Driving Permit, insurance coverage, vehicle registration document and a nationality sticker.

Parking: Road congestion is a problem in most town and city centres, which were certainly not designed for heavy traffic, and consequently parking is greatly restricted. Don't ever leave your car parked on a double yellow line, in a place marked for *permit holders only,* within a white zig-zag line close to a pedestrian crossing, or in a control zone. Also, don't park on a single yellow line when restrictions are in force, usually 8.30am to 6.30pm weekdays (consult signs on the curb). These are offences for which you can face a fine. Either use a meter or a municipal car park (distinguished by a white P on a blue background).

Pay particular attention if parking in central London; the traffic wardens are unforgiving and some seem over-eager to hand out tickets. In many areas, illegal parking may result in your car being wheel-clamped, immobilising it until you travel to a parking office and pay a hefty sum to have it released, which may not be for several hours (the inconvenience is part of the deterrent). Worse still, your car may be towed away.

Further information on driving in Britain can be found in *The Highway Code* published by Her Majesty's Stationery Office and widely available in bookshops and newsagents.

The **Road Traffic Hotline** provides information regarding any major disruptions on Britain's highways, tel: 0898-345367.

Breakdown: The following motoring organisations operate 24-hour breakdown assistance. All calls to these numbers are free.
AA, tel: 0800-887766.
RAC, tel: 0800-828282.
National Breakdown, tel: 0800-400600.

CAR RENTAL

To rent a car in Britain you must be over 21 years old (over 25 for some companies) and have held a valid full driving licence for more than one year. The cost of hiring a car will usually include insurance and unlimited mileage and road tax. It does not, however, include insurance cover for accidental damage to interior trim, wheels and tyres or insurance for other drivers without prior approval. It can be worth shopping around as some companies offer special weekend and holiday rates.

International companies such as Hertz, Avis, Budget Rent A Car and Europcar are particularly keen to encourage visitors to book in advance before they leave home and may offer holiday packages with discounts of as much as 40 percent on advance bookings through travel agents or branches in your own country. Another advantage of large international companies is that you can hire a car for a one-way trip if the company has an office at your destination.

Many rental firms provide child seats and luggage racks for a small charge.
Car rental firms:
Avis, tel: 081-848 8733.
Hertz, tel: 071-679 1799.
Swan National Eurodollar, tel: 071-730 8773.
Budget Rent A Car, tel: 0800-181181.
Guy Salmon Car Rentals, tel: 0483-757598.
British Car Rental, tel: 0203-633400.
Europcar, tel: 081-950 4080.
Eurodollar Rent A Car, tel: 0895-333000.

WHERE TO STAY

A variety of accommodation exists in Britain, from smart luxury hotels in stately homes and castles, to bed-and-breakfast (B&B) accommodation in private family homes or country farmhouses. More unusual accommodation, such as an *oast house*, can be arranged if you plan ahead.

By international standards, hotels in Britain are expensive, so if you are holidaying on a tight budget you should consider staying in bed-and-breakfast accommodation. Alternatively there are plenty of youth hostels throughout the country. Wherever you go, always ask to look at a room first before accepting it.

A word of warning: not all hotels include breakfast in their rates and they are also likely to add a service charge of 10–15 percent. However, all charges should be clearly displayed on the tariff. Tipping is at a guest's discretion.

It is always advisable to book a hotel in advance, particularly at Easter and in the summer, although during the rest of the year there is generally little difficulty in finding somewhere to stay. You can book a room through a travel agent, directly through a hotel or via the Tourist Board. Confirmation in writing and a deposit may be required.

However, if you do land in a place without a bed for the night, the local Tourist Information Centre may be able to help you. TICs displaying a **Local Bed Booking Service** sticker will book local accommodation for personal callers whereas those involved in the **Book-A-Bed-Ahead** scheme will reserve you somewhere suitable to stay in any area where there is another TIC involved in the scheme. All TICs have free lists of local accommodation. The **British Travel Centre** in Regent Street, London, provides an accommodation booking service for the whole of the country. A small deposit may be required which should later be deducted from your hotel bill.

Great Britain has no official classification system for the facilities and quality of accommodation an establishment has to offer, but several independent bodies run their own schemes. The AA (Automobile Association) and RAC (Royal Automobile Club) provide a simple scheme of awarding between one star (good, but basic) to five stars (luxury). Meanwhile the English, Welsh and Scottish tourist boards make life more confusing by awarding their very own Crowns, from one to five for facilities and services, and a separate measure of *Approved, Commended* and

Highly Commended for ambience and quality. However, a Michelin award is the accolade for which the most notable of hoteliers strive.

All establishments proudly display these awards outside and the thing to remember is that more does not necessarily mean better! A country inn with a mere 2 stars may prove to offer excellent and characterful accommodation, but lack facilities such as television and private bathrooms, whilst an impersonal concrete-block hotel with well-equipped shoe-boxes for rooms may boast 4 stars.

The **English Tourist Board (ETB)** produces a series of useful *Where To Stay* leaflets dealing with every type of accommodation in Britain, from farms to self-catering boating holidays. However, to be mentioned in these, an establishment has first to pay to be inspected and then pay to be included, so the leaflets are not exactly impartial.

The ETB also publishes *Bed and Breakfast Touring Maps* for seven different regions of England which are ideal if you are planning to tour. They pin-point hundreds of places to stay for under £20 as well as local places of interest. Areas are: *Yorkshire & Humberside; North West; North of England; Heart of Britain; East of England; West Country; South of England*. All the above are obtainable from TICs throughout the country or by writing to the tourist board in the appropriate area.

The tourist board also publishes a series of books which includes the following titles: *Hotels & Guesthouses in England* (£6.95), *Bed & Breakfast, Farmhouses, Inns & Hostels in England* (£5.95), *Self-Catering Holiday Homes in England* (£4.95), *Scotland – Hotels and Guest Houses* (£4.95). These guides are sold in bookshops, newsagents and most Tourist Information Centres or by post from the respective tourist boards.

Stately Homes: Britain has many grand stately homes and castles which have been converted into country-house hotels. This growing trend in luxury accommodation has saved many splendid historic buildings from dereliction. Most provide an extremely high standard of traditional accommodation and service, often with superb restaurants, hence a selection appear in the *Food Digest* section.

HOTELS

Hotels belonging to big chains such as Forte Group and Hilton abound and tend to offer a reliable, if at times impersonal, standard of service. In addition there are a host of individual private hotels. The business traveller on an expense account is increasingly well catered for, in both urban and country areas, where there are many hotels offering large conference rooms and health facilities in addition to fax and secretarial facilities. The following organisations have hotels in most parts of the country: **Forte Group**, tel: 081-567 3444, 0345-500400. **Intercontinental & Forum Hotels**, tel: 081-741 9000.

Hilton International, tel: 071-734 6000.
Holiday Inns, tel: 071-722 7755.
Crest Hotels, tel: 071-236 3242.
Rank Hotels, tel: 081-569 7120.

Many hotels offer special weekend and low-season breaks between October and April. Details can be obtained from individual hotels, chains of hotels or from the English Tourist Board which publishes a brochure, *Let's Go Short Breaks in England,* giving details of reduced rates at hundreds of hotels.

The following suggestions are for hotels in places which will serve as good bases for exploring the regions covered in the Guide's chapters. Prices quoted are the minimum for bed and breakfast for two people sharing. Unless otherwise stated, all the rooms in the following hotels have private facilities.

LONDON

The price of a hotel room in London is as high as the equivalent anywhere else in Europe. However, cost does not always mean quality, so look out for the LVCB membership sticker indicating that certain standards have been met and always try to view a room before accepting it. In the height of the summer season (April to September) it is advisable to book before you arrive as hotels fill up fast. The London Tourist Board provides a bed booking service through information centres or by telephone (credit cards only), tel: 071-824 8844.

The hotels listed below are located centrally and have been chosen either for their excellent positions or for providing welcoming English hospitality in characterful surroundings.

Many moderately priced hotels are small and don't have restaurant facilities, although they may provide room service. It is often worth calling into the more expensive hotels for afternoon tea or cocktails. Some hotels offer babysitting and booking services for theatres and restaurants, while smarter establishments are geared up for the business traveller with conference, fax and photocopying facilities.

Numerous hotels, including the Ritz and the Savoy, offer special weekend rates depending on the season. These are well worth checking out and may include extra incentives such as guided tours and Champagne dinners.

LUXURY: over £150

The Beaufort, 33 Beaufort Gardens, SW3, tel: 071-584 5252. Excellent small and homely luxury hotel in an elegant Knightsbridge square. Guests are given freedom of the house with own front door key and use of nearby health club. From £160.
The Berkeley, Wilton Place, SW1, tel: 071-235 6000. One of London's finest. High-class luxury, including Roman bath style roof-top pool, gymnasium and sauna. £200.

Blakes, 33 Roland Gardens, SW7, tel: 071-370 6701. Created by actress Anouska Hempel, this exotic, laid-back hotel is frequented by pop, media and showbiz types. 52 rooms. £195.
Brown's, Dover Street, W1, tel: 071-493 6020. Has expanded into 14 Mayfair Georgian town houses since it was opened in 1837 by James Brown, former manservant to Lord Byron. Very traditionally English. Magnificently furnished. 125 rooms. £205.
The Capital, Basil Street, SW3, tel: 071-589 5171. Courteous town-house hotel in heart of Knightsbridge with a high degree of *fin-de-siècle* elegance. Restaurant has one Michelin star. 60 rooms. £175.
The Goring, 15 Beeston Place, SW1, tel: 071-834 8211. Gracious hotel close to Buckingham Palace. This was the world's first hotel to install bathrooms and central heating in every room and it still maintains very high standards. 68 rooms. £175.
The Ritz, Piccadilly, W1, tel: 071-493 8181. Lavish hotel with overtones of sheer decadence which is synonymous with class and style the world over. Timeless, memorable and expensive. 130 rooms. £210.

EXPENSIVE: £100–£150

The Abbey Court, 20 Pembridge Gardens, W2, tel: 071-221 7518. Commendable B&B in restored town house delightfully furnished in English country style. 21 rooms (three with four-poster beds). £134.
The Basil Street Hotel, Knightsbridge, SW3, tel: 071-581 3311. Old-fashioned hotel with English country charm and character attracting regular clientele from the landed gentry. 94 rooms. £130.
The Cadogan, Sloane Street, SW1, tel: 071-235 7141. A fine Edwardian red-brick building which was once home to the actress and society beauty, Lillie Langtry. Now offers modern comforts combined with old-fashioned elegance. 122 rooms. £115.
The Coburg, Bayswater Road, W2, tel: 071-221 2217. Recently restored to its former glory, this Edwardian hotel overlooks Kensington Palace Gardens. 122 rooms. £115.
The Rubens, Buckingham Palace Road, Victoria, SW1, tel: 071-834 6600. Opposite the Royal Mews is this smart modernised hotel elegantly decorated with modern furniture and pastel shades. 188 rooms. £135.
Tower Thistle Hotel, St Katherine's Way, E1, tel: 071-481 2575. What this large modern hotel lacks in charm is compensated for by its breathtaking location on the north bank of the Thames, close to Tower Bridge and the Tower of London. 808 rooms. £128.

MODERATE: £70–£95

The Academy Hotel, 17–21 Gower Street, WC1, tel: 071-631 4115. Within two converted Georgian town houses in the heart of literary Bloomsbury. 33 rooms, most with private facilities. £95.

The Claverley, 13–14 Beaufort Gardens, SW3, tel: 071-589 8541. Respected Knightsbridge B&B hotel furnished in quaint English country style. 36 rooms, many with private facilities. £85.

Durrants Hotels, George Street, W1, tel: 071-935 8131. Discreet family hotel, just north of Oxford Street, which evokes the feeling of a country inn. Public rooms furnished with wood panelling and leather furniture. Bedrooms are comfortable. Well priced for the area. 93 rooms. £90.

Hazlitt's, 6 Frith Street, W1, tel: 071-434 1771. Characterful hotel occupying three historic town houses in Soho. 23 rooms, all with bathrooms, are charmingly furnished in classic period style, with antiques, potted plants and Victorian bath fittings. £90.

Portobello Hotel, 22 Stanley Gardens, W11, tel: 071-727 2777. Eccentric hotel, close to Portobello's antique market, furnished in a hybrid Victorian style. 25 rooms, all with private facilities, varying from tiny cabins to unusual suites. £96.

Wilbraham Hotel, Wilbraham Place, SW1, tel: 071-730 8296. Old-fashioned and dated, this privately owned hotel has a distinctive English charm. Good value in exclusive Belgravia. 50 rooms, most with bath. No credit cards. £70.

BUDGET: under £60

Abbey House, 11 Vicarage Gate, W8, tel: 071-727 2594. Inviting but basic B&B accommodation in a desirable Kensington residential street. Well maintained. 15 rooms. No credit cards. £42.

Eden House, 111 Old Church Street, SW3, tel: 071-352 3403. Pleasant town-house B&B in a quiet desirable location close to the fashionable King's Road in Chelsea. 14 rooms (5 family, 8 with bath). £55.

Edward Lear Hotel, 28–30 Seymour Street, W1, tel: 071-402 5401. Georgian house close to Marble Arch which was once inhabited by Victorian painter and poet Edward Lear. Tastefully refurbished in a comfortable modern fashion. 30 rooms. £50.

Elizabeth Hotel, 37 Eccleston Square, SW1, tel: 071-828 6812. Small and friendly hotel overlooking a grand period square close to Victoria. Use of private garden and tennis court. 25 rooms (7 with bath). £50.

Fielding Hotel, 4 Broad Street, WC1, tel: 071-836 8305. Covent Garden hotel in a quiet paved-over street close to the Royal Opera House. Small and rather frayed at the edges, it is excellent value for the location. 26 rooms (most with bath). £60.

The Willett, 32 Sloane Gardens, Sloane Square, SW1, tel: 071-824 8415. Small, tastefully modernised hotel in the fashionable neighbourhood of Sloane Square. 19 rooms (most with bath). £60.

The best areas for moderately priced **bed-and-breakfast** accommodation are Victoria, Knightsbridge, Earl's Court, Bayswater and Bloomsbury.

THAMES VALLEY & OXFORD

The Randolph Hotel, Beaumont Street, Oxford, Tel: 0865-247481. Grand Victorian hotel in central Oxford offering traditional service with all the trimmings. 109 rooms. £110.

The White Hart Hotel, Dorchester-on-Thames, Oxfordshire, tel: 0865-340074. Rambling old coaching inn surrounded by thatched cottages in a picturesque riverside village. Offers a high standard of accommodation with plenty of old-world charm. 20 rooms. £85.

Sir Christopher Wren's House Hotel, Thames Street, Windsor, tel: 0753-861354. Well located between the foot of the castle and the river, this fine hotel was once home to the architect, Sir Christopher Wren. Many original 17th-century features remain. Fine restaurant. 38 rooms. £99.

COTSWOLDS

The Shakespeare, Chapel Street, Stratford-upon-Avon, Warwickshire, tel: 0789-294771. This 17th-century half-timbered building is the best hotel in town and one of Stratford's most famous and beautiful buildings. Centrally located with large open fires and good restaurant. 70 rooms. £110.

The Snooty Fox, Market Place, Tetbury, Gloucestershire, tel: 0666-52436. Old Cotswold stone coaching inn on the square of this historic market town. Interior features oak panelling, log fires and is furnished with antiques. Fine restaurant. 12 rooms. £84.

The Grapevine, Sheep Street, Stow-on-the-Wold, Gloucestershire, tel: 0451-30344. Immaculately maintained hotel within an old stone building providing a good base from which to tour the Cotswolds. Guests are well catered for in the attractive conservatory restaurant. 23 rooms. £80.

SOUTHEAST

The Bow Window Inn, High Street, Littlebourne, Canterbury, Kent, tel: 0227-721264. Traditional English hospitality at this pretty old country inn with exposed beams and open fires situated 3 miles east of Canterbury. 8 rooms. £52.

The Mermaid Inn, Mermaid Street, Rye, tel: 0797-223065. Popular 15th-century inn in this ancient coastal port. Excellent restaurant. 28 rooms. £90.

The Ship Hotel, North Street, Chichester, tel: 0243 782028. Fine 18th-century Georgian town house, once the home of an admiral, situated in the centre of Chichester. Well furnished, it maintains its original character. 37 rooms. £66.

SOUTH & WEST

The Alexandra, Pound Street, Lyme Regis, Dorset, tel: 0297-42010. Large 18th-century white house, former home of Countess Poulet, set in fine grounds overlooking the bay. Comfortable and welcoming. 26 rooms. £80.

New Park Manor, Brockenhurst, New Forest, Hampshire, tel: 0590 23467. This excellent country retreat was once the hunting lodge of Charles II and is set in 6 acres of beautifully landscaped grounds in the heart of the New Forest. Facilities include excellent restaurant, stables, heated pool and tennis court. 25 rooms. £75.

Winchester, Wykeham Arms, 75 Kingsgate Street, Winchester, Hampshire, tel: 0962-53834. Popular old coaching inn crammed in a small street close to the Cathedral and College. Characterful with attentive service and comfortable rooms. 7 rooms. £66.

The Dukes' Hotel, Great Pulteney Street, Bath, Avon, Tel: 0225-463512. Hospitable Georgian town house hotel a short stroll from the heart of Bath. 22 rooms. £75.

The Royal Castle, 11 The Quay, Dartmouth, Devon, Tel: 0803-833033. This fascinating building on Dartmouth's quayside was originally a 17th-century coaching inn. Serves good Devon cuisine and award-winning traditional breakfasts. 25 rooms. £65.

The Queen's Hotel, The Promenade, Penzance, Cornwall, tel: 0736 62371. Grand English seaside hotel with wonderful views over Mounts Bay to St Michael's Mount in the distance. 71 rooms. £80.

WELSH BORDERS

The Castle Pool Hotel, Castle Street, Hereford, Herefordshire, tel: 0432-356321. This grand house was the former home of the Bishop of Hereford. Today it provides an excellent base in the centre of Hereford, a short walk from the cathedral. Particularly renowned for the excellence of its restaurant. 27 rooms. £80.

The Lion, Wyle Cop, Shrewsbury, Shropshire, tel: 0743-53107. Attractive 18th-century coaching inn located in the centre of this historic medieval town. Now owned by Trusthouse Forte. 59 rooms. £90

The Redland, 64 Hough Green, Chester, Cheshire, tel: 0244-671024. A curious and interesting interior lies behind the facade of this Victorian Gothic guesthouse which is delightfully furnished with quality Victorian and Edwardian antiques. 12 rooms. £50.

WALES

Ye Olde Bull's Head, Castle Street, Beaumaris, Anglesey, Gwynedd, tel: 0248-810329. Historic coaching inn at the centre of Beaumaris whose distinguished guests have included Charles Dickens. Comfortable Laura Ashley style bedrooms, fine restaurant and old-world charm. 11 rooms. £62.

Hotel Portmeirion, Portmeirion, Gwynedd, tel: 0766-770228. This eccentric hotel is central to Sir Clough Williams-Ellis's model fantasy village on the coast above Tremadog Bay. The interior has been decorated on exotic themes and each of the 14 rooms

has its own character. £97. 20 further rooms in the village are available from £72.

Waterwynch House Hotel, Narberth Road, Tenby, Dyfed, tel: 0834-2464. Inviting hotel surrounded by gardens, woods and beaches, in a picturesque cove on the Pembrokeshire coastal path. Good restaurant. 12 rooms (10 with private facilities). £30.

Fairyhill Country House, Reynoldston, Gower, Swansea, tel: 0792-390139. Twelve miles (20 km) west of Swansea, close to the breathtaking beaches of the Gower Peninsular, is this 18th-century country house peacefully situated within 24 acres (10 hectares) of parkland. Down to earth and friendly, with one of the best restaurants in the area. 11 rooms. £60.

Golfa Hall Hotel, Welshpool, Powys, tel: 0938-554777. Pretty white-washed country hotel with beautiful grounds overlooking a wooded valley west of Welshpool. Local produce is served in the restaurant. £60. 11 rooms.

Bryn-y-Bia Lodge Hotel, Craigside, Llandudno, Gwynedd, tel: 0492-49644. Attractive country house situated away from the bustle of this elegant seaside resort but still within easy access of the sea. Provides a high standard of service, food and accommodation. 14 rooms. £50

MERSEYSIDE

The Britannia Adelphi Hotel, Ranelagh Place, Liverpool, Merseyside, tel: 051-709 7200. Large and impressive, this is Liverpool's premier hotel and its grand classical stone facade provides a major landmark in the city centre. 390 rooms. £100 weekdays/£60 weekends.

PEAK DISTRICT

North Stafford Hotel, Station Road, Stoke-on-Trent, Staffs, tel: 0782-744477. This proud Jacobean-style Victorian red-brick hotel, opposite the main station, is ideally located for a visit to the Potteries. 69 rooms. £85

Old Hall Hotel, The Square, Buxton, Derbyshire, tel: 0298-22841. A landmark in Buxton since the 16th century, this dignified hotel is located on the town square overlooking the Pavilion Gardens with the Opera House close at hand. 37 rooms. £65.

EAST ANGLIA

Arundel House Hotel, 53 Chesterton Road, Cambridge, tel: 0223-67701. Privately owned terraced hotel overlooking the river Cam near the centre of the university town. 88 rooms (79 with private baths). £55.

The Georgian House Hotel, 32–34 Unthank Road, Norwich, Norfolk, tel: 0603-615655. Two Georgian houses have been combined to form this comfortable family-run hotel which is a stone's throw from the city centre. 27 rooms. £55.

Stuart House Hotel, 35 Goodwins Road, King's Lynn, Norfolk, tel: 0553-72169. This quiet, well cared-for hotel is ideal for exploring the Fens as well as the historic port of King's Lynn. 21 rooms (18 with private facilities). £50.

THE NORTH

Lady Anne Middleton's Hotel, Skeldergate, York, tel: 0904-632257. Family-run hotel in an attractive period house set in picturesque gardens close to the River Ouse and the centre of the city. 50 rooms. £60.
County Hotel, Priestpopple, Hexham, Northumberland, tel: 0434-602030. Excellent English hospitality at this friendly hotel in the market town of Hexham. Handy for exploring Hadrian's Wall, the Pennines and Southern Scotland. 12 rooms (9 with private showers). £70.
Lowbyer Manor, Alston, Cumbria , tel: 0498-81230. Characterful 17th-century manor house with exposed beams and inglenook fireplaces, once owned by the Earl of Derwentwater. Situated on the Pennine Way, it provides excellent hospitality and a good base from which to explore the Lake District, Northumbria and North Yorkshire. 11 rooms. £54.
The Blue Bell Hotel, Belford, Northumberland, tel: 0668-213543. Charming hotel within a picturesque 17th-century coaching inn on the east coast close to Holy Island. Interior is well furnished in period style. 15 rooms. £70.
Nanny Brow Country House Hotel, Ambleside, Cumbria, tel: 05394-32036. One of the best hotels in the Lakes, this Edwardian house is peacefully situated in lovely grounds, with stunning views. 19 rooms. £70.

SCOTTISH LOWLANDS

Scandic Crown, 80 High Street, The Royal Mile, Edinburgh, tel: 031-557 9797. Situated on the Royal Mile, a stone's throw from the castle, this grand hotel, opened in 1990, was designed to blend in with this historic area. Excellent service and facilities. 238 rooms. £100.
Sherbrooke Castle, 11 Sherbrooke Avenue, Glasgow, tel: 041-427 4227. Grand 19th-century baronial castle surrounded by its own grounds in a quiet residential area 3 miles (5 km) from the city centre. Well located for Pollock Country Park and the Burrell Collection. 25 rooms. £60.
Cringletie House Hotel, Peebles, Peebleshire, Borders, tel: 07213-233. Wonderfully located within a 28-acre estate, this turreted baronial mansion house has a reputation for outstanding cuisine and a great atmosphere. 13 rooms. £70.

SCOTTISH HIGHLANDS

The Lodge on the Loch, Creag Dhu, Onich, near Fort William, Inverness-shire, tel: 08553-237. In a stunning location, perched on the edge of Loch Linnhe, this provides a good base from which to explore the Western Highlands. Fine Scottish fare and warm hospitality. 18 rooms. £60.
Bunchrew House, Bunchrew, Inverness, tel: 0463-234917. Live like a lord at this 17th-century baronial turreted mansion where guests are given freedom of the estate for salmon fishing, golf and sailing. Traditional Scottish cuisine is served in the restaurant which overlooks the sea. 6 suites. £100.
Loch Duich Hotel, Ardelve, Kyle of Lochalsh, Wester Ross, tel: 059985-213. Wonderful food and good service at this congenial hotel just a short stroll from the fairytale Eilean Donan Castle and a ferry ride away from the Isle of Skye. 17 rooms. £50.
Knockomie Hotel, Grantown Road, Forres, Morayshire, tel: 0309-73146. A good starting point for the famous malt whisky trail, this delightful Edwardian country house hotel offers hearty hospitality and imaginative food. 7 rooms. £60

INNS & PUBS

The great institution of the British inn has in recent years become an increasingly popular choice of accommodation. Not only are inns cheaper and smaller than hotels but they may also offer charm, character and the opportunity of integrating with the local community, to which they are central.

Unique to Great Britain, the inn has a long history dating back to Roman times. Consequently there are many historic taverns, particularly in rural towns, villages and on road sides where travelling pilgrims may have rested in the Middle Ages or where stage coaches used to stop in the days of highwaymen. Many such inns have retained their old-world character and have welcoming open fires, low beams and a warm ambience combined with modern comforts. However, staying at an inn or pub may not always be such a cosy experience and in urban areas you are most likely to find pubs with an institutional feel. Standards vary from basic to sophisticated, with food facilities ranging from bar snacks to quality restaurants.

GUEST HOUSES

Somewhere between a hotel and a B&B in terms of size, price and facilities, guest houses are generally small and friendly, family-run businesses. Breakfast is usually included.

BED & BREAKFAST

These are generally private homes with a few rooms available for rent. As with all types of accommodation, standards will vary, but you can usually expect friendly hospitality, which will include a hearty English breakfast of eggs and bacon, and helpful advice on where to visit and eat in the area. Distinguished by a B&B sign placed outside, they are most abundant on the edge of towns and in prime tourist areas. B&Bs tend to be exceptional value and it is always advisable to book in advance during peak season. B&B accommodation is also available in many farmhouses, particularly in Wales, which provide the opportunity of rural accommodation with an insight into British farm life.

SELF-CATERING

The choice ranges from sophisticated town flats or quaint country cottages to unusual buildings such as oast houses (buildings which once contained kilns) and castles, or even canal barges. The English Tourist Board's guide to self-catering holidays in winter, *Home from Home,* lists around 200 self-catering properties from cliff-top fishermen's cottages to converted 19th-century barns and is part of their *Break with Tradition* campaign.

The National Trust and National Trust for Scotland have properties of historical interest to let. For further information write to: The National Trust, 36 Queen Anne's Gate, London SW1; The National Trust for Scotland, 5 Charlotte Square, Edinburgh EH2.

The Landmark Trust, Shottesbrooke, Maidenhead, Berkshire, tel: 0628-825925. This private charity, set up in 1965 to rescue small historic buildings in distress, now has over 200 properties of architectural or historical note available to let. Ranging from medieval castles and Gothic temples to water towers and lighthouses, all have been restored and furnished in keeping with the original character of the building. Prices range from £100 (two people sharing for 3 days) to £1,000 (12 sharing for a week in high season). Detailed information on each property is given in a handbook available by post for £7.50 (UK), £17 (USA), £18 (Australasia and Far East). Payment is accepted by sterling cheque or by credit card.

SELF-CATERING AGENCIES

Blakes Country Cottages, Wroxham, Norwich, Norfolk NR12, tel: 0603-783221. Over 1,000 cottages sleeping 2–8 people in pleasant areas of England. £131 (3 nights) to £560 (7 nights).

Cornish Traditional Cottages Ltd, Peregrine Hall, Lostwithiel, Cornwall PL22, tel: 0208-872559. 400 cottages, houses and apartments in Cornwall sleeping 2–12 people. £60 (4 nights) to £300 (7 nights).

Dales Holiday Cottages, 12 Otley Street, Skipton, North Yorkshire BD23 1DZ, tel: 0756-799821. Over 350 houses and cottages in Northumbria, Yorkshire Dales, moors and coast. Sleep 2–10. £60 (2 nights) to £450 (7 nights).

English Country Cottages Ltd, Dept E101, Fakenham, Norfolk NR21 8AS, tel: 0328-864041. Wide variety of over 2,000 country properties including oast houses, barns, castles and manor houses sleeping 2–22 people. £80 (3 nights) to £1,035 (7 nights).

Forest Holidays, Forestry Commission, 231 Corstorphine Road, Edinburgh EH12 7AT, tel: 031-334 0303. 5 or 6-berth cabins or cottages in Yorkshire, Cornwall and Scotland. Pets welcome. £60 (3 nights) to £105 (7 nights).

Hayward Cottage Holidays, Lansdowne Place, 17 Holdenhurst Road, Bournemouth, Dorset BH8 8EH, tel: 0202-555545. Over 200 holiday cottages in country and coastal areas in the south and southwest, from a medieval hall to an Elizabethan summer house. Sleep 2–12. £51 (3 nights) to £284 (7 nights).

Heart of the Lakes & Cottage Life, Rydal Holme, Rydal, Ambleside, Cumbria LA22 9LR, tel: 053 94-32321. Holiday homes in the centre of the picturesque Lake District. Sleep 2–10. £60 (2/3 nights) to £660 (7 nights).

Helpful Holidays, Coombe, Chagford, Devon TQ13 8DF, tel: 0647-433593. A wide variety of accommodation in the West Country's pretty villages and countryside. Sleep 2–20. £50 (3 nights) to £500 (7 nights).

Scottish Highlands Holiday Homes, Wester Altouriell, Abiachan, Inverness, tel: 9463-86247. Range of holiday homes and cottages in the Scottish Highlands.

LONDON

Holiday Flats Services Ltd, 16 Gloucester Place, London W1, tel: 071-486 8646. Have a large number of flats throughout Greater London from £300 for a studio to several thousand pounds for five-star luxury apartment.

Apartment Services, 2 Sandwich Street WC1, tel: 071-388 3558. 60 privately-owned flats in central London, particularly in Bloomsbury and Covent Garden. £150–£700 per week.

Holiday Flats, 1 Princess Mews, Belsize Crescent NW3, tel: 071-794 1186. 60 privately-owned 1–4 bed flats in Hampstead, St John's Wood and Bayswater. £250–£700 per week.

YOUTH HOSTELS

There are over 260 youth hostels in Britain ranging from town houses to beach chalets which are graded, *simple, standard* and *superior*. Facilities are very basic, but then accommodation is extremely cheap, usually comprising shared dormitories of bunk beds. Everyone is expected to do their fair share of the daily chores and therefore it is great for those who don't mind mucking-in, communal living and a shortage of creature comforts. The maximum length of stay in each hostel is three nights. You must be a national or international member to stay at a hostel, although anyone can join the association, overseas or in the UK.

Youth Hostel Association (YHA), head office: Trevelyan House, 8 St Stephen's Hill, St Albans, Herts, tel: 0727-55215.

For the fastest weekend refunds anywhere in the world.

Ensure your holiday is worry free even if
your travellers cheques are lost or stolen by buying
American Express Travellers Cheques from;

Lloyds Bank

Royal Bank of Scotland

Abbey National[*]

Bank of Ireland

Halifax Building Society[*]

Leeds Permanent Building Society[*]

Woolwich Building Society[*]

National & Provincial Building Society

Britannia Building Society[*]

American Express Travel Offices.

As well as many regional building societies and travel agents.

[*]Investors only.

Not all travellers cheques are the same.

AMERICAN
EXPRESS **Travellers
Cheques**
®

Our history could fill this book, but we prefer to fill glasses.

When you make a great beer, you don't have to make a great fuss

LONDON

36 Carter Lane, EC4, tel: 071-236 4965 (the largest in GB with 282 beds).
38 Bolton Gardens, SW5, tel: 071-373 3083 (111 beds).
4 Wellgarth Road, NW11, tel: 081-458 9054 (220 beds).
84 Highgate West Hill, N6, tel: 081-340 1831 (62 beds).
Holland House, Holland Walk, Kensington W8, tel: 071-937 0748 (190 beds).

FOOD DIGEST

To many, the thought of British food conjures up a picture of unappetising stodgy fare that rests heavy on the stomach, leaving taste buds asleep. However, whilst the tradition of uninspiring meals of "meat and two veg" will not be moved, a large proportion of the population have long been awake to outside international influences and, indeed, to making more imaginative use of traditional recipes.

This move has been led in recent years by a generation of talented modern British chefs who have injected new life into traditional recipes, combining them with French and international influences, to produce lighter and more delicately flavoured meals using the finest ingredients grown on British soil. Such fine produce includes succulent Welsh lamb, which is superb when served with mint sauce, and fine fruit and vegetables grown in Kent, the garden of England.

Scotland is famous worldwide for the quality of its beef. Cattle raised on the open Highlands produce coveted prime steak, unbeatable when served with cream, whisky and oatmeal sauce. Salmon from the lochs and rivers of Scotland is also internationally renowned as is the seafood from its shores. British farmers are justifiably proud of their labours, entering their produce in the many county shows which are held throughout the country in the summer months.

In Scotland the Taste of Scotland scheme, originally initiated by the tourist board, promotes hotels and restaurants which offer quality tradi-tional cooking using the best local ingredients. Look out for the blue-and-white stockpot symbol. An up-to-date guide listing 300 places is available from Taste of Scotland Scheme, 33 Melville Street, Edinburgh for £2.80 plus postage. A similar scheme is operated in Wales by the Welsh Tourist Board.

Naturally, since Britain is an island, seafood plays a major part in the daily diet. Fish such as haddock, cod and plaice are most common on the English dinner plate whilst oysters are a delicacy, eaten only during months with an r in them. Some of the best oysters come from North Farm, East Mersea in Colchester where tours of the oystery are given on the first Friday of each month.

British cheeses are particularly good. In addition to hard cheeses such as Cheddar, Double Gloucester and Wensleydale, there are also the famous, strongly flavoured blue Stilton cheese and fine Welsh goats' cheeses. To see cheese manufactured in the traditional way, visit Viscount Chewton's Cheese Dairy at Priory Farm, Chewton Mendip in Somerset or to sample the widest choice of British cheese and wine head down to The Nobody Inn at Doddiscombsleigh on Dartmoor where the selection includes over 30 Devonshire cheeses and many English wines.

You will be well set for a day of sightseeing after a full English breakfast of egg, bacon, sausage and grilled tomato with rounds of toast washed down with tea or coffee. Alternatively you may prefer porridge or kippers (smoked herrings).

Sunday lunch is a solid British tradition, bringing families together each week for a meal of roast meat and vegetables. Traditional weekly feasts are roast beef and Yorkshire pudding with horseradish sauce, roast pork with stuffing and apple sauce or maybe roast pheasant or duck, all served with gravy, roast potatoes and vegetables.

Many foreigners are amused at the British habit of taking afternoon tea – that is, until they try out a cream tea for themselves. This consists of scones, jam and cream (clotted cream in Devon and Cornwall) with a pot of tea. One of the best such teas is served at Primrose Cottage at Lustleigh near Dartmoor in Devon.

The traditional fast food is fish and chips. In the north they are cooked in beef dripping and an essential accompaniment is mushy peas, whilst in the south you are most likely to find them cooked in vegetable oil. One of the oldest, largest and most famous chippies is Harry Ramsdens at Guiseley in Leeds where people have been queuing for their fish and chips cooked the northern way for over 60 years.

They also know how to make a good sausage in Yorkshire. James Woodland Sausage Shop, Keighley, sells over 30 different varieties of sausage, including pork and leek, lamb and mint, gammon and pineapple.

In Staffordshire and Derbyshire oatcakes have been a major part of the staple diet for centuries and are a delicious snack when served hot with melted cheese. Another Derbyshire speciality is the almond pastry called **Bakewell Tart** and naturally the best are to be found in Bakewell, in the Peak District.

International **fast food chains** proliferate in every town centre, but for a quick and inexpensive bite to eat it is far more enjoyable and relaxing to go to a cosy café or pub serving homemade fare. A typical pub **bar snack** menu will offer wholesome food such as soups, steak-and-kidney and pork pies, lasagne, quiche, filled rolls and the ever-popular "ploughman's lunch" of bread, cheese, pickle and salad (the term is a cunning invention of marketing men and, in reality, has little to do with ploughmen's tastes). Particularly pleasant in summer is a pub lunch at a country pub with outside seating.

One legacy of the days of the British Empire is the wide variety of **ethnic restaurants** in Britain. Chinese and Indian are the most common and best value, almost every town has at least one. Most of the Chinese staff originally came from Hong Kong.

The British are probably one of the world's biggest consumers of **sweets**. Walk into any grocery store or newsagent and you will be bombarded by the choice of chocolate bars on offer. Cadbury's are one of the leading manufacturers and you can visit their Cadbury World visitor's centre at Bourneville, Birmingham, where there is a display of the history of chocolate, plus demonstrations and tastings.

When it comes to buying **groceries**, the small friendly neighbourhood baker, butcher and greengrocer has fallen victim to the large supermarkets, consumers having shifted their allegiance in the name of convenience. Stores such as Tesco and Sainsbury are the name of the game. Marks & Spencer's food departments are favoured by the middle classes because their groceries and pre-cooked meals undergo stringent quality controls (reflected in prices). In London the famous food departments in Harrods and in Fortnum & Mason's are particularly worth a visit; you can see a wide variety of delicacies on sale in elegant period surroundings.

The British are renowned for being keen **beer** drinkers. There are over 1,200 brands of beer on the market including bitter, lager, pale ale, stout and real ale. Fans of the latter, led by the Campaign for Real Ale (CAMRA), have promoted a greater appreciation of this traditional brew, which undergoes a second natural fermentation in the cask and is served without gas pressure. Many local breweries now produce their own real ale which is available from pubs in the area. However, three-quarters of the beer market is dominated by six national brewing companies, and weak, fizzy lagers have been winning an increasing share of the market. One of the big companies, Bass, has a museum at its brewery in Burton-on-Trent and conducts tours by arrangement.

Britons have also come to appreciate **wine**. Walk into any supermarket or off-licence and you will find a wide variety of wines from all over the world. England does, however, produce wine of its own, mainly in Kent where a dry white wine based on German grapes is made. There are numerous vineyards, such as those at Tenterden, Barkham Manor and Lamberhurst (England's largest vineyard) which welcome visitors, as does the English Wine Centre at Michelham Priory in East Sussex. The English are keen on brewing homemade wine made from fruit and flowers found in the hedgerows, such as elderberry, nettle and dandelion. Merrydown at Horam in East Sussex are makers of fruit wines and visitors can follow the wine-making process in their vats and press house.

The West Country (Devon, Somerset and Dorset) is known for its **cider** and **scrumpy** made from apples, brews which were undoubtedly brought across from France by the conquesting Normans in the 11th century. You can visit Dartington Cider Press Centre in Devon, Perry Cider Mills in Illminster, Somerset, or Mill House Cider Museum at Warmwell, Hampshire.

Whisky is the spirit of Scotland where over 100 distilleries produce their own distinctive single malts, the aristocrats of whiskies. Those who like a wee dram should consider taking the well-promoted whisky trail through the Spey Valley where half of Scotland's distilleries are concentrated. Many are keen to show visitors the secrets behind the making of their spirit. This is usually followed by a tasting.

WHERE TO EAT

The following is a selection of some of Britain's finest restaurants. Prices quoted are for an evening meal for two, although you will find set-lunch menus are considerably cheaper. Many are located within country-house hotels. A much fuller list of the capital's top restaurants can be found in Apa's *Insight CityGuide: London*.

LONDON

TOP-NOTCH

Chez Nico, 35 Great Portland Street, W1, tel: 071-436 8846. A passionate perfectionist, Nico Ladenis serves classic French cuisine which has earned him two Michelin stars. Closed weekends. From £100.
Le Gavroche, 43 Upper Brook Street, W1, tel: 071-408 0881. The only London restaurant to have ever been awarded three Michelin stars, thanks to the excellence of Albert Roux. From £100.
Harvey's, 2 Bellevue Road, SW17, tel: 081-672 0114. The hyped temperamental artist Marco Pierre White exhibits constant brilliance for which he has been awarded much acclaim, including two of those coveted Michelin stars. From £70.
Alastair Little, 49 Frith Street, W1, tel: 071-734 5183. Doyen of the new school of British cooking, Little presents imaginative and eclectic food within tasteful modern surroundings. £70.

TRADITIONAL

The English House, 3 Milner Street, SW3, tel: 071-584 3002. Quaint chintzy English dining room within a pretty Chelsea town house. Food has flair and a historic influence. £35 lunch/£55 dinner. Sister restaurant to **The Lindsay House**, 21 Romilly Street, W1.

Simpsons-in-the-Strand, 100 Strand WC2, tel: 071-836 9112. The Grand Divan Tavern is an Edwardian dining room renowned for serving the best roast beef in London. Staunchly traditional. Informal dress not acceptable. £51.

Wilson's, 236 Blythe Road, W14, tel: 071-603 7267. Serves one of the best Sunday lunches in town. A consistently high quality is maintained throughout the week in this dignified restaurant, where the eccentric patron may be seen wearing a kilt. £40 lunch/£60 dinner.

Rudland and Stubbs, 35–37 Greenhill Rents, Cowcross Street, EC1, tel: 071-253 0148. English and French-style fish dishes in an old-fashioned setting of tiled walls and bare floorboards. £37.

TRENDY

Langan's Brasserie, Stratton Street, W1, tel: 071-493 8822. Actor Michael Caine is one of the owners of this perennially fashionable brasserie where the reputation for attracting celebrities often overshadows the notable food. £55.

Hard Rock Café, 150 Old Park Lane, W1, tel: 071-629 0382. A shrine to rock music with an exceptional collection of memorabilia. Excellent hamburgers, long queues, high decibel level and great fun. £30.

Kensington Place, 205 Kensington Church St, W8, tel: 071-727 3184. Informal, bustling, New York-style restaurant. Modernist decor and adventurous food. £55.

The Ivy, 1 West Street, W1, tel: 071-836 4751. High-quality decor, gallery-worthy art and well thought-out food have made for the successful regeneration of The Ivy which re-opened its doors in 1990. Its relative, **Le Caprice** in Arlington Street, SW1, is another fashionable place to be seen.

The Dining Room (Vegetarian), Winchester Walk, SE1, tel: 071-407 0337. This unconventional basement restaurant makes imaginative use of whatever looks good at the neighbouring fruit and vegetable market. Daily changing menu is complemented by a range of organic wines. Closed weekends. £30.

CONTINENTAL

L'Artiste Assoiffé (French), 122 Kensington Park Road, W11, tel: 071-727 5111. Carousel horses and caged parrots adorn this delightful and entertaining restaurant close to Portobello's antique shops. £40.

La Bastide, 50 Greek Street, W1, tel: 071-734 3300. This charming restaurant located in one of Soho's oldest town houses serves traditional French regional cooking. £58.

Manzi's, 1–2 Leicester Street, WC2, tel: 071-734 0224. Timeless, Italian-run restaurant serving traditional fish dishes close to Leicester Square. £45.

Orso (Italian), 27 Wellington Street, WC2, tel: 071-240 5269. Basement Italian restaurant fashionable with the theatre and media crowd. £45. Related to American-style **Joe Allen**, 13 Exeter Street, WC2.

ETHNIC

Café Pacifico (Mexican), 5 Langley Street, W1, tel: 071-437 7144. Young and noisy Tex Mex joint with typical repertoire of *fajitas, enchiladas* and *tacos,* and, of course, those essential margaritas. Located in a converted warehouse in Covent Garden. £30.

Chiang Mai (Thai), 48 Frith Street, W1, tel: 071-437 7144. Modelled on a traditional stilt house, an extensive menu of good northern Thai cuisine. £30.

Fung Shing (Chinese), 15 Lisle Street, W1, tel: 071-437 1539. Has long been regarded as one of the best restaurants in Chinatown and is consequently always packed. £40.

The Red Fort (Indian), 77 Dean Street, W1, tel: 071-437 2410. Respected Soho restaurant which offers superb Mogul cooking in comfortably luxurious surroundings. £45. Related to the stylish **Wong Kei**, 41 Wardour Street, W1, tel: 071-437 8408. Regular crowds aren't deterred by the rude service for which this restaurant is famed. Huge, with three floors serving good value Cantonese food. Cash only. £20.

SOUTHERN ENGLAND

Thackeray's House, 85 London Road, Tunbridge Wells, Kent, tel: 0892-511921. Characterful house once inhabited by this famous novelist. This is not a theme restaurant and the food is to be taken seriously. £80.

La Vieille Auberge, 27 High Street, Battle, E. Sussex, tel: 0424-62255. Not far from Battle Abbey is this small, amiable and surprisingly good French restaurant. The food is excellent and the set-priced menus are exceptionally good value. Separate vegetarian menu. £45.

Gravetye Manor, Vowels Lane, East Grinstead, W. Sussex, tel: 0342-810567. A stunning Elizabethan manor house, beautifully decorated with wood-panelled rooms and surrounded by fine gardens, this is somewhere special. Equally pleasing is the excellent traditional and modern British cooking. £90.

Montagu Arms, Palace Lane, Beaulieu, Hampshire, tel: 0590-612324. Hotel and restaurant serving excellent English food. £70.

Le Poussin, 57 Brookley Road, Brockenhurst, Hampshire, tel: 0590-23063. Bland interior decoration is compensated for by first-rate French haute-cuisine of self-taught chef, Alex Aitkin, who skilfully incorporates organic local ingredients. Nicely located in a picturesque village not far from the coast and the New Forest. £100.

Chewton Glen, Christchurch Road, New Milton, Hampshire, tel: 0425-275341. Luxury country-house hotel with excellent leisure facilities and impeccable service. Food is equally faultless with a choice of vegetarian in addition to meat and seafood dishes. £90.

Gidleigh Park, Chagford, Devon, tel: 0647-32367. Set in 40 acres of beautiful grounds on the edge of Dartmoor, this picturesque mock-Tudor country-house hotel has a talented chef, Shaun Hill. £80.

The Carved Angel, 2 South Embankment, Dartmouth, Devon, tel: 0803-832465. Well established restaurant serving accomplished modern British cuisine in a picturesque setting overlooking Dartmouth harbour and the Dart estuary. £70.

CENTRAL ENGLAND

Oakes, 169 Slad Road, Stroud, Gloucestershire, tel: 0453-759950. Using only the best ingredients, Chris Oakes conjures up fine food on a modern British theme in unpretentious rustic surroundings. £60.

Redmond's at Malvern View, Cleeve Hill, Cheltenham, Gloucestershire, tel: 0242-672017. Situated high above the spa town of Cheltenham and overlooking the Malvern Hills, this restaurant has earned a fine reputation for superb modern British cooking. £60.

The Waterside Inn, Ferry Road, Bray-on-Thames, tel: 0628-20691. In an idyllic spot overlooking the Thames, this is one of England's most exceptional restaurants. The genius of Michel Roux has received great acclaim and several Michelin stars over the years. Over £120.

Le Manoir Aux Quat' Saisons, Great Milton, Oxfordshire, tel: 0844-278881. Widely considered to be Britain's Number 1 restaurant. Raymond Blanc uses his creative and unique talent to prepare exquisite meals in his beautiful Cotswold manor house. Over £130.

The Leatherne Bottle, Goring-on-Thames, Oxfordshire, tel: 0491-872667. A characterful olde-worldy riverside inn where the food is excellent and imaginatively produced with great care using the finest fresh ingredients. £50.

Hambleton Hall, Hambleton, Oakham, Leicestershire, tel: 0572-756991. Elegant dining-room, serving modern British cuisine, in a fine country-house hotel surrounded by delightful countryside. £75.

Hintlesham Hall, Hintlesham, Ipswich, Suffolk, tel: 0473-87334. Opulent classical country-house hotel in the peaceful Suffolk countryside serving high quality British food. £70.

NORTHERN ENGLAND

Bilbrough Manor, Bilbrough, York, tel: 0937-834002. Traditional English cuisine and good hospitality at this homely Edwardian country-house hotel. Set in 100 acres just outside York. £55.

McCoy's, The Cleveland Tontine, Staddlebridge, Northallerton, North Yorkshire, tel: 0609-82671. English eccentricity at its best. Lavish period surroundings, laid-back atmosphere and some of the most interesting food Britain has to offer. £65–£70.

Sharrow Bay Hotel, Howton Road, Ullswater, tel: 0853-6483. Eccentric country-house hotel offering 6-course fixed price menus of finely prepared modern and traditional British food, excellent sustenance for anyone touring the Lake District. £75.

SCOTLAND

The Altnaharrie Inn, Ullapool, Highland, tel: 0854-83230. From the pretty fishing village of Ullapool on Loch Broom it is worth the short boat ride or 4-mile (6-km) walk to sample some of the best cooking Scotland has to offer. Everything is homemade such as cloudberry icecream and herb-and-hawthorn soup. If you can't face the return journey you can always stay the night. £80.

The Champany Inn, nr Linlithgow, Lothian, Scotland, tel: 0506-834532. Famous for serving some of the best steaks in Britain, which are cut from prime Highland Aberdeen Angus cattle. £90.

Inverlochy Castle, Torlundy, Fort William, Highlands, tel: 0397-2177. Expect full pomp and ceremony at this Scottish castle located at the base of Ben Nevis where Graham Newbould (former chef to the Prince of Wales), cooks modern British food fit for royalty. £90.

The Peat Inn, Peat Inn, near Cupar, Fife, tel: 0334-84206. French cuisine of the highest quality served in complementary surroundings. Excellent wine list. £65.

WALES

Bodysgallen Hall, Llandudno, Gwynedd, tel: 0492-584466. Characterful 17th-century house adorned with antiques and surrounded by stunning gardens. Traditional Welsh recipes are prepared with the finest local produce. £50.

The Walnut Tree, Llandewi Skirrid, nr Abergavenny, tel: 0873-2797. Hospitable white-washed country inn offering excellent game and seafood prepared in a modern European style. £45.

THINGS TO DO

TOURIST ATTRACTIONS

According to the government statistical survey *Social Trends,* these are the country's top *free* attractions for visitors:

Blackpool Pleasure Beach, Lancashire, 6.5 million
British Museum, London, 4.7m
Strathclyde Country Park, Glasgow, 4.2m
National Gallery, London, 3.6m
Palace Pier, Brighton, 3.5m
Westminster Abbey, London, 3m
Pleasure Beach, Great Yarmouth, Norfolk, 2.6m
St Paul's Cathedral, London, 2.5m
York Minster, York, 2.5m
Canterbury Cathedral, 2.2m

Charging admission reduces the number of visitors. In the 1980s, entrance fees, some voluntary, began to be imposed on previously free national collections. As a result of such a charge the Natural History Museum in London has lost one-third of its visitors. Britain's top 10 attractions which *do* charge admission are:

Madame Tussaud's Waxworks Museum, London, 2.5 million
The Tower of London, 2.9m
Alton Towers Amusement Park, Staffordshire, 2.1m
Blackpool Tower, 1.5m
Natural History Museum, London, 1.5m
Chessington World of Adventure, Surrey, 1.5m
Royal Academy, London, 1.3m
Science Museum, London, 1.3m
London Zoo, 1.2m

STATELY HOMES

The three most visited stately homes in Britain – Warwick Castle, Leeds Castle and Blenheim Palace – all have spacious grounds and attract many more visitors than their rivals. Of the top 13 most popular places, five are in Scotland, none in Wales. The numbers of annual visitors are given by the Historic Houses Association.

Warwick Castle, Warwick, 685,000
Leeds Castle, Kent, 540,000
Blenheim Palace, Oxfordshire, 528,000
Castle Howard, Yorkshire, 221,000
Harewood House, Yorkshire, 181,000
Blair Castle, Perth, 171,000
Arundel Castle, West Sussex, 169,000
Bowood House, Wiltshire, 123,000
Dunvegan Castle, Inverness, 114,000
Exbury Gardens, Hampshire, 109,000
Glamis Castle, Angus, 109,000
Cawdor Castle, Nairn, 108,000
Scone Palace, Perth, 107,000

BRITISH HERITAGE & THE NATIONAL TRUST

There are two main organisations looking after Britain's old buildings, gardens and countryside. The Heritage organisations, which are government-funded, run key historic sites while the National Trust, a popular charity, runs stately homes and national parks.

English Heritage has more than 350 properties, including Stonehenge and Dover Castle. Single membership is £15, family membership £30, senior citizens £10.50. For further information: English Heritage, Key Sign House, 429 Oxford Street, London W1R 2HA, tel: 071-973 3000.

Historic Scotland has 330 properties including Glasgow Cathedral and Edinburgh Castle. Single membership is £11, family membership £18, senior citizens and students £7. Further information: Historic Scotland, 20 Brandon Street, Edinburgh EH3 5RA, tel: 031-244 3101.

Cadw (Welsh Heritage) has 127 properties from Roman sites to castles such as Caernarfon, Conway and Beaumaris and Tintern Abbey. Single membership £10, family membership £20, senior citizens £8. Further information: Cadw, Brunel House, 2 Fitzalan Road, Cardiff CF2 1UY, tel: 0222-465511.

The National Trust was founded in 1895 as an independent charity for the conservation of places of historic interest and natural beauty in England and Northern Ireland. It has over 260 properties open to the public, from large country houses and abbeys to lighthouses and industrial monuments. It also maintains over 550,000 acres (222,600 hectares) of countryside, including large expanses of shoreline and woodland. The majority of its funding comes from its 2 million members. Members of the National Trust are entitled to free entry to properties and a free copy of *The National Trust Handbook.* Annual membership is £19 for individuals and £34 for families, which can be recouped even on a two-week holiday if you visit several properties. Further information: The National Trust, 36 Queen Anne's Gate, London SW1H 9AS, tel: 071-222 9251.

The National Trust For Scotland is a separate body with over 100 properties covering 100,000 acres (40,500 hectares) and over 200,000 members. Properties in its care include castles, battlefields, islands, countryside and the birthplaces of several famous Scots. Single annual membership is £15, family membership is £24.50. For further information: The National Trust For Scotland, 5 Charlotte Square, Edinburgh EH2 4DU, tel: 031-226 5922.

The National Trust and the National Trust for Scotland have reciprocal free entry arrangements with each other and with many national trusts overseas, including Australia, India, New Zealand, Jamaica, Malaysia, Malta, Ireland and the Netherlands.

Visitors can also purchase a **Great Britain Heritage Pass** which allows unlimited access to more than 600 stately homes, castles, historic houses and abbeys in the UK. It costs £29 for 15 days or £43 for a month and is a definite bargain for the history-minded visitor. It's not available from all overseas offices of the BTA, but can be purchased on arrival from most tourist information centres.

Below are some of the National Trust's most visited sites:

ENGLAND

Brownsea Island, Poole, Dorset, tel: 0202-707744. This Island in Poole Harbour, with 500 acres (200 hectares) of heath, woodland and beaches, is a nature reserve and home to various species of wildlife. Reached by ferry from Poole Harbour or Sandbanks, it is a nice spot to picnic and bathe. Open: Mar–Sept 10am–dusk.

Chartwell, Sevenoaks, Kent, tel: 0732-866368. Fourteenth-century farmhouse much loved by Sir Winston Churchill who lived here for 40 years until the age of 90. Visitors are admitted to several rooms in the house which have been dedicated to the great man's memory, including his library and study. Also garden studio where he painted. Open: Apr–Oct from 12pm. Closed: Mon & Fri.

Corfe Castle, Wareham, Dorset, tel: 0929-480921. Ruins of a Norman fortress, standing amidst the Purbeck Hills, which has seen more than its share of bloodshed. Blown up by Roundhead troops in 1646, it was here that young King Edward was murdered in 978 under orders from his stepmother. Open: Feb–Oct 10am–5.30 p.m; Nov–Feb weekdays only 12 noon –3.30pm.

Fountains Abbey & Studley Royal, Ripon, North Yorkshire, tel: 076586-333. Beautiful ruins of one of England's greatest monasteries, founded by Cistercian monks in 1132. Formal landscaped gardens of Studley were laid out in the 18th century with classical temples, follies and lake. Also a deer park. Exhibition and film in Fountain's Hall. Open: daily 10am Closed: Fri in Nov, Dec and Jan.

Polesden Lacey, Great Bookham, near Dorking, Surrey, tel: 0372-52048. Regency villa containing fine paintings, furniture, porcelain and silver surrounded by lawns and flower gardens. Breathtaking views over the Downs. Open: Apr–Oct Wed–Sun; 1.30–5.30pm Mar; weekends only Nov. Grounds open: all year, daily 11am–sunset.

St Michael's Mount, Marazion, Cornwall, tel: 0736-710507. Fairytale castle and abbey set high on a granite mound overlooking Mount's Bay. Home of the 4th Lord of St Levan, it is reached by a granite causeway at low tide or a small ferry boat at high tide. The abbey, founded in the 5th century AD, is steeped in myths and legends and displays great similarities with Mont-St-Michel across the Channel in Normandy. Restricted opening, weekdays only.

Stourhead Gardens, Stourton, Wiltshire, tel: 0747-840348. Stunning landscaped grounds of an 18th-century Palladian villa (built by Colin Campbell), carefully laid out in the 1740s by banker Henry Hoare in collaboration with Henry Flitcroft. A fine example of English Romanticism with ornamental lakes, follies, classical temples, grottoes and bridges. House open: Apr–Nov 2–6pm. Closed: Fri. Grounds open: all year, daily.

Styal, Quarry Bank Mill & Country Park, Wilmslow, Cheshire, tel: 0625-527468. Water-powered spinning mill, built in 1784. Carefully preserved as a museum to the Industrial Revolution, it gives an insight into the working and living conditions of its mill workers. Situated in pleasant rural surroundings with its own village of workers housing. Open: 11am–5pm. Closed: Mon.

Tatton Park Garden, Knutsford, Cheshire, tel: 0565-54822. Magnificent mansion surrounded by 60 acres of gardens laid out by Joseph Paxton, including orangery and Japanese garden. The 1,000-acre (400-hectare) country estate includes deer park, lakes and a home farm which still operates as it did 50 years ago. Mansion open: Apr–Oct. Closed: Mon except Jul–Aug). Park and gardens: all year, daily.

Wakehurst Place, Ardingly, West Sussex, tel: 0444-892701. Picturesque gardens managed by the Royal Botanic Gardens at Kew with an important collection of exotic trees, shrubs and plants. Open: daily from 10am.

WALES

Chirk Castle, Chirk, Clwyd, tel: 0691-777701. Has survived a turbulent history since it was built in the 13th century. Six of its lords lost their heads in the Middle Ages and it suffered at the hands of both the Roundheads and Cavaliers in the Civil War. Has since become an elegant Georgian stately home with magnificent state rooms and formal 18th-century gardens and parkland. Open: Apr–Sept (not Sat and Mon); Oct–Nov weekends only, 12 noon–5pm.

Erddig, near Wrexham, Clwyd, tel: 0978-355314. Late 17th-century house which has remained unchanged for over 100 years and still has most of its original furniture. Out-buildings, including stables, smithy, laundry, kitchen and bakehouse, give a good insight into life of a bygone age. Extensive gardens and parkland. Open: Apr–Oct, 12 noon–5pm. Closed: Fri.

Penrhyn Castle, Bangor, Gwynedd, tel: 0248-353084. This rambling castle is a complete fake: not a Norman fortress, but the 19th-century home of a wealthy sugar merchant, George Pennant who built it as a display of his enormous wealth. Designed by Thomas Hopper in the 1820s and '30s, it is bold, large and highly decorated, displaying intricate and eccentric Victorian treatment of Norman motifs. It also houses a delightful collection of over 1,000 dolls from all over the world. Open: Apr–Oct, Wed–Mon 11am–5p.m.

Plas Newydd, Llanfairpwill, Anglesey, Gwynedd, tel: 0248-714795. Late 18th-century mansion, contains fine furniture and paintings including the most important Rex Whistler collection. Set in 168 acres (68 hectares). Open: Mar–Oct, 12 noon –5pm. Closed: Sat.

Powis Castle, Welshpool, Powys, tel: 0938-552554. Grand and opulent castle, originally a border fortress built by the medieval Princes of Upper Powys. Since the 16th century it has been the ancestral home of the Herberts who have turned it into a sumptuous stately home with a fine collection of furniture, paintings and, more recently, the Clive of India Collection of Treasures. Magnificent gardens laid out by Capability Brown. Open: Mar–Nov, 12 noon–5pm.

SCOTLAND

Bannockburn, Stirling, tel: 0786-812664. Site of one of the most important events in Scottish history when in 1314 Robert the Bruce defeated King Edward II, gaining freedom for the Scots from English domination. The Borestone site is claimed to have been Bruce's command post before the battle. Visitor Centre with exhibition. Open: all year, daily. Visitor Centre open: daily, Apr–Oct 10am–6pm.

Brodick Castle, Garden and Country Park, Isle of Arran, tel: 0770-2202. Ancient seat of the Dukes of Hamilton with parts dating back to the 13th century. Contains an impressive collection of antiques and paintings. Fine rhododendron garden in the grounds. Adventure playground. Open: Apr–Sept daily 1–5 p.m; Oct Mon, Wed and Sat only. Garden and country park open: all year, daily 9.30am–sunset.

Crathes Castle, Garden and Estate, Banchory, Grampian, tel: 033 044-525. In 1323 the lands of this estate (the lands of the Leys) were granted to the Burnett family by King Robert the Bruce. The castle was begun in the late 16th century and has exquisite painted ceilings. The 600 acres (240 hectares) of grounds include woodland, fields, over 3 acres (1.2 hectares) of walled gardens and great 18th-century yew hedges. Visitor Centre with exhibition. Open: Apr–Oct 11am–6pm. Gardens open: all year, daily 9am–sunset.

Culloden, Inverness, Highlands, tel: 0463-790607. The moorland site of the last major battle fought on mainland Britain where Bonnie Prince Charlie and the Jacobites were defeated by the government forces led by the Duke of Cumberland. See Old Leanach Cottage, the graves of the clans, the Well of the Dead and the memorial cairn. Visitor Centre with historical display. Open daily, all year. Visitor Centre open: Apr–Oct 9.30am–5.30pm.

Culzean Castle and Country Park, Kirkoswald, Ayrshire, tel: 065 56-269. Situated on a cliff top, this castle was built in the late 18th century for the 10th Earl of Cassillis by Robert Adam and is notable for its round drawing room and magnificent oval staircase. Surrounded by mature parklands, woodlands and shoreline. Adventure playground. Open: Apr–Oct daily from 10.30am Country Park open: daily all year, 9am–sunset.

Falkland Palace, Garden and Old Burgh, Kirkcaldy, Fife, tel: 033 757-397. Royal palace, built in the 16th century as a country residence of the Stewart monarchs who came here to hunt deer and wild boar in the Fife forest. The garden has the oldest tennis court in Britain, built in 1539. The King's Bedchamber, the Queen's Room and the Royal Chapel have all been restored. Open: Apr–Oct daily, 10am–6pm, Sun 2–6pm.

Glencoe, Highlands, tel: 085 52-307. This historic glen, where, in 1692, 40 members of the MacDonald clan were slaughtered by government soldiers, offers 14,200 acres (5,750 hectares) of some of the finest climbing and walking country in the Highlands. Wildlife includes red deer and golden eagles. Visitor Centre houses exhibition of mountaineering. Winter skiing. Open: all year, daily. Visitor Centre open: Apr–Oct, 10am–5.30pm.

Inverewe Gardens, Gairloch, Highlands, tel: 044-586-200. Created by Osgood MacKenzie in 1862, this beautiful garden is set on a peninsula on the shores of Loch Ewe. Native and exotic plants flourish throughout the year as a result of the excellent climatic conditions from the Gulf Stream. Visitor Centre. Open: all year daily, 9.30am–sunset.

Killiecrankie, Pitlochry, Tayside, tel: 0796-3233. One mile from the site of the Battle of Killiecrankie (1689), where the Jacobite Highlanders were victorious over King William's troops, is the 54 acres (2.2 hectares) of the Pass of Killiecrankie. See Soldier's Leap and the beautiful wooded gorge. Visitor Centre with battle exhibition. Open: all year. Visitor Centre open: Apr–Oct, 10am–5pm.

Threave Garden, Castle Douglas, tel: 0556-2575. Magnificent garden which is colourful all year, but most particularly in spring when the 200 varieties of daffodil come into bloom. The Victorian Threave House is home to the Trust's School of Horticulture. Visitor Centre with exhibition. Nearby is Threave Wildfowl Refuge. Garden open: all year, daily 9am–sunset. Visitor Centre open: Apr–Oct.

THEME & WILDLIFE PARKS

Alton Towers, Stoke-on-Trent, Staffordshire, tel: 0538-702200. The ancestral home of Earls of Shrewsbury has become Britain's premier leisure park. The magnificent gardens surrounding the shell of a neo-Gothic mansion contain over 120 rides and attractions. Long queues in summer. Open: daily, Mar–Oct from 10am.

Beaulieu, Beaulieu, Hampshire, tel: 0590-612123.

In the centre of the New Forest, Beaulieu (pronounced *bew-lee*) has a variety of attractions including Palace House, ancestral home of Lord Beaulieu's family since the 16th century; ruins of a Cistercian abbey dating from 1204, which houses an exhibition of monastic life and a motor museum, for which it is most famous. One of the finest in the world, it contains over 250 historic vehicles including Donald Campbell's land speed record breaker *Bluebird*, which can be viewed from the Monorail running overhead. Open: daily from 10am.

Blackpool Pleasure Beach, Blackpool, Lancashire. Lots of thrills and spills at this 40-acre (16-hectare) fun park on the sea front of northern England's most famous seaside resort.

Chessington World of Adventures, Chessington, Surrey, tel: 0372 727227. Situated on the A243 southwest of London (25 minutes from Waterloo Station by rail, then 10 minutes' walk), this is one of the closest children's amusement parks to the capital. Nine themed areas include "Transylvania", with a hanging roller-coaster. There's a zoo and an animal-free circus. Rides closed in winter.

Cotswold Farm Park, Guiting Power, Gloucestershire, tel: 0451-850307. This picturesque farm in the Cotswold Hills has the widest range of rare farm animals in Britain. Endangered breeds which the Rare Breeds Survival Trust has helped to save from extinction include Norfolk Horn Sheep, Castlemilk Moorit Sheep and Gloucester Cattle. Open: Mar–Sep 10.30am–6pm.

Drayton Manor Park, Tamworth, Staffordshire, tel: 0827-287979. Family leisure park promising lots of hair-raising adventures from the New Pirate Adventure to the Log Flume. Also Sir Robert Peel pictorial museum and exhibition of the history of the penny-slot machine, zoo, farm collection and nature conservation unit. Open: daily from 9am.

Slimbridge Bird Sanctuary, Slimbridge, Gloucestershire, tel: 0453-890100. The largest and most famous collection of wildlife in the world is here at the headquarters of the Wildfowl Trust. Open: daily.

West Midlands Safari and Leisure Park, Spring Grove, Bewdley, Worcestershire, tel: 0299-402114. The 195 acres (80 hectares) of big game reserves in the heart of England can be driven through. Also aquatic show, rides and amusements.

Whipsnade Wild Animal Park, nr Dunstable, Bedfordshire, tel: 0582-872171. Wild animals roam freely in the large enclosures of this 600-acre (240-hectare) estate. Open: from 10am daily.

SCOTLAND

Blair Drummond Safari and Leisure Park, Stirling, tel: 0786-841456. Scotland's only drive-through safari park has the additional trimmings of adventure playground and amusements. Open: Apr–Sept.

Landmark, Highland Heritage and Adventure Park, Carrbridge, Inverness-shire, tel: 047-984 613. Visitor Centre hosts an exhibition of the history of the Highlands, bringing alive the main events of Highland history and showing the impact of man on the land. Forestry Heritage Park tells the story of Scotland's forestry with demonstrations of traditional forestry skills in summer. Adventure playground, woodland maze and tree-top trail. Open: all year, daily.

HISTORIC HOUSES & CASTLES

LONDON

Chiswick House, Burlington Lane, Chiswick, W4, tel: 081-994 3299. Palladian villa designed by the third Earl of Burlington for himself as a temple to the arts in 1729. The interior was designed by his colleague, William Kent, and includes fine examples of furniture and decoration from the period. Open: daily. Admission: free. Tube: Turnham Green/British Rail: Chiswick.

Dickens House, 48 Doughty Street, WC1, tel: 071-405 2127. Regency house which has been faithfully restored as it would have been when Charles Dickens and his family lived here from 1837 to 1839. Here he wrote the novels *Nicholas Nickleby* and *Oliver Twist*. Contains a large array of memorabilia including his library, manuscripts, first editions, paintings and furniture. Closed: Sun. Tube: Russell Square.

Hampton Court, East Molesey, Surrey, tel: 081-977 8441. Great Tudor palace on the banks of the Thames, begun by Cardinal Wolsey, but persuasively taken over by Henry VIII. William and Mary later added state apartments designed by Wren, hoping to rival Versailles in France. The interior houses a fascinating collection of period furniture and detailing, while outside the formal gardens are equally delightful and contain the famous maze. Open: daily. BR: Hampton Court.

Hogarth's House, Hogarth Lane, Chiswick, W4, tel: 081-994 6757. Once the country home of the late 18th-century satirical artist William Hogarth, it has been carefully restored and now houses the largest public display of his work. Closed: Tue. Admission: free. BR: Chiswick.

Dr Johnson's House, 17 Gough Square, Fleet Street, EC4, tel: 071-353 3745. This fine example of a Georgian town house was once the home of the great 18th-century English essayist and lexicographer Samuel Johnson. It now contains a first edition of the famous dictionary he compiled here, and portraits of Johnson and friends. Closed: Sun. Tube: St Paul's/Chancery Lane.

Kensington Palace, Kensington Gardens, W8, tel: 071-937 9561. The primary sovereign residence from 1689 to 1760 and where Queen Victoria spent her childhood, this palace is now the London home of the Prince and Princess of Wales. The original Jacobean house has been remodelled over the years, including alterations by Wren and William Kent. The State Apartments are open to the public and include Queen Victoria's toys and the Court Dress Collection. Closed: Mon. Tube: High Street Kensington.

Kenwood House (The Iveagh Bequest), Hampstead Lane, NW3, tel: 081-348 1286. Elegant country house bequeathed to the state by Lord Iveagh along with his valuable collection of masterpieces by Rembrandt, Rubens, Vermeer, Turner, Reynolds and others. Remodelled by Robert Adam in the 18th century, the interior is an excellent example of this architect's distinctive decorative style. In the summer, open-air concerts are held in the grounds, laid out by Humphrey Repton. Open: daily. Admission: free. Tube: Golders Green/Archway.

Syon House, Syon Park, Brentford, Middlesex, tel: 081-560 0881. Remodelled by Robert Adam in 1766, this is one of the best examples of his work. The house is still home to the Duke of Northumberland. Open: Apr–Oct. Closed: Fri and Sat. The British Heritage motor museum is also in the grounds. Open: daily. BR: Syon Lane.

Tower of London, Tower Hill, EC3, tel: 071-709 0765. This imposing medieval fortress is London's principal tourist attraction. First built by William the Conqueror in 1066, the oldest remaining part is the White Tower which houses the Royal Armories. Particularly notorious as a prison and place of execution; those unfortunate enough to lose their heads on the block here included two of Henry VIII's wives. Don't miss the Crown Jewels and the ravens. The Beefeaters (Yeoman Warders in Tudor uniforms) give free guided tours. Long queues, especially in summer. Open: daily. Closed: Sun in winter. Tube: Tower Hill.

AROUND LONDON

Arundel Castle, Arundel, West Sussex, tel: 0903-883136. West Sussex's most notable attraction is this Norman castle overlooking the town of Arundel. Ancestral home of the Dukes of Norfolk, it was built in the 11th century but was later reconstructed in the 19th century. Contains a notable collection of paintings including works by Van Dyck, Reynolds and Gainsborough. Open: Mar–Oct afternoons only.

Berkeley Castle, Berkeley, Gloucestershire, tel: 0453-810332. Started life as a moated Norman fortress but has since evolved into a delightful stately home and has been inhabited by 24 generations of Berkeleys. It has an interesting history: Edward II was murdered here in 1327. Open: Apr–Sept 2–5pm. Closed: Mon Oct, Sun only 2–4.30pm.

Blenheim Palace, Woodstock, Oxford, tel: 0993-811325. Vanburgh's magnificent baroque palace, built in 1702 for the 1st Duke of Marlborough, is set within 2,500 acres (1,010 hectares) of parkland landscaped by Capability Brown. Built to rival Versailles, it is awesome in its size and opulence. Interior contains fine treasures including portraits by Reynolds and Sargeant and a series of tapestries depicting the Duke's victories. There is a Winston

Churchill exhibition and room where he was born. Palace open: Mar–Oct 10.30am–5.30pm. Park open: all year, daily 9am–5pm.

Castle Howard, Coneysthorpe, York, North Yorkshire, tel: 0653-84333. Another baroque masterpiece built on an enormous scale by Sir John Vanburgh (assisted by Nicholas Hawksmoor). This fine stately home contains priceless furniture and masterpieces by Van Dyck and Holbein and was the setting for the TV production of Evelyn Waugh's *Brideshead Revisited*. Costume museum in stable block and beautiful grounds. Open: Mar–Oct daily. Grounds from 10am, house and galleries from 11am.

Chatsworth House, Bakewell, Derbyshire, tel: 0246-582204. Chatsworth gracefully occupies beautiful grounds on the banks of the River Derwent. Built in the 17th century for the Duke of Devonshire, it was later extended. The grounds, laid out by Capability Brown, contain fountains and glass houses designed by Joseph Paxton. House contains a superb collection of furniture and the fine arts. Adventure playground, farming and forestry exhibitions. Open: daily, Mar–Oct from 11am.

Dover Castle, Dover, Kent, tel: 0304-201628. A medieval stronghold which has defiantly guarded the shortest crossing between Britain and France from its vantage point above the White Cliffs. Within the castle walls are a Norman keep, Saxon church, Roman lighthouse and a secret underground World War II base. Open: daily from 10am.

Harewood House, Harewood, Leeds, West Yorkshire, tel: 0532-886225. This grand house is the residence of the Earl of Harewood. Designed in 1759 by John Carr, it features magnificent interiors by Robert Adam and grounds landscaped by Capability Brown. Treasures include Chippendale furniture, Sevres and Chinese porcelain and paintings by Turner, Reynolds, Gainsborough and Bellini. Ceilings by Angelika Kauffman. Open: daily, Apr–Oct from 11am.

Lindisfarne Castle, Holy Island, tel: 0289-89244. 16th-century castle built high on a granite mound to defend Holy Island from the Scots (who never actually attacked). In 1903 it was sensitively restored by Sir Edwin Lutyens. Open: Apr–Sept 1pm–5.30pm. Closed: Fri. Open: Sat, Sun, Wed in October.

Ragley Hall, Alcester, Warwickshire, tel: 0789-762090. Magnificent Palladian home of the Marquess of Hertford which is particularly notable for the splendid ornate plasterwork in the Great Hall, designed by James Gibbs in 1750. The 400-acre (160-hectare) grounds were laid out by Capability Brown. Open: Apr–Sept. Closed: Mon and Fri. House open: 12 noon–5pm. Garden and park: 10am–6pm.

Royal Pavilion, Brighton, East Sussex, tel: 0273-603005. Magnificent eastern extravaganza, complete with domes and minarets, built for the Prince Regent (later George IV) by John Nash from 1815 to 1822. The spirit of eccentric fantasy continues inside where interiors are opulently decorated in a style of exotic *chinoiserie*. The structure of the building is an early example of the use of wrought-iron which is most evident in the kitchens where columns have become palm trees. Open: all year from 10am.

Warwick Castle, Warwick, Warwickshire, tel: 0926-495421. England's finest medieval castle and one of the country's greatest tourist attractions. Inhabited since the 14th century by the powerful Earls of Beauchamp, the castle is now owned by Madame Tussaud's which has restored it to its original grandeur and installed a lifelike waxwork recreation of "A Royal Weekend Party, 1898" throughout the state rooms. Also contains a splendid collection of medieval treasures, paintings, furniture and armour. Beautiful grounds include Peacock Garden and Pageant Field. Open: daily from 10am.

Windsor Castle, Windsor, Berkshire, tel: 0753-831118. A royal residence for over 900 years, the castle was founded by William the Conqueror in 1070 and has been added to by 40 other monarchs throughout history. Overlooks the Thames on one side and Windsor Great Park on the other. Richly decorated State Apartments contain priceless treasures and works of art, including drawings by Leonardo and Michelangelo. Queen Mary's dolls' house and Henry VIII's suit of armour are famous exhibits. Also on view: Waterloo Chamber and an exhibition of the Queen's Presents and Royal Carriages. St George's Chapel is being renovated following a 1992 fire. Changing of the guard takes place Mon–Sat at 11am. Open: all year, daily. Part of the castle is closed when the Queen is in residence.

Woburn Abbey, Woburn, Bedfordshire, tel: 0525-290666. Stately home of the Marquess of Tavistock. Designed by Henry Flitcroft, it is built on the site of a Cistercian monastery and is surrounded by a 3,000-acre (1,200-hectare) deer park landscaped by Humphrey Repton. The abbey contains an important collection of furniture and fine art, including paintings by Gainsborough, Rembrandt and Canaletto. Grounds are occupied by a safari park and wild animal kingdom. Abbey and Deer Park open: daily Apr–Oct.

WALES

Beaumaris, Bangor, Anglesey, tel: 0248-810361. The last of Edward I's great castles, this imposing medieval fortress, surrounded by a moat, was never finished despite the fact that more than 2,000 labourers spent over 35 years working on it. Open: daily from 9.30 a.m; Oct–Mar, Sun 2–4pm.

Caernarfon Castle, Gwynedd, tel: 0286-3094. One of Britain's largest and best preserved castles, built in 1283 by King Edward I, it was the setting for the investiture of Prince Charles as Prince of Wales in 1969. Open: Mar–Oct, daily 9.30am–6.30pm.

Cardiff Castle, City Centre, Cardiff, tel: 0222-822083. Originally a Roman fortress, the castle was rebuilt by the Normans, but today most of its character is derived from Victorian times when the wealthy Marquess of Bute commissioned the imaginative architect William Burgess to renovate and extend it. The two shared a passion in things medieval and Burgess was given free reign to create a distinctive High Victorian fantasy. The result is one of the most opulent Gothic Revival buildings of the period. Contains museums of the Welsh Regiment and The Queen's Dragoon Guards. Open: daily from 10am.

Conwy Castle, Gwynedd, tel: 0492-632358. One of Wales's greatest military castles, Conwy was built in the 13th century by Edward I as one of a series of nine fortifications to keep the Welsh at bay. Open: Mar–Oct, 9.30am–6.30pm.

Harlech Castle, Gwynedd, tel: 0766-780552. Another of the great Welsh medieval castles, this breathtaking fortress sits on a rocky crag on the northwest coast. It has been immortalised in the song *Men of Harlech*, which commemorates the surrender of the castle to the Yorkists in the 15th-century Wars of the Roses. Open: Mar–Oct, daily 9.30am–6.30 pm, Sun 2–6.30pm.

SCOTLAND

Blair Castle, Pitlochry, Tayside, tel: 079 681-207. Great white walled baronial castle which is the seat of the 10th Duke of Atholl. Leader of the Murray clan, he is privileged in being the only British subject allowed to have his own private army, the Atholl Highlanders. The castle can also claim fame for being the last British castle to be besieged. The 32 rooms on view contain a good collection of fine art, furniture, arms and armour. Open: Apr–Oct, daily from 10am.

Cawdor Castle, Inverness, tel: 06677-615. This 14th-century seat of the Thanes of Cawdor is famous for being the setting for Duncan's murder in Shakespeare's tragedy *Macbeth*. Surrounded by beautiful grounds with nature trail. Open: May–Sep 10am–5pm.

Craigievar Castle, Alford, Aberdeen, tel: 03398-83635. Fairytale castle standing in harmonious splendour unchanged since the day it was completed in 1625, to the extent that electric lighting has never been installed. Splendid original plaster ceilings. Open: daily Apr–Sept.

Dunrobin Castle, Golspie, Sutherland, tel: 04083-3177. Romantic castle overlooking the sea with fine formal apartments and gardens. Seat of the Earls and Dukes of Sutherland for over 800 years. Open: May–Sept from 10.30am, from 1pm Sun. Closed: Fri, Sat, Sun in May.

Edinburgh Castle, Castle Rock, Edinburgh, tel: 031-244 3101. This historic castle, strategically placed on top of volcanic rock above the city, is still used as a military barracks and piping school and is the location for the annual Edinburgh Military Tattoo. Contains Edinburgh's oldest building, 12th-century St Margaret's Chapel and the 15th-century

Palace Apartments where Mary Queen of Scots gave birth to James I of England. Also the Scottish Crown Jewels, Military Museum and the National War Memorial. Open: daily from 9.30am (12.30 on Sun).

Floors Castle, Kelso, tel: 0573-23333. Eighteenth-century William Adam mansion built for the Duke of Roxburghe. Later enhanced by William Playfair in the 19th century, its elegant apartments contain period furniture, porcelain and fine art. A tree in the park marks the spot where James II was killed in 1640 during the seige of Roxburghe Castle, supposedly by cannon fire. Open: May–Sept, 10.30am–5.50pm.

Glamis Castle, Dundee, tel: 030 784-242. Theatrical turreted castle, originating from the 11th century. However, it was remodelled in the 17th century and has sumptuous interiors. It has gained fame for being featured in Shakespeare's *Macbeth* and also for being the childhood home of Queen Elizabeth, the Queen Mother. Open: Apr–Oct daily, 12 noon–5.30pm.

Palace of Holyroodhouse, Canongate, Edinburgh, tel: 031-556 7371. Begun by James IV *circa* 1500, this royal palace is still used by the Queen when she visits Edinburgh. Visitors can see the State Apartments, Picture Gallery, Darnley Rooms and the Mary Queen of Scots suite. Open: from 9.30am.

Stirling Castle, Stirling, tel: 031-244 3101. This, the grandest of Scottish castles, has had a turbulent history, changing hands between the Scottish and English several times. It was favoured by the Stuart kings because of its strategic position on the Firth of Forth. James II was born here and Mary Queen of Scots was crowned here as a baby. Collection of buildings, principally from the 15th and 16th centuries, include the majestic Great Hall, the Chapel Royal, Royal Residence and the Regimental Museum of the Argyll and Sutherland Highlanders. Open: daily.

Scone Palace, Perth, Perthshire, tel: 0738-52300. Seat of the Murray family, the Earls of Mansfield, since 1600 although the present palace was built in the 19th century. It is famous for the being the place where the first Scottish meetings of parliament were held and where the Stone of Scone once resided. Later taken to Westminster Abbey, it was on this stone that Scottish royalty were traditionally crowned. Open: Mar–Oct, 10am–5.30pm, Sun 12 noon–5.30pm.

PRE-HISTORIC & ANCIENT TIMES

Avebury Stone Circle, Avebury, Wiltshire. Larger, older, yet lesser known than Stonehenge, this is the largest megalithic monument in England. With a circumference of a mile, it consists of 700 giant stones laid out in three concentric rings surrounded by a high earth wall and deep ditch. It is thought to be over 4,000 years old. Although very little is known about its purpose, some think it has cult origins.

Chedworth Roman Villa, Chedworth, Gloucestershire, tel: 0242-89256. The best preserved Roman domestic dwelling in the country. Built around AD 150, its painted walls and mosaic floors are still visible. Small museum. Open: Mar–Oct 10am–5.30pm. Closed: Mon.

Cirencester Corinium Museum, Cirencester, Gloucestershire, tel: 0285-655611. Good Roman collection from the time when this town was known as Corinium and second in importance only to Londinium. Includes mosaics, sculptures, antiquities and period reconstructions. Open: daily 10–5.30pm, Sun 2–5p.m. Closed: Mon in winter.

Cheddar Showcaves, Cheddar Gorge, Somerset, tel: 0934-742343. This dramatic gorge, flanked by enormous 450-ft (140-metre) high limestone cliffs, contains mysterious caves which were once inhabited by prehistoric man. The most impressive are Gough's and Cox's caves which have fine stalactites and stalagmites.

Hadrian's Wall. Stretching 74 miles (119 km) across the North of England, from Northumbria in the east to Cumbria in the west, this incredible fortification was built under orders of Emperor Hadrian in AD 122. It was in places as high as 20 ft (6 metres) and as wide as 10 ft (3 metres). 17 forts were built at 5-mile intervals, of which the best preserved is Housesteads, now in the care of the National Trust.

Maiden Castle, nr Dorchester, Dorset. The finest example of a prehistoric fortress in Britain. Situated on the hills outside Dorchester, it was originally a Neolithic camp and later an Iron Age fort, when the enormous earthworks and complicated entrances were constructed.

Roman Baths and Museum, Bath, tel: 0225-461111. The Romans first appreciated the springs of Bath, but Georgian England made them into a national attraction. The bath complex centres around a hot mineral spring which is dedicated to the Goddess Sulis Minerva and has remained intact over the years. Museum with fine collection of Roman artefacts. Open: daily 9am–5pm. Closed: Sun in winter.

Stonehenge, Amesbury, Wiltshire. Britain's most famous prehistoric monument stands as a series of mysterious stone circles on Salisbury Plain, the purpose of its origins unknown. For its own protection, it is now fenced off from the public.

ART GALLERIES

LONDON

Courtauld Institute, Somerset House, The Strand, WC2, tel: 071-872 0220. This fine collection, gathered by textile baron Samuel Courtauld, has moved from Woburn Place to the Strand. It contains many priceless masterpieces including the best collection of Post-Impressionist paintings in Britain. Open: daily. Tube: Temple.

National Gallery, Trafalgar Square, WC2, tel: 071-

839 3321. Home to the nation's most important – and indeed one of the world's greatest – collections of paintings. All the leading European schools and almost every artist of note from the 13th to the 19th century can be seen. Open: daily. Admission: free. Tube: Charing Cross/Leicester Square.

National Portrait Gallery, 2 St Martin's Place, WC2, tel: 071-930 1552. Anybody who is anybody in British history has their face on the wall, or at least in the archives, of this gallery. Here are paintings, photographs and sculptures of Britain's most famous and highly respected citizens from Tudor times to the present day, including monarchs, intellectuals and pop stars. Open: daily. Admission: free. Tube: Leicester Square/Charing Cross.

Queen's Gallery, adjacent to Buckingham Palace, SW1, tel: 071-930 4832. Temporary exhibitions of treasures from the Queen's private collection are shown in this gallery which used to be the Palace chapel. Closed: Mon. Tube: St James' Park/Victoria.

Tate Gallery, Millbank, SW1, tel: 071-821 1313. This is the storehouse for British art from the 16th century, including Blake, Constable, Reynolds and Gainsborough. It is also home to an important collection of international art that encompasses modern movements from French Impressionism to present day and is particularly strong on Cubism. The new Clore Gallery was designed by James Stirling to house the notable Turner collection. Open: daily. Admission: free. Tube: Pimlico.

OPEN DURING EXHIBITIONS

Barbican Art Gallery, Barbican Centre, EC2, tel: 071-638 4141. Large concrete complex built for the arts. The gallery, which is on the 8th floor, holds exhibitions of major importance. Tube: Barbican/Moorgate.

Hayward Gallery, South Bank, SE1, tel: 071-928 3144. Another concrete jungle built as a centre for the arts, but with the attractive location of the south bank of the Thames. The Hayward hosts exhibitions of international importance which most predominantly feature 20th-century art. Tube: Waterloo.

ICA (Institute of Contemporary Art), Nash House, The Mall SW1, tel: 071-930 3647. The ICA is the most avant-garde of London's major galleries. Two galleries show modern innovative work. Also live performance art, music, film and video. Tube: Charing Cross/Piccadilly Circus.

Royal Academy, Burlington House, Piccadilly W1, tel: 071-439 7438. Particularly well known for the large summer exhibition of works by both amateurs and professionals, all of which are for sale, from June to August. Unfortunately, this exhibition has a reputation for being more notable as a social event than for the quality of work exhibited. Tube: Green Park/Piccadilly Circus.

Serpentine Gallery, Kensington Gardens, Hyde Park W2, tel: 071-402 6075. Hosts interesting exhibitions of contemporary art within an airy gallery space in the centre of Hyde Park. Tube: Lancaster Gate.

Whitechapel Gallery, 80 Whitechapel High Street, E1, tel: 071-377 0107. Fabulous Art Nouveau gallery which holds exhibitions of work by major living artists. Tube: Aldgate East.

OUTSIDE LONDON

Arnolfini Arts Centre, Bristol, 16 Narrow Quay, Bristol, tel: 0272-299 191. Bristol's centre for the contemporary arts is located on the water's edge of its Docks. The café is particularly notable, designed by the artist Bruce McLean. Gallery open: daily 10am-7pm, Sun 12 noon–7pm.

Barbara Hepworth Museum, St Ives, Cornwall, tel: 0736-796226. Studio where the sculptress lived and worked from 1949 until her death. Contains 40 sculptures in addition to personal photographs and belongings. Open: all year from 10am. Closed: Sun (except Jul and Aug).

Birmingham Art Gallery & Museum, Chamberlain Square, Birmingham, tel: 021-235 2834. Houses a very good collection of art which is particularly rich in pre-Raphaelite paintings and drawings. It is also strong on natural history, archaeology and the decorative arts. Open: 9.30am–5pm, Sun 2–5pm.

Corner House, 70 Oxford Street, Manchester, tel: 061-228 7621. Opened in 1986 this is Manchester's very notable centre for contemporary art which hosts exhibitions of national importance. Open: Tue–Sun 12 noon –8pm.

Lady Lever Art Gallery, Port Sunlight Village, Wirral, Merseyside, tel: 051-645 3623. In the centre of this model workers' village, worth a visit in its own right, is this fine gallery founded by Viscount Leverhulme in memory of his wife. The gallery contains a particularly important collection of 19th-century British decorative arts and paintings, most notably works of the pre-Raphaelites and Wedgwood ware. It also contains 18th-century Chinese ceramics and Chippendale furniture. Open: daily 10am–5pm, Sun 2–5pm.

Leeds City Art Gallery & Henry Moore Centre, The Headrow, Leeds, West Yorkshire, tel: 0532)-462495. In addition to a notable collection of works by English masters including Gainsborough and Constable, this gallery houses a permanent exhibition of 20th-century sculpture in the Henry Moore centre with work by Moore (who studied art in Leeds) and Epstein. Open: daily.

The Museum of Modern Art, 30 Pembroke Street, Oxford, tel: 0865-722733. One of England's major modern art venues outside London, staging important exhibitions of painting, sculpture, photography and design. Open: 10am–6pm. Closed: Mon.

The Tate Gallery Liverpool, Albert Dock, Liverpool, tel: 051-709 3223. As the name implies, this new gallery is connected with its namesake in London and houses a major collection of contemporary art. In addition it hosts temporary exhibitions of work from the National Collection of Modern Art. Open: 11am–5pm. Closed: Mon.

Walker Art Gallery, William Brown Street, Liverpool, tel: 051-207 0001. England's most important gallery outside London with a rich collection of European old masters and Post Impressionist paintings. Excellent presentation of British work, most notably of the Pre-Raphaelites but also modern artists, Hockney, Lucien Freud and Gillian Ayres. Open: daily 10 a.m–5pm, Sun 2–5pm.

Whitworth Art Gallery, University of Manchester, Oxford Road, Manchester, tel: 061-273 5958. A fine collection of British work from the 18th century onwards. Particularly notable are watercolours and drawings by Blake, Turner, the pre-Raphaelites and, local hero, Lowry. Important collection of prints, textiles and wallpapers. Open: 10am–5pm. Closed: Sun.

SCOTLAND

The Burrell Collection, 2060 Pollokshaws Road, Glasgow, tel: 041-649 7151. Opened by the Queen in 1983, this purpose-built gallery houses the astounding and somewhat eccentric collection built up over 80 years by shipbuilding magnate Sir William Burrell. Although regarded by some as rather *too* eclectic, it includes many priceless treasures such as paintings by great masters, Rembrandt and Bellini and some superb furniture and stained glass. Open: daily 10am–5pm, Sun 12 noon–6pm.

Glasgow Art Gallery and Museum, Kelvingrove, Argyle Street, Glasgow, tel: 041-357 3929. The excellent collection of painting and sculpture includes major old masters, Impressionists and Post-Impressionists. Also extensive collections of decorative arts, including silver, porcelain and arms. Glasgow Style exhibition is devoted to the city's famous contribution to Art Nouveau by Charles Rennie Mackintosh and his contemporaries and contains a reconstruction of Mrs Cranston's Tearoom and other interior designs. Also collections concerning Scottish history, natural history, archaeology and ethnography. Open: from 10am, Sun from 12 noon.

Hunterian Art Gallery & Museum, University of Glasgow, tel: 041-330 5431. Despite housing works by major European masters such as Rembrandt, Reynolds, Pissarro and Rodin, this gallery is most notable for its outstanding collection of work by Mackintosh, including a reconstruction of a house he once lived in nearby. In addition, virtually unrivalled is the collection of paintings by Whistler, exhibited along with some of his personal possessions. It also holds the largest print collection in Scotland with works by Durer and Picasso. Open: from 9.30am. Closed: Sun.

The McManus Galleries, Albert Square, Dundee, tel: 0382-23141. Within this building built by George Gilbert Scott in 1867 is an excellent collection of 19th and 20th-century Scottish fine and decorative arts. Also contains collections relating to Dundee's human history from prehistoric times to the present day and archaeological finds from ancient Egypt. Open: 10am–5pm. Closed: Sun.

The National Gallery of Scotland, The Mount, Edinburgh, tel: 031-556 8921. This 19th-century building designed by William Playfair houses Scotland's most important collection of paintings. There are works by El Greco, Rembrandt, Constable, Titian and Velasquez as well as Post-Impressionists, Van Gogh, Cézanne and Gauguin, and an unparalleled collection of Scottish work. Open: daily 10am–5pm, Sun 2–5pm.

Scottish National Gallery of Modern Art, Belford Road, Edinburgh, tel: 031-556 8921. Contains work by many of Europe's leading 20th-century artists, including Picasso, Braque, Matisse, Derain, Giacometti, Mondrian, Moore, Hepworth and Hockney. Also holds a fine collection of Scottish work. Open: daily 10am–5pm, Sun from 2pm.

Scottish National Portrait Gallery, 1 Queen Street, Edinburgh, tel: 031-556 8921. The most famous and heroic figures in Scottish history, from the 16th century to present day, are immortalised on these walls. You can see Mary Queen of Scots, James I, Flora MacDonald, Robert Burns, Sir Walter Scott and many more. There are portraits by Raeburn, Reynolds and Gainsborough. Also houses the national collection of photography. Open: daily 10am–5pm, Sun from 2pm.

MUSEUMS

LONDON

British Museum, Great Russell Street, WC1, tel: 071-636 1555. A vast collection unrivalled anywhere in the world, set within Smirke's grand neoclassical building. Includes Egyptian mummies, the Elgin Marbles, Rosetta Stone and the Sutton Hoo ship burial. Also art, manuscripts, prints and drawings. Open: all year, daily. Admission: free. Tubes: Holborn, Tottenham Court Road.

Design Museum, Butlers Wharf, Shad Thames, SE1, tel: 071-403 6933. Modernist building overlooking the Thames devoted to the design progress of everyday domestic objects. There are regularly changing displays of graphic design and new design innovations. Closed: Mon. Tube: Tower Hill or London Bridge.

Imperial War Museum, Lambeth Road, SE1, tel: 071-735 84922. Totally redesigned in 1989, this excellent museum is as much about the frightening experience of war as it is about displays of arms and weapons. Contains works of art by the official war artists. The Blitz Experience is a main attraction, vividly simulating a London air-raid in World War II. Open: daily. Admission: free on Fri. Tube: Elephant and Castle.

London Transport Museum, The Piazza, Covent Garden, WC2, tel: 071-379 6344. The history of public transport in London dating from the early days of horse-drawn trams and the beginnings of the Underground to the present day. Many vehicles are on display along with exhibitions of graphics, including a collection of posters designed by leading artists of the 1930s. Open: daily. Tube: Covent Garden.

Museum of Mankind, 6 Burlington Gardens, Piccadilly, W1, tel: 071-437 2224. The British Museum's department of ethnography is particularly strong on exhibits relating to tribal and village cultures from America, Oceania and Africa, dating from ancient to modern times. Open: daily. Admission: free. Tube: Piccadilly Circus.

National Maritime Museum, Romney Road, Greenwich, SE10, tel: 081-858 4422. The biggest naval museum in the world with a large collection of exhibits relating to Britain's seafaring history. On show is a display of the Battle of Trafalgar, a gallery of model warships and many maritime instruments, weapons and paintings. The museum is in England's first Palladian-style house built for Queen Anne in the 17th century by Inigo Jones. Open: daily. BR: Greenwich/ Maze Hill.

Natural History Museum, Cromwell Road, SW7, tel: 071-589 6323. With an emphasis on man's evolution and biology, different departments are concerned with botany, zoology, mineralogy, palaeontology and entomology. Some of the most popular exhibits are the dinosaur and whale skeletons on the ground floor. Also incorporates the Geological Museum. Open: daily. Admission: free. Tube: South Kensington.

Science Museum, Exhibition Road, SW7, tel: 071-589 3456. This museum charts the history of science and technology up to the present day and analyses their influence on industry and everyday life. Highlights include the first steam locomotive, Stevenson's "Rocket", and space exploration memorabilia. Food, medicine and photography are also investigated. Open: daily. Tube: South Kensington.

Sir John Soane's Museum, 13 Lincoln's Inn Fields, WC2, tel: 071-405 2107. Home of one of Britain's greatest neoclassical architects and most passionate collectors. See his vast, valuable and eccentric collection of antiquities, books, drawings and paintings, including Hogarth's series of 12 paintings, *The Rake's Progress*, the Sarcophagus of Seti I, Wren's watch and Napoleon's pistol. Closed: Sun, Mon. Admission: free. Tube: Holborn.

Victoria and Albert Museum, Cromwell Road, SW7, tel: 071-938 8500. The arts treasure house of Britain and the finest museum of the decorative arts in the world. Initially founded in an attempt to raise the standard of design in British manufacturing, this vast collection, housed within 7 miles (11 km) of galleries, contains everything from medieval candlesticks and stained-glass windows to Chippendale furniture and Clarice Cliff ceramics. Closed: Fri. Voluntary donations. Tube: South Kensington.

OUTSIDE LONDON

Ashmolean Museum, Beaumont Street, Oxford, tel: 0865-278000. The country's oldest public museum, opened in the late 17th century, has important collections of antiquities from Rome, Greece and Egypt, fine British and European painting and sculpture, musical instruments and coins. These are now housed in a classical neo-Grecian building built by C.R. Cockerell in 1845. Open: 10am–4pm, Sun 2–4pm.

Bath Costume Museum, Assembly Rooms, Bennett Street, Bath, tel: 0225-461111. Undoubtedly one of the best costume museums in the world. 400 years of men's, women's and children's fashion and accessories are displayed in the elegant surroundings of the Georgian Assembly Rooms, designed by John Wood the Younger in 1769. Panorama Room with period settings and outdoor scenes of Bath from 1820–1939. Open: daily.

Beamish Open-Air Museum, Beamish, County Durham, tel: 0207-231811. Life in the North of England at the turn of the century is relived at this award-winning museum. A collection of original buildings have been brought together on this 260-acre (105-hectare) site to show a working community with an old town, home farm, railway station, trams, mine and colliery. Everything is real, right down to the dentist's surgery, printworks and original Co-op store. See demonstrations of traditional crafts such as mat, quilt and lace making. Open: daily 10am–5pm. Closed: Mon in winter.

Black Country Museum, Tipton Road, Dudley, West Midlands, tel: 021-557 9643. Working and living conditions of the Industrial Revolution are shown at this open-air canal-side museum close to the narrow Dudley Canal tunnel. Reconstructions of 18th and 19th-century houses, shops and pubs as well as displays of mining, boat building and chain making. Open: daily in summer 10am–5pm.

Duxford Airfield Imperial War Museum, Duxford, Cambridge, tel: 0223-833963. Britain's prime collection of military and civil aircraft housed in an enormous area along with military vehicles, tanks and guns. See inside Concorde and experience the flight simulator. The museum hosts special exhibitions and events. Adventure playground. Open: daily from 10am.

Ironbridge Gorge Museum, Ironbridge, Shropshire, tel: 095245-3522. This is the birthplace of the Industrial Revolution, where Abraham Darby invented a method of mass producing cast iron cheaply. Several sites are spread over 6 sq. miles (15 sq. km) centering around the Iron Bridge: Blists Hill open-air museum of a Victorian town, Museum of the River, Museum of Iron, Rosehill House (restored Ironmaster's house), Jackfield Tile Museum and Coalport China Museum. Open: daily 10am–6pm.

Jorvik Viking Centre, Coppergate, York, North Yorkshire, tel: 0904)-643211. Below ground at the site where excavations took place is a detailed reconstruction of Jorvik (York) as it was when inhabited by Vikings 1,000 years ago. Complete with authentic smells and noises, it includes houses and workshops containing everyday contents which were uncovered intact. Open: daily from 9am.

Maritime Museum, Haven Banks, Exeter, tel: 0392-58075. Britain's best collection of historic and unusual ships and boats from all over the world are displayed in a scenic location of warehouses on the banks of the River Exe. Open: daily 10am–5pm.

National Railway Museum, Leeman Road, York, North Yorkshire, tel: 0904-621261. Excellent collection of steam locomotives and carriages in this museum covering the history of train travel from its beginnings and its effect on society. Exhibits include Queen Victoria's personal luxury carriage and the speed record-breaking locomotive *Mallard*. Open: daily.

Royal Naval Museum, Royal Naval Base, Portsmouth, Hampshire, tel: 0705-733060. In addition to the museum which charts the history of the navy, you can see Nelson's ship *HMS Victory* and the *Mary Rose*. The latter was Henry VIII's flagship which sank in 1545 and its hull was salvaged in 1982 virtually intact along with her possessions and treasures. Open: daily 10am–5pm.

Stoke-on-Trent City Museum and Art Gallery, Hanley, Stoke-on-Trent, tel: 0782-202173. Award-winning museum located in the centre of the Potteries with an outstanding collection of fine and decorative arts. Not surprisingly the ceramic collection is of considerable world importance. Also natural history, social history and archaeology. Open: daily from 10.30am, Sun from 2pm.

York Castle Museum, The Eye of York, York, North Yorkshire, tel: 0904-653611. Britain's largest folk museum, dedicated to everyday life from Tudor to Edwardian times, is set in an old women's prison. Reconstructions of period settings include Victorian and Edwardian streets. Also sections are devoted to Yorkshire crafts, costume and military history. Open: daily.

SCOTLAND

Highland Folk Museum, Duke Street, Kingussie, tel: 0540-661307. Open-air museum of Highland life which includes an 18th-century shooting lodge and indoor exhibitions of farming. Highland tinkers, clothing, furniture and armour. Open: daily from 10am, Sun from 2pm.

Royal Museum of Scotland, Chambers Street, Edinburgh, tel: 031-225 7534. A large Victorian building houses this impressive Scottish collection of historical artefacts from all over the world. Natural history, ethnography, geology are mixed in with a fine collection of early machinery and scientific instruments. Open: daily 10am–5pm, Sun 2–5pm.

Scotch Whisky Heritage Centre, 358 Castlehill, Edinburgh, tel: 031-220 0441. Discover the secrets behind the national drink of Scotland. Displays

reveal its history and how it is made, complete with sound effects and aromas. Open: daily.

Scottish Tartans Museum, Davidson House, Drummond St, Comrie, tel: 0764-70779. Contains the world's largest collection of tartans and Highland dress. Run by the Scottish Tartans Society, it has historical displays and a reconstruction of a weaver's cottage. Open: Mon–Sat from 10am.

WALES

National Museum of Wales, Cathays Park, Cardiff, tel: 0222-397951. In addition to holding a collection of work by Welsh artists, the gallery holds an extremely valuable collection of French Impressionist paintings by Renoir, Monet and Manet and sculptures by Rodin and Dégas. There are also collections relating to the history and natural history of Wales. Open: daily 10 a.m–5pm, Sun from 2.30pm.

Welsh Folk Museum, St Fagans, South Glamorgan tel: 0222-555105. Open-air museum displaying Wales's rural history from farmers, millers and coopers to saddlers and clog-makers. Shown through a series of reconstructed and furnished typical workshops and dwellings. Open: daily from 10am. Closed: Sun, Nov–Mar).

Museum of the Welsh Woollen Industry, Llandysul, Dyfed tel: 0559-370929. Museum dedicated to the historic woollen industry of Wales with machinery and textile displays. Open: 10am–5pm. Closed: Sun (and Sat in winter).

Welsh Slate Museum, Llanberis, Gwynedd tel: 0286-870630. The Dinorwic Quarry and its workshops have remained unchanged since closing down in 1969 and stand as a museum to one of Wales's great industries. Open: daily 1.30–5.30pm.

PHOTOGRAPHY & FILM

The Ffotogallery, 31 Charles Street, Cardiff, tel: 0222-341667. This photographic gallery's major exhibitions often go on to tour the country. It covers most aspects of the photographic arts and has an extensive archive of photographs of the South Wales valleys which have been commissioned by the gallery over recent years. Open: Tue–Sat 10 a.m–5pm.

Lacock Abbey and Fox Talbot Museum, Lacock, nr Chippenham, Wiltshire, tel: 0249-73459. This abbey, founded in 1232 as a house for Augustan nuns, was the home of Henry Fox Talbot, the inventor of the negative/positive process of photography. Views of the abbey appear in the first photographically illustrated book, *The Pencil of Nature*, which Talbot produced in 1844. A converted barn houses the museum which commemorates his achievements. Open: Mar–Nov, daily 11am–5.30pm.

MOMI (Museum of the Moving Image), South Bank, London SE1, tel: 071-401 2636. Lively and fun museum of the history of cinema and television that explains the technological developments and what goes on behind the scenes. Visitors have a chance to sit in front of the camera themselves and become a newsreader or do a screen test for a Hollywood film. Closed: Mon. Tube: Waterloo.

National Museum of Photography, Film and Television, Prince's View, Bradford, West Yorkshire, tel: 0274-727488. A fascinating museum which covers the history of photography, film and television, and contains over 50,000 exhibits from the Kodak Collection. The range of superb hands-on displays includes being given the chance to be cameraman on a film set. Also houses the largest cinema screen in Britain (62ft x 52 ft/19 x 16 metres) with six-track stereo sound. Open: daily 11am–7.30pm. Closed: Mon.

Photographers' Gallery, 5 & 8 Newport Street, WC2, tel: 071-831 1772. London's photographic showcase usually presents at least two different exhibitions at any one time. The gallery's Print Room keeps an excellent selection of contemporary and historic prints for view and sale. Closed: Mon. Free. Tube: Leicester Square.

Portfolio Gallery, 43 Candlemaker Row, Edinburgh, tel: 031-220 1911. Set up in 1988, this prominent gallery presents a variety of exhibitions from the whole spectrum of photography, but most notably contemporary work. Publishes *Portfolio* magazine. Open: Tue–Sat 12 noon–5.30pm.

Royal Photographic Society, National Centre of Photography, The Octagon, Milsom Street, Bath, tel: 0225-62841. The society holds an exceptional collection of photographs, especially pictorial photography and the work of early British photographic pioneers. In keeping with the fact that the RPS is a functioning body for photographers, contemporary work is also exhibited. Open: 9.30am–5.30pm. Closed: Sun.

OTHER ATTRACTIONS

LONDON

Changing of the Guard at Buckingham Palace, The Mall, SW1, tel: 071-730 3488. The full pomp and ceremony of the Queen's Guards in their red uniforms and bearskins can be seen as they march between their barracks and the Palace accompanied by a military band for a change-over of guard duty. Changing of the guards can also be seen at Whitehall and the Tower 11.30am daily (alternate days in winter). Free. Tube: St James's Park.

Cutty Sark, King William Walk, Greenwich, SE10, tel: 081-853 3589. The last surviving tea-clipper, the *Cutty Sark* once held all the maritime speed records before the introduction of steam ships. She now lies as a museum in dry dock. Nearby is the *Gypsy Moth IV*, the yacht Sir Francis Chichester sailed single-handed around the world in 1966–67. Closed: Mon. BR: Greenwich.

Greenwich Royal Observatory, Greenwich Park, SE10, tel: 81-858 1167. Founded by Charles II, and built by Wren in 1685, this group of buildings is home to Greenwich Mean Time and the Prime Meridian. On display are early navigational, time-keeping and measuring instruments. In 1948 the Royal Observatory moved to Sussex and this group of buildings became part of the National Maritime Museum. Open: daily. BR: Greenwich.

London Planetarium and Laserium, Marylebone Road, NW1, tel: 071-486 1121. The solar-system is revealed with a spectacular display inside this large dome. The Laserium takes over in the evenings combining lasers and rock music. Open: daily. Tube: Baker Street.

Madame Tussaud's, Marylebone Road, NW1, tel: 071-935 6861. The world's best-known waxwork museum and one of London's greatest tourist attractions. Many famous personalities from history and the present day have been immortalised here, with varying degrees of visual authenticity. Open: daily. Tube: Baker Street.

Rock Circus, London Pavilion, Piccadilly Circus, W1, tel: 071-734 7203. Clever technology is combined with the artful waxworking of Madame Tussaud's. An interesting display of the history of rock and pop where stars, including Elvis, Madonna and the Beatles, "perform" rather more rigidly than usual. Open: daily. Tube: Piccadilly Circus.

St Paul's Cathedral, St Paul's Churchyard, EC4. Rebuilt by Sir Christopher Wren after the Great Fire of 1666, it is London's largest church. Also seat of the Bishop of London and church of the British Commonwealth. Prince Charles chose to marry Princes Diana here rather than the more traditional venue of Westminster Abbey. Crypt contains tombs of the Duke of Wellington, Lord Nelson and Wren himself. Open: daily 8am–6pm. Tube: St Paul's.

Westminster Abbey, Dean's Yard, SW1, tel: 071-222 5152. Fine example of English Gothic architecture, dating to the 13th century. Most English monarchs since 1066 have been crowned (and many married and buried) here. Also contains memorials to eminent British citizens, including Chaucer, Darwin, Newton, Dickens and Gladstone plus the Tomb of the Unknown Warrior. The Coronation Chair is on view with the Stone of Scone. There is a museum and Chapter House. Brass-rubbing in the cloisters. Closed: during Sunday services. Nave free. Tube: Westminster.

NATIONAL PARKS

Brecon Beacons. The Beacons (in South Wales) are a series of red sandstone mountains, many over 1,000 ft (300 metres) high, with the highest point, Pen-y-fan at 2,906 ft (885 metres). Comprising woodland, lakes, waterfalls, caves, farmland and the valley of the River Usk, this park covers an area of 519 sq. miles (1,345 sq. km) in Gwent, Powys and Dyfed.

Dartmoor. Dartmoor ponies roam freely across this expanse of 365 sq. miles (945 sq. km) of moorland in Devon with exposed granite *tors*, heath and peaty bogs. Highest point is High Willhays (2,038 ft/620 metres). Harsh home of Dartmoor prison and setting for Sherlock Holmes in *The Hound of the Baskervilles*.

Exmoor. Stretching over 265 sq. miles (685 sq. km) between Somerset and Devon with heathery moorland and breathtaking coastline. Gentle slopes give way to rugged upland wilderness. Home to Exmoor ponies, sheep, red deer and cattle.

Lake District. Some of Britain's most stunning and beautiful countryside stretches over 880 sq. miles (2,280 sq. km) in Cumbria, northeast England. 16 lakes are interspersed with high fells, the highest being Scafell Pike (3210 ft/980 metres). A haven for fishing, boating, climbing and swimming.

Northumberland. 398 sq. miles (1,030 sq. km) in Northumbria stretching north to the Cheviots at the Scottish border and westwards to Cumbria. Characterised by rugged stretches of moorland, it includes some of the most spectacular coastline in Britain and encompasses Hadrian's Wall. Wildlife includes grouse and roe deer.

North Yorkshire Moors. With a coastline of rugged cliffs stretching from Scarborough to Staithes, expanses of low moorland, deep valleys and heathered uplands, this national park covers 553 sq. miles (1,430 sq. km) in Yorkshire. This is James Herriot territory (made famous by several TV series based on the vet's books such as *All Creatures Great and Small*). It is also excellent walking country, with the 100-mile (160-km) long Cleveland Way.

Peak District. This well preserved area of natural beauty, covering 542 sq. miles (1,390 sq. km) at the tip of the Pennines between Sheffield, Derby and Manchester, was England's first designated national park. It is characterised by high wild and bleak moors of the Dark Peak, with peaks over 2,000 ft (600 metres), and low, gentle limestone countryside with dramatic wooded valleys and rivers.

Pembroke Coast. Remote and ragged coastal park which takes up most of the coast of Pembrokeshire, southwest Wales. Some 180 miles (290 km) long, the path stretches from sandy Amroth beach to Teifi near Cardigan. A variety of wildlife includes puffins, grey seals and kittiwakes. The park covers a total of 225 sq. miles (585 sq. km).

Snowdonia. A large and diverse area of stunning beauty covering 838 sq. miles (2,170 sq. km) in the northwest of Wales. It is characterised by a variety of geographical features including forests, lakes and torrential streams, but it is most admired for its craggy high peaks. There are 14 peaks over 3,000 ft (915 metres) high, whilst Mount Snowdon itself, at 3,560 ft (1,085 metres), is the highest south of the Scottish border. Excellent mountaineering, walking, pony trekking, canoeing, fishing and sailing.

Yorkshire Dales. This wild expanse of great natural beauty covers 680 sq. miles (1,760 sq. km) in the Pennine Hills. It encompasses Swaledale, Upper Ribblesdale, Wharfedale and Wensleydale and features deep dales, waterfalls, caves and quarries.

LITERARY PILGRIMAGES

Ayrshire: Robert Burns (1759–96). Scotland's literary hero, who championed the Scottish vernacular with his vivid descriptions of Scottish scenery and customs. His poems were mainly written in the Scottish dialect; the narrative *Tom o'Shanter* is the most celebrated. He wrote over 200 songs of which *Auld Lang Syne* is most famous. The original copy resides in the museum next door to the small white cottage where Burns was born in Alloway, near Ayr. During the last years of his short life, he lived in a small house in a back street of Dumfries which is now a museum. The Bachelor's Club in Tarbolton, a 17th-century thatched cottage where Burns and a group of friends formed a literary club in 1780, is now run by the National Trust.

Dorset: Thomas Hardy (1840–1928). Hardy spent most of his life in Dorset (Wessex) where he set many of his novels. He was born in Higher Bockhampton where he wrote *Far From the Madding Crowd* and *Under The Greenwood Tree*. He later lived in Dorchester where he studied to be an architect, building his own house at Max Gate on the Wareham Road in the late 19th century. The Dorset County Museum in Dorchester has a memorial collection devoted to Hardy. Hardy used The King's Arms, 30 High Street, Dorchester, an 18th-century coaching inn as a setting in the *Mayor of Casterbridge*. He also wrote *Return of the Native* and *Tess of the d'Urbervilles*.

Hampshire: Jane Austen (1775–1817). The daughter of a Hampshire clergyman, she grew up in the village of Steventon. Because she was a woman, Austen wrote all her novels, which are primarily concerned with the daily lives of ordinary people, anonymously and her true identity was not discovered until after her death. Between 1800 and 1817 she lived with her mother and sister in Chawton, Hampshire, where she wrote *Mansfield Park*, *Emma* and *Persuasion*. Now a museum (tel: 0420-83262), the house contains personal effects, letters and manuscripts. She also spent time in Bath and Lyme Regis, where she wrote much of *Persuasion* from Bay Cottage on The Parade. She is buried in Winchester Cathedral. She also wrote *Pride and Prejudice* and *Northanger Abbey*.

Kent: Charles Dickens (1812–70). Most of his life was spent in Kent and London. Born near Portsmouth, the son of a navy pay clerk. The house where he grew up is at No.11 Ordnance Terrace, Chatham, Kent. Between 1837 and 1839 he lived with his wife and son at 48 Doughty Street, London WC1, where he finished *Pickwick Papers* and wrote *Oliver Twist* and *Nicholas Nickleby*. The house now owned by the Dickens Fellowship contains a wide range of personal belongings, manuscripts and books. In 1856 Dickens moved to Gad's Hill Place near Rochester (now a girls' school), where he was to die. Dickens was fond of the seaside town of Broadstairs and went there to live in Bleak House to write part of *David*

Copperfield (in which the Dickens House museum appears as Miss Betsy Trotwood's house). Dickens also spent time in the Royal Albion Hotel there. His novels, such as *The Old Curiosity Shop, Our Mutual Friend, Great Expectations* and *Oliver Twist* reveal the harsh side of Victorian society and its underworld.

Lake District: William Wordsworth (1770–1850). The leading poet of the British Romantic period brought to life the dramatic landscape of the Lake District. In Main Street, Cockermouth, Cumbria, you can visit the house where he was born in 1770; it contains some of his personal belongings. Dove Cottage and Wordsworth Museum can be found in Town End, Grasmere, Cumbria where he lived with his sister Dorothy during the most creative years of his life. Works include *Guide Through the District of the Lakes,* 1810, and *Lyrical Ballads* with Coleridge.

Nottingham: D. H. Lawrence (1885–1930). The son of a Nottinghamshire miner, Lawrence grew up in a tiny house in Victoria Street, Eastwood, which has been restored to give an insight into his working class childhood (the Lawrence Birthplace Museum, tel: 0773-763312). Nearby at 28 Garden Road is *Sons and Lovers* Cottage where the Lawrence family lived between 1887 and 1891 and which can be seen as it was described in that novel (tel: 0773-719786; open by appointment). Also by Lawrence: *Lady Chatterley's Lover, The Rainbow* and *Women in Love.*

South Wales: Dylan Thomas (1914–53). Thomas was born in the industrial town of Swansea in Wales, growing up in 5 Cwmdonkin Drive in the Uplands district. He celebrates Welsh life in *Under Milk Wood* and *Collected Poems 1934–53.* Follow the Dylan Thomas Uplands Trail and visit the boat house where he lived and worked in Laugharne; it is now a museum.

Warwickshire: William Shakespeare (1564–1616). Stratford-upon-Avon is synonymous with Britain's greatest playwright and each year thousands make the pilgrimage to see where the famous bard was born. The Shakespeare Birthplace Trust (tel: 0789-204016) administers the following Tudor properties which have Shakespeare associations: Shakespeare's Birthplace, Henley Street; Anne Hathaway's Cottage, Shottery, where Shakespeare's wife grew up; Hall's Croft, Old Town; New Place/Nash's House, Chapel Street; Mary Arden's House and the Shakespeare Countryside Museum, Wilmcote, the house where Shakespeare's mother grew up.

Yorkshire: The Brontë Sisters: Anne (1820–49), **Charlotte** (1816–55), **Emily** (1818–48). All were born in Thornton, West Yorkshire, although their family home was at the Parsonage in Haworth, West Yorkshire (tel: 0535-42323). Now a museum looked after by the Brontë Society, it has been restored to the way it was when this famous literary family lived here (1820–61) and contains some of their furniture, manuscripts and personal belongings. *Wuthering Heights* by Emily Brontë. *Jane Eyre, Shirley, Villette, The Professor* by Charlotte Brontë. *Agnes Grey, The Tenant of Wildfell Hall* by Anne Brontë.

CULTURE PLUS

THEATRE

Britain's rich dramatic tradition is reflected in the excellent quality and range of its theatre. Although London is naturally the centre, most towns and cities have at least one theatre which hosts productions from their own theatre company or from touring companies which might include the Royal Shakespeare Company (RSC) and the National Theatre (NT). Britain's leading contemporary playwrights include Tom Stoppard, Harold Pinter and Alan Ayckbourn. On the middle-brow musicals scene, Andrew Lloyd Webber has been dominant for many years.

Half of London's theatres – which amount to over 100, including fringe and suburban theatres – are to be found in the West End, centred around Shaftesbury Avenue and Covent Garden. Here the many shows tend to be "safe" and they include long runners such as *Phantom of the Opera, Cats, Les Misérables* and *The Mousetrap.*

West End shows are very popular and as a result good tickets can be hard to obtain. If you cannot book a seat through the theatre box office (credit card bookings by telephone accepted) try **Ticketmaster** (tel: 071-413 3550) and **First Call** (tel: 071-240 7200) before going to other agencies which may charge a hefty fee. Avoid ticket touts unless you're rich or desperate; their tickets are usually genuine enough, but they will demand anything from £70 to £120 for a best-seat ticket that would cost £25 at the box office. **SWET Ticket Booth** at Leicester Square has unsold tickets available at half price on the day, from 12 noon for matinées and from 2pm for evening performances. Be prepared to pay cash only and for long queues. Some theatres, such as the National, keep back a certain amount of tickets for each performance to sell at the box office from 10am on the day.

For fringe theatre bookings, go to the **Fringe Theatre Box Office** at the Duke of York's Theatre, St Martin's Lane, WC2, tel: 071-379 6002, although there is usually no problem in buying a ticket on the door. Consult the listings in the weekly *Time Out* magazine or quality newspapers for what's on in the West End and at the many fringe theatres around London.

On a summer's evening Shakespeare's plays are performed at the open-air theatre in **Regent's Park**.

The Barbican Centre, Barbican, EC2, tel: 071-638 8891. Purpose-built concrete arts complex containing the Barbican Theatre, Concert Hall and The Pit which are well thought-out and comfortable with good acoustics, although somewhat sterile. Because of financial difficulties, the Royal Shakespeare Company is not always able to maintain performances throughout the winter. 24-hour information, tel: 071-628 2295. Tube: Moorgate.

National Theatre, South Bank, SE1, tel: 071-928 2252. A wide range of modern and classical plays can be seen at three repertory theatres housed within this massive concrete structure on the banks of the Thames: the Olivier, the Lyttelton and the Cottesloe. Tube: Waterloo/Embankment.

Royal Court Theatre, Sloane Square, SW1, tel: 071-730 1745. Home to the English Stage Company who produce plays by contemporary playwrights. Tube: Sloane Square.

The Royal Shakespeare Theatre, Stratford-upon-Avon. The Royal Shakespeare Company (RSC), famous the world over, performs a repertoire of plays by the Bard at the Royal Shakespeare Theatre, while works by his contemporaries are staged across the river at the Swan Theatre (an Elizabethan-style playhouse). Nearby, at The Other Place, modern productions are performed. The RSC season at Stratford runs from March to September and they also perform for a certain period of the year at the Barbican Centre in London and at Newcastle-upon-Tyne.

Box office, tel: 0789-295623 (credit card bookings accepted). 24-hour booking information, tel: 0789-69191. Shakespeare overnight packages, tel: 0789-295333

It is always advisable to book tickets in advance, either from the box office or through commercial ticket agents in major cities. On weekdays, visitors can tour behind the scenes and see the RSC collection of costumes, props and paintings.

CLASSICAL CONCERTS

Many British cities have their own professional orchestras and promote seasons of concerts. These include the **Royal Liverpool Philharmonic**, **The Hallé** in Manchester and the **City of Birmingham Symphony Orchestra** (directed by Simon Rattle) among others. In London there are the **London Philharmonic** and, at the Barbican, the **London Symphony Orchestra**.

In the summer the **Scottish National Orchestra** (SNO) presents a short Promenade season in Glasgow, while in London the BBC sponsors the **Henry Wood Promenade Concerts** at the Royal Albert Hall, Kensington. The BBC also funds several of its own orchestras, the **BBC Symphony** and the **BBC Scottish Symphony Orchestra** and broadcasts about 100 hours of classical music on Radio 3 each week.

Chamber music has considerable support in Britain and there are several professional string and chamber orchestras such as the **English Chamber Orchestra** and **The Academy of Ancient Music**.

Major venues outside London which attract world-class performers include **St David's Hall** in Cardiff and the **Glasgow International Concert Hall**.

THE MAIN LONDON VENUES

Barbican Hall, Silk Street, EC2 (tel: 071-638 8891) is home to the London Symphony Orchestra and the English Chamber Orchestra. **Royal Festival Hall**, South Bank, SE1 (tel: 071-928 8800) is London's premier classical music venue. Also within this arts complex are the **Queen Elizabeth Hall** where chamber concerts and solos are performed, and the small **Purcell Room**. **Wigmore Hall**, 36 Wigmore Street, W1 (tel: 071-935 2141) is an intimate hall renowned for its lunchtime and Sunday chamber recitals.

Royal Albert Hall, Kensington Gore, SW7 (tel: 071-589 3202) is a circular hall which Queen Victoria dedicated to the memory of her husband. It comes alive each summer for the Henry Wood Promenade Concerts, simply known as the "Proms".

In the summer, open-air classical concerts are performed at the picturesque **Kenwood Lakeside Theatre**, Hampstead Lane, NW3 and in **Holland Park**, Kensington, W8.

OPERA

The **Royal Opera** and the **English National Opera** are among the world's finest opera companies and perform regular seasons in London. The Royal Opera resides at the **Royal Opera House** in Covent Garden, a magnificent theatre where it produces lavish performances of operas in their original language. Dress is generally formal and tickets very expensive. Not far away at **The Coliseum**, an elegant Edwardian theatre, the English National Opera (ENO) puts on less traditional performances in English. London's **Sadler's Wells Opera Company** is based at the Sadler's Wells Theatre which also stages performances by visiting companies.

The **D'Oyly Carte** is Britain's leading light-opera company mainly concerned with performances of the humorous Gilbert & Sullivan operettas. After a period of closure due to financial difficulties the company has recently come back to life and has set up home at the **Alexandra Theatre** in Birmingham.

The Welsh are renowned for their fine voices. Most districts of Wales have a choir of some sort and there are more than 100 male voice choirs. The **Welsh National Opera** has gained an excellent reputation worldwide and performs regular seasons at the **New Theatre** in Cardiff and at the **Grand Theatre** in Swansea.

Scotland, too, has its own opera company, **Scottish Opera**, based at the **Theatre Royal** in Glasgow. It tours Scotland and the north of

England, performing several short seasons in Edinburgh throughout the year.

There are several regional opera companies including **Opera North**, which is based in Leeds and tours the north of England. **Opera 80**, which performs operas in English, tours the country and puts on a season at the Sadler's Wells Theatre in London each year.

In summer, **Glyndebourne** in Sussex is a major feature on the opera map, hosting a season which attracts artists of international standing, while in **Buxton**, Derbyshire, the Opera House hosts a major opera festival.

BALLET & DANCE

As with opera, the major venues for ballet are the Royal Opera House and The Coliseum, home to the **Royal Ballet** and the **Royal Festival Ballet** respectively. The **Sadler's Wells Royal Ballet** has moved from the Sadler's Wells Theatre to the Birmingham Hippodrome where it is now known as the **Birmingham Royal Ballet**, sister company to the Royal Ballet. However, the Sadler's Wells Theatre continues to be London's leading dance venue, presenting dance of all styles. With regular seasons from the Birmingham Royal Ballet, Rambert Dance Company, London Contemporary Dance Theatre and Whirligig, the theatre also hosts international dance companies such as Lindsay Kemp, Merce Cunningham and Cumbre Flamenca.

Manchester is where the **Northern Ballet Company** resides when it is not touring throughout England. In Wales, leading ballet companies perform at the New Theatre in Cardiff and the Grand Theatre in Swansea.

The **Scottish Ballet**, based in Glasgow, performs regularly at the Theatre Royal and the Robin Anderson Auditorium. It also tours Scotland, and presents a series of performances in Edinburgh twice a year.

FESTIVALS

There are hundreds of arts festivals for music, dance, theatre and literature held throughout the country each year. The most famous is the **Edinburgh International Festival** and **Fringe Festival**. It takes place for a period of 3 to 4 weeks between August and September when Edinburgh becomes a hub of cultural activity. The city also hosts jazz, folk and film and TV festivals at other times during the year. Glasgow hosts the **Mayfest** in May as well as its own jazz and folk festivals.

The **Royal National Eisteddfod of Wales** dates back to 1176 and is the most important of the hundreds of *eisteddfodau* which take place in Wales annually. It is a festival devoted entirely to music and literature in the Welsh language and is held for a week in August in a different venue each year.

The **Llangollen International Eisteddfod**, which takes place in the picturesque town of Llangollen in north Wales each July, was established after World War II to bring nations from all over the world together in a festival of song, dance and music.

Other notable arts festivals are held at **Chichester**, **Brighton**, **Buxton**, **Malvern**, **Salisbury**, **Harrogate** and **York**. Music festivals are held at **Aldeburgh**, **Cheltenham**, **Stratford** and **Bath**.

JAZZ

There are many pubs and clubs which host live jazz and festivals are held annually throughout the country, most notably at **Camden**, London; **Bracknell**, Berkshire; and in **Edinburgh**. **Ronnie Scott's** in the heart of London's Soho is Britain's best known jazz venue and features international artists and the ubiquitous Ronnie Scott himself.

DIARY OF EVENTS

For further information on events in the different regions of Britain contact the local tourist board.

JANUARY

Burns Night (25th): Scotland.
International Boat Show: Earl's Court, London.

FEBRUARY

Chinese New Year Celebrations: in London and Manchester Chinatowns.
Crufts Dog Show: NEC, Birmingham.
Shrove Tuesday (41 days before Easter): various old customs celebrate "Pancake Day".

MARCH

Edinburgh International Folk Festival.
Ideal Home Exhibition: Earl's Court, London.
London International Book Fair: Olympia, London.
Royal Shakespeare Theatre: Stratford-upon-Avon, opens the new season.
Sheffield Chamber Music Festival.

APRIL

April Fool's Day (1 April): the day when practical jokes are sanctioned (at least until noon). Most national newspapers include a spoof story or two (which can be hard to separate from the absurdity of the real news).
Harrogate Spring Flower Show: North Yorkshire.
Queen's Birthday (21 April): celebrated with a gun salute in Hyde Park and at the Tower of London.

MAY

Bath International Festival: choral and chamber music.

Beating Retreat: Horse Guards Parade, Whitehall, London.
Brighton Arts Festival.
Chelsea Flower Show: Royal Hospital, Chelsea, London.
Glyndebourne Festival: opera season opens (until August).
Mayfest Festival, Glasgow.
Nottingham Festival.
Perth Festival of Arts: Tayside,Scotland

JUNE

Appleby Horse Fair: Cumbria.
Beating Retreat by the Household Division: Horse Guards Parade, Whitehall, London.
Biggin Hill International Air Fair: Biggin Hill, Kent.
Bournemouth Music Festival.
Exeter Festival: Devon.
Fine Art and Antiques Fair: Olympia, London.
Glasgow Show: Bellahouston Park, Glasgow.
Glastonbury Pilgrimage: Abbey Ruins, Glastonbury, Somerset.
Grosvenor House Antiques Fair: London.
Royal Academy of Arts Summer Exhibition: Piccadilly, London.
Royal Cornwall Show: Wadebridge, Cornwall.
Royal Highland Show: Ingliston, Newbridge, Edinburgh.
Trooping the Colour: for a close-up view of Her Majesty on horseback, you will need to apply for tickets in January by writing to: The Brigadier Major, HQ Household Division, Horse Guards Parade, Whitehall, London.

JULY

Birmingham International Jazz Festival.
Cambridge Festival.
Cheltenham International Festival of Music: Gloucestershire.
Henley Royal Regatta: Henley-on-Thames.
Llangollen International Musical Eisteddfod: Llangollen, Wales.
Robin Hood Festival: Sherwood Forest, Nottinghamshire.
Royal Tournament: Earl's Court, London.
York Early Music Festival.

AUGUST

Edinburgh International Festival.
Edinburgh Military Tattoo: Edinburgh Castle.
Highland Games at Dunoon: Perth and Aboyne in Scotland.
Notting Hill Carnival: Ladbroke Grove, London (bank holiday weekend).
Royal National Eisteddfod of Wales.

SEPTEMBER

Braemar Royal Highland Games: Balmoral, Scotland.
Cardiff Festival.
Cornish Gorsedd: (celebration of ancient Cornish traditions).
Farnborough Air Show: Surrey.
Salisbury Festival: Wiltshire.

OCTOBER

Birmingham International Film and TV Festival.
Canterbury Festival.
Cheltenham Festival of Literature.
Motor Show: Earl's Court, London.
National Gaelic Mod: Strathclyde, Scotland.
Norwich Jazz Festival.
Nottingham Goose Fair: Forest Recreation Ground, Nottingham.
Nottingham Real Ale Festival.
Opening of pheasant shooting season.
Stratford Mop Fair: Stratford-upon-Avon.
Swansea Music Festival.
Trafalgar Day Parade: Trafalgar Square, London.

NOVEMBER

Armistice Day (nearest Sunday to the 11th): Remembrance Service for those who died in two world wars, Cenotaph, Whitehall, London.
Cardiff Festival of Music: St David's Hall, Cardiff.
Christmas Lights: switched on in Oxford and Regent Streets, London.
Guy Fawkes Day (5th), firework celebrations to commemorate the failure of Mr Fawkes to blow up Parliament in 1605.
London Film Festival: South Bank, London SE1.
London to Brighton Veteran Car Run (1st Sunday): leaves from Hyde Park in London.
Lord Mayor's Show: The City, London.
Military International Tattoo: NEC, Birmingham.
State Opening of Parliament: House of Lords, Westminster, London.

DECEMBER

Hogmanay: New Year's Eve revels in Scotland.
New Year's Eve: exuberant celebrations in London's Trafalgar Square.

SHOPPING

If you are looking for something typically British to take back home, you will not have to look far. To start with there are quality **wools** and **clothes**, including the wonderful hand-knitted woollens from the Scottish islands of Shetland, Arran and Fair Isle, and the Guernsey and Jersey sweaters of the Channel Islands. There is fine Harris Tweed cloth from Lewis. You can seek out a kilt made in your own clan tartan, choose a town tartan or a plaid commemorating an individual event. The scenic Orchil Hills outside Edinburgh have a long tradition of woollen production where visitors can "do" The Scottish Mill Trail.

Another important centre for the cloth and wool industry is Bradford through which 90 percent of the wool trade passed in the 19th century. The area's many mill shops are a bargain-hunter's paradise where lengths of fabric, fine yarns and fleeces from the Yorkshire Dales can be bought. Some mills give guided tours. The British Wool Centre is here in Clayton and has a historic display and items on sale from the British Wool Collection. Wales, too, has many mills which produce colourful tapestry cloth in striking traditional Celtic designs.

Nottingham is the traditional manufacturing centre for **shoes** and **lace** and at the Lace Hall, High Pavement, you can watch lace being made, learn its history and, of course, buy gifts.

The flagship of Britain's bespoke **tailoring** industry is Savile Row in London where gentlemen come from all over the world to have their suits crafted. Other outlets for traditional British attire are Burberry's (for raincoats), Aquascutum, Austin Reed and Jaeger which have branches in Piccadilly in London and in many cities nationwide. The best stores for feminine clothes in pretty floral prints are Laura Ashley and Liberty's. For those with a more contemporary taste in clothing, Britain has a thriving young **fashion market** with leading designers such as Katherine Hamnett, Paul Smith and Vivienne Westwood and trendy outlets such as Jigsaw, Warehouse and Next. Many top international haute-couture designers can be found in Knightsbridge and Mayfair. For quality everyday clothing Marks & Spencer's chain stores have a longstanding reputation, particularly for their jumpers and underwear.

Top-price **china**, **glass** and **silver** items can be found in Regent Street and Mayfair in London at exclusive shops such as Waterford Wedgwood, Thomas Goode, Aspreys and Garrards. Stoke-on-Trent (in "the Potteries") is the home of the great china and porcelain houses, including Wedgwood, Minton, Royal Doulton, Spode, Portmeirion, Coalport and Royal Stafford. All these have visitor centres where you can often pick up some real bargains. You can also visit the Caithness Glass factory at Wick in Scotland and Dartington Crystal at Great Torrington in Devon.

The centre for British **jewellery** production is in Hockley, Birmingham, an industry which developed here in the 18th century along with other forms of metal working such as brass founding and gun smithing. Today more than 200 jewellery manufacturers and 50 silversmiths are based here.

English **flower perfumes** make a delightful gift. The most exclusive of these come from Floris in Jermyn Street, London, whilst the Cotswold Perfumery in the picturesque village of Bourton-on-the-Water, Gloucestershire, makes its own heavenly perfumes on site.

If you are coming to Britain to look for **antiques** it is worth getting in touch with the London and Provincial Antique Dealers' Association, 535 King's Road, London, SW10, tel: 071-823 3511. They run an up-to-date computer information service on the antiques situation throughout the country and also publish their own comprehensive booklet, *Buying Antiques in Britain* (£3 plus postage). A number of antique fairs are held nationwide throughout the year and many towns such as Bath, Harrogate and Brighton have their own antique centres and markets.

Consumable British delights which are easy to take home include Twinings or Jacksons **tea**, Scottish **whisky** and **shortbread** and numerous brands of **chocolate**. Bentick's are famous for their after dinner **mints**, Thornton's produce fine confectionery made from fresh ingredients, while on a more popular level, Cadbury's is a national favourite.

Every town has a **street market** once a week where cheap clothes and domestic ware can be bought and there may also be a good presence of **local craft** and homemade produce. There are many workshops in rural areas of Britain where potters, woodturners, leatherworkers, candlemakers and other craftsmen can be seen producing their wares. A free map of these can be obtained from the Crafts Council, 12 Waterloo Place, London SW1, tel: 071-930 4811.

Pop music is one of Britain's greatest exports and consequently the record shops here are excellent. Virgin, HMV and Our Price are the largest chains and Tower Records megastore in Piccadilly Circus, London, is open until 11pm.

SPORTS

Many international sports were introduced by the British who take their leisure time very seriously. Extensive television coverage is given to a wide variety of sports but most particularly to football, rugby, cricket, racing, tennis, athletics, snooker and skiing. Facilities for participation in indoor sports, such as badminton, squash, volleyball and swimming are good throughout the country. Every town and city has at least one sports centre and swimming pool. There are also plenty of facilities for golf and tennis, or for the more outward bound, climbing, sailing and windsurfing.

For information on public sports and leisure facilities in each area you can contact the local council's sport department. Alternatively, contact **The Sports Council**, 16 Upper Woburn Place, London, WC1, tel: 071-388 1277. The British Tourist Board has introduced a new *Family Leisure Guide* series of books giving information on individual sports in the country. Initially this includes editions on golf and horse racing which are available by post from The Pen & Ink Company Ltd, Whitewell Chambers, Ferrars road, Huntingdon, Cambridgeshire costing £9.95 (including postage within the UK).

The British Sports Association for the Disabled was founded in 1961 to encourage and provide opportunities for people with disabilities. For further information, contact the Council at 34 Osnaburgh Street, London NW1, tel: 071-383 7277.

Tickets for major sporting events can be purchased from commercial agents such as Keith Prowse, tel: 071-793 0800.

FOOTBALL

The most popular sport in Europe, has its traditional home in England where it was developed in the 19th century. In the past British football has gained a bad reputation due to the behaviour of hooligans on the terraces, but great efforts have been made to curb disruptions in recent years and things have improved considerably, particularly since the excellent performance of the English team in the 1990 World Cup.

The professional football season runs from August until May. England and Scotland have separate football associations (FA) with four divisions in England and three in Scotland. The climax to the season is the **English FA Cup** played at Wembley in London and the **Scottish FA Cup** played at Hampden Park in Glasgow.

Teams which continue to dominate the top of English first division are Liverpool, Manchester United, Tottenham Hotspur and Arsenal, although just about every town and city has its own team.The top teams in Wales are Cardiff, Swansea and Wrexham which play in the English league. In Scotland, Rangers and Celtic are great rivals.

For further information, contact **The Football Association**, 16 Lancaster Gate, London W2, tel: 071-262 4542.

RUGBY

This game was invented at Rugby School in Warwickshire in the early 19th century, hence its name. There are two different forms of rugby in Britain: **Rugby Union**, a 15-a-side game played by amateurs and **Rugby League**, a 13-a-side game played by both professionals and amateurs. The former is governed by the Rugby Union, based at Whitton Road, Twickenham, tel: 081-892 8161.

International Rugby Union matches are played at Twickenham, Murrayfield and Cardiff Arms Park. Rugby League is mainly played in the north of England and in Wales where it is the national game. The British Lions play annually against teams from Australia, New Zealand and Papua New Guinea. In the late 1980s a national league of 10 teams was launched with a nationwide league championship playing towards the **Rugby League Challenge Cup** Final at Wembley. The rugby season is between September and May.

CRICKET

The sport of English gentlemen, has been in existence since the 16th century and there is no more pleasing experience on a summer's afternoon than watching a match on a village green while having afternoon tea. Nationally, 17 county teams play 3 and 4-day matches to compete for the **Britannic Assurance County Championships**. On an international level, 5-day **Cornhill Test Matches** are played against touring teams from Australia, India, New Zealand, Pakistan, Sri Lanka and the West Indies.

The Marylebone Cricket Club (MCC), based at **Lords** cricket ground at St John's Wood in north London, is the governing body for the world game. International cricket matches are played at half a dozen grounds in Britain including Lords and the Oval in London, Edgbaston in the Midlands and Headingly in Leeds.

TENNIS

Although this sport has been played for centuries, the modern game originated in England in the late 19th century. **Wimbledon fortnight** takes place on grass courts at the All England Club in Wimbledon, South West London in June. The ground can accommodate over 30,000 spectators, but tickets can be hard to obtain. To buy them in advance, contact the **All England Lawn Tennis and Croquet Club**, Church Road, Wimbledon, London SW19, tel: 081-946 2244. Alternatively, tickets can be obtained from agents in London such as Ticketmaster, tel: 071-379 6433 or First Call, tel: 071-240 7200.

HORSE SPORTS

Horse racing is a major British industry and takes two forms:

Flat racing takes place between March and early November. The most important races are the Derby and Oaks at Epsom, the St Leger at Doncaster and the 1,000 and 2,000 Guineas held at Newmarket. The Royal Ascot meeting is quite a spectacle and a major social event where race-goers dress up in their finest regalia in the presence of the Queen.

Steeplechasing and **hurdle racing** take place between September and early June. The National Hunt Festival meeting at Cheltenham in March is the most important event where the highlight is the Gold Cup. The most famous steeplechase in Britain (dating from 1837) is the hair-raising Grand National held at Aintree in Liverpool where a large field of horses race over enormous fences.

Show Jumping: nearly 2,000 shows are held throughout the country each year, but the major events are the Royal International Horse Show at the NEC in Birmingham, the Horse of the Year Show at Wembley, London and the Olympia International Show Jumping Championships in London.

Polo: matches take place at Windsor Great Park or Cowdray Park, Midhurst, West Sussex on summer weekends. The Governing body is the Hurlingham Polo Association, Ambersham, Midhurst, West Sussex.

Horse Trials are held in spring and autumn nationwide. The major 3-day events (cross-country, show jumping and dressage) are at Badminton in Avon, Windsor in Buckinghamshire, Bramham in Yorkshire, Burghley in Lincolnshire and Chatsworth in Derbyshire.

The main equestrian body in Britain is **The British Horse Society** which governs the Pony Club and Riding Club. It also runs the British Equestrian Centre at Stoneleigh in Warwickshire where it is based. For further information, tel: 0203-696697.

There are plenty of **public riding stables** if you want to go out for a hack in the countryside. However, stables are unlikely to let riders out unaccompanied. **Pony trekking** is particularly popular on Dartmoor, Exmoor, in the New Forest and in Wales.

FIELD SPORTS

These include fox-hunting, shooting and falconry. **Fox-hunting** on horseback with a pack of hounds takes place between autumn and spring and is still very popular despite fierce opposition from animal rights activists and anti-bloodsport campaigners. For those who have no qualms about such sports, a "meet" is an impressive spectacle.

The **shooting** of game such as grouse, pheasant and ptarmigan is protected by law and you must have a licence. Shooting can only take place during the open season. In the close season birds are bred on estates under the care of gamekeepers.

At the **Falconry Centre**, Newent, Gloucestershire, tel: 0531-820286, there are rare and endangered species of birds of prey from all over the world. There is also the opportunity to see displays using falcons, eagles, hawks and owls and find out more about the sport.

Field sports are governed by the **British Field Sports Society**.

ANGLING

Freshwater fishing for salmon, trout (**game fishing**) or for perch, pike or bream (**coarse fishing**) on rivers, lakes and lochs in Britain will usually have to be paid for and you will either have to join a club, or buy a temporary permit. The coarse fishing season runs from June to March. For further information, contact local tourist offices or the **National Anglers Council**, 11 Cowgate, Peterborough, Cambridgeshire, tel: (0733) 54084. For **sea angling**, contact the **National Federation of Sea Anglers**, 26 Downsview Crescent, Uckfield, East Sussex, tel: (0825) 763589.

ATHLETICS

Athletics in Britain are governed by the **Amateur Athletics Association** (AAA). There is a considerable following and participation of athletics in this country, which is further encouraged by wide television coverage and the success of British athletes. The main national sports centre for athletics is at **Crystal Palace** in South London. For further information contact the AAA, Edgbaston House, 3 Duchess Place, Hadley Road, Edgbaston, Birmingham, tel: 021-456 4050.

Highland Games are held in Scotland between August and September when they coincide with the annual gatherings of clans. Activities include tossing the caber and throwing the hammer as well as dancing and piping competitions. The best known games are at Braemar, near Balmoral, in September and there are also gatherings at Aboyne, Argyllshire and Cowal.

SNOOKER

Thought to have been invented by Sir Neville Chamberlain in India in 1875, snooker has gained considerable prestige and popularity over the past two decades and has now become a major national sport. Professional players compete for very high stakes, of which the annual **Embassy World Professional Championships** held in Sheffield is the tops. There are snooker halls in all towns and cities, and the **Billiards & Snooker Control Council**, Coronet House, Queen Street, Leeds, West Yorkshire, tel: 0532-440586, can supply a list of clubs.

GOLF

The home of golf is Scotland where the game has been played since the 17th century and naturally the oldest golf club in the world is there: The Honourable Company of Edinburgh Golfers. The most important national event is the Open Championship with the Walker Cup for amateurs and the Ryder Cup for professionals. There are hundreds of courses around the country which welcome visitors. Wales alone has over 100 courses – as does Scotland, where even the most famous courses such as St Andrew's are open to the public. Courses close to London are generally heavily booked.

For more information concerning dates and venues of tournaments contact the **Professional Golfer's Association**, Apollo House, The Belfry, Sutton Coldfield, West Midlands, tel: 0675-70333.

WATERSPORTS

Britain offers plenty of opportunities to those interested in sailing, particularly on the south coast and around Pembrokeshire, south west Wales, but also on the lakes and lochs of the north of England and Scotland. There are also excellent facilities for canoeing, windsurfing, jet skiing and boating on Britain's many inland waters. Information on clubs for sailing, power boating and windsurfing can be obtained from the **Royal Yachting Association**, RYA House, Romsey Road, Eastleigh, Hampshire, tel: 0703-629962.

The most important annual **sailing** event is the Cowes Regatta held at the Isle of Wight, whilst the Henley Regatta on the Thames in July is an international rowing event and a major mark on the social calender.

Canoeing: The British Canoe Union, Mapperley Hall, Lucknow Avenue, Nottingham, tel: 0602-691944, can give information on events and other matters concerning this sport. One of the main canoeing sites is at the Canolfan Tryweryn National White Water Centre, Frongoch, near Bala, Gwynedd, tel: 0678-520826, where world slalom and white water racing championships have been held.

There is **jet skiing** at the Cotswold Jet Ski Club (best to book first), Lake 11, Spine Road, Cotswold Water Park, Cirencester, Gloucestershire, tel: 0285-861345. Alternatively, try the Tallington Lakes Jet Ski Club, Stamford, Lincolnshire, tel: 0778-341144.

National Water Sports Centres are at Great Cumbrae Isle, Firth of Clyde, Scotland and at Holme Pierrepont, Nottinghamshire.

ANNUAL SPORTING EVENTS

FEBRUARY

Skiing: at Fort William and Aviemore in Scotland.
Snooker: Benson and Hedges Masters, Wembley Conference Centre.

MARCH

Racing: Cheltenham Gold Cup, Cheltenham, Gloucestershire.
University Boat Race: Oxford and Cambridge, on the Thames between Putney and Mortlake, London.

APRIL

Football: Littlewoods Cup Final, Wembley, London.
Horse Racing: Grand National Race Meeting, Aintree, Liverpool.
London Marathon, Greenwich Park, London.
Rugby League: Silk Cut Challenge Cup Final, Wembley.
Rugby Union: Pilkington Cup Final, Twickenham.

MAY

Cycling: The Milk Race, starts from Westminster Bridge, London.
Football: FA Cup Final, Wembley.
Horse Trials: Badminton, Avon.
Horse Racing: 1,000 & 2,000 Guineas Stakes, Newmarket, Suffolk.
Royal Windsor Horse Show, Home Park, Windsor.
Snooker: London Masters Final, Café Royal, London.

JUNE

Cycling: London to Brighton cycle ride.
Golf: British Masters.
Horse Racing: Royal Ascot, Ascot, Berkshire.
Horse Racing: The Derby, Epsom, Surrey.
Horse Racing: The Oaks, Epsom, Surrey.
Polo: Queen's Cup, Windsor Great Park.
Show Jumping: Royal International Horse Show, NEC, Birmingham.
Tennis: Stella Artois Tournament, Queen's Club, London.
Tennis: Wimbledon Lawn Tennis Championships, All England Lawn Tennis & Croquet Club, London.
Sailing: Round the Island Yacht Race, Cowes, Isle of Wight.

JULY

Athletics: Grand Prix, Crystal Palace, London.
Cricket: Benson & Hedges Cup Final, Lords Ground, London.
Motor Racing: British Grand Prix, Silverstone, Northamptonshire.
Rowing: Henley Regatta Week, Henley-on-Thames.

AUGUST

Motor racing: Birmingham Motor Prix.
Sailing: Cowes Week Regatta, Isle of Wight.

SEPTEMBER

Cricket: Nat West Trophy final, Lord's Grounds, London.

OCTOBER

Show Jumping: Horse of the Year Show, Wembley Arena, London.
Golf: Dunhill Cup Final, St Andrew's, Fife.
Golf: World Matchplay, Wentworth, Surrey.

NOVEMBER

Lombard RAC Car Rally, Harrogate, North Yorkshire.

DECEMBER

Olympia International Show Jumping, Olympia, London.

USEFUL ADDRESSES

INFORMATION CENTRES

There are over 800 Tourist Information Centres (TICs) throughout Britain which provide free information and advice to visitors on local sights, activities and accommodation. Many offer the **Book A Bed Ahead** service whereby they will find you a suitable place to stay in other towns where there is a TIC involved in the scheme.

Although opening times vary from region to région and change between peak and off-season, most TICs are open office hours, which are extended to included weekends and evenings in high season or in areas where there is a high volume of visitors all year round. Some TICs close in winter between October and March. TICs are generally well signposted and denoted by the distinctive italic i symbol (*i*).

The following are information offices for the different regions of Britain which you can write to or telephone for information. Unless otherwise stated, they are administrative offices only and therefore cannot be visited in person.

English Tourist Board/British Tourist Authority: Thames Tower, Black's Road, London W6 9EL. Tel: 071-730 3488.
London Tourist Board and Convention Bureau: 26 Grosvenor Gardens, London SW1V ODU. Tel: 071-730 3450.
East Anglia Tourist Board: Toppesfield Hall, Hadleigh, Suffolk IP7 5DN. Tel: 0473-822922.
South East England Tourist Board: The Old Brewhouse Warwick Park, Tunbridge Wells, Kent TN2 5TU. Tel: 0892-540766.
Southern Tourist Board: 40 Chamberlayne Road, Eastleigh, Hampshire SO5 5JH. Tel: 0703-620006.
West Country Tourist Board: 60 St David's Hill, Exeter, Devon EX4 4SY. Tel: 0392-76351.
Heart of England Tourist Board: Woodside, Larkhill Road, Worcester WR5 2EF. Tel: 0905-763436.
East Midlands Tourist Board: Exchequergate, Lincoln LN2 1PZ. Tel: 0522-531521.
Yorkshire & Humberside Tourist Board: 312 Tadcaster Road, York, North Yorkshire YO2 2HF. Tel: 0904-707961.
Northumbria Tourist Board: Aykley Heads, Durham DH1 5UX. Tel: 091-384 6905.
North West Tourist Board: Swan House, Swan Meadown Road, Wigan, Lancashire WN3 5BB. Tel: 0942-821222.
Scottish Tourist Board: 23 Ravelston Terrace, Edinburgh EH4 3EU. Tel: 031-332 2433.
Wales Tourist Board: Brunel House, 2 Fitzalan Road, Cardiff CF2 1UY. Tel: 0222-499909.

LONDON

The following **tourist boards** deal with written, personal and telephone enquiries:
Scottish Tourist Board: 19 Cockspur Street, London SW1Y 5BL. Tel: 071-930 8661.
Wales Information Bureau: British Travel Centre, 12 Regent Street, London SW1. Tel: 071-409 0969.
British Travel Centre: 12 Regent Street, London SW1. Tel: 071-730 3400. Personal callers only. Represented here in addition to the British Tourist Authority are British Rail, American Express and Room-Centre offering a booking service for rail, air and sea travel, sightseeing tours, theatre tickets and accommodation throughout Britain. There is also a currency exchange bureau. Open: 9am–6.30pm Monday–Friday, 10am–4pm weekends.

At the following centres the **London Visitor and Convention Bureau** (LVCB) provides general information and booking services for hotels, theatres, and sightseeing tours: Victoria Station, Heathrow terminals 1, 2, 3 (underground station concourse), Selfridges, Harrods and the Tower of London.

London Regional Transport (LRT) publish a map and guide for visitors which is available from tourist and travel information centres at the following underground stations: Piccadilly Circus, Oxford Circus, Heathrow and at major British Rail stations in the capital.

BRITISH TOURIST AUTHORITY OFFICES OVERSEAS

Australia: 8th Floor, 210 Clarence Street, Sydney, NSW 2000. Tel: 2-267 4555.

Chicago: 625 N Michigan Avenue, Suite 1510, Chicago, IL 60611. Tel: 312-787 0490.

France: 63 Rue Pierre-Charron, 75008 Paris. Tel: 42 89 11 11.

Germany: Taunusstrasse 52–60, 6000 Frankfurt am Main 1. Tel: 69-23 80 711.

Japan: Tokyo Club Building, 3-2-6 Kasumigaseki, Chiyoda-Ku, Tokyo 100. Tel: 3-3581 3603.

Los Angeles: Suite 450, 350 South Figueroa Street, Los Angeles, CA 90071. Tel: 213-628 3525.

New York: 40 West 57th Street, New York, NY 10019. Tel: 212-581 4700

New Zealand: Suite 305, 3rd Floor, Dilworth Building, corner Queen and Customs streets, Auckland 1. Tel: 9-303 1446.

The Netherlands: Aurora Gebouw (5th floor), Stadhouderskade 2, 1054 ES Amsterdam. Tel: 20-85 50 51.

Singapore: 24 Raffles Place, 20-01 Clifford Centre, Singapore 0104. Tel: 535 2966.

USEFUL NUMBERS

London Regional Transport (24 hours): tel: 071-222 1234.

National Trust: stately home information, tel: 071-222 9251.

London Tourist Board: 071-730 3488.
English Tourist Board: 071-824 8000.
Welsh Tourist Board: 0222-499909.
Scottish Tourist Board: 031-332 2433.

Phone Guide to London: (36/48p a minute). Dial 0839-123 followed by any of two dozen numbers, for example: 400 What's On This Week; 403 Current Exhibitions; 407 Sunday Outings; 422 Rock and Pop Concerts; 423 Theatre; 428 Markets.

SPECIAL INFORMATION

DISABLED

More care and attention is being paid to providing better general day-to-day facilities for the disabled in Britain. Trains and buses are being better designed and equipped, and many museums and public places have been made more accessible and provide separate facilities. Many TICs have leaflets giving details of disabled access and facilities at places of interest.

Free holiday information on a variety of holidays for people with specialist needs, from the disabled and elderly to one-parent families, is available from Holiday Care Service, 2 Old Bank Chambers, Station road, Horley, Surrey, tel: 0293-774535.

The **Royal Association for Disability and Rehabilitation** (RADAR), 25 Mortimer Street, London W1, tel: 071-637 5400, acts as an information service and can provide a free list of publications it has available concerning matters for the disabled.

EMBASSIES & CONSULATES

If you lose your passport or run into legal or medical trouble during your stay, you should contact your country's embassy or consulate. Most countries have diplomatic representation in London which can be found through the *Yellow Pages* or via telephone Directory Enquiries (192). Many also have consulates in Edinburgh and Cardiff.

LONDON

Australia: Australia House, Strand WC2, tel: 071-379 4334.

China: 31 Portland Place W1, tel: 071-636 5637.

Egypt: 26 South Street W1, tel: 071-499 2401.

France: 58 Knightsbridge SW1, tel: 071-235 8080.

Germany: 23 Belgrave Square SW1, tel: 071-235 5033.

Hong Kong: 6 Grafton Street W1, tel: 071-499 9821.

India: India House, Aldwych WC2, tel: 071-836 8484.

Indonesia: 38 Grosvenor Square W1, tel: 071-499 7661.

Japan: 46 Grosvenor Street W1, tel: 071-493 6030.

Netherlands: 38 Hyde Park Gate SW7, tel: 071-584 5040.

Russia: 13 Kensington Palace Gardens W8,
tel: 071-229 3628.
Saudi Arabia: 27 Eaton Place SW1,
tel: 071-235 8431.
South Africa: South Africa House, Trafalgar Square
WC2, tel: 071-930 4488.
United States: 24 Grosvenor Square W1,
tel: 071-499 9000.

CARDIFF

Belgium: Empire House, Docks, tel: 0222-488111.
Costa Rica: 62 St Mary Street, tel: 0222-226554.
Denmark: 70 James Street, tel: 0222-480003.
Finland: Mount Stuart Square, tel: 0222-480704.
Liberia: Cory Buildings, tel: 0222-481141.
Netherlands: 113–116 Bute Street,
tel: 0222-488636.
Norway: Empire House, tel: 0222-489711.
Turkey: Empire House, Docks, tel: 0222-461144.

EDINBURGH

Australia: Hobart House, Hanover Street,
tel: 031-226 6271.
Austria: 33 Charlotte Street, tel: 031-225 1516.
Belgium: 89 Constitution Street, tel: 031-554 3333.
Denmark/Finland/Norway: 50 East Fettes Avenue, tel: 031-552 7101.
France: 7 Weymss Place, tel: 031-225 7954.
Germany: 116 Eglinton Crescent,
tel: 031-337 2323.
Greece: 9 Regent Terrace, tel: 031-556 1701.
Iceland: 50 Grange Road, tel: 031-667 2166.
Italy: 6 Melville Crescent, tel: 031-226 3631.
Portugal: 167 Glasgow Park, tel: 031-339 5345.
Spain: 51 Lauderdale Street, tel: 031-447 1113.
Sweden: 6 St John's Place, tel: 031-554 6631.
Switzerland: 6 Moston Terrace, tel: 031-667 2386.
United States: 3 Regent Terrace, tel: 031-556 8315.

FURTHER READING

OTHER INSIGHT GUIDES

Other *Insight Guides* which highlight destinations in
this region are:

Also in print:
CityGuides to Oxford,
Edinburgh and
Glasgow, and *Insight
Guide*: Channel Islands.

ART/PHOTO CREDITS

INDEX

Y

A
B
C
D
F
G
H
I
J
a
b
c
d
f
g
h
i
j
k
l

INSIGHT *Pocket* GUIDES

•••••••••••••••••••••••••••••

United States: **Houghton Mifflin Company, Boston MA 02108**
Tel: (800) 2253362 Fax: (800) 4589501

Canada: **Thomas Allen & Son, 390 Steelcase Road East**
Markham, Ontario L3R 1G2
Tel: (416) 4759126 Fax: (416) 4756747

Great Britain: **GeoCenter UK, Hampshire RG22 4BJ**
Tel: (256) 817987 Fax: (256) 817988

Worldwide: **Höfer Communications Singapore 2262**
Tel: (65) 8612755 Fax: (65) 8616438

66 I was first drawn to the Insight Guides by the excellent "Nepal" volume. I can think of no book which so effectively captures the essence of a country. Out of these pages leaped the Nepal I know – the captivating charm of a people and their culture. I've since discovered and enjoyed the entire Insight Guide Series. Each volume deals with a country or city in the same sensitive depth, which is nowhere more evident than in the superb photography. **99**

Sir Edmund Hillary